To Terry

Happy the husband of a good wife,
Twice-lengthened are his days;
A worthy wife brings joy to her husband,
Peaceful and full is his life.

A good wife is a generous gift
Bestowed upon him who fears the Lord;
Be he rich or poor, his heart is content,
And a smile is ever on his face.

Sirach 26:1-4

CATHOLIC REPLIES

*Answers to over 800 of the
most often asked questions
about religious and moral issues*

JAMES J. DRUMMEY

C.R. Publications
345 Prospect Street
Norwood, MA 02062

C.R. Publications
345 Prospect Street
Norwood, MA 02062

Cover design by Jeff Giniewicz
Printed in the United States of America

ISBN 0-9649087-0-0

Contents

Acknowledgements

This book began with questions and answers in my parish bulletin in the fall of 1987. Eventually, replies were provided for bulletins in about a dozen parishes. Space considerations being what they are in parish bulletins, however, it soon became obvious that questions requiring lengthy answers could not be treated adequately in such a limited format.

So early in 1991, *The Wanderer* was approached about the possibility of adding a question-and-answer column to the pages of that national Catholic weekly. The first column appeared on April 25, 1991, and more than 1,000 questions have been answered since then. I am very grateful to all those readers who have taken the time to send me their questions on an amazing variety of religious topics.

Gratitude and appreciation are also due to several people who have played an active part in the success of "Catholic Replies." First is my former pastor, Msgr. Robert J. Sennott, who got me started and encouraged me in those early years.

Second is the Very Rev. Robert J. Sullivan, whose advice and suggestions have been most helpful in the preparation of these replies over the years.

Third is A.J. Matt Jr., editor of *The Wanderer*, who gave me the opportunity to bring this apostolate to the national, and international, readership of his fine newspaper.

And fourth are those men and women who so willingly agreed to say some very kind things about "Catholic Replies" in the foreword and on the back cover of the book. It is a joy and a privilege to be associated with persons who are such articulate and vigorous proponents of our Catholic Faith.

It is my prayer that the contents of this book will help the reader always to be "ready to give an explanation to anyone who asks you for a reason for your hope" (1 Peter 3:15).

James J. Drummey
August 15, 1995

Foreword

"Quite early on," says the *Catechism of the Catholic Church* in sections 4 and 5, "the name *catechesis* was given to the totality of the Church's efforts to make disciples, to help men believe that Jesus is the Son of God so that believing they might have life in his name, and to educate and instruct them in this life, thus building up the Body of Christ (*Catechesi tradendae* 1; 2).

"'Catechesis is an *education in the faith* of children, young people, and adults which includes especially the teaching of Christian doctrine imparted, generally speaking, in an organic and systematic way, with a view to initiating the hearers into the fullness of Christian life'" (*CT* 18).

In the broad sense, this book is a work of catechesis. It collects and presents, in a "systematic way," answers on a wide range of subjects from Mr. Drummey's "Catholic Replies" column in *The Wanderer.* I have known Jim Drummey well for more than three decades, and I was one of those who encouraged him to publish his column in *The Wanderer.* His execution of the project has fully met the high expectations of those who urged him to do it, and this book will make those columns permanently and easily accessible.

For a lay person to write a question-and-answer column on the Catholic Faith is a perilous undertaking, but Mr. Drummey has certainly handled the task well. His columns are concise, clear, and accurate. He selects and answers questions that are practically relevant. He is afraid neither to take on the tough questions nor to admit it when he is unable to provide an adequate answer.

Mr. Drummey recognizes that he is not the Pope, but his answers can be relied upon to provide authentic Church teaching from authentic sources, including, as appropriate, experts whom he has personally consulted.

Mr. Drummey also writes in clear and uncluttered English. He wants to inform and he does so with consistently good effect because he goes right to the point of the question without attempting to impress with any display of empty erudition.

I rely on Jim Drummey's columns. This book, as a systematic compilation of those columns, provides an important service toward the "education in the faith of children, young people, and adults."

Charles E. Rice
Professor of Law
Notre Dame Law School

Author's Note

Most of the questions and answers in this book are reproduced as they originally appeared in parish bulletins or in *The Wanderer*, except for minor editing to fit the book format or when it was necessary to combine several questions or answers dealing with the same subject matter.

In many cases, however, new material has been introduced from such important Church documents as the *Catechism of the Catholic Church*, *Evangelium Vitae*, and *Veritatis Splendor*, which were not in existence when some of the replies were first prepared. This material was added to the text to make the replies as current and as authoritative as possible.

Chapter 1

Father, Son, and Holy Spirit

Q. If God knows everything, then He knows who will go to Heaven and to Hell. So it really doesn't matter what a person does if that person is predestined for Hell, right? — M.B., Massachusetts

A. Wrong. You are confusing predestination with God's foreknowledge. Yes, God knows who will be saved and who will be lost, but He does not cause anyone to go to Hell. Suppose you have considerable knowledge of the stock market and predict that within six months a certain stock will go up 20 points. And suppose that in six months that stock is indeed up 20 points. Did you cause the stock to increase in value, or was it just your superior knowledge of market conditions that enabled you to predict this would happen?

God predestines no one to go to Hell, says the *Catechism of the Catholic Church* (n. 1037). It says that one must willfully turn away from God (the definition of mortal sin) and persist in mortal sin until the end in order to deserve punishment in Hell. That is why the Church implores the mercy of God, who "wants none to perish but all to come to repentance" (2 Peter 3:9).

God did not want us to be puppets, so He gave each of us a free will. He wants us to choose Him freely. He gives us all the grace we need to be saved. He shows love and concern for us even when we turn away from Him. He says to the sinner, "Come now, let us set things right .... Though your sins be like scarlet, they may become white as snow" (Isaiah 1:18).

God "wants all men to be saved and come to know the truth," said St. Paul (1 Timothy 2:4). He said that God has "predestined us through Christ Jesus to be his adopted sons" (Ephesians 1:5). If we leave ourselves open to His grace and love, receive His sacraments frequently, and follow the teachings of His Church, then Heaven will be our final destination.

Q. I am 65 years old and have never really understood how God can know who will eventually wind up in Heaven or Hell and how we can still have free will. — J.M., New York

A. First of all, God is all-knowing and knows the fate of each and every person from the beginning to the end of time. He does not see history as a series of consecutive events, one following upon another over many millenia, but rather God views the entire panorama of human history at once. Perhaps the following analogy will help to illustrate this.

Suppose you are walking through a cemetery and you pass by a series of gravestones bearing the chronological dates of 1900, 1930, 1950, 1975, and 1990. You see each of those stones one by one, over the period of time that it takes you to walk by them. But if you flew over that cemetery in a helicopter, you would see all of the stones at once. That is how God sees our lives and the choices we make, not over a span of time but all at once, because He is outside of time.

Now the same God who knows the choices that we will make, whether for good or evil, has given us a free will to make those choices. He did not create a race of robots, but rather a race of people capable of thinking and reasoning, evaluating and deciding whether to do good and avoid evil, or vice versa. God wants us to choose Him freely, and He gives us all the graces we need to make the correct choices. He pursues us down through the years, like Francis Thompson's "hound of Heaven," never giving up on us, no matter what we do, and always reaching out to us, seeking our repentance and our return to His loving care.

Q. It is obvious that the Trinity had foreknowledge that the chief priests and Pontius Pilate would exercise their free will and act as they did in putting Jesus to death. Jesus was willing to expose Himself to the cross out of love for fallen humanity, but was the Crucifixion an anticipated but not planned occurrence? If it was planned, would this not have meant that God willed that the chief priests and Pilate commit this terrible crime? Would the Incarnation without the Crucifixion have atoned for original sin? — A.O., Ohio

A. God could have exercised only His mercy and pardoned our sins without the Crucifixion and death of Jesus. But God is all-just as well as all-merciful and, to satisfy the requirements of justice, both the Incarnation and the Crucifixion were necessary. Jesus could have chosen another way to die, but once He had made the free decision to sacrifice Himself for our sins, His death on the cross was the logical consequence of that decision. And perhaps He exposed Himself to a horrible death by crucifixion to make clear both the terrible evil of sin and His deep and abiding love for us.

While it is true that God knew the kind of death that Jesus would suffer, and knew the events and decisions that would lead to the death of His Son, it is not true that God willed the actions of Judas, Annas and Caiaphas, and Pilate. These men were guilty of evil dispositions that were contrary to the will of God, but their free choices to act on those evil dispositions were not directly willed by God.

The Father, who sees all things simultaneously, sent the Son into a wicked world in need of redemption and into the midst of men who were disposed to engineer His death. But the decision to kill Jesus was the fault of those men, not of God. God did not cause or will the evil, but He permitted it to happen so that good might come from it.

Q. If God knows that certain persons are going to end up in Hell, where is the justice and love in allowing those persons to be born and to live out a life in a miserable world and then go on to a more miserable one? No matter what that person were to do with his life, it wouldn't change God's knowledge or that person's destination. Isn't that cruel? I have a real problem with this and need to try to understand it. — J.O., Arkansas

A. You are correct that God's knowledge of what choices we make in life cannot change because God sees all of those choices at once, not as a series of events. But you are not correct in saying that it doesn't matter what a person does with his life. Of course it matters. If a person continually strives to choose good and avoid evil, to do what God wants and to repent of those choices that go against the love and law of God, then that person is destined for Heaven.

The other question is whether it is cruel and unjust of God to bring into the world persons who will ultimately reject the Creator and deliberately choose an eternity in Hell. That's looking at things from a negative perspective. Look at it from the positive side and ask whether it is loving and just of God to bring into the world persons who will ultimately embrace the Creator and deliberately choose an eternity in Heaven.

That's the true picture of God. The God who gave us free will to choose Him; the God who sent His only Son to die for us and give all of us the opportunity to get to Heaven; the God who knows that over the course of human history, no matter how many people lose their souls, good will far outweigh evil.

It's a mistake to think primarily of those who will choose Hell, even though there is no need for them to do so. Let us think instead of the multitudes who will choose Heaven. Should they be deprived of eternal happiness because some members of the

human race choose eternal misery? And might we say paren-
thetically that many of those who wind up in the miserable
world of Hell probably did not live a miserable existence in
this life? We suspect that those living in misery in this life are
probably a lot closer to God than those persons who are living
in luxury.

Be that as it may, it is not for us to say that God should not
have created certain individuals knowing that they would wind
up in Hell. Our inadequate human feelings are no match for the
infinite wisdom of a God who says that "my thoughts are not
your thoughts, nor are your ways my ways" (Isaiah 55:8). God
sees the whole picture; we see only a few tiny details. God sees
that the general good will outweigh the individual losses.

Or look at it this way. If I had a great-grandfather who lost
his soul, that would be his own fault. There was no need for it
to happen, but it was his decision to choose evil over a God
who is all-good. And now he is suffering the consequences of
his free choice. But that's not the end of the story. Because my
great-grandfather existed, my grandfather, my father, myself,
and my children will all have the opportunity to save our souls.
Should we be deprived of eternal happiness (if we get to
Heaven) because my great-grandfather chose eternal damnation (if he did)?

**Q. Can you explain why God permits evil and suffering?
— P.M., Florida**

A. The presence of evil and suffering in the world is a
mystery that we will not fully understand until the final
judgment, but Holy Scripture and the teaching of the Church
can shed some light on it. Consider the following points:

(1) God created the first humans in a state of holiness, but
Adam and Eve, at the urging of Satan, set themselves against
God and brought evil into the world. As a result of their sin,
said the Second Vatican Council, "men have frequently fallen
into multiple errors .... The result has been the corruption of
morals and human institutions and not rarely contempt for the
human person himself" (*Decree on the Apostolate of the Laity*,
n. 7). Thus, the evils of the world are traceable not to God but
to original sin and the personal sins we commit.

(2) While God is not the cause of evil and suffering, He
permits these afflictions in order to draw some good out of
them. For instance, out of the suffering and death of Jesus
came eternal salvation. If Jesus did not die on the cross, we
could not get to Heaven.

(3) If we join our sufferings with those of Christ, they will bring us closer to Him. Who knows more about homelessness and poverty than our Lord, who was born in a stranger's cave and buried in a stranger's grave? Who knows more about loneliness than our Lord, who was abandoned by all His friends? Who knows more about injustice than our Lord, who was falsely accused and wrongfully convicted of criminal activity? Who knows more about physical pain than our Lord, who underwent excruciating torture and death? "Come to me, all you who are weary and find life burdensome," Jesus says to us, "and I will refresh you" (Matthew 11:28).

(4) In his Apostolic Letter *On the Christian Meaning of Human Suffering*, Pope John Paul II said that "suffering is present in the world in order to release love, in order to give birth to works of love toward neighbor, in order to transform the whole of human civilization into a 'civilization of love'" (n. 30). Thus, suffering can be beneficial if it stirs in us a spirit of compassion, love, and sacrifice toward others.

(5) Patient suffering can prepare us for the life to come. If we suffer with Christ, says St. Paul, we will be "glorified with him. I consider the sufferings of the present to be as nothing compared with the glory to be revealed in us" (Romans 8:17-18).

For more insights into the problem of suffering, see Peter Kreeft's excellent book *Making Sense Out of Suffering* (Servant Books).

Q. Lately I've been hearing more and more that "God's love is unconditional." No one will deny that Christ came into this world freely, while we were still sinners, and that by His life, death, and resurrection merited for mankind the gift of regeneration. However, after Baptism, or regeneration in the divine life of grace, men by personal mortal sin can lose this gift. This being so, it seems to me that after Baptism, God's love is conditioned by our repentance, confession, and the reception of absolution in order for us to regain the divine life of grace. Would you please comment? — J.J.L., Missouri

A. We are talking about two different things here: God's love for us and our response to that love. You are correct that we can by mortal sin lose our share in the divine life and can regain that state of grace only through sorrow and repentance for sin. However, while we are changing from friend to foe to friend of God again, He remains unchanged. He continues to love us with an everlasting and unconditional love. Scripture tells us that "God is love" (1 John 4:8), that He will always remain faithful to us no matter what we do (Exodus 34:6-7), and that His love for us is so great that He sent His only Son "as an offering for our sins" (1 John 4:10).

Q. Why have pronouns referring to the Almighty been reduced to lower case when they were always capitalized in the past? — E.W.M., Missouri

A. The trend in English grammar is toward a general reduction in the capitalization of words. As part of this trend, standard usage now prints all pronouns and pronominal adjectives referring to God in the lower case. The International Committee on English in the Liturgy has elected to follow this usage, although it does capitalize nouns referring to God, such as Lord, Father, Son, etc. We have elected to continue capitalizing the pronouns as well.

Q. I have heard people refer to God as "God the Mother" and say that God is a spirit who has within Himself the qualities of men and women. Is this correct? — Name Withheld, Nebraska

Q. I was told by the Office of Worship in my diocese that my worship of an image of God the Father was pagan worship. If Jesus had that image when He walked on earth, why is it wrong for us? — C.P., Pennsylvania

A. God is a living spirit with no gender or sexuality. We can come to know Him by applying the natural light of human reason to the wonders of His creation and by listening to Divine Revelation, particularly to the words of Jesus, the Son of God. When Scripture says that we are made in the image and likeness of God (Genesis 1:26), it means that we have a spirit like His that allows us to think, to choose, and to love. We do not resemble God in our bodies since He does not have a material body.

While we cannot know everything about God, we can know something about His qualities. The First Vatican Council (1869-1870) listed 15 attributes of God, including that He is "one, true, and living ... almighty, eternal, beyond measure, incomprehensible ... infinite in intellect, will, and in every perfection ... entirely simple and unchangeable ... and inexpressibly exalted over all things that exist or can be conceived other than Himself."

We call God "Father" not as any affront against mothers or

womanhood, or as a form of "pagan worship," but because Jesus told us to call God "our Father" (Matthew 6:9). This was not a declaration that God is male, but rather an analogy to help us understand something about the nature of God. We associate certain good qualities with fathers, such as protective love, fidelity, leadership, strength, security, and stability.

There are also verses in the Bible in which God is identified with feminine characteristics, such as the tenderness and concern of a mother (Isaiah 49:15 and Matthew 23:37), but to use the expression "God the Mother" would contradict the teaching and example of Jesus.

"In no way is God in man's image," says the *Catechism of the Catholic Church* (n. 370). It says that God is neither man nor woman but rather a pure Spirit in which there is no place for the difference between the sexes. The respective "perfections" of man and woman, the *Catechism* says, are but a reflection of the "infinite perfection of God: those of a mother and those of a father and husband."

Q. If God is a spirit and has no bodily parts, how can Jesus be seated at His right hand? — E.M.C., New York

A. To be placed at the right hand of a king or ruler has always been considered a sign of high esteem and, in Jewish families, the honor of sitting "at the right hand of the father" was accorded to the oldest son. You are correct in saying that God does not have a right hand; the expression is meant to signify that Jesus, as God's only Son, is equal to His Father and occupies the highest place in Heaven. In the words of St. John Damascene:

"By 'the Father's right hand' we understand the glory and honor of divinity, where he who exists as Son of God before all ages, indeed as God, of one being with the Father, is seated bodily after he became incarnate and his flesh was glorified" (*De fide orth.*, 4, 2: PG 94, 1104C).

Q. The phrase in the Our Father, when we say "lead us not into temptation," puzzles me. Why would God lead us into temptation? — A.R., Florida

A. You are quite correct that God would never lead us into temptation; only the Devil would try to do that. As St. James has told us: "No one who is tempted is free to say, 'I am being tempted by God.' Surely God, who is beyond the grasp of evil, tempts no one. Rather the tug and lure of his own passion tempt every man" (James 1:13-14).

The confusion arises because temptation can mean two different things: an inducement or enticement to evil, or a trial or test of faith. It is the latter meaning that Jesus had in mind when He taught us the Our Father. In fact, the phrase in the New American Bible version of the Lord's Prayer reads, "... subject us not to the trial" (Luke 11:4), rather than "lead us not into temptation."

For a good analysis of the Our Father, see paragraphs 2759-2865 of the *Catechism of the Catholic Church*. Regarding the petition in question, the *Catechism* says that when we say "lead us not into temptation," we are asking God not to allow us to take the path that leads to sin. This petition implores the Spirit of discernment and strength; it requests the grace of vigilance and final perseverance (n. 2863). See also pages 189-238 of Peter Kreeft's book *Fundamentals of the Faith* (Ignatius Press).

Q. The Church celebrates feast days in honor of Jesus and the Holy Spirit, but is there one for God the Father? — R.F.K., New York

A. There is no specific feast for God the Father. The closest to one is the feast of the Most Holy Trinity, which is celebrated on the first Sunday after Pentecost. This should not be interpreted, however, as some kind of neglect of the Father. Because the Church calendar celebrates the events of our redemption, it reflects primarily those events and the persons connected with them, as well as outstanding examples of Christian living (the saints). It does not reflect thoroughly the whole history of salvation (there are no feast days for Moses or Abraham, for example) or the work of the Father since we live in an age in which all things have been handed over to Christ.

You will have noticed that virtually the entire Mass is addressed to the Father, with only a few prayers addressed to Jesus or to the congregation, and none to the Holy Spirit. This does not of course imply their inferiority to the Father; it is simply the liturgical tradition. And that tradition is not based on proportionality, but rather on the faith experience of the community gathered around Christ.

Q. If A.D. began with the birth of our Lord, what was the last year B.C.? — C.B., Florida

A. In our day, most people divide history into two time periods: B.C., which means before Christ, and A.D., which means *anno Domini*, or in the year of our Lord. While A.D.

goes forward in time, from 1 to the present year, B.C. goes backwards, from 500 B.C. to 100 B.C., as it moves closer to our time. So the last year before the birth of Jesus was 1 B.C.

We do not know the exact year in which our Lord was born. In the sixth century, a monk named Dionysius the Little fixed the birth of Christ in the Roman year 754, but scholars today agree that Dionysius miscalculated by a few years. In his excellent book *Catholic Apologetics Today* (Tan Books), Fr. William Most summarizes (pages 251-254) the evidence presented by E.L. Martin that points toward 3 B.C. as the year in which Jesus was born. That summary is too long to repeat here, but interested readers are urged to consult Fr. Most's book, as well as Martin's own book, *The Birth of Christ Recalculated.*

Q. I was taught in my childhood that to show reverence to Jesus we should bow our head slightly at the mention of His name. Now you can count on one hand the number of people who do that. How come? — C.A., Florida

A. A number of religious gestures and signs of reverence have sadly fallen into disuse in recent decades as more and more people have become very careless in their use of God's name and in their behavior in church. You would think that some of them were at the local McDonald's the way they dress, talk, and act in church. About the only thing they don't do in front of the Blessed Sacrament is genuflect. It is up to pastors and priests to remind people that the church is God's house and that reverential behavior is not only expected but is required of those who call themselves followers of Christ.

One of the great paradoxes of history is that the name of the holiest Person who ever lived on this earth is used to express fear, anger, disgust, and other emotions. Even Catholics who should know better misuse the name of their Lord and Savior. St. Paul said that "at Jesus' name every knee must bend in the heavens, on the earth, and under the earth" (Philippians 2:10). Those who don't bend their knee on hearing the name of Jesus ought at least to bow their heads slightly in reverence.

Q. I can't find in the synoptic Gospels where Jesus claimed to be God. Jesus never intended to be worshiped as a god. — B.C.B., Massachusetts

A. There are few things clearer in the synoptic Gospels of Matthew, Mark, and Luke than the fact that Jesus did indeed claim to be God on several occasions. For instance, there was the time in the synagogue at Nazareth when He read the prophecy from Isaiah about the Messiah and then said to His listeners: "Today this Scripture passage is fulfilled in your hearing" (Luke 4:21). He was claiming to be the promised Messiah.

On another occasion, He told His disciples: "Whoever acknowledges me before men I will acknowledge before my Father in heaven" (Matthew 10:32).

And of course at His trial before the Sanhedrin on the night before His death, Jesus was asked by the high priest: "Are you the Messiah, the Son of the Blessed One?" Our Lord, knowing that His words would mean certain death, replied: "I am; and you will see the Son of Man seated at the right hand of the Power and coming with the clouds of heaven" (Mark 14:61-62).

The enemies of Jesus had no doubts about the meaning of His words for they found Him guilty of blasphemy — of claiming to be God — and they sentenced Him to die for making that claim.

Q. Why was our Lord called "Son of Man"? When one criticizes dissenting theologians like Fr. McBrien and his orchestra, isn't that what Jesus warned against when He said not to judge others lest you be judged? — P.C.G., Pennsylvania

A. (1) The phrase "Son of Man," which appears dozens of times in the Gospels, is a title Jesus used to indicate His messianic mission of bringing salvation to the people of God and His role as judge at the end of the world. "If anyone in this faithless and corrupt age is ashamed of me and my doctrine," Christ said, "the Son of Man will be ashamed of him when he comes with the holy angels in his Father's glory" (Mark 8:38). The title also emphasizes the humanity of Jesus, just as "Son of God" emphasizes His divinity.

One of the most powerful uses of the phrase can be found in chapter 7 of Daniel, where the prophet had a vision of God sitting on His throne and being ministered to and attended by "thousands upon thousands" and "myriads upon myriads" of angels. As the visions continued, said Daniel, "I saw one like the son of man coming on the clouds of heaven; When he reached the Ancient One and was presented before him, He received dominion, glory, and kingship; nations and peoples of every language serve him. His dominion is an everlasting dominion that shall not be taken away, his kingship shall not be destroyed."

(2) Jesus' warning against judging others referred to judging

a person's motives rather than his actions. We can say that abortion is objectively evil without delving into the subjective reasons why a person would choose to have an abortion. So there is nothing wrong with criticizing a Fr. McBrien for statements that ridicule the Pope or reject Church teachings as long as we don't attempt to guess at his motives. Only God knows why people say or do certain things, and He will judge them accordingly.

Q. Where does it say in the Gospels or the Epistles that Jesus had to come down to earth to die for our sins? — G.M.G., Illinois

A. There are a number of places in the New Testament where it talks about Jesus dying for our sins. In the Gospel of John, for instance, our Lord told Nicodemus: "Yes, God so loved the world that he gave his only Son, that whoever believes in him may not die but may have eternal life. God did not send the Son into the world to condemn the world, but that the world might be saved through him" (John 3:16-17).

And in Paul's letter to the Romans, it says: "At the appointed time, when we were still powerless, Christ died for us godless men. It is rare that anyone should lay down his life for a just man, though it is barely possible that for a good man someone will have the courage to die. It is precisely in this that God proves his love for us: that while we were still sinners, Christ died for us. Now that we have been justified by his blood, it is all the more certain that we shall be saved by him from God's wrath" (Romans 5:6-9).

Q. Did Jesus ever state that "either you are with me or you are against me," and where can I find this statement? — C.N., New Jersey

A. This saying of our Lord can be found in Matthew's Gospel (12:30) and in Luke's Gospel (11:23). It reads as follows: "He who is not with me is against me, and he who does not gather with me scatters."

Q. Why is John the disciple Jesus loved? Did He not love the other eleven disciples too, even Judas Iscariot? — F.J.C., Massachusetts

A. Jesus certainly did love all of the Apostles, including Judas, but He apparently had a special affection for John, perhaps because John was reportedly the youngest member of the Twelve. Our Lord also seemed to favor Peter, James, and John over the other Apostles since He included only them in such important moments in His life as the Transfiguration and the Agony in the Garden. Because Jesus was just like us in all things but sin, He liked some people more than others. But He loved everyone, even those who betrayed Him and executed Him.

Q. Regarding the controversy over *The Last Temptation of Christ*, the film that showed Christ as being subject to sinful passions and desires, has the Catholic Church ever addressed the issue of our Lord giving in to temptation? — W.R.A., Oklahoma

A. Although Jesus was tempted in the desert (Matthew 4:1-11) and in the Garden of Gethsemani (Luke 22:39-46), it was never possible for Him to commit a sin because it would have meant that God was capable of sinning against Himself. Since Christ was a divine Person, whose every act was an act of God, He could not sin. "In him there is nothing sinful," says John (1 John 3:5). And Paul says: "For we do not have a high priest who is unable to sympathize with our weakness, but one who was tempted in every way that we are, yet never sinned" (Hebrews 4:15).

When we are tempted, our will waivers and we find ourselves leaning toward evil. However, there was no wavering will in Christ, no inclination toward sin, no struggle in choosing between good and evil. Jesus had both a human will and a divine will, but as the Third Council of Constantinople (680-681) taught, Christ's human will "does not resist or oppose but rather submits to his divine and almighty will." (See the *Catechism of the Catholic Church*, n. 475.)

Why did our Lord subject Himself to these temptations? Perhaps to show us how to overcome them in our own lives. "Since he was himself tested through what he suffered," said St. Paul, "he is able to help those who are tempted" (Hebrews 2:18).

Q. If Jesus was sinless, why was He baptized by John in the Jordan River? — A.C., Idaho

A. Jesus was indeed sinless and had no need of baptism, but the reasons for His action can be found in section 536 of the *Catechism of the Catholic Church*, which sees the baptism of our Lord as the acceptance of His mission as God's suffering Servant as foretold in chapter 53 of Isaiah. Jesus allows Himself to be numbered among sinners and becomes "the Lamb of God, who takes away the sin of the world" (John 1:29).

According to the *Catechism*, Jesus was already anticipating the baptism of blood at the time of His death and, in perfect submission to His Father's will, He would out of love for sinful humanity consent to this "baptism of death" for the remission of our sins.

That the Father was pleased with the Son's acceptance of this baptism of blood is shown by the words that came from Heaven: "You are my beloved Son. On you my favor rests" (Luke 3:22). At the same time, the Holy Spirit descended on Jesus in the visible form of a dove, signifying that Jesus would be the source of the Spirit for all people for all time. The heavens that had been closed by Adam's sin were now opened.

Q. Could you clarify when it was that Jesus knew He was part of a triune God of all creation? — J.T., New Jersey

A. Jesus always knew this. In the words of the *Catechism of the Catholic Church* (nos. 473-474):

"'The human nature of God's Son, *not by itself but by its union with the Word*, knew and showed forth in itself everything that pertains to God.' Such is first of all the case with the intimate and immediate knowledge that the Son of God made man has of his Father. The Son in his human knowledge also showed the divine penetration he had into the secret thoughts of human hearts (cf. *Mk* 2:8; *Jn* 2:25; 6:61, etc.).

"By its union to the divine wisdom in the person of the Word Incarnate, Christ enjoyed in his human knowledge the fullness of understanding of the eternal plans he had come to reveal. What he admitted to not knowing in this area, he elsewhere declared himself not sent to reveal" (cf. *Mk* 13:32; *Acts* 1:7).

Q. I have been told that Christ only gradually became aware of His divine nature and His mission, but I contend that He knew of His divine nature from the beginning. Can you give me some information to prove this? — R.R.C., Pennsylvania

A. It is the teaching of the Catholic Church that Jesus, because He was a divine Person with both a divine nature and a human nature, knew of His divinity and His mission from the beginning. He had two kinds of knowledge, human and divine, and three kinds of human knowledge: (1) He had the Beatific Vision, which is an immediate face-to-face knowledge of God (He knew that He and the Father were one). (2) He had infused supernatural knowledge, which was knowledge conferred on Him by God without previous human experience or reflection on His part (He was able to read the hidden thoughts of His listeners and could predict future events). (3) He had acquired knowledge "about what one in the human condition can learn only from experience," in the words of the *Catechism of the Catholic Church*, n. 472 (He learned how to read and write and become a carpenter).

In his *Question and Answer Catholic Catechism*, Fr. John Hardon offers this summary of Christ's knowledge:

"Christ, as God, knew all things, past, present, and future. And even as man, because his humanity was united to the Word of God, he had access to all knowledge; but since the nature he assumed was finite, his human knowledge was not infinite. Therefore, he could develop as man through the kind of experience he had as he grew from infancy, through childhood, and into adult age. But never was Christ ignorant of anything he could have known, as though he were not God-made-man from the first moment of the Incarnation; or ignorant of anything he should have known, as though his human nature was blinded, like ours, by original or personal sin."

For further information about Jesus' knowledge, see paragraphs 472-474 of the *Catechism of the Catholic Church* and Fr. William G. Most's book *The Consciousness of Christ* (Christendom College Press).

Lastly, we also have the statement of Pope John Paul II that Jesus first proclaimed His Messiahship publicly in the temple at the age of 12 when He told Mary and Joseph, "Did you not know I had to be in my Father's house?" (Luke 2:49). This response, said the Holy Father, was our Lord's "manifestation of his awareness that he was the 'Son of God' and thus of his duty to be 'in his Father's house,' the temple, to 'take care of his Father's business' (according to another translation of the Gospel phrase). Thus Jesus publicly declared, perhaps for the first time, his Messiahship and his divine identity."

Q. In Colossians 1:24, St. Paul says something that has puzzled me for some time. How could there be anything lacking in the sufferings of Christ? — J.G.F., New Jersey

A. The passage in question reads: "Even now I find my joy in the suffering I endure for you. In my own flesh I fill up what is lacking in the sufferings of Christ for the sake of his body, the church." Paul did not mean that Christ's sufferings were not infinitely valuable and sufficient for our redemption, because they were. What the Apostle meant was that we can add our sufferings to those of Christ so that the fruits of His Redemption can be applied to people everywhere.

In his letter on suffering, *Salvifici Doloris*, Pope John Paul dwelt at some length on the meaning of these words of St. Paul. Among other things, the Holy Father said: "The sufferings of Christ created the good of the world's Redemption. This good in itself is inexhaustible and infinite. No man can add anything to it. But at the same time, in the mystery of the Church as his Body, Christ has in a sense opened his own redemptive suffering to all human suffering. Insofar as man becomes a sharer in Christ's sufferings — in any part of the world and at any time in history — to that extent he in his own way completes the suffering through which Christ accomplished the Redemption of the world.

"Does this mean that the Redemption achieved by Christ is not complete? No. It only means that the Redemption, accomplished through satisfactory love, remains always open to all love expressed in human suffering. In this dimension — the dimension of love — the Redemption which has already been completely accomplished is, in a certain sense, constantly being accomplished. Christ achieved the Redemption completely and to the very limit; but at the same time He did not bring it to a close. In this redemptive suffering, through which the Redemption of the world was accomplished, Christ opened himself from the beginning to every human suffering and constantly does so. Yes, it seems to be part of the very essence of Christ's redemptive suffering that this suffering requires to be unceasingly completed" (n. 24).

Q. In my parish bulletin, "Dear Padre" answered a question about organized religion by saying that "most Scripture scholars readily admit that Jesus did not come to earth specifically to start a new religion with an elaborate code of rules, regulations, and various classes and social structures. His main purpose, aside from gaining the gift of salvation, was to show people a new way to live in the world." This doesn't sound right to me. — R.D., Massachusetts

A. It doesn't sound right to us, either. Jesus indeed came to show people a new way to live in the world, but He also established a new covenant (1 Corinthians 11:25) and a new religion or church (Matthew 16:18) as the vehicle for salvation. In the words of the Second Vatican Council's *Dogmatic Constitution on the Church*:

"Christ, the one Mediator, established and ceaselessly sustains here on earth his holy Church, the community of faith, hope, and charity, as a visible structure. Through her He communicates truth and grace to all .... This is the unique Church of Christ which in the Creed we avow as one, holy, catholic, and apostolic. After his Resurrection, our Savior handed her over to Peter to be shepherded (Jn. 21:17), commissioning him and the other apostles to propagate and govern her (cf. Mt. 28:18 ff.). Her He erected for all ages as 'the pillar and mainstay of the truth' (1 Tim. 3:15). This Church, constituted and organized in the world as a society, subsists in the Catholic Church, which is governed by the successor of Peter and by the bishops in union with that successor" (n. 8).

Q. The Apostles Creed used to say that Jesus descended into Hell; now it says that He descended to the dead. Why the change? — T.K., Arizona

A. To clarify the fact that Jesus did not descend to the Hell of eternal damnation, but rather to the abode of the dead, or "lower regions" of the earth where the souls of the just were waiting to be redeemed and taken to Heaven.

According to the *Catechism of the Catholic Church* (n. 633), the Bible calls the abode of the dead "hell," which is *Sheol* in Hebrew or *Hades* in Greek, because those who wind up there are deprived of the vision of God. This was true for all those people, whether evil or good, who had died before Jesus' redeeming death on the cross.

Their state was not the same, however, as Jesus illustrated through the parable of the poor man Lazarus, who after death was received into "the bosom of Abraham" but remained separated by "a great abyss" from the rich man who had ignored his plight while they lived on earth (Luke 16:19-31). It was these just souls in Abraham's bosom (called the "spirits in prison" in 1 Peter 3:19) whom Jesus delivered when He descended into "hell."

Q. What did Jesus mean when He said, "In my Father's house there are many mansions"? — M.T., Massachusetts

A. When our Lord told the Apostles at the Last Supper that there were many mansions or "dwelling places" (John 14:2) in Heaven, He meant that not all will have the same degree of happiness there. Although each person will be perfectly happy in knowing and loving God, and will have all the joy that he or she can bear, the degree of happiness will vary according to the life we lived on earth. "Even among the stars," St. Paul told the Corinthians, "one differs from another in brightness. So it is with the resurrection of the dead" (1 Corinthians 15:41-42).

In other words, those who loved God ardently on earth, who bore trials and crosses patiently, and who seldom offended God through sin will have a higher degree of happiness in Heaven than those who led sinful lives but turned back to God and saved their souls. In the words of St. Paul: "He who sows sparingly will reap sparingly, and he who sows bountifully will reap bountifully" (2 Corinthians 9:6).

Q. What did Jesus mean by saying, "I have other sheep that do not belong to this fold"? — E.S., Ohio

A. In chapter 10 of John's Gospel, Jesus talked about the role of the shepherd in taking care of his sheep, protecting them from harm. "I am the good shepherd," He said. "I know my sheep and my sheep know me in the same way that the Father knows me and I know the Father; for these sheep I will give my life. I have other sheep that do not belong to this fold. I must lead them, too, and they shall hear my voice. There shall be one flock then, one shepherd."

The "other sheep" are the Gentiles, all those who are not Jews. The mission of Jesus was to bring all people into His Church so that one day there would be one Church and one Shepherd, Christ Himself.

Q. Jesus said that we should not call anyone on earth our father, so is it all right for us to call a priest "Father"? — A.M.R., New Hampshire

A. If we consider the context of our Lord's remarks, we see that He was denouncing the Pharisees for requiring people to perform hard tasks while avoiding such works themselves. Instead of helping people lighten their burdens, said Jesus, the Pharisees were "fond of places of honor at banquets and the front seats in synagogues, of marks of respect in public and of being called 'Rabbi.'

"As to you," Jesus told the crowds and His disciples, "avoid the title 'Rabbi.' One among you is your teacher, the rest are learners. Do not call anyone on earth your father. Only one is your father, the One in heaven. Avoid being called teachers. Only one is your teacher, the Messiah. The greatest among you will be the one who serves the rest. Whoever exalts himself shall be humbled, but whoever humbles himself shall be exalted" (Matthew 23:1-12).

What our Lord was doing was using hyperbole, engaging in extravagant speech to make a point. His point was not that the use of such titles as father and teacher is wrong (it is what we commonly call our male parent or those who instruct children in school); He was criticizing the Pharisees for abusing the authority attached to these titles. He was saying that those in authority are supposed to serve others, not impose heavy burdens on them while at the same time looking for public recognition and praise.

St. Stephen called the members of the Sanhedrin "my brothers! Fathers!" (Acts 7:2). St. Paul addressed a crowd in Jerusalem as "my brothers and fathers" (Acts 22:1). And St. John said in his first letter: "Fathers, I address you, for you have known him who is from the beginning" (1 John 2:13).

St. Paul also had no problem with being considered as a father to the people of Thessalonica. "You likewise know," he said to them, "how we exhorted every one of you, as a father does his children — how we encouraged and pleaded with you to make your lives worthy of the God who calls you to his kingship and glory" (1 Thessalonians 2:11-12).

Q. My parish priest said that Veronica accompanied Christ to Calvary and offered Him a towel on which He left the imprint of His face. This event is commemorated in the sixth Station of the Cross, but it is not mentioned in the Bible. Do you know where the veil is kept today? — J.F., New York

A. According to pages 55-57 of Joan Carroll Cruz's book *Relics* (Our Sunday Visitor), Veronica's veil was bequeathed to Pope Clement I and kept in the catacombs during the first three centuries of the Church's existence. It was later placed in the Basilica of St. Peter and is preserved today, says Cruz, "in the chapel constructed in one of the four enormous pillars that sustain the cupola of St. Peter's. Adorned by Bernini with balustrades and niches and surrounded by twisted columns from the ancient church, the pier is fronted by an enormous statue of Veronica that stands 16 feet tall. It seems one of movement captured in stone. With her extended arm producing a sweep of the veil, Veronica seems to have been halted between the excitement of her discovery and her eagerness to exhibit the holy treasure of the Lord's likeness."

Cruz says that "a door arranged at the base of the statue gives access to two corridors, one leading to the Vatican grottoes where the relics of St. Peter repose, the other ascending to the interior niche where the Holy Icon is kept." The veil is exposed from the high balcony each year on Good Friday.

Veronica is not mentioned in the Gospel account of our Lord's painful walk to Calvary. The incident of the veil has come down to us through Tradition, and the woman has been given the name Veronica because the Latin words for the true image that appeared on her veil are *vera icon*.

Q. One of our priests said we are not supposed to have fear of the Lord, but isn't this a gift of the Holy Spirit? — J.F.M., Wisconsin

A. Sacred Scripture tells us that "the fear of the LORD is the beginning of wisdom" (Psalm 111:10). But fear in this sense does not mean an irrational fright or terror. It means rather a reverential awe of God along with a recognition of our all-too-frequent failure to live the way He wants us to live. This gift of the Holy Spirit instills in us a desire not to offend or displease God in any way.

A holy and just fear of the Lord, Pope John Paul II has said, "does not exclude the trepidation that arises from an awareness of the faults committed and the prospect of divine chastisement, but mitigates it with faith in the divine mercy and with the certitude of the fatherly concern of God who wills the eternal salvation of each one."

Q. Just what is meant by a sin against the Holy Spirit that cannot be forgiven either in this world or in the next world? — K.J., Minnesota

A. In Matthew 12:31-32, Jesus says that "every sin, every blasphemy, will be forgiven men, but blasphemy against the Spirit will not be forgiven. Whoever says anything against the Son of Man will be forgiven, but whoever says anything against the Holy Spirit will not be forgiven, either in this age or in the age to come." It seems probable that this passage refers to the sin of final impenitence, the obstinate rejection of God's mercy and love even at the moment of death. While a person who is truly sorry for sin will always be pardoned, the person our Lord was talking about does not even seek pardon and completely and finally rejects the assistance the Holy Spirit offers to turn that person away from evil and back to God.

Q. In your recent explanation of what is meant by a sin against the Holy Spirit that cannot be forgiven, you gave the right answer. But there is more to it, as Pope John Paul II said in his encyclical, "On the Holy Spirit in the Life of the Church and the World." — H.M.N., Texas

A. Thank you for reminding us of the Holy Father's remarks, particularly when he says: "Blasphemy against the Holy Spirit, then, is the sin committed by the person who claims to have a 'right' to persist in evil — in any sin at all — and who thus rejects Redemption. One closes oneself up in sin, thus making impossible one's conversion, and consequently the remission of sins, which one considers not essential or not important for one's life. This is a state of spiritual ruin because blasphemy against the Holy Spirit does not allow one to escape from one's self-imposed imprisonment and open oneself to the divine sources of the purification of consciences and of the remission of sins" (n. 46).

Q. Does the Holy Spirit first enter the soul at Baptism? Does the spirit or soul exist at conception? Is there any Church authority that claims the spirit or soul exists prior to birth? — W.J.M., Florida

A. In his nighttime conversation with Nicodemus, Jesus said that "no one can enter into God's kingdom without being begotten of water and Spirit" (John 3:5). St. Paul said that God "saved us through baptism of new birth and renewal by the Holy Spirit. This Spirit he lavished on us through Jesus Christ our Savior" (Titus 3:5-6). And in the Rite of Baptism, there are several references to the child receiving new life in and through "water and the Holy Spirit."

While the Church has explicitly stated that the soul is infused at Baptism with the grace of the Holy Spirit, it has not declared precisely when God infuses the soul into the body. It is the common theological view that this infusion takes place at the moment of conception. This makes good sense since we know that human life begins at that point and that the soul is the life principle. If there is a growing and developing life in the womb, then obviously the soul is present long before the birth of the child.

Chapter 2

Sacred Scripture

Q. What is a good Bible to follow? Is the King James version okay for Catholics? — J.R.A., Alabama

Q. Is it true that the only Bible sanctioned by the Catholic Church is the Douay-Rheims translation? — J.W.S, Indiana

A. No, it is not true. The Douay-Rheims translation, which is still popular with some Catholics, goes back to the beginning of the 17th century. It was revised and issued by Bishop Richard Challoner in 1749 and 1750 and was the standard Catholic English version for about 200 years. In 1970, the first English translation ever made from the original languages under Catholic auspices was published as the New American Bible and, in 1987, another translation of the New Testament of the NAB, featuring some gender-exclusive language, was published. Also sanctioned for use in the liturgy are the Revised Standard Version and the Jerusalem Bibles, but the 1970 version of the NAB remains as the text most frequently used in the liturgy at the present time.

The King James Bible, originally published in 1611 and primarily used by Protestants, is incomplete. It omits or includes in a separate section as not authentic seven books that are found in the Old Testament section of Catholic Bibles, namely Tobit, Judith, Wisdom, Sirach (Ecclesiasticus), Baruch, and 1 and 2 Maccabees, as well as the last six chapters of Esther and parts of Daniel (chapter 3:24-90 and chapters 13 and 14).

A variety of Catholic Bibles are available in hard or soft cover, in regular print or large print, at any Catholic bookstore.

Q. Your statement that the New American Bible issued in 1970 was the first English translation ever made from the original languages is not accurate. Monsignor Ronald Knox translated the Bible from the original languages for the English hierarchy. — M.A.H., New York

A. Actually, the English translation published by Monsignor Knox in 1949 was taken from St. Jerome's Vulgate, a Latin version of the Bible that Jerome had translated from Greek and Hebrew between 390 and 405 A.D. Since Latin was considered at that time a vulgar language, or the language of the common people, Jerome's translation was called the "Vulgate." So it is correct to say that Monsignor Knox did not work from the original languages, but from Latin.

Editor's Note: Regarding a question about recommending a good Catholic Bible, Edith Myers of Texas, a knowledgeable and frequent contributor to Catholic publications, sends along these helpful comments:

"The New Testament of the New American Bible, revised from the 1970 edition and given an imprimatur in 1986, does not have inclusive language (or if in rare instances it does, they are hard to find), and is a tremendous improvement over the 1970 version. In many places it returns to traditional language, and some strange translations that were in the earlier version have been corrected. The 1986 translation of the New Testament is in all the New American Bibles that are being sold today, but unfortunately it has never been put into the Missal. At Mass we still have the 1970 translation.

"It is the Book of Psalms in the N.A.B., revised in 1991, that has the inclusive language, and that also, I am sorry to say, is in all the currently printed New American Bibles. It employs inclusive language in passages referring to God, as well as to people, and in the resulting awkward translation destroys the beauty of the psalms.

"Probably the best Catholic Bible we have now is the Ignatius Bible, which is a reprint of the 1966 Revised Standard Version, Catholic Edition. It differs in translation in a number of places from the original R.S.V. (e.g., "full of grace" instead of "favored one").

"There is also a Catholic edition of the New Revised Standard Version, but it doesn't have a different Catholic translation. The N.R.S.V. has some inclusive language, but applying only to people, not to God.

"The International Student Bible for Catholics (a New Testament only) is good for young people because it is in everyday language and has a section of 125 pages in the front explaining Catholic beliefs, doctrinal and moral."

Q. Is there a specific translation of the Bible that would be best for apologetics work? — G.J.L., Louisiana

A. Karl Keating, one of the Church's premier apologists, says that the best version of the Bible "will be the version you will read." He says that it might also be wise to purchase several translations of the Bible in order to compare the way different passages are translated, and to pick up an inexpensive copy of

the King James version since that is the one most Fundamentalists use. Keating also recommends buying a commentary
on the Bible, either *A New Catholic Commentary on Holy
Scripture* or *The Jerome Biblical Commentary*, as well as Fr.
William Most's book *Free From All Error* (Franciscan Mary-
town Press).

**Q. I was asked what the "Geneva Bible" was. Do you have
any information about this? — A.J.G., Montana**
    A. According to Fr. John Hardon's *Modern Catholic
Dictionary* (Doubleday), the Geneva Bible is "an English translation of the Bible, under Protestant auspices, published in
Geneva in 1560. It was the first English edition to use verse
divisions, had a strong Calvinist tone, and is popularly known as
the "Breeches Bible" because of its translation of Genesis 3:7,
'they ... made themselves breeches.'"

**Q. How can I find out about the *Didache*? Where can I find
out about the books that were not put into the Bible? —
J.M., California**
    A. The *Didache* is a summary of the teachings of the twelve
Apostles. It was compiled in the first and second centuries but
was not published until 1883 following its discovery by a Greek
Orthodox Metropolitan in an 11th century manuscript. Excerpts
from the *Didache* can be found in Volume I of *The Faith of the
Early Fathers* (Liturgical Press) by William A. Jurgens.
    Those writings that were not put into the Bible because their
sacred or inspired character was in doubt are called the
Apocrypha. There are dozens of apocryphal works, according to
the Catholic Church. They include the Books of Adam and Eve,
Martyrdom of Isaiah, Testament of the Patriarchs, Assumption of
Moses, Gospel of Peter, Gospel of James, Gospel of Thomas,
History of Joseph the Carpenter, Acts of John, Acts of Paul, Acts
of Peter, Acts of Andrew, and many more.
    In Protestant usage, the term Apocrypha refers to several Old
Testament works that appear in Catholic Bibles, but which have
been excluded by Protestants as uninspired books. These works
are Tobit, Judith, 1 Maccabees, 2 Maccabees, Wisdom, Sirach,
Baruch, and parts of Esther and Daniel.

**Q. What are the Dead Sea Scrolls? — F.A.F., California,
and J.J., Oregon**
    A. The Dead Sea Scrolls are a collection of manuscripts,
written mostly in Hebrew, that were discovered in caves near the

Dead Sea beginning in 1947. Dating from the first century before and the first century after Christ, the scrolls contain portions of virtually every book of the Old Testament, including a complete text of Isaiah, as well as writings about the Essenes, a strict Jewish sect that lived in that region from the second century B.C. to the second century A.D.

Bible scholars have been poring over the manuscripts and fragments of manuscripts since they were first discovered, and there has been considerable controversy over who should have control of them and what the scrolls tell us about the Old Testament and about the history of the Jewish people at the beginning of the Christian era. We can expect to hear more about these documents in the future.

Q. Did Moses and Jesus belong to the Essene brotherhood? A book I read recently said that the Benedictine monasteries were modeled after the Essenes and that St. Francis of Assisi's *Canticle to the Sun* is essentially identical to the Essene Gospel. — C.A.H., Pennsylvania

A. The Essenes were groups of Jewish ascetics who lived in Palestine from about the second century before Christ until the second century after Christ, when they disappeared from history. They are not mentioned in Scripture, but are referred to by ancient writers, such as Josephus (A.D. 37c-100), who said that there were about 4,000 of them in the latter part of the first century A.D. There is no evidence that Moses, Jesus, the Benedictines, or St. Francis had any connection with this sect.

According to Fr. John Hardon's *Modern Catholic Dictionary*, the Essenes "were an exclusive society, engaged mainly in agriculture. In general they renounced marriage, without denying its value, and recruited their ranks by adopting young children. They practiced the strictest community life, and also a vigorous caste system. Along with considerable superstition, they believed in Yahweh and in immortality."

Fr. Hardon said that "they had been almost forgotten in religious history until the discovery of the Dead Sea Scrolls in 1947. Almost certainly it was a community of Essenes that produced the treasure of literature found at Qumran, near the Dead Sea."

Q. Can you respond to the footnote in this book, which says that the Council of Toulouse in 1229 prohibited laypeople from possessing copies of the Bible and forbade them to have copies in the vernacular. It also said that the

Church in more recent times has condemned Bible societies and that the Pope in 1866 classed these societies with Communism, saying that "pests of this sort must be destroyed by all means." — R.S.R., Illinois.

A. Karl Keating, on pages 45-46 of *Catholicism and Fundamentalism* (Ignatius Press), has refuted the first charge. He explains that the Council of Toulouse (a local council, not an ecumenical council) was called to deal with the Albigensian heresy, which contended that the flesh was evil and, therefore, that marriage was evil and fornication and ritual suicide were not immoral. To justify their theories, the Albigensians used vernacular versions of the Bible and twisted them to support their immoral views. So the bishops meeting at Toulouse restricted the use of the Bible until the heresy was ended, and their action affected only the people of southern France.

As for the second charge, various Popes did condemn Protestant Bible societies because some of them circulated inaccurate translations and all of them promoted the interpretation of Scripture according to each individual's own private judgment. Pope Pius VII said that private interpretation of the Bible was contrary to these words of St. Paul: "I beg you, brothers, in the name of our Lord Jesus Christ, to agree in what you say. Let there be no factions; rather, be united in mind and judgment" (1 Corinthians 1:10). The Pope also quoted St. Augustine as having said that "heresies would not have arisen unless men had read good Scripture badly, and rashly asserted their own mistakes to be the truth."

Q. How do we know that the Bible is the inspired word of God? — R.J.S., Massachusetts

A. We know this because the Catholic Church, which Jesus established and guaranteed would always teach the truth, tells us that the Bible is the inspired word of God. Here are the steps leading to that conclusion:

(1) If we look at the Bible as a collection of books about religious history, we find in existence today several thousand partial and complete manuscripts, in many languages, going back over 2,000 years. A comparison of those manuscripts with each other, with the writings of Roman and Jewish historians, and with archaeological findings in the Middle East shows that the Bible gives us an accurate historical account of many persons, places, and events.

(2) If we look at the Gospels as reliable history books, they tell us about a man named Jesus who claimed to be God and proved

His claim with spectacular miracles, including His own resurrection from the dead. The Gospels tell us that Jesus established a Church (Matthew 16:18), and promised that it would last until the end of the world (Matthew 28:20) and would always teach the truth (John 14:16-17).

(3) For about three centuries after Christ, many manuscripts were circulated as the inspired word of God. These included not only the Gospels of Matthew, Mark, Luke, and John, but also "Gospels" attributed to Peter, James, and Thomas. The Catholic Church ended this confusion late in the fourth century (at the Councils of Hippo in 393 and Carthage in 397) by declaring which books were truly inspired by God and which were not. The Church gave us the very same Bible that Catholics use today, with 46 books in the Old Testament and 27 in the New Testament.

(4) Not only did the Catholic Church decide which books belonged in the Bible, but it has preserved the Bible through the centuries. If it were not for the Catholic Church, there would be no Bible. The Church has also been the reliable interpreter of biblical passages, according to the Second Vatican Council's *Constitution on Divine Revelation* (see also sections 85-86 of the *Catechism of the Catholic Church*):

"'The task of authentically interpreting the Word of God, whether written or handed on, has been entrusted exclusively to the living teaching office of the Church, whose authority is exercised in the name of Jesus Christ. This teaching office is not above the word of God, but serves it, teaching only what has been handed on, listening to it devoutly, guarding it scrupulously, and explaining it faithfully by divine commission and with the help of the Holy Spirit; it draws from this one deposit of faith everything which it presents for belief as divinely revealed" (n.10).

The document went on to say that "sacred tradition, sacred Scripture, and the teaching authority of the Church, in accord with God's most wise design, are so linked and joined together that one cannot stand without the others...." (*Ibid.*).

Q. I have a friend who claims that the Bible is the sole rule of faith and the only guide to heaven. Is my friend right? — P.J.H., New Jersey

A. No, your friend is wrong, and the Bible itself makes no such claim. Your friend may disagree and point to Paul's second letter to Timothy, where the saint says that "all Scripture is inspired of God and is useful for teaching — for reproof, correction, and training in holiness" (2 Timothy 3:16). But to say that Scripture is "useful" (other translations say "profitable") is not the same as saying that it is the *only* source of truth.

Catholics believe that we get divine truth not only from the Bible but also from sacred Tradition. This kind of Tradition, says the *Catechism of the Catholic Church* (n. 83), comes from the Apostles and hands on what they received from Jesus' teaching and example and what they learned from the Holy Spirit. It says that the first generation of Christians did not yet have a written New Testament, and that the New Testament itself demonstrates the process of living Tradition.

Since sacred Tradition and sacred Scripture flow "from the same divine wellspring," said Vatican II's *Constitution on Divine Revelation*, both "are to be accepted and venerated with the same sense of devotion and reverence" (n. 9).

Now your friend might say that Jesus condemned tradition (Matthew 15:3), but our Lord was referring to human traditions or customs that can be modified or even abandoned over time, such as the ritual washing of hands. When Catholics use Tradition with a capital "T", they mean what St. Paul meant when he told the Thessalonians to "hold fast to the traditions you received from us, either by our word or by letter" (2 Thessalonians 2:15). Or when he told Timothy: "The things which you have heard from me through many witnesses you must hand on to trustworthy men who will be able to teach others" (2 Timothy 2:2).

Finally, it doesn't make sense to claim that the Bible is the only guide to salvation. Jesus never said it was. He told the Apostles to go forth and teach, not to go forth and write a book. Furthermore, millions of people have lived and died without ever seeing a Bible, either because one was not available to them or because they could not read.

Jesus established the Catholic Church to help us get to Heaven by acting as an authentic and living interpreter of the Bible and Tradition. Rather than having each person try to decide what a biblical passage means — the disastrous results of that approach can be seen in the hundreds of religious denominations that have sprung up in recent centuries — Jesus gave us an infallible teaching authority to tell us how God wants us to live and what we must do to get to Heaven.

Q. Can you suggest any books that use biblical quotations that would help Catholics defend their beliefs when questioned by those of other faiths? — M.L., Florida

A. You could start with Karl Keating's book, *Catholicism and*

Fundamentalism, as well as his monthly magazine *This Rock*, which is available for $24 a year from P.O. Box 17490, San Diego, California 92177. Or a book by Mr. Keating's colleague, Patrick Madrid, who edited the stories of 11 converts to the Catholic Church in *Surprised by Truth* (Basilica Press), which contains hundreds of biblical quotes.

Available from Our Sunday Visitor are the books of Fr. Albert J. Nevins (*Answering a Fundamentalist* and *Strangers at Your Door*) and Fr. Peter Stravinskas (*The Catholic Answer Book, The Catholic Response*, and *The Catholic Church and the Bible*). And there is Fr. Robert Fox's *Protestant Fundamentalism and the Born-Again Catholic* (Fatima Family Apostolate).

Fr. Stravinskas also edits *The Catholic Answer*, a magazine published six times a year by Our Sunday Visitor, 200 Noll Plaza, Huntington, Indiana 46740, at an annual rate of $15.

Q. If Cain and Abel were the only children of Adam and Eve, how were their heirs produced? — C.B., Florida
A. First of all, Cain and Abel were not the only children of Adam and Eve. They had other sons and daughters, including a son named Seth (Genesis 5:3-4). Where did their descendants come from? There are two possible explanations: (1) They married other human beings on earth who did not take their origin from Adam and Eve. (2) The descendants of Adam and Eve produced heirs by marrying among themselves.

There is a theological problem with the first explanation. In his 1950 encyclical *Humani Generis*, Pope Pius XII said that Catholics could not "embrace that opinion which maintains either that after Adam there existed on earth true men who did not take their origin through natural generation from him as from the first parent of all, or that Adam represents a certain number of first parents" (n. 37). That opinion is known as polygenism, and the Holy Father said that it cannot be reconciled with the Church's teaching on original sin, "which proceeds from a sin actually committed by an individual, Adam, and which through generation is passed on to all and is in everyone as his own."

There is a moral problem with the second explanation, according to modern standards, but God permitted the marriage of brothers and sisters, nephews and nieces, for a limited time in order to propagate the human race. He most certainly protected the earliest human beings from the evils usually associated with intermarriage in families and, when these special circumstances were no longer necessary, God forbade such intermarriage.

Q. I was taught that because of the sin of Adam and Eve, we are born into the world with original sin and cannot get to Heaven unless we are baptized. Now I am led to believe that we no longer have to believe in Adam and Eve, original sin, or limbo, and that anyone can go to Heaven, even if they haven't been baptized. Please explain. — E.T., New Jersey

A. What you were once taught is still true, and anyone who has tried to tell you otherwise is wrong. The Second Vatican Council, recent Popes, and the *Catechism of the Catholic Church* have restated the Church's belief in the sin of our first parents, Adam and Eve, and the necessity of baptism to get to Heaven. Limbo, the theory that there is a place of natural happiness for infants who die without having been baptized, is only theological speculation; it has never been a defined doctrine of the Church.

Regarding children who have died without Baptism, the *Catechism* (n. 1261) says that the Church can only entrust them to the mercy of God, as she does in her funeral rites for them. It reminds us of the great mercy of God, who "wants all men to be saved" (1 Timothy 2:4), and Jesus' tenderness toward children which caused Him to say, "Let the children come to me and do not hinder them" (Mark 10:14).

These Scripture passages, says the *Catechism*, allow us to hope that there is way for unbaptized children to be saved.

The effects of original sin on the human race were spelled out by Vatican II in its *Pastoral Constitution on the Church in the Modern World* (n. 13) and the *Decree on the Apostolate of the Laity* (n. 7), by Pope Paul VI in his Credo of the People of God, by Pope John Paul II on several occasions, including in 1986 when he said that "as a result of original sin, human beings are born in a state of hereditary moral weakness and they easily follow the path of personal sin if they do not correspond with the grace offered by God to humanity by means of Christ's redemption," and by the *Catechism of the Catholic Church* (nos. 402-409).

For instance, the *Catechism* (n. 403) follows the lead of St. Paul in teaching what the Church has always taught, namely, that the overwhelming misery which oppresses men and women, and their inclination toward evil and death, cannot be understood apart from their connection with Adam's sin and the fact that he has transmitted to us a sin with which we are all born afflicted. This is why the Catholic Church baptizes even tiny infants who have not committed personal sin.

Baptism is still required to get to Heaven, but it can be baptism of water, of blood (martyrdom), or desire (a wish to belong to the

Church of Christ, even if one does not know what Church that is but still sincerely strives to do God's will by acting on the graces which God makes available to them). See the section on salvation in chapter 4 for more information on this matter.

Q. What is the Church's teaching on evolution of humans and animals from primitive lower life forms? Is evolution to be pushed and the Genesis account shunned? — M.S., Washington

A. The Church's position is that evolution is a theory that offers a possible explanation regarding the growth and development of animals and humans from earlier and more primitive organisms. While many people and many textbooks present evolution as a scientifically demonstrable fact, there is a growing body of material that raises questions about the evolutionary hypothesis. See, for example, such books as Michael Denton's *Evolution: A Theory in Crisis* (Adler & Adler) and Phillip E. Johnson's *Darwin on Trial* (Regnery Gateway).

At a general audience on April 16, 1986, Pope John Paul II said that the theory of evolution is "only a probability, not a scientific certainty." He went on to say that "the doctrine of faith, however, invariably affirms that a human's spiritual soul is directly created by God. According to the hypothesis mentioned, it is possible that the human body, following the order impressed by the Creator on the energies of life, could have been gradually prepared in the forms of antecedent living beings. But the human soul, on which man's humanity definitively depends, cannot emerge from matter because it is of a spiritual nature."

In other words, God could have fashioned the universe through an evolutionary process. But whether He did it that way or by direct creation, He still must be acknowledged as its Maker. With this basic premise established, the Church encourages scientists and scholars to continue their investigation so that someday we may know with certainty the method God used to bring human beings and the universe to their present state of development. The ultimate answer will involve no conflict between scientific and religious truth, for God is the Author of both.

The Genesis account of creation is not to be shunned. Nor is it to be regarded as a scientific and anthropological account of the origins of the universe and the human race. Rather, the beautiful and inspiring passages in Genesis are to be read as religious history in which the author used figurative language and popular descriptions to teach fundamental religious truths about salvation. Some of those truths are that God in His goodness created the universe out of nothing; that everything He created was good; that He created the first humans in His image and likeness; that those first humans lost their state of perfect happiness through the sins of pride and disobedience; that the whole human race suffers from the consequences of their sins; and that one day there will be a Redeemer for fallen humanity.

Q. Your recent reply about evolution makes it clear that mankind was probably not created in one day, as taught by the ancient Hebrews in Genesis. Since this was the only teaching of the Church on man's creation for many centuries, does this mean that doctrine does change and evolve, so that silencing of theologians with new ideas damages true religion? — J.T., New Jersey

A. The Genesis account of the creation of the world in six days was never a doctrine of the Church, so if scientists come up with some new evidence about when creation occurred, or how long it took, it will not mean that a doctrine of the Church has changed or evolved. The early chapters of Genesis do not contain scientific facts, but rather religious truths. Fr. William Most has summarized those truths in his fine book on the Bible entitled *Free From All Error*:

"God made all things; in some special way, He made the first human pair; He gave them some command (we do not know what the command was — the garden and the fruit are part of the stage setting); they violated the command and fell from favor" (p. 61).

These truths are doctrines that have been taught by the Church for nearly 20 centuries. Those who deny or cast doubt on them would be guilty of undermining some fundamental teachings of the Church.

Q. I recently read a short book entitled *Catholic Answers to Fundamentalists' Questions* by Philip St. Romain. I had problems with different parts of the book, especially the chapter entitled "Human Origins and Destiny." Could you comment on the book? — W.H.B., California

A. We also had problems with the book, and with a list of suggested readings that included the *Dutch Catechism* and books by Raymond Brown, Hans Kung, and Richard McBrien. As for the chapter you mentioned, St. Romain says on page 45:

"The theory of evolution is considered by scientists to be a credible explanation for the diversification of life forms. Catholic teachers of science would be terribly remiss if they withheld exposure to it from their students."

There are scientists who consider evolution a credible theory, but Mr. St. Romain would have done his readers a service by pointing out that an increasing number of scientists are finding the theory of evolution incredible. See, for example, the books *Evolution: A Theory in Crisis* by Michael Denton and *Darwin on Trial* by Phillip E. Johnson.

On page 47, St. Romain says that the story of Adam and Eve "is really the story of all of humanity," not just that of "two people only." He says that "as scientists continued to amass a wide variety of data strongly confirming the evolutionary hypothesis, theologians began working more freely on the polygenic alternative" to the Catholic teaching that original sin stemmed from Adam and not from multiple first parents of the human race. St. Romain concedes that "no polygenic explanations have been given full affirmation" by the Church, but says that "theologians have pointed out that God may well have chosen only one male and female out of a humanoid population to bear the consciousness of his image and likeness."

That's possible, but another suggested explanation, that "freedom was misused by one or perhaps many human beings, with the result that eventually we have all been affected and left short of the marks of innocence, justice, and immortality for which we were destined," does not square with the official Catholic attitude on polygenism as stated by Pope Pius XII in paragraph 37 of his encyclical *Humani Generis*.

Q. Why are we being punished for Adam's sin? Romans 3:23 and 5:12, as well as 1 Corinthians 15:22, state that all have sinned in Adam, but Deuteronomy 24:16 and Ezekiel 18:20 state that the children shall not be punished for the father's sin. This appears to be a contradiction. Besides, Adam ate the fruit. Why should a just God judge us guilty for a crime we didn't commit? — B.C.B., Massachusetts

A. Suppose you had a rich uncle who promised to give you a million dollars if you went to Mass every Sunday for ten consecutive years. Let's say that you kept your part of the bargain for a few years, but then went to Mass only sporadically, and lost out on the million dollars. If you had remained faithful to your promise, not only would you have benefited from the money, but so would your wife and children. Since you were not faithful, your family was not able to share in the promised wealth. But your uncle did not do your children any injustice since they had no right to the money.

So, too, with the human race. We are born in a state of original sin, not through any fault of our own, but because we receive the human nature which Adam and Eve had to give us. If they had remained faithful to God, we would have received a reward for their fidelity, and probably would not have complained that we didn't deserve any reward since we had done nothing ourselves to earn it. If we would gladly have accepted a reward for something we didn't do, we really cannot object to missing out on a reward because of something our first parents did. This is particularly true since we ourselves often fail to do what God wants us to do, just as Adam and Eve did.

The good news is that God did not abandon us after Adam and Eve disobeyed Him. He sent His only Son to die for our sins so that one day we would be able to enjoy the wonderful paradise that Adam and Eve lost because of their sin. Because Jesus laid down His life for us, said St. Paul, "all men are now undeservedly justified by the gift of God, through the redemption wrought in Christ Jesus" (Romans 3:24). Yes, "a single offense brought condemnation to all men," but it is equally true that "a single righteous act brought all men acquittal and life" (Romans 5:18).

As for the verses cited from Deuteronomy and Ezekiel, they have to do with miscellaneous laws and ordinances governing the Jewish people, not with the sin which we inherit as a result of our origin from Adam.

Q. Why was the book of Ecclesiasticus renamed Sirach? — H.B., Delaware

A. The book of Sirach or Ecclesiasticus has long been known by both names. It was at one time called *Liber Ecclesiasticus*, which means "church book," because it was used extensively in presenting moral teaching to catechumens and to the faithful. Its earliest title may have been Wisdom of the Son of Sirach, and it is called Sirach now because the man who translated the book from Hebrew into Greek sometime after 132 B.C. was the grandson of Sirach, a wise man who lived in Jerusalem and wrote the book sometime between 200 and 175 B.C.

Q. The first reading at Mass recently was taken from the book of Exodus, chapter 40, verses 16-21 and 34-38. But in my copy of the Bible, chapter 40 of Exodus contains only 36

verses. **Where are the other two? — H.B., Delaware, and M.K., Colorado**

A. Chapter 40 of Exodus contains 38 verses in the New American, King James, and Confraternity of Christian Doctrine translations of the Bible, but only 36 verses in the Douay-Rheims Bible. T.S. of Massachusetts has provided us with the following explanation:

"The versions of the Bible which you consulted are based on the Hebrew Masoretic text for much of the Old Testament, including the book of Exodus, while the Douay-Rheims version is a translation of St. Jerome's Latin Vulgate, which depended upon the Greek Septuagint for the Old Testament (although not completely). This resulted in a number of differences (major and minor) between the two texts, especially in the number or numeration of verses in chapters of the Old Testament.

"In the specific case of Exodus 40, the Douay-Rheims consolidates the concept expressed in verses 12-15 of the versions based on the Masoretic text ... and renders this in two verses (12-13). Verses 14-36 in the Douay-Rheims continue in the same manner as verses 16-38 in the versions which you consulted."

Q. Can you help me with a scriptural conundrum? Doesn't 1 Corinthians 15:22 contradict Deuteronomy 24:16? — B.C.B., Massachusetts

A. In his first letter to the Corinthians, Paul says: "For just as in Adam all die, so too in Christ shall all be brought to life." The passage in Deuteronomy reads: "Fathers shall not be put to death for their children, nor children for their fathers; only for his own guilt shall a man be put to death."

As illustrated in Joshua 7:24 and 2 Samuel 21:5, the primitive tribal law of Israel permitted the punishment not only of the guilty person but also of his family. Deuteronomy 24:16 is speaking of the criminal code and execution as the penalty for specific criminal acts, and makes clear that such a practice is wrong.

Paul is not saying that we die because Adam sinned, but that the way we experience death is conditioned by the fallen state of our nature. If Adam had not sinned, he would still at some point have been united with God by a transcendent act of surrender — death and transformation. The Redemption restores to humans that final condition as the God-willed end now available again because of the death of Jesus, the new Adam.

Q. Can you tell me what happened to the tablets on which the Ten Commandments were written and where they might be now? — M.B., New Jersey

A. Those stone tablets were carried about by the Israelites for many years in the Ark of the Covenant, a chest of acacia wood that God ordered Moses to build (Exodus 25:10-22). King David brought the Ark to Jerusalem (2 Samuel 6), and it remained there until the destruction of the temple and the city in 587 B.C., when it disappeared from history. The long-lost chest was the reason for the fictional perils of Indiana Jones in the movie *Raiders of the Lost Ark.*

Q. Are Catholics expected to believe in all of the Bible, part of it, or none of it? Catholics are taught that their God is a God of love, kindness, and mercy, but the God of Deuteronomy is a cursing God that wants to kill everything that breathes. — G.M., Louisiana

A. Catholics are expected to believe in all of the Bible because "all Scripture is inspired of God and is useful for teaching — for reproof, correction, and training in holiness so that the man of God may be fully competent and equipped for every good work" (2 Timothy 3:16-17).

You exaggerate in calling the God of Deuteronomy a cursing God who wants to kill everyone. Yes, there are places where those who do evil are cursed (Deuteronomy 27:14-26). But read Chapter 4, where Moses summarizes God's fidelity and love for his people. And read Chapter 30, verses 15-20, where Israel is given the choice between "life and prosperity, death and doom." Those who walk in the ways of the Lord will "live and grow numerous," while those who turn away from God and serve other gods "will certainly perish."

The choice before Israel is our choice as well: "I have set before you life and death, the blessing and the curse. Choose life, then, that you and your descendants may live, by loving the LORD, your God, heeding his voice, and holding fast to him. For that will mean a long life for you to live on the land which the LORD swore he would give to your fathers Abraham, Isaac, and Jacob."

Q. What is the Church's official teaching on Noah's Ark? A priest said that it was only a myth, but after watching a documentary on television recently, it would appear that the ark has been found. — M.B., California

A. We have seen films and pictures of an object high up in the mountains in Turkey that some believe is Noah's Ark. Expeditions have been launched in an effort to reach that remote spot and confirm the presence of the ark once and for all, but political objections by neighboring governments and extreme weather conditions have kept all such expeditions from reaching their goal.

These claims and ventures are fascinating, to say the least, but we are not aware of any hard evidence to prove that the shadowy object captured on film is in truth Noah's Ark.

As for the Church's position on Noah's Ark, it teaches what the Bible teaches — that there was a time of great wickedness on earth and that God decided to destroy the wicked with a flood, sparing only a good and blameless man named Noah and his family by telling them to build an ark to ride out the flood. Catholics are not required to take literally all the details of the story, e.g., whether Noah took two of every kind of animal on earth into the ark, or just the animals in his own region of the world; whether the flood covered the entire earth, or whether it covered only the whole of the particular area where Noah lived.

The real message of the Genesis account has less to do with historical details than with man's capacity for evil and God's justice and mercy. There is a lot of symbolism in the story, too, with the waters of the flood foreshadowing the waters of Baptism, and with the ark typifying the Church in a world of wickedness.

So it would be wrong to describe the story of Noah's Ark as a myth in the sense that the word is used today to mean something imaginary or fictitious. As Pope John Paul II has said, "the term 'myth' does not designate a fabulous content, but merely an archaic way of expressing a deeper content" (General Audience, November 7, 1979, as quoted in Fr. William G. Most's book *Free From All Error*, p. 64).

Q. Recently I heard one priest say that the biblical story of Jonah was a myth, and another priest say that there were many illnesses in biblical days, and that is what is meant when the Bible talks about devils and evil spirits being cast out. What is a person to believe? — M.P., Kansas

A. We are talking about two different things here. In the case of Jonah surviving three days in the belly of a whale, Catholics are free to view the incident reported in the Old Testament as didactic fiction, i.e., a story told to make a religious point, or they can believe that the event really happened.

Is such a thing possible? Certainly. The same God who raised Lazarus after four days in the grave could also have preserved Jonah for three days inside a sea creature. Or it could even be a completely natural occurrence. The *People's Almanac* reported the true story of a seaman named James Bartley who disappeared in 1891 after his shipmates had caught an 80-foot sperm whale. They thought that he had drowned, but when the crew cut the whale open the next day, Bartley was found alive inside the huge fish.

Jonah's time inside the whale may not have been three 24-hour days; it could have been less than half that if we count the time, like our Lord's three days in the tomb, as parts of three distinct days.

As for the contention that the exorcisms reported in the Bible did not really involve the casting out of evil spirits, that implies that Jesus could not tell the difference between someone with mental problems and someone possessed by the devil. Read some of the accounts of exorcisms performed by our Lord (Mark 1:23-27, 5:1-20, 9:14-29) and see if it seems that these persons were merely suffering from psychological illnesses.

Q. A friend of mine is bothered by the disturbing thought that the Apostles may have made up the whole story about Christ and that it never really happened at all. Can you help debunk these thoughts which bedevil my friend? — J.J.C., Ohio

A. There have been people down through the centuries who have advanced this theory of a conspiracy by the Apostles and the early Church. Some have contended that everything in the Gospels was invented; others have accepted the existence of Jesus as a good man, but have rejected His miracles and His resurrection. There are several things wrong with such conspiracy theories, however, including an abundance of historical evidence that supports the existence of a God-Man named Jesus who performed extraordinary wonders and founded a Church that has spread His teachings and brought His life-giving Sacraments to hundreds of millions of people over two millenia.

The Gospels a hoax? Look at what happened to the Apostles for telling others about Jesus. They were harassed, persecuted, and put to death. What conspirators would be willing to undergo a brutal and painful death for a lie? People may be willing to lay down their lives for the truth, but not for a lie.

More evidence of the pre-eminent place of Jesus in human history comes not from Christian sources, but from non-Christian and even pagan authorities. The existence of Jesus as a historical figure is confirmed in the writings of Tacitus, the Roman historian of the second century, and Josephus, the Jewish historian of the first century. And then there are the numerous archaeological explorations in the Holy Land that have corroborated time and again the places and events described in the New Testament.

H.V. Morton, the famous travel writer who visited all of the localities associated with the origins of Christianity, said that "one has to visit Palestine to understand how meticulously accurate is the Bible." In his book *In the Steps of the Master* (Dodd, Mead), Morton said that he could read pertinent passages from the Gospels while standing at Jacob's Well or in the Garden of Gethsemani and feel as if he had been transported back to the time of Christ, so accurately had the Evangelists described these places.

Among many other books that will provide your friend with historical facts to debunk conspiracy theories about the Gospels, you might consult *The Bible as History* by Werner Keller (William Morrow), volumes one and two of *Jesus and His Times* (E.P. Dutton Company) by Henri Daniel-Rops, *Daily Life in the Time of Jesus* (Hawthorn Books) by Daniel-Rops, *Life of Christ* (McGraw-Hill) by Fulton J. Sheen, and *The Life of Christ* (Bruce Publishing Company) by Giuseppe Ricciotti.

Q. A Jesuit priest told a friend of mine that none of the authors of the Gospels had ever actually met Jesus. When I told my friend that at least St. John the Apostle, the beloved disciple, had spent a great deal of time with our Lord, he countered by saying that St. John the Apostle and John the author of the fourth Gospel were two different people. What are we to believe? — T.K., Missouri

A. What this Jesuit priest, and other priests, theologians, and Scripture "scholars" are doing to the faith of Catholics today is a scandal. Instead of providing healthy food to those hungry for the truth, they are feeding the faithful the poison of error and fanciful theories. Here are the facts as the magisterium of the Church has affirmed them in Vatican II's *Constitution on Divine Revelation*:

"The Church has always and everywhere held and continues to hold that the four Gospels are of apostolic origin. For what the Apostles preached in fulfillment of the commission of Christ, afterwards they themselves and apostolic men, under the inspiration of the divine Spirit, handed on to us in writing the foundation of faith, namely, the fourfold Gospel, according to Matthew, Mark, Luke, and John" (n. 18).

Two footnotes accompany this passage. The first one says that apostolic men "refers to the generation partly contemporary with the Apostles, but younger than they; e.g., Mark and Luke." Thus, Mark and Luke were not Apostles, but got the information for their Gospels from persons who were eyewitnesses to the events in the life of Christ. Luke confirms this when he tells us in the preface to his Gospel that the events he recorded "were transmitted to us by the original eyewitnesses and ministers of the word" (Luke 1:2).

The other footnote cites the second century work of St. Irenaeus, *Against Heresies*. Irenaeus was a pupil of St. Polycarp, who knew John the Apostle. This connection would seem to make Irenaeus a reliable source of information about the authorship of the Gospels, and that is surely why his work is cited in the *Constitution on Divine Revelation*. Here is what Irenaeus said in *Against Heresies*:

"Matthew also issued among the Hebrews a written Gospel in their own language, while Peter and Paul were evangelizing in Rome and laying the foundation of the Church. After their departure, Mark, the disciple and interpreter of Peter, also handed down to us in writing what had been preached by Peter. Luke also, the companion of Paul, set down in a book the Gospel preached by him. Afterwards, John, the disciple of the Lord who reclined at his bosom, also published a Gospel, while he was residing at Ephesus in Asia."

It has been the clear teaching of the Church from the beginning that the Gospels were written by two Apostles, Matthew and John, and two "apostolic men," Mark and Luke. Those bent on ignoring or rejecting this constant teaching, and on upsetting the faith of ordinary Catholics with their novel speculations, ought to consider the warning issued by the Pontifical Biblical Commission in its 1964 *Instruction on the Historical Truth of the Gospels*. After emphasizing the need for "the greatest prudence" when presenting scriptural matters to the ordinary Catholic, the *Instruction* said:

"This virtue of prudence must especially be cultivated by those who write for [or speak to] the faithful at the popular level .... They must consider it a sacred duty never to depart in the least from the common doctrine and tradition of the Church. Yes, they may turn to their own use the real advances in biblical knowledge ... but must avoid altogether the rash fancies of innovators. They are strictly charged not to give in to a dangerous itch for novelty, recklessly disseminating attempts at the solution of difficulties without prudent sifting and serious discrimination — disturbing the faith of many."

Q. Some modern Bible scholars say that St. Luke did not know St. Paul. Is that true? — M.O., Massachusetts

A. It has been the unanimous tradition of the Catholic Church for nearly 1,900 years that Luke was a physician from Antioch who accompanied Paul on his journeys and based his Gospel on what Paul said about Jesus. This tradition is supported by St. Irenaeus, who died around 200 A.D. and who wrote in *Against Heresies*: "Luke also, the companion of Paul, set down in a book the Gospel preached by him."

Paul also mentions Luke in three of his letters: "I have no one with me but Luke," he says in 2 Timothy 4:11. He calls Luke one of "my fellow workers" in Philemon 1:24. And in Colossians 4:14, Paul says that "Luke, our dear physician, sends you greetings." There is no concrete evidence to support the modern theory that this is not the same Luke who wrote the third Gospel and the Acts of the Apostles.

Q. Does the Bible forbid the use of alcohol? — J.S., Ohio

A. Nowhere in Scripture is the use of alcohol prohibited. Drunkenness or misuse of alcohol is condemned (1 Corinthians 6:10), but not the moderate use of drink. Would Jesus have changed water into wine at Cana (John 2:1-11) if the Bible prohibited alcohol? Our Lord Himself drank wine and was falsely accused by His enemies of being a drunkard (Matthew 11:19).

Throughout the Bible you will find the clear distinction between the use and abuse of alcohol. See, for instance, Proverbs 20:1 and Proverbs 31:6-7. In the New Testament, St. Paul told the Ephesians to "avoid getting drunk on wine" (Ephesians 5:18), but he also told Timothy: "Stop drinking water only. Take a little wine for the good of your stomach, and because of your frequent illnesses" (1 Timothy 5:23).

Q. What is the Church's teaching regarding Elijah coming back as John the Baptist (Matthew 17:12-13)? Is this to be taken literally or figuratively? — J.D.T., North Dakota

A. This statement of our Lord is to be taken figuratively. Elijah and John the Baptist were two distinct individuals with the same mission: to prepare the way for the coming of the

Messiah. After referring to the Jewish tradition that Elijah was to come as a precursor of the messianic age, Jesus explained that the Old Testament prophet had come in the person of the Baptist.

Q. My niece who left the Catholic Church to join a Fundamentalist church wrote me a letter saying that all I had to do to be saved was to accept Jesus as my personal Savior. She cited as proof of this John 3:16: "For God so loved the world that he gave his only begotten Son, that whosoever believeth in him should not perish, but have everlasting life." Isn't she confusing redemption with salvation? — A.M., California

A. Yes, she is. Jesus did redeem us by His death on the cross, but salvation does not come simply through one act of accepting Christ as our Savior. The Catholic Church has always taught that our salvation depends on the condition of our soul at the moment of death. It must be free from sin and filled with sanctifying grace. We must make a lifelong effort to follow Jesus faithfully by keeping His commandments and adhering to the blueprint He laid down in the Sermon on the Mount.

St. Paul, great saint that he was, did not think that his salvation was assured by his born-again experience on the road to Damascus. He told the Philippians to "work with anxious concern to achieve your salvation" (Philippians 2:12). Other translations say, "Work out your salvation with fear and trembling."

A good discussion of this point of contention can be found in chapter 13 of Karl Keating's book *Catholicism and Fundamentalism.* It was Mr. Keating who suggested that the next time a Fundamentalist asks if you have been saved, you reply: "I am redeemed and, like the Apostle Paul, I am working out my salvation in fear and trembling, with hopeful confidence — but not with a false assurance — and I do all this as the Church has taught, unchanged, from the time of Christ."

Q. Would you please explain Matthew 10:28? I understand the soul to be immortal, hence indestructible. Is the passage correct, and does "him" refer to God? Also, is there a book you could recommend that would be helpful in answering such questions? — H.B., Delaware

A. Here is the verse in question: "Do not fear those who deprive the body of life but cannot destroy the soul. Rather, fear him who can destroy both body and soul in Gehenna."

When Jesus warned against those who could destroy the soul, He did not mean destroy in the sense of annihilating or putting it out of existence. The soul is immortal and will last forever, either in Heaven or Hell. Our Lord used destroy in this case to mean that the soul will fail to achieve its goal of union with God for all eternity, that it will wind up in Gehenna, a Hebrew word that came to mean Hell in the New Testament.

The word "him" in the verse does not refer to God; it refers to whomever can cause us to choose Hell over Heaven, either another person or perhaps the devil.

One book that would be helpful in understanding scriptural passages is the *Jerome Biblical Commentary*, which should be available through any Catholic bookstore or even your local public library.

Q. Can you explain the meaning of Jesus' words in chapter 23, verse 31 of St. Luke, and chapter 19, verses 26-27 of St. John? Why did Jesus call Mary "Woman" instead of "Mother"? — L.E.W., New York

A. In the first instance, Jesus had stopped on His way to Calvary to talk with the women of Jerusalem. After warning them of the calamities to come, our Lord said: "If they do these things in the green wood, what will happen in the dry?" He was saying that if the innocent, like Himself, must undergo many sufferings, those guilty of sin would be even more severely punished.

In the second instance, Jesus' use of the term "woman" for his mother ("Woman, there is your son") sounds disrespectful to us today, but at that time it was a common and rather formal way of speaking. In his encyclical *Mother of the Redeemer*, Pope John Paul II explains the signficance of the word:

"Jesus highlights a new relationship between mother and Son, the whole truth and reality of which he solemnly confirms. One can say that if Mary's motherhood of the human race had already been outlined, now it is clearly stated and established .... The mother of Christ ... is given as mother to every single individual and all mankind....

"The words uttered by Jesus from the cross signify that the motherhood of her who bore Christ finds a 'new' continuation in the Church and through the Church, symbolized and represented by John. In this way, she who as the one 'full of grace' was brought into the mystery of Christ in order to be his mother and thus the Holy Mother of God, through the Church remains in that mystery as 'the woman' spoken of by the book of Genesis (3:15) at the beginning and by the Apocalypse (12:1) at the end of the history of salvation. In accordance with the eternal plan of Providence, Mary's divine motherhood is to be poured out upon the Church, as indicated by statements of Tradition, according to which Mary's 'motherhood' of the Church is the reflection and extension of her motherhood of the Son of God."

Q. In the Gospel read on Palm Sunday, the centurion said of Jesus, "Surely this was an innocent man." Is this supposed to be a more accurate translation or is it another attempt to detract from the divinity of Christ? — J.G.F., New Jersey
A. Neither; it is a case of three evangelists giving slightly different versions of the same quotation. The New American Bible translation from Luke's Gospel that was read on Palm Sunday is very close to the pre-Vatican II translation, which said, "Truly this was a just man" (Luke 23:48).

What you are thinking of is the centurion's words as recorded in Matthew 27.54 ("Clearly this was the Son of God") and in Mark 15:39 ("Clearly this man was the Son of God"). In the translations that preceded the New American Bible, this statement was rendered, "Truly he was the Son of God" (Matthew) and "Truly this man was the Son of God" (Mark). So there has been no substantial change in the statement of the centurion as reported in the Gospels of Matthew, Mark, and Luke.

Q. Our daughter was very upset over a Gospel passage from Luke 12:49-53 because it sounded as if Jesus was trying to break up families. Can you clarify that passage? — W.B.P., Minnesota
A. In the passage from Luke, Jesus said that He had not come to establish peace on earth, but rather "for division. From now on, a household of five will be divided three against two and two against three; father will be split against son and son against father, mother against daughter and daughter against mother, mother-in-law against daughter-in-law, daughter-in-law against mother-in-law." A similar passage can be found in Matthew 10:34-39.

Jesus is not saying that He wants to break up families, but rather that there will be division in families among those who want to keep His teachings and follow His law and those who don't. For instance, there could be splits between a father and son over Mass attendance, between a mother and daughter over abortion, between a mother-in-law and daughter-in-law over divorce and remarriage.

Jesus does not desire these splits, but He is reminding us that they are inevitable unless all members of a family conform their lives to His divine plan. "Whoever loves father or mother, son or daughter, more than me is not worthy of me," Christ said. "He who will not take up his cross and come after me is not worthy of me" (Matthew 10:37-38).

Q. In Matthew 13 and Mark 4, Jesus told the Apostles, "To you the mystery of the reign of God has been confided. To the others outside it is all presented in parables, so that they will look intently and not see, listen carefully and not understand, lest perhaps they repent and be forgiven." Didn't Jesus want understanding, repentance, and healing? Are biblical parables used to *hide* moral precepts, or to *reveal* them? — F.J.C., Massachusetts

A. The purpose of a parable is to use a familiar life situation to teach a spiritual lesson. In both Matthew 13 and Mark 4, Jesus explains the parable of the sower and the seed to the Apostles but not to the crowd. The reason is that the disciples were well-disposed to accept the teachings of Jesus, while the crowds were not. Their hearts were still hardened and their minds were still darkened to an understanding of the mystery of the reign of God, and they would require a more gradual unveiling of that mystery.

Jesus wants understanding, repentance, and healing, but only when we have set aside all obstacles and are truly open to His love. Then the moral precepts hidden in the parables will be fully revealed to us.

Q. While visiting an unfamiliar parish recently, I heard the priest say, with reference to the Gospel reading (Matthew 5:17-37), that it consisted of "Aramaic exaggeration" and was not to be taken literally. What is "Aramaic exaggeration" and how is it relevant to the Gospel passage cited? — M.S., Maryland

A. The passage in question is from the Sermon on the Mount. Among other things, Jesus said that keeping the commandments against murder and adultery is not enough; we must also avoid anger and abusive speech and lustful thoughts. He then said that if a person's eye or hand leads one into sin, it would be better to gouge out that eye or to cut off that hand than to have one's entire body cast into Hell.

We are not familiar with the expression "Aramaic exaggeration," but if the priest was saying that our Lord here was using hyperbole or extravagant speech to make a point, the priest was right. Jesus was saying that eternal damnation is such a terrible punishment that a person would be better off in the long run to gouge out an eye or cut off a hand and go through life maimed rather than let that eye or hand lead to an eternity in Hell. Christ was not advocating such an extreme course of action, but He was trying to warn His listeners of the consequences of unforgiven sin.

Q. A recent Gospel reading (John 4:4-42) was about Jesus meeting with a Samaritan woman. Who were the Samaritans, why were Jews not supposed to socialize with them, and did they also believe in a Messiah? — J.L.N., New Jersey

A. The ancient conflict between the Jews and the Samaritans was both religious and political. Four centuries before Christ, the Samaritans, who were a mixed population of Jews not deported from the northern kingdom by its Assyrian conquerors and non-Jews resettled there by Assyria, made a complete break with the Jewish temple in Jerusalem and built their own temple on Mount Gerizim. They worshiped Yahweh, acknowledged only the first five books of the Old Testament, and considered themselves the only true descendants of the Hebrew patriarchs. Their temple was destroyed by John Hyrcanus, who ruled Judea from 134 to 104 B.C.

This longtime enmity between Jews and Samaritans was the reason why a Samaritan town refused hospitality to Jesus and the Apostles on another occasion (Luke 9:51-56), and why the woman at the well was so surprised that a Jew would speak to her. It was taboo for a Jewish rabbi to speak to any woman in public, let alone a Samaritan woman who was considered by the Jews to be ritually impure. Yet Jesus revealed to her that He was the Messiah the Samaritans had been waiting for, and this most unlikely disciple proceeded to persuade many of the people in her town to believe in our Lord.

Q. Enclosed are questionable articles from two issues of *The Catholic Communicator*, which is published by the Archdiocese of Santa Fe. Would you comment on them? — A.S.J., New Mexico

A. In the article about the miracle of the loaves and fishes, the writer said that one interpretation of the event was that "most of the people had actually brought food with them, but were afraid to let it be known, lest they lose it to the hungry crowd around them. But when the little boy came forward and gave his lunch to Jesus that it might be shared with everyone, his generosity shamed their selfishness, and they began to share with each other. Once the spirit of sharing and caring took over, it turned out there was food enough and to spare. In fact, there were twelve baskets left over."

That may be one interpretation of the miracle, but it is certainly not compatible with Catholic teaching since it implies that there was no miracle at all, that Jesus did not feed more than 5,000 people with five loaves of bread and two fish in a foreshadowing of the Eucharist.

The other article said that Jesus never got all the things He wanted during His life on earth and that a study of His life would show that "many, if not most, of His plans did not work out." This conclusion is nonsense. Jesus knew from His birth exactly what God's plan was and how it would affect His life. He wasn't some mindless robot caught up in events of which He had no knowledge and over which He had no control.

Jesus freely chose to do the will of His Father (Luke 22:42), which meant suffering and dying for our sins. His plans were His Father's plans, and they worked out exactly as He and His Father wanted them to work out.

Q. Can you explain why chapter 1, verse 5 in the Gospel of St. John was changed after Vatican II? One gets two different meanings. — A.F., Wisconsin

A. In the Confraternity of Christian Doctrine version published before Vatican II, the verse reads: "And the light shines in the darkness; and the darkness grasped it not." In the New American Bible translation of 1970, the verse reads: "The light shines on in darkness, a darkness that did not overcome it."

One does get two different meanings because the original Greek can be translated in different ways, according to the explanatory footnotes in both editions of the Bible. The footnote in the CCD translation says that "grasped may refer to man's failure to appreciate the light" of God's revelation and grace, but that "the Greek term can convey the idea of the darkness not restraining the light."

The footnote in the NAB version says that if the word overcome is used, "hostility between darkness and light is indicated, perhaps a reference to the sin of Gn 3. Other possible translations — 'grasp,' 'comprehend,' 'receive' — are preferred by those who regard the verse as referring to the ministry of Jesus."

Q. One of our local priests says that when St. Paul talked about wives being submissive to their husbands, he didn't mean men and women but was really talking about the Church. Is that true? — E.C., Pennsylvania

A. St. Paul was talking about both married couples and the Church, but some people who refer to his remarks in chapter 5 of his letter to the Ephesians usually quote only the admonition that "wives should be submissive to their husbands." It is necessary, however, to read the whole passage (verses 22-33) to get the true sense of what Paul was saying.

The apostle did not say that wives were inferior to their husbands, but rather that they should serve their husbands as the Church serves Christ. He also said that husbands should love their wives as Christ loves the Church. How did our Lord show His love for the Church? He suffered and died for it in the greatest demonstration of love the world has ever known.

The true meaning of St. Paul's words is that Christian marriage symbolizes the intimate relationship between Christ and the Church. This means that wives should serve their husbands in the same spirit that the Church serves Christ, and that husbands should love and care for their wives with the same devotion that our Lord has for His Church. What other analogy could Paul have used that would have conferred higher praise on husbands and wives?

Q. I understand that, according to the traditional teaching of the Church, the theological virtues of faith and hope do not exist in Heaven. The only virtue that exists there is charity or love. But doesn't this contradict 1 Corinthians 13:13, where St. Paul says: "There are in the end three things that last: faith, hope, and love, and the greatest of these is love"? — W.F.H., Rhode Island

A. "In the end" does not mean "in eternity," but rather at the end of any argument, discussion, or train of thought about these virtues. The sense of this verse is clearer in the Greek, which says, "but now remains ... faith (etc.)," and in the Confraternity of Christian Doctrine translation from 1961, which says, "So there abide faith, hope, and charity, these three; but the greatest of these is charity."

For further explanation of these theological virtues, with a great many Bible verses cited, see *The Teaching of Christ* (Our Sunday Visitor) by Lawler, Wuerl and Lawler, pp. 294-313, and the *Catechism of the Catholic Church*, nos. 1812-1829.

Q. What are we to think about the passage from 1 John 5:16-17? People I pray for frequently are steeped in mortal sin. Are we to despair of them? — R.S.F., Washington

A. Here is the passage: "Anyone who sees his brother sinning, if the sin is not deadly, should petition God, and thus life will be given to the sinner. This is only for those whose sin is not deadly. There is such a thing as a deadly sin; I do not say that one should pray about that."

While it is not completely clear what St. John means by sin in the first instance, he is probably referring to mortal sin since "life will be given to the sinner" who petitions God through the sacrament of Penance. The "deadly sin" probably refers to apostasy (the total rejection of the Catholic Faith by one who was baptized in that Faith) or to final impenitence (rejection of God's love and mercy at the moment of death).

John is not saying that we shouldn't pray for those who are steeped in mortal sin because only God knows whether a person is finally impenitent or not. We know from our Faith that God wants everyone to be saved: "As I live, says the Lord GOD, I swear I take no pleasure in the death of the wicked man, but rather the wicked man's conversion, that he may live" (Ezekiel 33:11).

Q. I have come across several interpretations of the last book of the Bible, each claiming to be the official Catholic interpretation, each boasting an imprimatur, and each contradicting the others. Does a truly official Catholic interpretation for the symbolism found in the last book of the Bible actually exist? — T.A., Missouri

A. Strictly speaking, no. The book of Revelation is one of the most difficult books in the Bible to understand because it is filled with extravagant symbolism and apocalyptic imagery surrounding the battle between good and evil and the ultimate triumph of Christ over Satan. Much of the book symbolically reinterprets conditions contemporary with the times during which it was written. Both the Douay and the New American Bible translations have extensive notes explaining the symbolism of John's visions, and those notes are as close as you will get to an official Church interpretation of the final book of the Bible.

Chapter 3

Church and Papacy

Q. I would like to know who became the first priests after the Apostles. In Acts 6:6, we read about the Apostles imposing hands upon seven men who are commonly referred to as deacons, so when did the first priests come into being after the Apostles? — A.O., New York

A. In the May 1993 issue of *This Rock*, Karl Keating provides us with this explanation:

"The English word 'priest' is derived from the Greek word *presbuteros*, which is commonly rendered into Bible English as 'elder' or 'presbyter.' The ministry of Catholic priests is that of the presbyters mentioned in the New Testament (Acts 15:6, 23). The Bible says little about the duties of presbyters, but it does reveal they functioned in a priestly capacity.

"They were ordained by the laying on of hands (1 Tim. 4:14, 5:22), they preached and taught the flock (1 Tim. 5:17), and they administered sacraments (Jas. 5:13-15). These are the essential functions of the priestly office, so wherever the various forms of *presbuteros* appear — except, of course, in instances which pertain to the Jewish elders (Matt. 21:23, Acts 4:23) — the word may rightly be translated as 'priest' instead of 'elder' or 'presbyter.'"

Q. When was the title "father" first used for priests? — J.B.L., Massachusetts

A. According to *The Jerome Biblical Commentary*, the use of the title "father" began in monasteries as a form of address to the abbot as father of the monastic family. It was then extended to other monks who served as spiritual directors, and later generally applied to the clergy. There is no date given, but since the Rule of Benedict (circa 525) already speaks of the paternal role as typical, the use of "father" probably began in the fifth century, if not earlier. (See pages 25-26 for the answer to those who say that Jesus told us to call no one "father.")

Q. I know there are sinners in the Church, but is it correct to call the Church sinful? — M.M.D., Virginia

A. There are sinners in the Church, but to describe as sinful what St. Paul called "the Body of Christ" (1 Corinthians 12:27) would be wrong. In the words of Vatican II's *Constitution on the Church* (see the *Catechism of the Catholic Church*, n. 823):

"Faith teaches that the Church ... is holy in a way which can never fail. For Christ, the Son of God, who with the Father and the Spirit is praised as being 'alone holy,' loved the Church as His Bride, delivering Himself up for her. This He did that He might sanctify her (cf. Eph. 5:25-26). He united her to Himself as His own body and crowned her with the gift of the Holy Spirit, for God's glory. Therefore in the Church, everyone belonging to the hierarchy, or being cared for by it, is called to holiness..." (n. 39).

Pope Paul VI, talking about the holiness of the Church in his *Credo of the People of God*, said the Holy Spirit "gives her life and movement. She is therefore holy, though she has sinners in her bosom, because she herself has no other life but that of grace; it is by living by her life that her members are sanctified; it is by removing themselves from her life that they fall into sins and disorders that prevent the radiation of her sanctity."

Q. Why do Catholics believe that their Church is the one, true Church founded by Jesus? — M.E.T., Massachusetts

A. The Gospels tell us that Jesus founded a Church while He was on earth when He said to Peter, "You are 'Rock' and on this rock I will build my church" (Matthew 16:18). Jesus indicated that His Church would last forever when He said, "I am with you always, until the end of the world" (Matthew 28:20).

Catholics believe that their Church was founded by Christ because the current leader of the Catholic Church is the historical successor of St. Peter and because it alone possesses four signs or marks — one, holy, catholic, and apostolic — that point to the Church of Christ.

(1) Our Lord said that His Church would have unity ("There shall be one flock then, one shepherd" — John 10:16), and this unity or oneness in leadership, worship, and belief is most evident in the Catholic Church.

(2) Since Jesus is holy, His Church must be holy in its members and its miracles. The Catholic Church can claim an extraordinary number of saints and martyrs and holy men, women, and children who have faithfully followed the teachings of our Lord. As for Christ's promise that "signs like these will accompany those who have professed their faith ... the sick upon whom they lay their hands will recover" (Mark 16:17-18), the Catholic Church has from the beginning been blessed with thousands of miraculous cures all over the world.

(3) Jesus indicated that His Church would be catholic, or universal, when He said that it would last "until the end of the world" and when He told the Apostles to spread it to "all the nations" (Matthew 28:19). Only the Catholic Church has existed since the time of Christ and exists everywhere in the world today.

(4) Only the Catholic Church is apostolic in that its bishops can trace their historical succession back to the Apostles, who were the first bishops of Christ's Church, and the bishops today are teaching the same things that the Apostles taught. For proof of this, compare the Apostles' Creed from the first century with the Nicene Creed from the fourth century and the Credo of the People of God issued by Pope Paul VI in 1968.

That is why Vatican II's *Declaration on Religious Freedom* (and the *Catechism*, n. 2105) said that the "one true religion subsists in the catholic and apostolic Church" (n. 1).

Q. I recently heard a priest say that in his opinion there are no longer four marks of the Church. We are only holy, catholic, and apostolic, he said, but no longer one. Who instituted the concept of the four marks, and isn't the priest guilty of heresy? — D.I.F., California

A. The four marks or signs by which we can recognize the Church founded by Jesus Christ appear first in the creed which came out of the Councils of Nicea and Constantinople in the years 325 and 381. Near the end of that creed, or Profession of Faith, we express our belief in "one, holy, catholic, and apostolic Church."

That belief is spelled out in great detail in paragraphs 811-870 of the *Catechism of the Catholic Church*, beginning with the statement: "This is the sole Church of Christ, which in the Creed we profess to be one, holy, catholic, and apostolic. These four characteristics, inseparably linked with each other, indicate essential features of the Church and her mission" (n. 811).

Heresy means a denial of some truth of the Catholic Faith, but we can't tell from the question whether the priest is obstinately rejecting unity as a mark of the true Church, or whether he might have meant that the unity willed by Christ for His Church (John 17:20-21) is being seriously undermined today by people who call themselves Catholics but whose words and actions are far from the teachings of our Lord, as expressed by the Holy Father, the Vicar of Christ, and those in communion with him.

But whatever the priest had in mind, unity remains one of the four essential marks of the Church.

Q. How do you answer those folks who say that the Catholic Church is wealthy and should sell its treasures to help the poor and homeless? — W.J., Arizona

A. First of all, the Catholic Church is not wealthy in the usual sense of the word. Yes, the Church does have a worldwide network of churches, schools, convents, monasteries, hospitals, orphanages, and homes for the aged, the troubled, and the dying. But these physical structures are not used to make anyone rich; they are used to bring the teachings and love of God to the people of every nation. It costs a huge amount of money to maintain these buildings and operate the agencies and programs they house, and the universal Church, which exists to save souls, not to make a profit, runs a large deficit every year.

Second, while the Catholic Church does own many valuable books, works of art, and historical treasures, it serves only as a depository for them. It was the Church that saved these masterpieces from barbarian invaders centuries ago, and it is the Church that preserves them today for all to enjoy.

Third, even if the Church did sell all these priceless artifacts and gave the money to the poor, the proceeds would provide hardly more than a day's food to the millions of hungry people around the world. They would be hungry again the next day, but the marvelous treasures of our civilization would be in the hands of private individuals and no longer available to the public.

Fourth, we must bear in mind that no one has done more for the needy of the world than the Church, thanks to the tremendous generosity of millions of faithful Catholics. The Church does not have to apologize to anyone for failing to assist the least of our brothers and sisters.

Finally, did you ever wonder why those who want the Catholic Church to sell its treasures never make the same demand of governments or museums? Is it possible, as Bishop Fulton Sheen once suggested, that some of these critics don't really care about the poor, but attack the Church because they don't like its teachings against abortion, contraception, divorce, homosexual behavior, or some other issue?

Q. Would you please name all 12 Apostles and when and how they died. Also, please name the first 10 Popes and the years of their reigns. — T.F., New York

A. The names of the Apostles, as they are listed in chapter 10 of Matthew's Gospel, are Simon, also known as Peter, and his brother Andrew; James, Zebedee's son, and his brother John;

Philip and Bartholomew, Thomas and Matthew the tax collector; James, son of Alphaeus, and Thaddaeus; Simon the Zealot Party member, and Judas Iscariot.

There are no historical accounts of when and how the Twelve died, but tradition says that Peter was crucified in Rome sometime between 64 and 67; Andrew was martyred in Patras around 70; James the Greater was beheaded in Jerusalem in 44; John died a natural death at Ephesus about 100; Philip was crucified in Phrygia; Bartholomew (Nathaniel) was flayed and beheaded in Armenia; Thomas was martyred in India; Matthew was killed with a spear in Ethiopia; James the Less was either stoned to death in 62 or thrown from the top of the temple in Jerusalem in 66; Thaddaeus (Jude) was killed with a halberd in Persia; Simon was sawed in two in Persia; and Judas hung himself in Jerusalem in 30.

The first 10 Popes were St. Peter (30-64 or 67), St. Linus (67-76), St. Anacletus (76-88), St. Clement (88-97), St. Evaristus (97-105), St. Alexander I (105-115), St. Sixtus I (115-125), St. Telesphorus (125-136), St. Hyginus (136-140), and St. Pius I (140-155).

Q. After attending a course in Christology and the Church, which seemed to contradict official Catholic teaching, I am concerned that liberal elements in the Church could overturn divinely revealed truth. Is this possible? — F.D., New York

A. No, it is not possible. Jesus promised that the gates of Hell ("jaws of death") would never prevail against His Church (Matthew 16:18). This is not to say that heresies (denials of one or more of the Church's divinely revealed truths) could not become widespread in the Church, as did Arianism, which denied the divinity of Jesus, in the fourth century. Or in our own time when many truths of the Faith are being denied, distorted, or denigrated by persons who purport to speak as representatives of the Church.

This current situation, to which F.D. referred, has caused the Holy Father and the magisterium of the Church, particularly the Sacred Congregation for the Doctrine of the Faith, to issue various statements and documents exposing the falsity of some modern interpretations of Catholic doctrines and beliefs. Pope Paul VI issued his Credo of the People of God in 1968 for the specific purpose of quieting the "disturbance and perplexity in many faithful souls" caused by those who were loudly disputing Church teachings.

And since that time, there have been such documents as *Errors Concerning the Mysteries of the Incarnation and the Trinity*, the *Declaration in Defense of the Catholic Doctrine on the Church Against Some Present-Day Errors*, the *Declaration on Procured Abortion*, *Christian Faith and Demonology*, the *Declaration on Certain Problems of Sexual Ethics*, *The Reality of Life After Death*, the *Declaration on Euthanasia*, *The Splendor of Truth*, and of course the *Catechism of the Catholic Church*, which Pope John Paul II called "a sure and authentic reference text for teaching Catholic doctrine" (n. 3).

Faithful Catholics know that the deposit of divinely revealed truth will never be overturned or replaced because there will always be an infallible teaching authority to steer the Barque of Christ through the storms of heresy. Remember that Jesus promised to be with His Church "always, until the end of the world!" (Matthew 28:20), and to give His Church "another Paraclete — to be with you always: the Spirit of Truth" (John 14:16-17). We can take comfort in these promises of our Lord while at the same time praying and working to keep members of the Church faithful to the truths handed down to us from the Apostles.

Q. What is the Affirmation Creed and is it binding on Catholics? — T.T.H., Pennsylvania
A. We are not familiar with an "Affirmation Creed." You may be thinking of the Athanasian Creed, a statement of beliefs attributed to St. Athanasias (296-373) but possibly written or revised by St. Ambrose. That Creed, which has the official approval of the Church and once had a place in the Liturgy of the Hours, focuses almost exclusively on the Trinity and the Incarnation. It also contains numerous anathemas condemning those who would reject its doctrinal statements.

Q. As a recent newcomer to the Catholic Faith, I would like to know where did the tradition of having a Pope originate? — M.L., Alberta
A. The tradition of having a Pope began when Jesus chose Peter to be the head of His Church by changing his name from Simon to Peter, calling him the "rock" on which the Church of Christ would be built, and giving him authority over that Church (Matthew 16:15-20). Peter's role as supreme leader of the new Church was indicated time and again in the Acts of the Apostles (e.g., Acts 1:15-26; 5:1-10; 15:6-12).

Since the time of Peter, the record shows a long line of men who have taken his place as Bishop of Rome, and the manner in which they have exercised their reponsibility has developed historically. The only one man in all the world today who even claims to be filling Peter's shoes is Pope John Paul II, who has on many occasions specifically called himself the successor of Peter. For example, during a visit to Detroit in 1987, the Holy Father said: "I come to you as the successor of St. Peter, and therefore, as the [Second Vatican] Council reaffirms, as the Vicar of Christ and pastor of the whole Church, as shepherd of all Christ's flock. This is because in St. Peter the Lord set up a lasting and visible source and foundation of our unity in faith and in communion."

Q. How many of the more than 260 Popes would you characterize as being corrupt? — G.P., Florida

A. It is generally agreed by historians that four or five Popes were guilty of serious moral lapses. Some critics of the Church have tried to use this information to undermine the Catholic teaching on infallibility. But they are confusing infallibility (the inability of the Holy Father to teach error when he speaks on a matter of faith and morals) with impeccability (the inability of the Holy Father to commit a sin). The Church has never claimed impeccability for any Pope, although many of them have lived lives of extraordinary holiness, because we are all sinners, but it has claimed the charism of infallibility for every Pope because of Christ's promises to be with His Church all days, and never to let the gates of Hell prevail against it.

The fact that some Popes were wicked in their private lives is no argument against the truth of the Catholic Church, anymore than immoral conduct by an American President is an argument against the goodness of the United States. In fact, it is an argument for the reliability of the Church since it continued during the reign of those unworthy Popes to teach faithfully the truths handed down by Christ and the Apostles and suffered no lasting harm from the immoral conduct of a tiny percentage of its leaders.

Q. A co-worker who is Baptist and is heavy in the study of the end of the world recently asked me if I knew any facts that the Antichrist will come out of Rome. Can you shed some truth on this? — P.A.S., Iowa

A. The Antichrist is specifically mentioned only in the letters of St. John (1 John 2:18, 2:22, 4:3, and 2 John 7), and John identifies this person as "he who denies that Jesus is the Christ."

St. Paul doesn't use the word "Antichrist," but talks about "the man of lawlessness ... that son of perdition and adversary who exalts himself above every so-called god proposed for worship, he who seats himself in God's temple and even declares himself to be God" (2 Thessalonians 2:3-4).

Paul goes on to say that the lawless one will be revealed in time, "and the Lord Jesus will destroy him with the breath of his mouth and annihilate him by manifesting his own presence. This lawless one will appear as part of the workings of Satan, accompanied by all the power and signs and wonders at the disposal of falsehood — by every seduction the wicked can devise for those destined to ruin because they have not opened their hearts to the truth in order to be saved" (2 Thessalonians 2:8-10).

While some historical figures, such as Nero, have been labeled as antichrists, and there are those who foolishly think that the Pope is the Antichrist (hence your friend's question about whether the Antichrist will come out of Rome), the common Catholic interpretation is that the Antichrist is a real person who will engage in a final apocalyptic struggle with Christ before the end of the world. The *Catechism of the Catholic Church* talks about "a final trial that will shake the faith of many believers" (n. 675). It refers to a religious deception that will offer human beings an apparent solution to their problems at the price of apostasy from the truth. But the supreme religious deception, the *Catechism* says, will be the Antichrist, a pseudo-messiah whom people will follow instead of following God and the true Messiah, His Son Jesus.

The Church, the *Catechism* says, will enter the glory of the kingdom only after passing through this final Passover, when she will follow her Lord in His death and resurrection. Then the kingdom will be fulfilled by God's victory over the final unleashing of evil, which will cause Jesus to come down from Heaven. God's triumph over the revolt of evil, says the *Catechism*, "will take the form of the Last Judgment after the final cosmic upheaval of this passing world" (n. 677).

Q. I reluctantly admit that my faith was shaken after reading a book called *National Sunday Law* by an A. Jan Marcussen, especially the interpretation of "Vicarius Filii Dei" as Roman numerals that add up to 666. Can you comment? — M.Y., Maryland

A. We are not familiar with the book, but the ludicrous, if not malicious, attempt to equate the Holy Father with Satan (666 is reputed to be the mark of the beast, according to Revelation 13:18) has been convincingly demolished by Karl Keating on pages 221-222 of *Catholicism and Fundamentalism.*

One of the titles of the Pope is Vicar of Christ (*Vicarius Christi*), but the numerical value of those letters do not add up to 666. So anti-Catholics like Ralph Woodrow, author of *Babylon Mystery Religion*, have invented a new title for the Pope, Vicar of the Son of God (*Vicarius Filii Dei*) because those letters do add up to the number of the beast.

The most commonly accepted theory is that the beast of Revelation was the Emperor Nero Caesar, who was an unmerciful persecutor of the early Christians and whose name adds up to 666. But if you want to play games with people's names, says Karl Keating, there are lots of individuals who could be identified as the beast, including Martin Luther, whose name in Latin also totals 666!

Q. I am writing to ask you about the papal title "Vicarius Filii Dei." A letter from Bill Jackson quotes you as saying: "... anti-Catholics like Ralph Woodrow have invented a new title, Vicar of the Son of God," etc. He then quotes from "Our Sunday Visitor" (April 18, 1915) that "the letters inscribed on the Pope's miter are Vicarius Filii Dei." I have come to understand over recent years that the number 666 can be applied to a multitude of names, so I have no desire to make some big point regarding a papal title. But can you clarify the above discrepancy? Was "Our Sunday Visitor" in error or has it, perhaps, been misquoted? Is it possible that both titles have been used within the Roman Catholic Church? — Ralph Woodrow, California

A. Mr. Woodrow is head of an organization called the Evangelistic Association and author of *Babylon Mystery Religion*, a book that, as Karl Keating has demonstrated in *Catholicism and Fundamentalism*, is filled with erroneous statements about the Catholic religion, including the allegation that one of the Pope's titles is Vicar of the Son of God. If numerical values are assigned to the Latinized version of that title (*Vicarius Filii Dei*), said Mr. Woodrow in his book, the letters add up to 666, which Revelation 13:18 tells us is the number of the beast. This "revelation" has led many gullible people to believe that the Pope is the beast.

We are happy to know that Mr. Woodrow has come to realize that the number 666 can be applied to a multitude of names, and we are glad to have the opportunity to respond to his question about the quote that reportedly appeared in *Our Sunday Visitor*.

We called the *Sunday Visitor* and spoke to Robert P. Lockwood, president of the OSV corporation. Mr. Lockwood told us that he had looked into this allegation before and discovered that Fr. John Noll, in a column entitled "Bureau of Information" that appeared in the April 18, 1915 issue of *Our Sunday Visitor*, had indeed said that the letters inscribed on the Pope's miter are *Vicarius Filii Dei*.

Mr. Lockwood said that he did not know what Fr. Noll's source was, that there is no way of discovering his source since then-Archbishop Noll died in 1956, and that it was surely just a mistake made by a very busy priest, one who wrote virtually all the copy for the newspaper in its early years (OSV began publication in 1912).

That assigning the title "Vicar of the Son of God" to the Holy Father may have been a mistake is further indicated by the fact that Fr. Noll, in the same column, said that "the Bishop of Rome, as head of the Church, was given the title 'Vicar of Christ,'" which in Latin is *Vicarius Christi* and does not add up to 666. That, of course, is the correct title, and not Vicar of the Son of God.

We can also assume that it was a mistake from the fact that we have found no corroboration anywhere that any Pope was ever called Vicar of the Son of God. A recent (1967) edition of the *Catholic Encyclopedia* lists the following titles of the Holy Father: Bishop of Rome, Vicar of Jesus Christ, Successor of the Chief of the Apostles, Supreme Pontiff of the Universal Church, Patriarch of the West, Primate of Italy, Archbishop and Metropolitan of the Roman Province, and Sovereign of the State of Vatican City.

Well, maybe Vicar of the Son of God was a title in use when Fr. Noll wrote his column. Not true. According to the 1911 edition of the *Catholic Encyclopedia*, the title pope was used "solely to denote the Bishop of Rome, who, in virtue of his position as successor of St. Peter, is the chief pastor of the whole Church, the Vicar of Christ upon earth. Besides the bishopric of the Roman Diocese, certain other dignities are held by the pope as well as the supreme and universal pastorate: he is Archbishop of the Roman Province, Primate of Italy and the adjacent islands, and sole Patriarch of the Western Church."

The same article lists the "most noteworthy" titles of the Holy Father as Papa, Summus Pontifex, Pontifex Maximus, and Servus Servorum Dei. Another article, under the heading "Vicar of Christ," said that some popes had been called Vicar of

St. Peter and Vicar of the Apostolic See, and Pope Nicholas III (1277-1280) was known as Vicar of God. But no pope was called Vicar of the Son of God.

We also looked into whether titles of any kind have appeared on miters, the liturgical headdress worn by popes, cardinals, abbots, and bishops of the Latin Rite. While miters were of different shapes over the centuries, and were sometimes adorned with gold embroidery and even precious stones, there is no indication of any words or titles being written on them.

In the 1911 *Catholic Encyclopedia*, for example, there are sketches of ten miters of various shapes that were in use from the 11th to the 20th century, with no writing on them. There is also a picture of an elaborate 16th-century miter with paintings of scenes from our Lord's life, but no words or titles.

And if you want to see a papal miter up close, you can visit the Shrine of the Immaculate Conception in Washington, D.C., and view the miter worn by Pope Paul VI during his pontificate. The miter is enclosed in a glass case and, as you walk around the case, you will not see any writing on his miter.

So those who base their charge that the Pope is the beast of Revelation solely on a single mistake in a column written eight decades ago are on very shaky ground. Their case is further shredded by a total lack of historical evidence to back up their allegation.

Finally, the charge is contrary to all common sense. In just our own century, for example, please tell us what Pontiff resembles the evil beast of Revelation? Pope St. Pius X? Benedict XV? Pius XI? Pius XII? John XXIII? Paul VI? John Paul II? How many magnificent documents have these men written, reaffirming teachings that go back to Christ Himself? How many thousands of talks have they given, calling people to holiness? How many thousands of miles has John Paul II traveled, urging those on every continent to follow Christ?

Have those who believe the Holy Father to be an agent of Satan ever listened to one of his talks and wondered how a man who sounds so good could be so bad? Have they ever noticed how often the Pope quotes from the Bible that they revere? Did they watch the way that John Paul challenged President Clinton to his face on the evil of abortion in Denver in August 1993? Did they watch the way the Holy Father called the youth of the world to serve Christ, and the tremendous enthusiasm this septuagenarian was able to generate among teenagers and young adults?

The man has an aura of goodness and holiness about him, and

that is why people of all faiths, and of none, are so attracted to him and to what he says. He is a moral and spiritual lighthouse in a world that is foundering on the rocks of sin and secularism. All faithful Catholics and other Christians ought to be thrilled to have a spiritual leader who has the courage to proclaim "the splendor of truth" to a culture steeped in falsehood.

Satan is the "father of lies" (John 8:44), our Lord said. John Paul is an apostle of truth, guided to all truth by the "Spirit of truth" promised by Jesus at the Last Supper (John 16:13). This makes the Holy Father not an ally but an enemy of Satan. Are those who denounce the Pope so blind, so caught up in an unreasonable hatred of the papacy, that they cannot recognize that he is doing the work of God and not the work of the Devil?

Mr. Woodrow, Mr. Jackson, and others are certainly free to disagree with the teachings of the Pope and the Catholic Church, but they ought to make sure that their reasons for disagreement are not based on falsehood. For in disputing the Catholic Church, they are disputing what St. Paul called "the pillar and bulwark of truth" (1 Timothy 3:15).

Q. Would you please tell us about the Papal Coronation Oath, its history and significance with respect to succession to the papacy? — P.M.D., Kansas

A. There is no oath involved in the coronation of a pope. You may be thinking of the words pronounced by the second cardinal deacon as he placed the papal tiara on the new Pope's head: "Receive the tiara adorned with three crowns, and know that you are the father of princes and kings, ruler of the earth, and earthly vicar of our Savior Jesus Christ, to whom is honor and glory forever. Amen."

The last Pope to be crowned with the papal tiara, a tall headdress ornamented with precious stones, was Paul VI, who later gave the tiara to the poor. When Pope John Paul I assumed office on September 3, 1978, he was installed with the pallium, a circular band of white wool ornamented with six small crosses that is worn about the neck and shoulders as a symbol of the fullness of episcopal authority.

Pope John Paul II, who was invested in similar fashion on October 22, 1978, said of the tiara: "This is not the time to return to a ceremony and an object considered — perhaps wrongly — to be a symbol of the temporal power of the popes. Our time calls us, urges us, obliges us, to gaze on the Lord and to immerse ourselves in humble and devout meditation on the mystery of the supreme power of Christ himself."

Q. I have always been perplexed and saddened by the controversy about Pope Pius XII's role in the "Final Solution." This was certainly a moral problem on which the Pope should have spoken out. Is it possible that the disobedience and disloyalty exhibited so publicly today had the seeds of its beginning 50 years ago? If Pope John Paul I could be murdered in his own apartment, why couldn't "business as usual" be done without Pope Pius XII being aware of it? — M.S.B., Arizona

A. First of all, there is no convincing evidence that Pope John Paul I was murdered. He died from a pulmonary embolism on September 28, 1978, just 34 days after being elected Pope. Six years later, a man named David Yallop wrote a book, *In God's Name*, suggesting that the Holy Father had been murdered and offering a list of six possible suspects. In 1989, after a careful investigation of the charges, British author John Cornwell showed in his own book, *A Thief in the Night*, that Yallop's theory was false, that there was no plot to kill the Pontiff, and that he died of natural causes.

Second, it is demonstrably false that Pope Pius XII failed to speak out or to help persecuted Jews during World War II. In fact, the Holy Father spearheaded an effort to rescue Jews from the Nazis that included hiding them in his own residence, as well as in Catholic convents and monasteries, and ordering sacred vessels at the Vatican to be melted down for gold to ransom Jews from the Nazis. In his book *Three Popes and the Jews*, former Israeli diplomat Pinchas Lapide estimated that Pius XII saved 860,000 Jews from death.

When the Holy Father died in 1958, Israeli delegate to the United Nations Golda Meir eulogized him: "We share the grief of the world over the death of His Holiness Pius XII. During a generation of wars and dissensions, he affirmed the high ideals of peace and compassion. During the ten years of the Nazi terror, when our people went through the horrors of martyrdom, the Pope raised his voice to condemn the persecutors and to commiserate with their victims."

For more information on how the Holy Father helped Jewish and other victims of Nazi terror, see the books *Pius XII and the Holocaust*, which is published by the Catholic League for Religious and Civil Rights, 1100 West Wells Street, Milwaukee, WI 53233, and *The Pope and the Holocaust*, by Fr. John S. Rader and Kateryna Fedoryka, which is available from the Family Apostolate, Post Office Box 55, Redfield, South Dakota 57469.

Q. I have heard repeated references by Evangelical Protestants to a concordat signed between Pope Pius XII and Adolf Hitler shortly before World War II. There is the suggestion that this was an evil agreement. Is the text of that concordat available? I would like to be able to read what it said. — L.A.D., Pennsylvania

A. During the pontificate of Pope Pius XI (1922-1939), when Eugenio Cardinal Pacelli, the future Pope Pius XII, was Vatican Secretary of State, a concordat was signed by the Vatican and Nazi Germany. Previous Vatican-German concordats had become inoperative after Hitler came to power in 1933. The new agreement was a typical European arrangement, basically guaranteeing "uninhibited freedom of action for all Catholic religious, cultural, and educational organizations, associations, and federations." This excerpt comes from page 40 of *The Pope and the Holocaust*, which cites as its source a 1973 book by Anthony Rhodes entitled *The Vatican in the Age of the Dictators* (Holt, Rinehart and Winston).

Those who conclude from this that the future Pius XII somehow approved what the Nazis were doing don't know their history. For example, on April 28, 1935, Cardinal Pacelli told 250,000 pilgrims at Lourdes that the Nazis "are in reality only miserable plagiarists who dress up old errors with new tinsel. It does not make any difference whether they flock to the banners of the social revolution, whether they are guided by a false conception of the world and of life, or whether they are possessed by the superstition of a race and blood cult."

On March 3, 1939, the day after Pacelli was chosen to succeed Pius XI, the Berlin Nazi newspaper *Morgenpost* said that "the election of Cardinal Pacelli is not accepted with favor in Germany because he was always opposed to Nazism and practically determined the policies of the Vatican under his predecessor."

Following his Christmas message in 1941, an editorial in the December 25th *New York Times* praised the Holy Father for being "about the only ruler left on the Continent of Europe who dares to raise his voice" against Nazism. "In calling for a 'real new order' based on 'liberty, justice, and love,' to be attained only by a 'return to social and international principles capable of creating a barrier against the abuse of liberty and the abuse of power,'" said the *Times* editorial, "the Pope put himself squarely against Hitlerism."

For more on this matter, see the two books cited in the previous reply.

Q. Can you explain the meaning of the Pope's infallibility? — J.T., Indiana

A. According to the *Catechism of the Catholic Church*, papal infallibility means that the Pope is preserved from error when, as supreme pastor and teacher of all the faithful — who confirms his brethren in the faith — he proclaims by a definitive act a doctrine pertaining to faith or morals (n. 891).

Infallibility *does not mean* that the Pope cannot sin. The Holy Father goes to Confession frequently and acknowledges his sinfulness at Mass when he asks God to "wash away my iniquity, cleanse me from my sins." Nor does infallibility mean that the Pope cannot make a mistake when he talks about science, politics, economics, or other non-religious matters.

To teach infallibly, the Pope must speak on faith or morals; he must speak with his full authority as the Successor of Peter and head of the Church on earth; he must make a final pronouncement on the doctrine at issue; and he must bind all Catholics to accept his teaching or fall away "entirely from the divine and Catholic Faith."

That last phrase is from the infallible declaration of Pope Pius XII in 1950 when he defined the dogma of the Assumption, saying that at the end of her life, the Blessed Mother "was taken up to heavenly glory both in body and soul." A reading of that proclamation makes clear that the Holy Father was acting as the supreme shepherd and teacher of the faithful, was confirming his brethren in the faith, and was proclaiming by a definitive act a doctrine of that faith.

Evidence that Jesus intended to preserve Peter and his successors from error can be found in our Lord's statement to Peter: "Whatever you declare bound on earth shall be bound in heaven; whatever you declared loosed on earth shall be loosed in heaven" (Matthew 16:19). Jesus would hardly give approval in Heaven to bad decisions by Popes on earth, so He provided protection against that happening.

Does the current Holy Father enjoy the same infallibility given to St. Peter? Certainly. After all, Jesus promised that He would be with His Church "always, until the end of the world" (Matthew 28:20), and that His Father would "give you another Paraclete — to be with you always: the Spirit of truth" (John 14:16-17).

The Spirit of truth, the Holy Spirit, has been with the Catholic Church since Pentecost, and the record of the past 2,000 years shows that no Pope has ever made a false statement on faith or morals.

Q. I was told that the Popes have only spoken *ex cathedra* twice in 2,000 years. Is that true? How do we know when the Pope is speaking *ex cathedra*? — J.M., California, and J.R.H., Washington

Q. Is it correct to claim that all encyclicals addressed to the world on matters of faith and morals are infallible? How can I explain to a friend the problems with "humble dissent" from Church teachings? She showed me a book with a chapter on infallibility, which included a paragraph on "humble dissent," and she said that since the book had an imprimatur, it was without error. — M.E.C., California

A. *Ex cathedra* means "from the chair," or seat of authority, of St. Peter and usually refers to the Pope's exercise of infallibility. We know that he is speaking infallibly when he fulfills all of the conditions mentioned in the previous reply. The closest thing to a list of infallible pronouncements would be Dr. Ludwig Ott's masterful compilation, *Fundamentals of Catholic Dogma* (Tan Books). He lists not only the doctrines defined by Popes, but also the infallible declarations of many of the Church's general councils.

Some examples of infallibly defined doctrines, in addition to Pope Pius IX's definition of the Immaculate Conception in 1854 and Pius XII's definition of the Assumption in 1950, include the nature of God, the Trinity, angels, grace, the fall, redemption, the humanity and divinity of Christ, the Sacraments, Heaven, Hell, and Purgatory.

It should be noted that the charism of infallibility is not restricted to the Pope. The infallibility promised to the Church is also present in the body of bishops when, together with the successor of St. Peter, they exercise the supreme *Magisterium*, especially in an ecumenical council, according to the *Catechism of the Catholic Church* (n. 891).

Vatican II's *Constitution on the Church* also explained that while individual bishops do not enjoy the prerogative of infallibility, they "can nevertheless proclaim Christ's doctrine infallibly," either when "gathered together in an ecumenical council" or "even when they are dispersed around the world, provided that while maintaining the bond of unity among themselves and with Peter's successor, and while teaching authentically on a matter of faith or morals, they concur in a single viewpoint as the one which must be held conclusively" (n. 25).

It is not correct to say that every encyclical letter addressed to the world on matters of faith and morals is infallible, but if the Supreme Pontiff restates a long-held teaching of the Church (for example, the evil of artificial contraception in *Humanae Vitae* or that priestly ordination is reserved to men in *Ordinatio Sacerdotalis*), a good case can be made for the infallibility of that restatement, even if the Pope does not specifically identify his encyclical as infallible, since he is definitively proclaiming that a certain doctrine of faith or morals is to be believed.

Furthermore, Catholics cannot disregard non-infallible statements either because divine assistance is also given to the Pope and the bishops in communion with him when they propose in the exercise of the ordinary *Magisterium* a teaching that leads to a better understanding of Revelation in matters of faith and morals. Thus, the faithful are to submit humbly and adhere sincerely to the teachings of the Holy Father, even when he is not speaking infallibly, because his ordinary teaching is an extension of his extraordinary charism (*Catechism of the Catholic Church*, n. 892).

As for the notion of "humble dissent," Pope John Paul had this to say in an address to the U.S. Bishops in Los Angeles on September 16, 1987: "This is a grave error that challenges the teaching office of the bishops of the United States and elsewhere .... Dissent from Church doctrine remains what it is, dissent; as such it may not be proposed or received on an equal footing with the Church's authentic teaching."

M.E.C. will also have to inform her friend that, unfortunately, an imprimatur on a book is no longer a guarantee that the book is free from doctrinal errors.

Q. I have been taught that a defined dogma of the Church must be believed by all the faithful under pain of excommunication and that no defined dogma of the Church can be circumvented or declared null. Can you comment? — S.A.B., Massachusetts.

A. What you have said is true. For instance, after defining the Assumption, Pope Pius XII said: "Hence if anyone, which God forbid, should dare willfully to deny or to call into doubt that which we have defined, let him know that he has fallen away completely from the divine and Catholic Faith" (n. 45).

Of course, the person denying the defined dogma must understand exactly what he or she is doing, must willfully or deliberately do it, and must know that the penalty for this action is excommunication in order to be separated from the Church.

Q. Are you aware of any Church doctrines that have been changed over the years in such a way as to show that the

Catholic Church might have taught error in doctrine? —
B.S., California

A. No, we are not aware of any change in doctrine, nor is it possible for such a thing to happen. To suggest that the Catholic Church could teach error would mean that Jesus, the Founder of the Church, lied when He promised to be "with you always, until the end of the world" (Matthew 28:20), and to ask the Father to "give you another Paraclete — to be with you always: the Spirit of truth" (John 14:16-17).

Our grasp of a particular doctrine, like the Immaculate Conception, may change as we study it and reflect upon it, but this is not a change in the doctrine itself, but rather a growth in our understanding of the words and realities that were always there but may have been obscure to us. For some good insights into the "development of doctrine," see chapter 11 of Karl Keating's *Catholicism and Fundamentalism* and the introduction to Ludwig Ott's *Fundamentals of Catholic Dogma.*

Q. Isn't it true that an imprimatur of a bishop can be withdrawn by order of the Holy Father? I believe there was recently such a case. Isn't it also true that papal definition precludes any further interpretation of dogma, that no matter how much a doctrine may be developed or meditated upon, its meaning can never be changed? — G.M., New York

A. We don't know if the Holy Father would personally order withdrawal of an imprimatur, but his Sacred Congregation for the Doctrine of the Faith could. In fact, there was a case in New Jersey in 1983 where the SCDF told the Archbishop of Newark to remove an imprimatur from a book because it contained theologically incorrect teachings. The norms governing the publication of books on religious and moral topics, and the need to obtain ecclesiastical approval, can be found in canons 824-832 of the Code of Canon Law.

Papal definition of a dogma is supposed to preclude further debate or disputation about a doctrine. This does not mean, however, that efforts cannot be made to gain a better understanding of a doctrine that has come down to us through Sacred Scripture or Sacred Tradition. Vatican II put it this way:

"This tradition which comes from the Apostles develops in the Church with the help of the Holy Spirit. For there is a growth in the understanding of the realities and the words which have been handed down. This happens through the contemplation and study made by believers, who treasure these things in their hearts (cf. Luke 2:19, 51), through the intimate understanding of spiritual things they experience, and through the preaching of those who have received through episcopal succession the sure gift of truth. For, as the centuries succeed one another, the Church constantly moves forward toward the fullness of divine truth until the words of God reach their complete fulfillment in her" (*Constitution on Divine Revelation*, n. 8).

Q. When should books concerning Catholic doctrine bear an imprimatur? Are there any requirements concerning the imprimatur that the faithful (both writers and readers) are bound by? Is an Archbishop required to obtain an imprimatur for his own books? — D.A.P., Indiana

A. It is more common these days to see in a book the words "with ecclesiastical approval" rather than the word imprimatur ("Let it be printed"), though they mean essentially the same thing. Canon 827 of the Code of Canon Law says that the approval of the local ordinary is necessary for the publication of "catechisms and other writings dealing with catechetical formation"; for textbooks dealing with "sacred Scripture, theology, canon law, church history," or "religious or moral disciplines" that are used in elementary, middle, or higher schools; and for "books and other writings which treat of questions of religion or morals" that are "exhibited, sold, or distributed in churches or oratories."

If books covering these subjects are not to be employed as textbooks for teaching, paragraph 3 of canon 827 recommends that they be "submitted to the judgment of the local ordinary," but it is not mandatory.

In answer to D.A.P.'s last question, an Archbishop would need ecclesiastical approval for his own book if it were to be used as a catechism or as a textbook, or if it treated questions of religion and morals and was to be exhibited, sold, or distributed in churches or oratories.

Q. What does "published with ecclesiastical approval" mean in the missalette? — M.M., Virginia

A. It means that the content of the missalette has been approved by the local bishop or someone designated by him. The more familiar terms are imprimatur ("Let it be printed"), which is what the bishop says after his Censor Deputatus (delegated censor) has approved a book by declaring Nihil Obstat ("Nothing stands in the way" of publication).

These terms normally appear at the front of a book along with the statement: "The Nihil Obstat and Imprimatur are official declarations that a book or pamphlet is free of doctrinal or moral error. No implication is contained therein that those who have granted the Nihil Obstat or Imprimatur agree with the contents, opinions, or statements expressed."

Q. Why does the sexist, all-male Roman Catholic hierarchy think that it has a right to dictate to Americans what they can and cannot do in regards to abortion, birth control, and the like? Why does the Roman Church think it has the right to violate the First Amendment and try to censor the works of authors it disagrees with? Why does the Roman Church refuse to recognize women's rights of equality in church governance, becoming priests, etc.? Why should any well-educated, thinking person who appreciates the First Amendment and religious liberty remain in the Roman Church? — Puzzled, North Carolina

A. (1) The Catholic Church does not dictate to anyone. As the Body of Christ on earth, it presents to the world the teachings of its Founder, Jesus Christ, the Son of God, on the dignity of all human life, born and unborn, and on the proper use of the sexual faculties given to us by God. Each one of us has a free will and may reject the teachings of Christ and risk the eternal consequences of that rejection.

(2) The Catholic Church does not have any military or police power to censor the works of authors it disagrees with. What it has in America is the right, under the First Amendment, to try to persuade people not to patronize authors whose works ridicule religious beliefs or glorify immoral behavior.

(3) The Catholic Church believes in the equality of all its members, male and female. Its refusal to ordain women has nothing to do with equality; the Church is simply following the example of Jesus, who chose not to ordain women even though there were some highly qualified women in His company, including His own mother. As for women in positions of Church governance, women in this country are already serving in such key posts as those of judicial vicar and chancellor.

(4) One would expect well-educated and thinking persons to remain in the Catholic Church because they would know that faithful members of that Church have the best chance of getting to Heaven. There is no conflict between being a practicing Catholic and at the same time a believer in religious liberty and the First Amendment.

Q. Why doesn't the Pope do more to stop the spread of the Modernist heresy in the Catholic Church, especially in the United States? — M.L., California, and E.M., Montana

A. Modernism refers to some theories about the origins and teachings of the Church that were prominent early in the 20th century. Among other things, the Modernists of those days, as well as those in our own time, held that the existence of a personal God could not be demonstrated, that the Bible was not inspired by God, that Christ was not divine, and that He did not establish a Church or the Sacraments. What makes Modernism so difficult to combat is that it uses Catholic terms, but empties them of their traditional meanings.

In responding to what he called the "synthesis of all heresies," Pope St. Pius X in 1907 issued two documents — the decree *Lamentabili* and the encyclical *Pascendi* — condemning 65 propositions of Modernism and explaining why these propositions were in error. A reading of these documents, which should be available through a Catholic bookstore, will provide a better idea of what Modernism is.

M.L.'s frustration at the continuing spread of this heresy is compounded many times over, we are sure, by the frustration felt by the Holy Father. He has battled the Modernists day in and day out during his pontificate through numerous encyclicals (notably *Veritatis Splendor*), weekly public audiences, speeches on every continent, documents issued with his approval by various Vatican congregations, the silencing of some dissident theologians, and publication of the *Catechism of the Catholic Church* and *Crossing the Threshold of Hope*, both of which have become international best-sellers.

Even a secular journal like *Time* magazine recognized the great contribution the Holy Father is making in promoting the religious and moral teachings of the Catholic Church when it named Pope John Paul its 1994 Man of the Year. He needs our continued prayers and support for the strength and courage to remain steadfast in his role as the Vicar of Christ on earth.

Q. After John Paul II, how many more Popes will there be until the end of the world, according to the prophecy of St. Malachy? — L.C., New York

A. St. Malachy (1095-1148) was a holy and dedicated bishop who restored religious fervor to Ireland in the 12th century. He is reputed to have performed miracles, and he died in the arms of St. Bernard at Clairvaux. But Malachy is better known today for the alleged prophecies about those who would be Pope from the time of Celestine II, who died in 1144, to the end of the world.

According to the alleged list, which was not discovered until more than four centuries after Malachy's death, there would be 112 Popes after Celestine, ending with Peter the Roman, "who will feed his flock amid many tribulations, after which the seven-hilled city [Rome] will be destroyed and the dreadful Judge will judge the people."

Peter the Roman is the only Pope listed by name; the others are described by short phrases that lend themselves to varied interpretations. "Apostolic Pilgrim" is applied to Pius VI because he made a trip to Germany; "Burning Fire" to Pius X because he restored devotion to the Eucharist; and "Pastor and Sailor" to Pius XII because he traveled to America by boat before he became the Supreme Pontiff.

One list applies "Pastor and Sailor" to John XXIII because of his travels on the waterways of Venice. Then "Flower of Flowers" would be assigned to Paul VI, who had lilies on his coat of arms; "From the Middle of the Moon" to John Paul I, who reigned for just over a month; "From the Labor of the Sun" to John Paul II, either because of his devotion to Mary, the "woman clothed with the sun," or because the phrase could mean that the sun's energy is like atomic energy, which could destroy the world in the form of nuclear bombs.

According to Malachy's alleged list, there are only two Popes to go until the end of the world, but he doesn't make clear whether there might be additional Popes between the next one and Peter the Roman. In any case, the prophecies are so vague, and require such imagination to fit them to modern-day Pontiffs, that they are probably spurious.

The smartest thing to do is to heed the words of our Lord: "As for the exact day or hour, no one knows it, neither the angels in heaven nor the Son, but the Father only" (Matthew 24:36). "Stay awake, therefore! You cannot know the day your Lord is coming" (Matthew 24:42).

Q. Can you explain how the Fathers of the Church were identified and what qualified them to be considered Fathers of the Church? Who are the Doctors of the Church and how did they get that title? — J.M., California

A. The title of "Father of the Church" has been applied to scores of intellectually brilliant and extraordinarily holy individuals whose writings and sermons helped the Church to defend itself against heresies and to grow and flourish during its early centuries. Nearly 100 persons have been given that title because of their orthodoxy, sanctity, and antiquity. The patristic age is considered to have ended in the West with the death of St. Isidore of Seville in 636 A.D. and in the East with the death of St. John Damascene in 749 A.D.

Other well-known Fathers include Sts. Ambrose, Athanasius, Augustine, Basil the Great, Benedict, Clement of Rome, Cyprian, Gregory the Great, Ignatius of Antioch, Irenaeus, Jerome, John Chrysostom, Justin Martyr, Peter Chrysologus, and Polycarp.

Some of these individuals have also been named "Doctors of the Church" (a title granted for a long time by a consensus of the Church and more recently by papal proclamation) for their outstanding writing or preaching, but that title has been more commonly applied to more than a score of persons who lived after the patristic age. These include Sts. Albert the Great, Alphonsus Liguori, Anselm, Anthony of Padua, Bernard of Clairvaux, Bonaventure, Catherine of Siena, Francis de Sales, John of the Cross, Peter Canisius, Robert Bellarmine, Teresa of Avila, and Thomas Aquinas.

The writings of the Fathers have been compiled by William A. Jurgens in his three-volume work *The Faith of the Early Fathers* (Liturgical Press). The doctrinal index for each volume can be of immense value to those seeking the ancient roots of our Catholic beliefs.

Q. Would you please tell me who writes canon law and if there is an obligation to abide by it? — F.C., Ohio

A. The first official book of canons, or laws, of the Catholic Church was compiled by St. Raymond of Penafort in 1234 and approved by Pope Gregory IX. In 1917, the *Decretals of Gregory IX*, along with other canons, regulations, and legislation that had been enacted by Popes and ecumenical councils since 1234, were systematically arranged and promulgated as the first Code of Canon Law. Pope John XXIII called for a revision of that Code in 1959 and appointed a Pontifical Commission for the Revision of the Code of Canon Law.

Under the chairmanship of Pericle Cardinal Felici (1966-1982), the Commission was organized into ten study groups to review different sections of the 1917 Code. Special groups of consultors, including bishops, priests, religious, and laypersons, prepared drafts of proposed changes and submitted them for evaluation by bishops' conferences throughout the world, the superiors of religious and secular institutes, the departments of the Roman Curia, and pontifical universities and faculties. These groups in turn consulted with canon lawyers, theologians, and pastoral leaders before sending their comments to the Pontifical Commission.

Other drafts were prepared, the membership of the Commission was expanded from 59 to 74 in 1980 in order to obtain more input into the revisions, and the final proposal was presented to Pope John Paul II on October 29, 1981. The Holy Father spent one year personally studying the revised Code and made several changes in the text before promulgating it on January 25, 1983.

Regarding our obligation to abide by the new Code, John Paul said in his apostolic constitution (*Sacrae Disciplinae Leges*) promulgating it: "I command that for the future it is to have the force of law for the whole Latin Church, and I entrust it to the watchful care of all those concerned in order that it may be observed."

Q. What was supposed to come out of the Second Vatican Council? Did it change traditional practices and beliefs? — I.E.C., Pennsylvania

Q. Can you tell me in two paragraphs what was so bad about the Church before Vatican II and what happened as a result of Vatican II? — E.J., New Jersey

A. Many books have been written about the Second Vatican Council without covering the subject completely, but we will try to give a capsule summary (in about seven paragraphs) of that 21st Council in the Church's history.

Vatican II, which was held in Rome from 1962 to 1965, was attended by more than 2,500 bishops from all over the world. It issued 16 documents reaffirming the traditional beliefs of the Catholic Church and urging renewed fervor in bringing the Gospel of Christ to the modern world in order to, in the words of Pope John XXIII, "make men, families, and peoples really turn their minds to heavenly things."

The documents — two dogmatic and two pastoral constitutions, nine decrees, and three declarations — called for updated Catholic rituals and practices, better ways of presenting the ancient doctrines of the Church without distorting them or watering them down, and efforts to bring about the unity of all Christians.

These documents deal with the Church itself, divine Revelation, the liturgy, bishops, priests, Religious men and women, the laity, Christian education, communications, the missions, ecumenism, the Eastern churches, non-Christians, religious freedom, and the Church in the modern world.

The best way to find out what Vatican II said is to read the documents. They should be available in any Catholic bookstore. Then you won't be deceived when some priest, Religious, or layperson tries to justify some aberration in doctrine or liturgy, education or ecumenism, by referring to the "spirit of Vatican II." Reading the *Catechism of the Catholic Church* would be helpful, too, since that compendium of Catholic teaching contains numerous quotations from the Council.

There wasn't anything "bad" about the pre-Vatican II Church; in fact, it was flourishing. There was, however, a widespread unease among the bishops in northern Europe, a sense that the Church was not prepared for a coming crisis of faith and that it needed to address new and sometimes complex issues. Since the Council, the Church has gone through considerable agony because of those who have distorted its teachings and done bizarre things with its liturgical life.

Nevertheless, said Pope John Paul II in *Crossing the Threshold of Hope*, "the Second Vatican Council was a great gift to the Church." He added, however, that it must be interpreted correctly and defended "from tendentious interpretations" (p. 157).

The Holy Father also said that "the Spirit who spoke through the Second Vatican Council did not speak in vain. The experience of these years allows us to glimpse the possibility of a new openness toward God's truth, a truth the Church must preach 'in season and out of season' (cf. 2 Tim. 4:2). Every minister of the Gospel must be thankful and feel constantly indebted to the Holy Spirit for the gift of the Council. It will take many years and many generations to pay off this debt" (p. 165).

Q. In reading through the various constitutions of Vatican II, there is a marked absence of statements on the primacy of the Holy Father. It is apparent that the Fathers of Vatican II intended via ambiguity to allot to themselves the supreme and sole authority of everything in their dioceses. They successfully emasculated the Holy Roman Pontiff's authority and reduced him to a figurehead, a bishop like they are, to whom they pay lip service while they ignore him. — J.P.K., New York

A. You have not read the documents of Vatican II carefully enough. Please reread paragraphs 18 to 29 of the *Constitution on the Church* and also paragraphs 4 to 11 of the *Decree on the*

Bishops' Pastoral Office in the Church. For instance, consider these words from paragraph 22 of the *Constitution on the Church*:

"But the college or body of bishops has no authority unless it is simultaneously conceived of in terms of its head, the Roman Pontiff, Peter's successor, and without any lessening of his power of primacy over all, pastors as well as the general faithful. For in virtue of his office, that is, as Vicar of Christ and pastor of the whole Church, the Roman Pontiff has full, supreme, and universal power over the Church .... Together with its head, the Roman Pontiff, and never without this head, the episcopal order is the subject of supreme and full power over the universal Church. But this power can be exercised only with the consent of the Roman Pontiff. For our Lord made Simon Peter alone the rock and keybearer of the Church (cf. Mt. 16:18-19), and appointed him shepherd of the whole flock (cf. Jn. 21:15ff)."

Q. Does an archbishop have any authority over the Catholic schools and colleges located in his see? — R.J.M., Massachusetts

Q. To whom in the Catholic hierarchy are Catholic colleges and universities answerable? — D.M., Massachusetts

A. The norms for Catholic universities and all other Catholic institutions of higher learning are spelled out in canons 807-814 of the Code of Canon Law and in Pope John Paul II's apostolic constitution on Catholic universities (*Ex Corde Ecclesiae*), which was issued by the Vatican's Congregation for Catholic Education on August 15, 1990.

In the latter document, which the Holy Father called a "magna carta" for Catholic institutions, he said that "each bishop has a responsibility to promote the welfare of the Catholic universities in his diocese and has the right and duty to watch over the preservation and strengthening of their Catholic character. If problems should arise concerning this Catholic character, the local bishop is to take the initiatives necessary to resolve the matter, working with the competent university authorities in accordance with established procedures and, if necessary, with the help of the Holy See."

This responsibility applies also to elementary and secondary schools, both those owned by other corporations and those owned by the diocese. In the latter instance, the bishop would also have the final responsibility for compensation, maintenance, etc. not as bishop but as proprietor of the institution.

The problem today is that many so-called Catholic colleges and universities have sacrificed their Catholic character in the pursuit of government and foundation grants and secular approval. Their faculties, invited speakers, and honorary degree recipients often include persons who have publicly rejected Catholic teachings on faith and morals. Some local bishops have taken these institutions to task for abandoning their catholicity, but the problem seems to be getting worse.

Let us pray that all bishops will have the courage and the perseverance to carry out the Holy See's desire that colleges and universities in their dioceses maintain their Catholic identity.

Q. When someone claims to have received a private revelation, what kind of jurisdiction does the local bishop have in deciding the authenticity of the revelation? — W.R.A., Oklahoma

A. As the chief spiritual shepherd and guide for the faithful of a particular region, the local bishop is bound to present and explain the truths of the Faith and to safeguard their integrity through all suitable means (canon 386). Therefore, the bishop has the responsibility to determine the authenticity of any private revelations reported in his diocese since these can have an effect on the beliefs and practices of the faithful under his jurisdiction.

Q. What specifically are the rights and duties of a permanent deacon? — F.X.W., New Jersey

A. In June of 1967, Pope Paul VI issued a document (*Sacred Order of the Diaconate*) permitting men to become permanent deacons to help carry on the work of the Church. Preparation for the diaconate involves several years of study and formation and those eligible must be 25 years of age if unmarried or 35 years if married (the prospective deacon must obtain the consent of his wife). An unmarried deacon cannot marry after ordination and a married deacon whose wife dies may not remarry.

Permanent deacons work in a variety of apostolates, including parish, campus, and prison ministries, as well as with the sick in hospitals and nursing homes. They can preach at Mass and distribute Holy Communion, officiate at baptisms and weddings, preside over wake and burial services (but not celebrate the funeral Mass), and hold certain church offices, including director of a parish where there is no permanent pastor.

Q. What are the responsibilities of a Pastoral Associate? In my parish, the Pastoral Associate is a religious. She has given a sermon at Mass and, during 40 hours devotion, she was dressed in an alb, led the prayers, gave a sermon, carried the monstrance in procession, and gave the blessing — all in the presence of a priest. — A.S., Illinois

A. According to the Archdiocese of Boston's *Guidelines for Pastoral Associates*, "The Pastoral Associate is a non-ordained, full-time or part-time, salaried/stipended person who is a member of the parish staff, sharing responsibility for the daily pastoral care of the faithful."

The possible specific areas of responsibility include evangelization (convert instruction through the Rite of Christian Initiation of Adults), parish outreach (visits to homes, hospitals, nursing homes and interreligious gatherings), adult enrichment (sacramental catecheses, Scripture study, prayer groups, retreats), family life (pre-Cana programs, parenting groups, and work with bereaved, separated, divorced, remarried), peace and justice (education in social justice and projects to help the needy), organization and administration (parish office administration and personnel work), and religious education (programs for children, youth, and adults).

The other major area of responsibility for Pastoral Associates is worship and spirituality. This includes planning liturgies, leading prayer services and other devotions, organizing rehearsals for weddings and baptisms, administering the Eucharist when a priest or deacon is not available, and training lectors and Extraordinary Ministers.

In light of these guidelines and Church law, the Pastoral Associate in A.S.'s parish has exceeded her responsibilities. Only a priest or deacon may give a sermon or homily at Mass. If no priest or deacon is present at Eucharistic adoration or benediction, an acolyte, Extraordinary Minister of the Eucharist, or member of the faithful may expose and repose the Blessed Sacrament, but they may not give the blessing (see canon 943 of the Code of Canon Law and paragraphs 82-100 of the liturgical document *Rite of Holy Communion and Worship of the Eucharist Outside Mass*). Since a priest was present, and assuming that he was physically able, there is no justification for the actions of the Pastoral Associate.

Q. What are the rules or customs concerning greeting priests, monsignors, bishops. archbishops, and cardinals? I know that one is supposed to rise when a priest enters a

room, and it is customary to kiss the Pope's ring, but what else is appropriate? And how do you address a bishop? — M.F., Virginia

A. One should greet any member of the clergy cordially and politely, calling them Father, Monsignor, Bishop, Archbishop, or Cardinal. A bishop and archbishop may also be addressed as "Your Excellency," a Cardinal as "Your Eminence," and the Pope as "Your Holiness." It used to be customary to kiss the ring of bishops, archbishops, and cardinals, but that custom is no longer widely practiced, at least in the United States, but there is no reason why a person cannot do so as a sign of respect and reverence.

Q. Please explain the history and the function of theologians in the Catholic Church. What constitutes a theologian, what is their official role in the Church, and why are some dissident theologians tolerated for such a long time? — R.A.L., New York

A. In the *Catholic Encyclopedia* edited by Fr. Peter Stravinskas, a theologian is described as "a person who is formally trained in theology, which studies God, His attributes and relations to the universe. Catholic theology is divided into five areas: (1) dogmatic (including Christology and soteriology), (2) moral, (3) pastoral, (4) ascetical, and (5) mystical. The theologian must possess a doctorate or a least a licentiate degree. The theologian's function is to explain and defend the Church's official teachings and to express better some of the Church's teachings in the light of today's terminology and discoveries."

A more thorough explanation of the role of theologians can be found in an instruction (*The Ecclesial Vocation of the Theologian*) issued by the Sacred Congregation for the Doctrine of the Faith on May 24, 1990. The text of that instruction, which includes a discussion on dissent and the duty of theologians to conform their views to the divinely assisted magisterium of the Church, appeared in the November/December 1990 issue of *The Pope Speaks* (Our Sunday Visitor, 200 Noll Plaza, Huntington, IN 46750, $4.00 per copy).

Q. What exactly is meant by the term "corporation sole"? If a bishop who is the corporation sole of a diocese is excommunicated for some grave action, can he claim the property of the diocese as his own? Do the faithful and the successor bishop have any special rights in regard to their

parish churches or financial holdings? — S.J.C., Illinois

A. Some American dioceses are organized in civil law as corporation soles, for example, Roman Catholic Archbishop of Boston, Inc., corporation sole. The individual bishop controls the corporation while he is bishop of the diocese. The corporation sole is a civil law device which centralizes ownership of diocesan resources and property. Procedural details vary by state, but civil law recognizes the Church's right to confide to and withdraw from a bishop authority over the corporation, and would not permit him to take the assets with him if he were excommunicated.

The rights of parishioners and successor bishops are extensive and various in canon law, which does not recognize the corporation sole, but treats each parish as a distinct legal entity. Canons 1273-1298 of the 1983 Code of Canon Law deal with the management and disposal of the temporal goods of the Church.

Q. I wonder about some small towns that have several priests assigned to a parish when there is no apparent need for that many priests. How does this fit in with the shortage of priests? — M.C., Maryland

A. The staffing of parishes is the decision of the ordinary of the diocese acting on the advice of his personnel board, which studies the needs of individual parishes. The guideline in some dioceses is the "sacramental index," i.e., the number of baptisms, weddings, funerals, etc., that take place in a parish. The higher the sacramental index, the greater the number of priests assigned to a parish.

As for apparent overstaffing, it could be that the priests are working in other ministries (prisons, hospitals, chanceries) and living there, are retired from active ministry, are on "limited duty" for health reasons, or are part of a religious order parish where the priests often live in larger communities than the equivalent diocesan rectory.

Q. I love your column, and agree that priestesses are theologically impossible as well as socially undesirable, but I wonder about your statement that the Catholic Church believes in the equality of all its members. How can that be when we are not equal in any sense? — L.H.R., Alabama

A. We are equal in the sense that each one of us possesses a rational soul, that each is created in the image of God, that each has been redeemed by Christ, and that each enjoys the same divine calling and destiny. In the words of the Second Vatican Council's *Dogmatic Constitution on the Church*, n. 32:

"The chosen People of God is one: 'one Lord, one faith, one baptism' (Eph. 4:5). As members, they share a common dignity from their rebirth in Christ. They have the same filial grace and the same vocation to perfection. They possess in common one salvation, one hope, and one undivided charity. Hence, there is in Christ and in the Church no inequality on the basis of race or nationality, social condition or sex, because 'there is neither Jew nor Greek; there is neither slave nor freeman; there is neither male nor female. For you are all "one" in Christ Jesus' (Gal. 3:28, Greek text; cf. Col. 3:11)."

Q. What is the difference between schism and heresy? — M.M., Massachusetts
A. Heresy is the obstinate denial by a baptized Catholic of some truth which must be believed by divine and Catholic faith, or the obstinate doubt about some truth. Schism is the refusal to subject oneself to the authority of the Pope or refusal to maintain communion with the members of the Church subject to the Supreme Pontiff. Those guilty of heresy or schism automatically incur the penalty of excommunication.

Q. In a reply some months ago, you stated that "schism is the refusal to subject oneself to the authority of the Pope." In view of the recent controversy regarding Archbishop Lefebvre and the Society of St. Pius X, I thought your definition somewhat lacking. May I suggest Fr. Yves Congar's *Dictionary of Catholic Theology*, which defines schism as "a refusal to accept the existence of legitimate authority in the Church." — P.J.R., New Hampshire
A. You may indeed since different dictionaries give slightly different definitions of schism, although the general sense of each of them is the same — a stubborn refusal to submit to the authority of the Pope or those in communion with him. One can use whatever definition makes the point best, whether it's that of Fr. Congar, or Fr. John Hardon's *Modern Catholic Dictionary* ("a willful separation from the unity of the Christian Church"), or the *Catholic Almanac* ("formal and obstinate refusal by a baptized Catholic, called a schismatic, to be in communion with the Pope and the Church").

Q. Who has the authority to excommunicate someone? What must be done to justify it? — S.H., Minnesota

A. The authority to excommunicate a person from the Catholic Church is reserved to the Pope or to the bishop of the person who has committed the offense that calls for excommunication, although in certain cases (such as abortion) the person is automatically cut off from the Church as soon as the action has been committed provided that the person knew in advance of the penalty attached to the action, but went ahead and performed it anyway.

In addition to procurement of abortion, other sins warranting excommunication include apostasy, heresy, and schism; desecration of the Holy Eucharist; pretended celebration of the Eucharist or conferral of absolution by one who is not a priest; physical attack on the Pope; absolution of an accomplice in a sin against the Sixth Commandment; violation of the seal of the confessional; and unauthorized ordination of a bishop.

To obtain formal excommunication of a person, one would have to produce evidence of the sinful action and bring it to the attention of a bishop. The purpose of the penalty is to show the sinner how wrong the action was and to bring about the sinner's repentance and reconciliation with the Church.

Q. I would like to become involved with a third order that would be suitable for me. Where can I find information on their rules, vows, names, addresses etc.? — P.Z., Connecticut, and J.O., Arkansas

A. Secular orders or third orders are societies of the faithful that were established by religious orders for those laypeople living in the world who wish to deepen their faith and their commitment to the work of Christ and His Church while continuing their secular lives. They are called third orders because their creation came after the foundation of first orders (for men) and second orders (for women).

Some of the best known third orders, and the addresses where you may contact them, are the Lay Carmelites (8501 Bailey Road, Darien, Illinois 60561), the Discalced Carmelites (P.O. Box 3420, San Jose, California 95156), the Dominicans (487 Michigan Avenue, N.E., Washington, DC 20017), the Franciscans (3191 71st Street East, Inver Grove Heights, Minnesota 55076), the Third Order of Mary (Marist Fathers, 518 Pleasant Street, Framingham, Massachusetts 01701), and the Secular Order of Servants of Mary (3121 West Jackson Boulevard, Chicago, Illinois 60612).

Chapter 4

Salvation and Ecumenism

Q. How do you answer those who say that "one church is as good as another"? — S.M.K., Washington
A. This matter of religious indifferentism, which says that all religions are the same, that it really doesn't matter which one you belong to, is not an easy topic to discuss because some people have a problem distinguishing between the beliefs of a particular church and the sincerity of the church members who hold those beliefs. In the comments that follow, we will be looking at the beliefs of certain religions strictly from an objective point of view, without trying to decide who is right and who is wrong.

If you say that one church is as good or true as another, then you must agree that vice is as good as virtue, and falsehood is on a par with truth. For there are churches today that teach absolutely contradictory things — that Jesus is God, that Jesus is not God; that Hell exists, that Hell does not exist; that infant Baptism is right, that infant Baptism is wrong; that abortion is evil, that abortion is good; that homosexual behavior is sinful, that homosexual behavior is not sinful.

For the purposes of our discussion, it does not matter who is right in each of these areas. The point is that both sides cannot be right — a square cannot be a circle — no matter how sincerely adherents of these opposing views believe in them. Either Jesus is God, or He isn't. Two completely contradictory statements cannot be equally correct or truth has lost all meaning.

There are good and sincere persons in all religions, and God will reward them accordingly. However, their sincerity cannot change what is objectively false. God has revealed certain teachings to us. Will He give His approval to those who say that it really doesn't matter what we believe?

The dangers of religious indifferentism, of saying that one church is as good as another, were summarized by Pope John XXIII in his 1959 encyclical letter *Ad Petri Cathedram* ("Near the Chair of Peter"):

"To reckon that there is no difference between contraries and opposites has surely this ruinous result, that there is no readiness to accept any religion either in theory or in practice.

For how can God, who is Truth, approve or tolerate the heedlessness, neglect, and indolence of those who, when it is a question of matters affecting the salvation of us all, give no attention at all to the search for and the grasp of the essential truth, nor indeed to paying the lawful worship due to God alone?"

Q. A priest told a friend of mine that because the Church recognizes Protestant Baptism as valid, and their rites and ceremonies are basically the same as ours, all religions are equal. Can you reply to this? — J.B., New York

Q. In explaining the Church's teaching on ecumenism, a popular column by a priest said: "Protestant churches are now regarded as valid Christian communities within the Body of Christ." Shouldn't this require some additional explanation? — P.M., Nebraska

A. Yes, it should, and the additional explanation can be found in the Second Vatican Council's *Decree on Ecumenism*. Paragraph 3 of that document states that Protestants who "have been properly baptized are brought into a certain, though imperfect, communion with the Catholic Church," and "are properly regarded as brothers in the Lord by the sons of the Catholic Church."

But just because the Church recognizes the validity of Baptism in those Christian churches that use water and the trinitarian formula ("I baptize you in the name of the Father, and of the Son, and of the Holy Spirit"), it does not mean that all Christian denominations are equally true.

For the *Decree on Ecumenism* also says that while these "separated churches and communities" possess many endowments of the Catholic Church, such as "the written word of God, the life of grace, faith, hope, and charity," they still suffer from certain defects in their understanding of doctrine, discipline, and the structure of the Church, and "are not blessed with that unity which Jesus Christ wished to bestow on all those whom he has regenerated and vivified into one body and newness of life — that unity which the holy Scriptures and the revered tradition of the Church proclaim. For it is through Christ's Catholic Church alone, which is the all-embracing means of salvation, that the fullness of the means of salvation can be obtained" (n. 3).

According to the *Catechism of the Catholic Church*, the Holy Spirit uses these churches and ecclesial communities as means of salvation, whose power derives from the fullness of grace and truth that Christ has entrusted to the Catholic Church. The *Catechism* says that these blessings come from Christ and lead to Him, and are in themselves calls to Catholic unity (n. 819).

Vatican II stated clearly in the *Constitution on the Church* (see also section 816 of the *Catechism*) that "the unique Church of Christ" is the one handed over by Jesus to Peter after the resurrection. This Church, the Council said, constituted and organized in the world as a society, "subsists in the Catholic Church, which is governed by the successor of Peter and by the bishops in union with that successor" (n. 8).

Q. Pope John Paul has repeated the ancient Church teaching on "no salvation" outside the Catholic Church. Aren't many souls lost because parish priests are silent about this teaching? — C.M.S., New Jersey

A. You are correct in stating that the Church has long taught that it is only through the Church founded by Jesus that we can attain salvation. Writing in the third century, St. Cyprian said: "Outside the Church there is no salvation." This was repeated by the Fourth Lateran Council in 1215, the Council of Florence in 1442, the Council of Trent a century later, and by the Second Vatican Council and the *Catechism of the Catholic Church*.

For instance, the *Catechism*, under a bold-faced subhead that reads, **"Outside the Church there is no salvation,"** asked how one is to understand this statement that has been often repeated by the Church Fathers. Restating it positively, the *Catechism* says it means that "all salvation comes from Christ the Head through the Church which is his Body" (n. 846).

Does this mean, as some insist, that in order to get to Heaven one must be enrolled in a Catholic parish? No, it does not. This false idea was rejected by the Vatican's Holy Office in 1949, and those who still promote it make God out to be an uncaring Creator who consigns to Hell hundreds of millions who have lived and died without ever knowing of the Catholic Church.

What the doctrine of no salvation outside the Church does mean is that everyone is saved through the Catholic Church, either as faithful members of that Church, or as members of churches which contain some significant elements of truth and sanctification found in the Catholic Church, or as persons who, through no fault of their own, do not know the Gospel of Christ or His Church, but who nevertheless seek God with a sincere heart and, moved by grace, try in their actions to do His will as they know it through the dictates of their conscience (*Catechism*, n. 847).

This in no way mitigates the claim of the Catholic Church to be the one, true Church; nor does it mean that all Catholics are automatically saved. On the first point, Vatican II (and the *Catechism*, n. 846) taught that "the Church, now sojourning on earth as an exile, is necessary for salvation. For Christ, made present to us in His Body, which is the Church, is the one Mediator and the unique Way of salvation. In explicit terms He Himself affirmed the necessity of faith and baptism (cf. Mk. 16:16; Jn. 3:5) and thereby affirmed also the necessity of the Church, for through baptism as through a door men enter the Church.

"Whosoever, therefore, knowing that the Catholic Church was made necessary by God through Jesus Christ, would refuse to enter her or to remain in her could not be saved" (*Constitution on the Church*, n. 14).

On the second point, Vatican II emphasized that mere membership in the Catholic Church is not enough to be saved. It said that Catholics wishing to get to Heaven must possess the "Spirit of Christ," accept the "entire system and all the means of salvation" given to the Church, and "persevere in charity" (*Ibid.*).

The same paragraph also warned all members of the Church to "remember that their exalted status is to be attributed not to their own merits but to the special grace of Christ. If they fail moreover to respond to that grace in thought, word, and deed, not only will they not be saved but they will be the more severely judged."

Yes, this teaching should be more widely disseminated, but it must also be correctly explained. In his best-selling book *Crossing the Threshold of Hope*, Pope John Paul put this doctrine very succinctly: "It is therefore a revealed truth that there is salvation only and exclusively in Christ. The Church, inasmuch as it is the Body of Christ, is simply an instrument of this salvation" (p. 136).

The Holy Father also said that "people are saved *through* the Church, they are saved *in* the Church, but they always are saved *by the grace of Christ*. Besides formal membership in the Church, the sphere of salvation can also include other forms of relations to the Church. Paul VI expressed this same teaching in his first encyclical, *Ecclesiam Suam*, when he spoke of the various circles of the dialogue of salvation (nos.101-117), which are the same as those indicated by the [Vatican] Council as the spheres of membership in and of relation to the Church. This is the authentic meaning of the well-known statement, 'Outside the Church there is no salvation'" (pp. 140-141).

Q. Does the doctrine of "no salvation outside the Church" mean that all non-Catholics who are good-living people are destined for eternal damnation? What is the answer? — E.M.D., Massachusetts

Q. I just read a book called *Letter to a Fallen-Away Catholic*. Among other things, it says that baptism of desire and baptism of blood are false teachings that originated with Archbishop Gibbons of Baltimore in 1884 to make Roman Catholicism merge more freely with Americanism. Is this accurate? — E.W., California

A. No, it is not accurate. Baptism of blood and/or desire was taught by such Church Fathers as Irenaeus in the second century, Tertullian and Cyprian in the third century, Cyril of Jerusalem and John Chrysostom in the fourth century, Augustine in the fifth century, and the Council of Trent in the 16th century. Writing about Baptism in the year 400, for instance, St. Augustine said: "I find that not only suffering for the name of Christ can supply for that which is lacking by way of Baptism, but even faith and conversion of heart if, perhaps, because of the circumstances of the time, recourse cannot be had to the celebration of the mystery of Baptism."

In *The City of God*, Augustine wrote: "Those who, though they have not received the washing of regeneration, die for the confession of Christ — it avails them just as much for the forgiveness of their sins as if they had been washed in the sacred font of Baptism."

The answer to E.M.D. is that everyone's salvation — Catholic and non-Catholic — is through the Catholic Church, either as faithful members of the Church (baptism of water), or as good-living persons who give their life for Christ (baptism of blood) or who would belong to the Catholic Church (baptism of desire) if they knew it was the true Church founded by Jesus Christ to help us get to Heaven. To interpret the doctrine literally, as you suggest, would be to damn hundreds of millions who never heard of the Catholic Church, including, for example, all the inhabitants of the Western Hemisphere before 1492.

Q. At a recent meeting of one of our parish organizations, we were advised not to use the expression, "one, true Church" because it smacked of "triumphalism." What is triumphalism and aren't we still the one, true Church? — N.R.F., New Jersey

A. In his excellent *Modern Catholic Dictionary*, Fr. John A. Hardon defines triumphalism as "a term of reproach leveled at the Catholic Church for the claim that she has the fullness of divine revelation and the right to pass judgment on the personal and social obligations of humankind." It would be wrong to claim to be the one, true Church if the claim were false. But the claim is accurate, as Vatican II made clear when it said: "God himself has made known to mankind the way in which men are to serve him, and thus be saved in Christ and come to blessedness. We believe that this one true religion subsists in the catholic and apostolic Church, to which the Lord Jesus committed the duty of spreading it abroad among all men" (*Declaration on Religious Freedom,* n. 1).

Q. Who belongs to the Body of Christ? A nun friend of ours says all the people of the world, but I say only those people baptized in Christ. — F.S.D., New York
A. The Second Vatican Council said that "they are fully incorporated into the society of the Church who, possessing the Spirit of Christ, accept her entire system and all the means of salvation given to her, and through union with her visible structure are joined to Christ, who rules her through the Supreme Pontiff and the bishops" (*Constitution on the Church,* n. 14).

As for Christians who are separated from the Catholic Church, the Council said that those "who believe in Christ and have been properly baptized are brought into a certain, though imperfect, communion with the Catholic Church" and "are properly regarded as brothers in the Lord by the sons of the Catholic Church" (*Decree on Ecumenism,* n. 3).

A footnote to this section in the Abbott translation of the Vatican II documents said that the decree probably stopped short of calling these separated Christians members of the Body of Christ because of this sentence in the 1943 encyclical of Pope Pius XII on the Mystical Body (*Mystici Corporis*): "Only those are to be included as real members of the Church who have been baptized and profess the true faith and have not been so unfortunate as to separate themselves from the unity of the Body or been excluded from it by legitimate authority for serious faults."

Q. In paragraph 16 of *Lumen Gentium* from Vatican II, it says that Moslems who worship in the religion of Abraham may share in salvation. I didn't think Moslems worshiped in the religion of Abraham, plus I thought unbaptized souls could not go to Heaven. Could you explain? — D.B., Ohio

A. In the paragraph cited, the Council said that "the plan of salvation also includes those who acknowledge the Creator. In the first place among these are the Moslems, who, professing to hold the faith of Abraham, along with us adore the one and merciful God, who on the last day will judge mankind." There is further clarification of this in Vatican II's *Declaration on the Relationship of the Church to Non-Christian Religions*:

"Upon the Moslems, too, the Church looks with esteem. They adore one God, living and enduring, merciful and all-powerful, Maker of heaven and earth and Speaker to men. They strive to submit wholeheartedly even to his inscrutable decrees, just as did Abraham, with whom the Islamic faith is pleased to associate itself. Though they do not acknowledge Jesus as God, they revere him as a prophet. They also honor Mary, his virgin mother; at times they call on her, too, with devotion. In addition they await the day of judgment when God will give each man his due after raising him up. Consequently, they prize the moral life, and give worship to God especially through prayer, almsgiving, and fasting" (n. 3). See also paragraph 841 of the *Catechism of the Catholic Church*.

Jesus taught that Baptism is necessary for salvation, but His Church has taught that it can be baptism of water, blood, or desire. Thus, Moslems not baptized with water, who adore and worship the one God and try, with the graces God gives them, to live a moral life, exhibit what is equivalent to a desire to belong to the Church of Christ, even if they do not know what Church that is. Such sincere efforts would include them in the plan of salvation.

Editor's Note: To a recent question about the possibility of salvation for those not baptized with water, specifically those who practice the Moslem religion, we quoted paragraph 16 of Vatican II's *Dogmatic Constitution on the Church* and paragraph 3 of the *Declaration on the Relationship of the Church to Non-Christian Religions*. These two documents state that the plan of salvation includes not only practicing Catholics, but also those who acknowledge the Creator and who strive wholeheartedly to live up to His decrees. We also pointed out in that reply that persons not baptized with water can still attain salvation through baptism of blood (martyrdom) or through baptism of desire (a sincere desire to belong to the Church of Christ).

Some of our readers have written to take issue with the idea of baptism of desire and have sent along statements by Popes and

Councils that these readers believe rule out baptism of desire. The teaching on baptism of desire, however, goes back to the early Church and was included in the statements of the Council of Trent (see chapter 14 of the *Decree Concerning Justification*, which was promulgated by that Council at its sixth session on January 13, 1547).

The teaching was reaffirmed by Pope Pius XII in his 1943 encyclical on the Mystical Body (*Mystici Corporis*) and by the Vatican's Supreme Sacred Congregation of the Holy Office in a letter to Archbishop Richard J. Cushing of Boston, dated August 8, 1949. The full text of the letter can be found in the October 1952 issue of *The American Ecclesiastical Review*, pages 311-315. Here are the pertinent excerpts from that letter:

"We are bound by divine and Catholic faith to believe all those things which are contained in the word of God, whether it be Scripture or Tradition, and are proposed by the Church to be believed as divinely revealed, not only through solemn judgment but also through the ordinary and universal teaching office.

"Now, among those things which the Church has always preached and will never cease to preach is contained also that infallible statement by which we are taught that there is no salvation outside the Church.

"However, this dogma must be understood in that sense in which the Church herself understands it. For, it was not to private judgments that Our Saviour gave for explanation those things that are contained in the deposit of faith, but to the teaching authority of the Church.

"Now, in the first place, the Church teaches that in this matter there is question of a most strict command of Jesus Christ. For He explicitly enjoined on His apostles to teach all nations to observe all things whatsoever He Himself had commanded (Matt. 28:19-20).

"Now, among the commandments of Christ, that one holds not the least place, by which we are commanded to be incorporated by Baptism into the Mystical Body of Christ, which is the Church, and to remain united to Christ and to His Vicar, through whom He Himself in a visible manner governs the Church on earth.

"Therefore, no one will be saved who, knowing the Church to have been divinely established by Christ, nevertheless refuses to submit to the Church or withholds obedience from the Roman Pontiff, the Vicar of Christ on earth.

"Not only did the Saviour command that all nations should enter the Church, but He also decreed the Church to be a means of salvation, without which no one can enter the kingdom of eternal glory.

"In His infinite mercy God has willed that the effects, necessary for one to be saved, of those helps to salvation which are directed toward man's final end, not by intrinsic necessity, but only by divine institution, can also be obtained in certain circumstances when those helps are used only in desire and longing. This we see clearly stated in the Sacred Council of Trent, both in reference to the Sacrament of Regeneration [Baptism] and in reference to the Sacrament of Penance.

"The same in its own degree must be asserted of the Church, in as far as she is the general help to salvation. Therefore, that one may obtain eternal salvation, it is not always required that he be incorporated into the Church actually as a member, but it is necessary that at least he be united to her by desire and longing.

"However, this desire need not always be explicit, as it is in catechumens; but when a person is involved in invincible ignorance, God accepts also an implicit desire, so called because it is included in that good disposition of soul whereby a person wishes his will to be conformed to the will of God.

"These things are clearly taught in that dogmatic letter which was issued by the Sovereign Pontiff, Pope Pius XII, on June 29, 1943, *On the Mystical Body of Jesus Christ.* For in this letter the Sovereign Pontiff clearly distinguishes between those who are actually incorporated into the Church as members, and those who are united to the Church only by desire.

"Discussing the members of which the Mystical Body is composed here on earth, the same august Pontiff says: 'Actually only those are to be included as members of the Church who have been baptized and profess the true faith, and who have not been so unfortunate as to separate themselves from the unity of the Body, or been excluded by legitimate authority for grave faults committed.'

"Toward the end of this same Encyclical Letter, when most affectionately inviting to unity those who do not belong to the body of the Catholic Church, he mentions those who 'are related to the Mystical Body of the Redeemer by a certain unconscious yearning and desire,' and these he by no means excludes from eternal salvation, but on the other hand states that they are in a condition 'in which they cannot be sure of their salvation' since 'they still remain deprived of those many heavenly gifts and helps which can only be enjoyed in the Catholic Church.'

"With these wise words he reproves both those who exclude from eternal salvation all united to the Church only by implicit desire, and those who falsely assert that men can be saved equally well in every religion.

"But it must not be thought that any kind of desire of entering the Church suffices that one may be saved. It is necessary that the desire by which one is related to the Church be animated by perfect charity. Nor can an implicit desire produce its effect, unless a person has supernatural faith: 'For he who comes to God must believe that God exists and is a rewarder of those who seek Him' (Hebrews 11:6). The Council of Trent declares (Session VI, chap. 8): 'Faith is the beginning of man's salvation, the foundation and root of all justification, without which it is impossible to please God and attain to the fellowship of His children.'"

The letter concluded with a very strong warning to those who would call this teaching of the Church into question:

"Therefore, let them who in grave peril are ranged against the Church seriously bear in mind that after 'Rome has spoken' they cannot be excused even by reasons of good faith. Certainly, their bond and duty of obedience toward the Church is much graver than that of those who as yet are related to the Church 'only by an unconscious desire.'

"Let them realize that they are children of the Church, lovingly nourished by her with the milk of doctrine and the sacraments, and hence, having heard the clear voice of their Mother, they cannot be excused from culpable ignorance, and therefore to them applies without any restriction that principle: submission to the Catholic Church and to the Sovereign Pontiff is required as necessary for salvation."

Q. I am interested in the fate of the controversial Jesuit, Fr. Leonard Feeney, who taught that there was no salvation outside the Catholic Church. I know that the Holy Office of the Vatican in 1949 presented an explicit explanation of the Church's teaching on salvation. What is this teaching exactly, and whatever happened to Fr. Feeney? — E.D.V., Louisiana, and J.P., Massachusetts

A. It is true that the Holy Office, in a letter to then-Archbishop Richard Cushing of Boston that was quoted in the previous reply, condemned Fr. Feeney's teaching that one had to be enrolled in a Catholic parish in order to be saved. Fr. Feeney was excommunicated, but was reconciled with the Church, through the personal efforts of Humberto Cardinal Medeiros, before he died in 1978. Feeney's community has since divided into five groups, with the two largest also now reconciled and living as male and female Benedictine communities in Still River, Massachusetts.

Editor's Note: Regarding a previous reply on the status of Fr. Leonard Feeney at the time of his death in 1978 and the present status of the order that he and Sister Catherine (Goddard Clarke) founded, the Slaves of the Immaculate Heart of Mary, we have received the following information from S.A.M. of Massachusetts.

After noting that the censures imposed on Fr. Feeney in 1949 by the Vatican's Holy Office "were lifted in 1972 through the instrumentality of Cardinal Medeiros of Boston and Cardinal John Wright of the Sacred Congregation for the Clergy in Rome," and that "Father was not asked to change his teaching on the necessity of belonging to the Roman Catholic Church for salvation," S.A.M. went on to say that her order, the Slaves of the Immaculate Heart of Mary, "was approved by Cardinal Ratzinger's office in 1988, through the efforts of Bishop Harrington of Worcester. Although many (but not all) of the Brothers had in the meantime become Benedictines, the Sisters had not, and we still live in the original convent in Still River [Massachusetts]."

Sister also enclosed a letter from the Reverend Lawrence A. Deery, Vicar for Canonical Affairs for the Diocese of Worcester, to the Reverend John B. McCormack, Secretary of Ministerial Personnel for the Archdiocese of Boston, regarding the regularization of the order. In the letter, dated May 4, 1988, Fr. Deery wrote:

"1) The Sisters were asked to 'understand' the letter of the-then Holy Office dated 8 August 1949. They were not asked to 'accept' its contents.

"2) The Sisters were asked to make a Profession of Faith. Nothing else was required.

"It would seem that the Congregation for the Doctrine of the Faith holds the doctrine ["Outside the Church there is no salvation"] to have been defined and consequently definitive. It is its theological interpretation and speculation which they see as problematical.

"In our discussions with the Congregation, it seemed rather clear that proponents of a strict interpretation of the doctrine should be given the same latitude for teaching and discussion as those who would hold more liberal views.

"Summarily, Mother Theresa [Superior of the order] and her community in no manner abandoned Father Feeney's teachings. Consequently the Sisters do a good deal more than keep the memory of Father Feeney. They now actively proclaim his teachings as they did before the regularization."

Q. In the past you have dealt with questions concerning the possibility of salvation for those of other faiths, and those not baptized with water. I do not recall ever hearing or reading an explanation about the conditions of souls of those who, because of place of birth, such as on an isolated island, and before the time of the world explorers and consequent evangelization of these areas, never had the opportunity to know of God and the story of salvation. Can you please tell me what the Church teaches about these souls? — W.E.M., Indiana

A. In his Credo of the People of God, Pope Paul VI said that "the divine design of salvation embraces all men; and those who without fault on their part do not know the Gospel of Christ and His Church, but seek God sincerely, and under the influence of grace endeavor to do His will as recognized through the promptings of their conscience, they, in a number known only to God, can obtain salvation."

The Second Vatican Council said much the same thing and then added: "Nor does divine Providence deny the help necessary for salvation to those who, without blame on their part, have not yet arrived at an explicit knowledge of God, but who strive to live a good life, thanks to His grace. Whatever goodness or truth is found among them is looked upon by the Church as a preparation for the gospel. She regards such qualities as given by Him who enlightens all men so that they may finally have life" (*Constitution on the Church*, n. 16).

Q. A woman convert who leads our Bible study group says that in order to be saved, one must have a "born-again" experience. This sounds to me like something out of evangelical Protestantism. Is there anything in Catholic doctrine to support her assertion? — M.J.S., Maryland

A. The expression "born again" comes from Jesus' conversation with Nicodemus when our Lord said, "I solemnly assure you, no one can enter into God's kingdom without being begotten [born again] of water and Spirit" (John 3:5). Some Protestants interpret this to mean that one must make a concrete decision to accept Christ as one's personal Savior in order to be saved, and that nothing else is necessary. Such an interpretation overlooks St. Paul's warning that "every one of us will have to give an account of himself before God" (Romans 14:12).

Catholics believe that they are "born again" when they are baptized, and that they receive the Holy Spirit again in a special way when they are confirmed. They know, however, that Baptism is not enough since we must also live according to God's plan. In other words, Baptism makes it possible for us to be saved, but we still must, in the words of St. Paul, "work with anxious concern" to achieve our salvation (Philippians 2:12). We do this by keeping the commandments and receiving the sacraments, particularly the Holy Eucharist, which involves the acceptance of Christ as our personal Savior every time we take Him, Body and Blood, Soul and Divinity, into our hearts.

So there is a sense in which the leader of your study group could be correct, but one must be careful to distinguish the Catholic meaning of a "born-again" experience from the Protestant understanding of it.

Q. Where can I get brochures or articles or information on how to answer the views of the Fundamentalists? — D.K., Wisconsin

A. You can start with such books as *Catholicism and Fundamentalism* by Karl Keating; *Answering a Fundamentalist* and *Strangers at Your Door* (Our Sunday Visitor), both by Albert J. Nevins, M.M.; *Rome Sweet Home* (Ignatius Press) by Scott and Kimberly Hahn; and *Surprised by Truth* (Basilica Press), which was edited by Patrick Madrid. These books should be available through your local Catholic bookstore.

For briefer articles dealing with specific objections to Catholicism by Fundamentalists, write to Mr. Keating at This Rock, P.O. Box 17490, San Diego, CA 92177 and ask for a list of the tracts he has prepared on a variety of subjects, particularly the booklet entitled *Pillar of Fire, Pillar of Truth*. You might also want to subscribe to *This Rock*, his monthly magazine.

Q. My brother wishes to get involved in the RCIA program at his parish and asked what I knew about it. I have heard that it is a "feel-good" program that has very

little doctrinal content. Can you comment? — C.L., Ohio

A. The Rite of Christian Initiation of Adults (RCIA) is a program of rites and instructions by which unbaptized persons, known as catechumens, can become members of the Catholic Church by receiving the sacraments of initiation, Baptism, Confirmation, and the Holy Eucharist, usually at the Easter Vigil. There is available from any Catholic bookstore a 375-page study edition of the program (*Rite of Christian Initiation of Adults*), complete with the text of the rite, additional rites, and the "National Statutes for the Catechumenate," which were approved by the National Conference of Catholic Bishops in 1986 and confirmed by the Holy See in 1988.

Certain aspects of the RCIA can be adapted for non-Catholics who have been baptized and seek full communion in the Catholic Church, and for Catholics who may have been baptized but were never catechized and who wish to receive the sacraments of Confirmation and the Eucharist. The program includes rites for the preparation of adults, as well as of children who have reached catechetical age, or what used to be called the age of reason, i.e., about seven years.

How the program of instruction is carried out depends on the people in charge in a particular parish or diocese. Some programs are heavy on sharing faith stories and life experiences and light on doctrine. Some steer clear of such potentially controversial matters as sin and Confession, artificial contraception, divorce, devotion to the Blessed Mother, etc., and give catechumens and candidates for full communion a picture of Catholicism that is hardly distinguishable from other Christian religions.

On the other hand, there are good programs that give a balanced presentation of Catholicism. A sound program of instruction should focus on apologetics, provide solid explanations of Catholic doctrines, and give reasoned answers to the tough questions raised by critics of Catholicism. People who come to inquiry sessions, the first stage of the RCIA process, want answers to their questions, and it is a mistake to tell the inquirers that the answers will come later because the questioners may not come back later.

So tell your brother to check into the RCIA program in his parish. If it's a good one, tell him to get involved. There's no better feeling than assisting someone in becoming a full member of Christ's Church. If the program in his parish is not a good one, and he can't do anything to improve it, he'll have to go elsewhere.

Q. As a lifelong Episcopalian, I am thinking of converting to the Catholic Church. What is the procedure involved? Would I have to receive the sacraments of Baptism and Confirmation again? — D.R.D., Tennessee

A. You would not have to be baptized again, but you would have to be confirmed. The Catholic Church recognizes as valid a baptism performed in another Christian denomination if it was by immersion or pouring and the words were those of the trinitarian formula. You will be required to produce a baptismal certificate as proof of your Baptism in the Episcopal Church.

The Catholic Church does not recognize the validity of confirmation in other Christian denominations, except for the Orthodox Church, in which a child is confirmed by a priest at the same time as the Baptism. For more details, see *Principles and Norms of Ecumenism*, the revised Ecumenical Directory that was approved by the Holy Father on March 25, 1993, and the *Rite of Christian Initiation of Adults*.

As for the procedure for conversion, you should contact a Catholic priest and tell him of your intentions. Since you are not a catechumen, i.e., an unbaptized person, but rather a candidate for full Catholic communion, it is not necessary that you undergo the full RCIA program of instruction and preparation.

According to the "National Statutes for the Catechumenate," which were approved by the U.S. Bishops in 1986, "Those who have already been baptized in another church or ecclesial community should not be treated as catechumens or so designated. Their doctrinal and spiritual preparation for reception into full communion should be determined according to the individual case, that is, it should depend on the extent to which the baptized person has led a Christian life within a community of faith and been appropriately catechized to deepen his or her inner adherence to the Church " (n. 30).

Q. If a Catholic attends a funeral in an Episcopal church and the officiating minister invites all to receive communion, may she do so? — M.D.G., New York

A. A Catholic should not receive communion in an Episcopal church since it implies that it is the same thing as receiving the Eucharist in a Catholic church. Catholics believe that the bread and wine truly become the Body and Blood of Christ, while most other Christian denominations consider the Species to be only symbols of our Lord's Body and Blood.

The Catholic Church considers intercommunion a result of unity in faith and worship, not a means of achieving it, and the

Church asks Catholics to refrain from intercommunion while praying for that full unity willed by our Lord.

Q. My husband is a baptized non-Catholic who has devoutly attended Mass for seven years, instructs our children in Catholic catechism, and follows the teachings of the Holy Father. Our priest said it would be all right for him to receive Communion because he has been reciting the Creed. Is the priest corrrect.? — J.R.H., Washington

A. While your husband is certainly well on his way toward becoming a Catholic, he has not yet been formally accepted into the Church and, therefore, should not be receiving the Eucharist. Recitation of the Creed and all the other good things your husband is doing are wonderful, but he is not yet fully united with the Catholic Church. He lacks that unity of faith that is necessary for reception of Holy Communion.

Why not have the priest give your husband the instructions he needs for full membership in the Church, instead of urging him to take an incorrect shortcut?

Q. The Episcopalian husband of a Catholic friend died recently and was given a funeral Mass in my parish church. Is this allowable? — M.T., Massachusetts

A. Yes, it is allowable. According to Canon 1183 of the Code of Canon Law, the local bishop can on a case-by-case basis permit a baptized non-Catholic to receive the funeral rites of the Catholic Church if there is no indication that the deceased would have been opposed to a Catholic service and if the person's own minister is not available.

The absence of the non-Catholic minister could be either a physical unavailability (no minister living in the area) or a moral unavailability (there is a minister of the non-Catholic deceased in the area, but the deceased had not been attending services at that church). If the deceased person had not been, in this case, a practicing Episcopalian, then it can be presumed that he was not opposed to a Catholic funeral.

Q. A priest told me it is no longer wrong to go to another church's services. Is this true? — Name Withheld, Washington, and J.M., New York
Q. Should a parent allow a child to be taken to non-Catholic Sunday services by a non-Catholic relative when the child is visiting that relative? — B.M., Missouri
A. According to the Ecumenical Directory published in 1993

by the Pontifical Council for Promoting Christian Unity, Catholics may attend the non-sacramental liturgical services of other denominations and may even "take part in the psalms, responses, hymns, and common actions of the church in which they are guests. If invited by their hosts, they may read a lesson or preach." This presupposes, of course, that the responses, hymns, and common actions are not at variance with the Catholic Faith.

While Catholics may share in sacramental life with members of the Eastern Churches, which possess true Sacraments, Catholics may not share in sacramental life with Christians of other churches because that would signify a unity of faith, worship, and life that does not exist at the present time.

As for letting a relative take a child to a non-Catholic service, it would depend on the age of the child and how often this happens. An occasional trip to the relative's church for a boy or girl who has not made First Communion would not be a problem. But a youngster who has received First Communion ought to be attending Mass every weekend, so if the child were visiting a non-Catholic relative on a weekend, the parents of the child should make sure that he or she gets to Mass.

Q. Is it permissible to allow the use of a Catholic church for the consecration of an Episcopal bishop because it can seat more people? — L.B., Illinois, and J.A.J., Arizona

A. Yes, it is permissible. In the words of the 1993 Ecumenical Directory:

"Catholic churches are consecrated or blessed buildings which have an important theological and liturgical significance for the Catholic community. They are therefore generally reserved for Catholic worship. However, if priests, ministers, or communities not in full communion with the Catholic Church do not have a place or the liturgical objects necessary for celebrating worthily their religious ceremonies, the diocesan bishop may allow them the use of a church or Catholic building and also lend them what may be necessary for their services."

Q. Our parish hosted a community-wide worship service featuring four Protestant pastors, including a female Methodist minister. Given the feminist thrust for women's ordination, wasn't this invitation insensitive and lacking in good judgment? — T.D., Arkansas

A. We don't think so. Hosting an ecumenical service means inviting the leaders of other denominations, some of whom may be female. But this does not mean that the Catholic parish has compromised the Church's opposition to female clergy. The reasons for that opposition have been clearly stated for a long time, and we don't believe that inviting a woman minister from another denomination to participate in a service in a Catholic church is either insensitive to the Catholic position or lacking in good judgment.

Q. One of our Parish Council members has been hired as a pastoral assistant at a local Lutheran church, and she will make home visitations for them. Is she permitted to do this? — A.K., Alaska

A. It doesn't make much sense for a Catholic to go around promoting Lutheranism, which does not have the fullness of the means of salvation. She should be evangelizing for the one, true Church founded by Jesus — the Catholic Church.

Q. At a Catholic church in Little Rock, Arkansas, some time ago, President Clinton, a Protestant who does not believe in the Real Presence, received Holy Communion. Are Protestants permitted to receive Holy Communion in Catholic churches? — T.T.H., Pennsylvania

A. If this did in fact happen, then the priest who gave Mr. Clinton Communion was wrong. In the missalettes that are used in many Catholic churches, the "Guidelines for Receiving Communion" are spelled out. The policy regarding other Christians says that "it is a consequence of the sad divisions in Christianity that we cannot extend to them a general invitation to receive Communion. Catholics believe that the Eucharist is an action of the celebrating community, signifying a oneness in faith, life, and worship of the community. Reception of the Eucharist by Christians not fully united with us would imply a oneness which does not yet exist, and for which we must all pray."

Q. In your January 20th column, you stated that the priest who gave President Clinton Communion did wrong. It seems to me that this priest may well have been correct, according to the 1983 Code of Canon Law. Canon 844.4 mentions that "Catholic ministers may licitly administer these sacraments to other Christians who do not have full communion with the Catholic Church, who cannot approach a minister of their own community and on their own ask for it, provided they manifest Catholic faith in these sacraments and are properly disposed." Could you

please inform me if, in your opinion, I read this canon errantly? — F.D., Ohio

A. In quoting canon 844.4, you left out the first part of that provision, which says that Communion can be given in such a situation only "if the danger of death is present or other grave necessity, in the judgment of the diocesan bishop or the conference of bishops." Grave necessity could mean persons in prison or undergoing persecution. Obviously, President Clinton would not qualify under these conditions.

The other requirements are proper disposition, manifestation of Catholic belief that the Eucharist is the Body and Blood of Christ, and inability to approach one's own minister, usually because a person is a great distance from their own church. Without judging whether Mr. Clinton was properly disposed, and without knowing whether he holds the same faith in the Eucharist as Catholics do, we can say that in Little Rock, Arkansas, he was not sufficiently distant from his own church that his own minister was unavailable to him.

Since neither the danger of death nor grave necessity were present, we stand by our earlier reply that President Clinton should not have been given Holy Communion, if in fact that did happen.

Q. I have seen news reports of meetings between the Pope and other religious leaders which refer to the universal Church as a "denomination," putting it on a par with the 2,500 churches of our separated brethren. This does not seem to reflect the truth of the situation. Can you comment? — R.D.H., Maine

A. You raise an interesting point. Webster's *New Collegiate Dictionary* defines a denomination as "a religious organization uniting in a single legal and administrative body a number of local congregations." On the other hand, Fr. John Hardon's *Modern Catholic Dictionary* defines the word as "a legally distinct group of believers, especially among Protestants. Different denominations exist within a single Protestant tradition, e.g., Lutheran. They are not necessarily different, though they generally are, in their faith, worship, and form of church government."

It is common in secular news reports to use the term "denomination," but Catholic sources should be more careful in their choice of words. Vatican II suggested such synonyms for the Church as sacrament, kingdom of heaven on earth, sheepfold, flock, tract of land, vineyard, edifice of God, mother, community of faith, hope and charity, visible structure, society, Mystical Body of Christ, and People of God, but perhaps it would be simpler to use the word "Church."

Q. How can the Catholic Church participate in the ecumenical movement in light of 2 John 10-11? — G.P., Florida

A. The verses in question read: "If anyone comes to you who does not bring this teaching, do not receive him into your house; do not even greet him, for whoever greets him shares in the evil he does."

What teaching was John talking about? In verse seven, he warned against those "deceitful men ... who do not acknowledge Jesus Christ as coming in the flesh." He was referring to the fierce struggle in the early Church with those heretics (Docetists) who contended that Christ was not really a man, that He only seemed to be human. John linked these heretics with "the antichrist" and urged the faithful not to show any hospitality to these false teachers lest they infiltrate the Christian community and lead its members astray.

It would be wrong to compare the life-and-death situation John was talking about at the end of the first century to efforts at the end of the 20th century to bring about unity among Christians who agree on the teaching that Jesus Christ is true God and true man. Authentic ecumenical efforts seek to hasten the day when there will be one flock and one shepherd (John 10:16) and do not hesitate to assert that "it is through Christ's Catholic Church alone, which is the all-embracing means of salvation, that the fullness of the means of salvation can be obtained" (Vatican II, *Decree on Ecumenism*, n. 3).

Q. I have been asked by a Methodist to join his Bible study group. Is this permitted by the Church and should I do so for ecumenical reasons? — J.M.G., Pennsylvania

A. There is no Church prohibition of participation in Bible study with other Christians, but whether you should take part depends on who is leading the study group and on your knowledge of the Catholic Faith and of the Catholic interpretation of Scripture. If the person conducting the study is honestly trying to develop an appreciation of and love for the Word of God, and is not trying to force a particular viewpoint on the members of the group, then it could be a positive and beneficial experience for you.

On the other hand, if the person in charge of the group is

trying to proselytize the group, and if you are not that knowledgeable about your own Faith, you could leave yourself open to being swayed against Catholic teachings. Remember that non-Catholic Christians use a different Bible than we do, one that leaves out seven Old Testament books (Tobit, Judith, Wisdom, Sirach, Baruch, and 1 and 2 Maccabees), and most non-Catholics disagree with the Catholic view of certain key passages. So if you think that the Catholic view will be disputed, and if you are not intellectually prepared to defend that view, then you should not participate, even for ecumenical reasons.

Q. When I told my daughter she was wrong to send her children to a Baptist Bible study group, she called the chancery office in Chicago. A priest there told her that she was doing the right thing. How can I convince my daughter that this was bad advice? — R.E.L., Illinois

A. Assuming that you are not talking about preschoolers, who would very likely be exposed to Bible stories on a level that would not raise denominational issues, you are right to be concerned. While Catholics and Baptists do hold some beliefs in common (the Trinity, the divinity of Christ, original sin, the Virgin Birth, Heaven, and Hell), there are significant areas of disagreement. For instance, Baptists recognize only two sacraments — Baptism and the Lord's Supper — which they call "ordinances." They do not believe in baptism of infants and they see bread and wine only as symbolic of Christ's Body and Blood.

Baptists consider the Bible to be the sole rule of faith and the only guide to human conduct. They recognize no universal spiritual leader and teacher, all authority rests in the local congregation, and the will of the majority is final in all matters of church law and doctrine.

Any good Baptist, like any good Catholic, believes that his church is the surest way to salvation and will use Bible study classes to prove that point. Thus, a Catholic child attending these classes will get the Baptist view of Scripture, which is often contrary to the Catholic view.

How will your grandchildren reconcile what they hear in the Baptist classes with what they hear in Catholic classes? When they ask their mother why the Catholic Church baptizes infants, what will she tell them? When they ask why Baptists don't believe that Jesus is really present in the Eucharist, what will she say?

There are enough confused Catholics in the land today; let's not add to their numbers. Your daughter would not think of sending her children to classes where conflicting theories of math or science were taught. Why do it with something as important as religion?

And while we're on the subject, why not suggest to your daughter that she ask for Bible classes for Catholic children in her own parish? Then she won't feel the need to send her youngsters to a Baptist program.

Q. Although I am not a member of your Church, I enjoy reading your section in *The Wanderer* because the answers you give are accurate, clear, and not "nuanced" into incomprehensibility. From your replies I have learned much about the Catholic Church which was unknown to me previously. One thing puzzles me. I can't understand why Catholic bishops in America follow the doctrines, policies, and practices of Liberal Protestantism when they can see before their eyes how Liberalism is destroying the Episcopal Church. Many Catholic bishops and priests preach and teach what is preached and taught in the Protestant denominations and, that being the case, I don't understand why a Protestant would need to be converted to Catholicism. — R.T., California

A. R.T., an Episcopal clergyman, raises a very good point. It is analogous to the cry of certain Americans for more socialism in this country when socialism has been so thoroughly discredited elsewhere in the world. We don't know why some Catholics — bishops, priests, and laity — either promote or allow to be promoted doctrines, policies, and practices that have caused such damage to Protestant churches because we can't look into their minds and hearts. But we do know that what they are doing is harmful to the Catholic Church and may be keeping converts away. It was just such schizophrenic behavior that for a long time kept the late British journalist and television commentator Malcolm Muggeridge from becoming a Catholic.

What we can say to R.T., as *The Wanderer* has been telling its readers for years, is to follow the lead of the Holy Father and those bishops, priests, and laypeople who are faithful to him. Pope John Paul, through his encyclicals, apostolic exhortations, speeches in numerous nations, and weekly audiences, has been raising a standard to which all faithful Catholics, and all those who seek the truth, can rally.

Judge the Catholic Church by those who try to follow all the teachings of Jesus, not just those which suit them. And come to the Catholic Church because it is the Church that Jesus promised to be with "always, until the end of the world" (Matthew 28:20), to which He said His Father would give "another Paraclete — to be with you always: the Spirit of Truth" (John 14:16-17), and which St. Paul called "the pillar and bulwark of truth" (1 Timothy 3:15).

Q. What is meant by the term Anglican-Catholic? — P.A.R., Massachusetts
Q. Is the Anglo-Catholic Mass valid? — G.K., Virginia
A. According to Our Sunday Visitor's *Catholic Encyclopedia*, which was edited by Fr. Peter Stravinskas, "the Anglo-Catholics are a small minority of the worldwide Anglican Communion. After the Oxford Movement [in the last century], this party was interested in the restoration of Catholic doctrinal and devotional practices. By the end of the twentieth century, the groups finds itself increasingly frustrated, especially with the ordination of female clergy (of every rank) in various member churches of the Communion. Anglo-Catholics have generally favored corporate reunion with Rome and for this reason have continued their separate identity. But a number of them have converted to the Roman Church as individuals, especially after the Pastoral Provision was approved for the United States [in 1981]. According to this arrangement, married clergymen who convert may be ordained (if invalidly ordained) as Catholic priests.

"Parishes may be set up, and the form of the Mass and of the sacraments retains some elements of traditional Anglican usage found in the Prayer Book.

"An organization known as S.S.C. or the Society of the Holy Cross is a group of Anglo-Catholic clergy who generally accept Catholic doctrine and moral practice, including *Humanae Vitae*, and who await the day of full communion with Rome. Some Anglo-Catholics joined the Continuing Anglican Movement after 1975, when the first female clergy were ordained in the United States. Others have gone in different directions, even joining the Eastern Orthodox Church, which accepts the Pope of Rome as 'first among equals.'"

Q. The liturgy in the two Catholic churches near me is so bad that my family and I have joined an Anglican Catholic Church in the community, which is traditional, conservative, and orthodox, and more Catholic than the Roman

Catholic churches in the area. We are very happy there, but I still believe the Roman Catholic Church is the true Church, and I wonder if it is a sin for me to go to this Anglican Church. I don't know what to do. Please advise me. — D.A.B., Virginia

A. Your plight is shared by other Catholics across the country who find themselves in parishes where liturgical abuses are rampant and where going to Mass is a traumatic rather than an uplifting experience. But while you find many things to enjoy and agree with at the Anglican Catholic Church in your community, it is not the Church founded by Jesus and it does not possess the fullness of truth or a valid Sacrifice of the Mass.

If you truly believe that the Roman Catholic Church is the true Church of Christ, then it is wrong for you to attend another church. Our sympathy and our prayers go out to you, and to all others going through a similar trial, but we could never advise anyone to leave the only Church founded by Jesus because of abuses initiated or condoned by certain priests and bishops. When Jesus asked the Apostles if they intended to leave Him because of His teaching on the Eucharist, Peter replied: "Lord, to whom shall we go? You have the words of eternal life" (John 6:68).

"Where Peter is, there is the Church" is an ancient truism. The Church headed today by the successor of Peter, Pope John Paul II, is the only sure road to Heaven, even though some members of that Church are ignoring the Holy Father and are creating liturgical and moral potholes for faithful Catholics traveling that difficult road. The Good Friday that the Church is suffering through today will pass and be followed by the glory of Easter, but we must pray constantly for priests and bishops that they will give to their people the marvelous spiritual heritage that has been handed down to them.

Q. Would you please explain how the Orthodox religion came about, what they practice and believe in, and how they are related to the Roman Catholic Church? — D.C., Vermont

A. The Orthodox Church, which has valid orders and valid sacraments and shares many of the beliefs of Catholics, officially separated from the Roman Catholic Church in 1054. The reasons for the split included married clergy, the use of leavened bread for the Eucharist, and disagreement over the use of the word *filioque* in the Creed. *Filioque* means "and from the Son" and refers to the Catholic belief that the Holy Spirit proceeds from the Father and the Son. The Orthodox Church believes that the Holy Spirit proceeds through the Son.

Other differences between the two Churches, according to the *Catholic Encyclopedia* edited by Fr. Peter Stravinskas, include "the acceptance by the Orthodox of only the first seven ecumenical councils, their rejection of any single supreme head of the Church, the remarriage of divorced individuals, and the questioning of such Catholic dogmas as Purgatory, papal infallibility, and the Immaculate Conception."

Recent Popes and Patriarchs have tried hard to reconcile the two Churches, and Pope John Paul II has made the development of better relations a priority of his pontificate.

Q. Is it permissible for a Catholic couple to occasionally fulfill their Sunday Mass obligation at a nearby Greek Orthodox church, including the reception of Holy Communion, if the closest non-Modernist Catholic church is an hour's drive away? The local Orthodox priest has been a friend for some years and knows we are loyal to Rome and have no intention of converting to Orthodoxy. He is aware of the problems in our local parish and has agreed to give us Communion. — J.S., California

Q. I have been told it is permissible to attend Orthodox services inasmuch as they have valid orders and sacraments. Are there any conditions to this permission? — L.D.B., Minnesota

A. The general rule is that Catholics should receive the sacraments from Catholic ministers (canon 844.1). But Catholics may receive sacraments from ministers of other churches which possess valid orders and true sacraments, such as the Eastern Orthodox Churches, under the conditions stated in the revised Ecumenical Directory issued in 1993 by the Pontifical Council for Promoting Christian Unity:

"Whenever necessity requires or a genuine spiritual advantage suggests, and provided that the danger of error or indifferentism is avoided, it is lawful for any Catholic for whom it is physically or morally impossible to approach a Catholic minister, to receive the Sacraments of Penance, Eucharist, and Anointing of the Sick from a minister of an Eastern Church."

Assuming that there is no danger of error or indifferentism, Catholics wishing to attend Orthodox services and receive the Eucharist must do so out of necessity, genuine spiritual advantange, or physical or moral inaccessibility to a Catholic priest. Such necessity could mean persons in danger of death, in prison, or in countries where the Church is persecuted; genuine spiritual advantage could mean the situation described by J.S.; physical impossibility could mean no access to a Catholic minister; moral impossibility could mean a psychological aversion to a Catholic minister or church.

It must be emphasized that Catholics receiving sacraments in the Orthodox Church do so only by way of exception to the general rule. There must be serious reasons and, according to the Ecumenical Directory, "it is strongly recommended that the diocesan bishop ... establish general norms for judging situations of grave and pressing need and for verifying the conditions" mentioned above.

Editor's Note: In a recent reply, we stated that while Catholics should normally receive the sacraments from Catholic ministers, they were permitted to receive them from ministers of other churches which possess valid orders and true sacraments, such as the Eastern Orthodox Church, provided that it was physically or morally impossible to approach a Catholic minister, that the danger of error or indifferentism was avoided, and that there was a genuine necessity or spiritual advantage involved (canon 844).

That may be true from the Catholic viewpoint, says Fr. Stephen Morris, an Eastern Orthodox priest in New York City, but "you failed to point out that this is a totally unacceptable practice according to Orthodox canon law and spiritual practice. The Orthodox Church sees Holy Communion as the seal of unity in a common faith already achieved and not an individualistic act in which any priest may give Holy Communion to any person who wishes to receive a 'dose of grace,' as it were.

"Any Orthodox priest who would agree to give Holy Communion to non-Orthodox (as the Catholic couple involved pointed out, they had no intention of converting to Orthodoxy and had made this clear to the Orthodox priest) is introducing 'modernistic,' 'relativistic,' and 'synchretistic' practices into the life of the Church. As I understand from your columns, this is the very thing you condemn the Roman Catholic priests in this country for doing so eagerly. How can you condemn a Roman priest for ignoring the various injunctions of the Church and yet encourage an Orthodox priest to violate the injunctions of the Church?

"In answering a question about Roman Catholic priests giving Holy Communion to non-Roman Catholic Christians, you cited various Roman rulings that this was not acceptable. The reasons given sounded very Orthodox, as they had mostly to do with Communion presupposing a unity of faith (which was clearly not shared by a non-Roman Catholic Christian). Again, it seems to me inconsistent at best to say Roman Catholic priests ought to obey the canons, but Orthodox ought not, and that Catholic laity should ask (and encourage) Orthodox priests to do the very thing these same laymen refuse to countenance in Roman priests.

"I would like to request that you clear up this matter in a future column and point out that Roman Catholics ought not receive (or ask to receive) the sacraments from Orthodox priests, if only out of respect for Orthodox practice."

Fr. Morris expresses his viewpoint very well, and that is why we have quoted at length from his letter. We would, however, make three comments: (1) Our obligation in writing this column is to point out what is acceptable *Catholic* canonical and liturgical practice, not what is acceptable to those of other faiths, although we are happy to give Fr. Morris his say. (2) We don't condemn anyone, priest or otherwise, for flouting Church law and practice. We do point out where they have strayed from Church teaching and leave condemnation of them up to God since only He knows the motivations of these people. (3) We have on more than one occasion carefully made the distinction between receiving sacraments from ministers of churches with valid orders and true sacraments (Eastern Orthodox) and receiving them from, or giving them to, persons from churches without valid orders or true sacraments (Protestant churches).

Q. Jesus Christ, His mother, stepfather, Apostles, Rabbi Paul, the first Pope, and early disciples were all Jews. Why do Christian religions, including Roman Catholicism, deemphasize this fact, as well as the obligation to monotheistic Judaism? — T.F.O., Massachusetts

A. This fact was not deemphasized by the Second Vatican Council. In its *Declaration on the Relationship of the Church to Non-Christian Religions*, the Council Fathers recalled "the spiritual bond linking the people of the New Covenant with Abraham's stock"; acknowledged that "the beginnings of her faith and her election are already found among the patriarchs, Moses, and the prophets"; said that "from the Jewish people sprang the Apostles, her foundation stones and pillars, as well as most of the early disciples who proclaimed Christ to the world"; and declared that "the Church awaits that day, known to

God alone, on which all peoples will address the Lord in a single voice and 'serve him with one accord'" (n. 4).

Referring to this same paragraph, the *Catechism of the Catholic Church* (n. 839) says that when the Church, which it calls the People of God in the New Covenant, delves into her own background, she discovers her link with the Jewish people, who were the first to hear the Word of God. To the Jews, the *Catechism* says, belong the sonship, the glory, the covenants, the giving of the law, the worship, the promises, and the patriarchs. And from their race, according to the flesh, is the Christ, for as St. Paul said, "God's gifts and his call are irrevocable" (Romans 11:29).

Q. My son-in-law, who is a convert to Catholicism, is being pressured to join the Masons. Is there something you could recommend that would explain the Church's opposition to the Masons? — J.A.K., Texas

Q. What are the actual facts on Catholics being permitted to join the Masons? — J.C., Maine

Q. The enclosed letter to the editor in the *San Antonio Express-News* says that Catholics are free to be Masons. How can this be? — B.E.D., Texas

Q. A Mason told me that the Pope has rescinded his prohibition of Catholics joining Freemasonry. What is the present Church position? — S.B., New York

Q. Are Catholics prohibited from enrolling in Masonic associations? — T.T.H., Pennsylvania

Q. Has the ban on Freemasonry been lifted? I have been told that Pope John Paul II removed the ban. — A.O., Ohio

Q. Several Sundays ago, I received Holy Communion from a man with a Masonic ring on his hand. I asked him about it, and he said he had been a Mason for over ten years. Is it possible for him to give out Holy Communion? — G.C.G., Michigan

A. Freemasonry originated in London in the early 1700s and has usually been hostile to religion in general and the Catholic Church in particular. Eight Popes have condemned it, beginning with Clement XII in 1738. During the 1970s, there was a perception that Catholics could join Masonic lodges that were not anti-Catholic, but in 1980 the Sacred Congregation for the Doctrine of the Faith called this perception false. The Congregation restated the ban on Masonic membership in a declaration issued on November 26, 1983, with the approval of Pope John Paul II.

The declaration said that "the Church's negative position on Masonic associations ... remains unaltered since their principles have always been regarded as irreconcilable with the Church's doctrine. Hence, joining them remains prohibited by the Church. Catholics enrolled in Masonic associations are involved in serious sin and may not approach Holy Communion. Local ecclesiastical authorities do not have the faculty to pronounce a judgment on the nature of Masonic associations which might include a diminution of the above-mentioned judgment."

In June 1985, the National Conference of Catholic Bishops called Freemasonry "irreconcilable" with Catholicism because "the principles and basic rituals of Masonry embody a naturalistic religion, active participation in which is incompatible with Christian faith and practice. Those who knowingly embrace such principles are committing a serious sin."

Two good books on Freemasonry are William J. Whalen's *Christianity and American Freemasonry* (Our Sunday Visitor) and Paul A. Fisher's *Behind the Lodge Door: Church, State and Freemasonry in America.*

Q. One of the organizations that receives charitable contributions through my place of work is the Shriners Children's Hospitals, which are affiliated with the Masons. Knowing the problems with Freemasonry, are Catholics permitted to financially assist any of their charities? Or what about charities connected with the Mormons or other non-Christian religions? — D.A.P., Indiana

Q. My two handicapped children have received assistance from the Shriners. Is it permissible for a Catholic family to accept help from this organization in light of its affiliation with the Masons? — B.A.M., Rhode Island

Q. My Knights of Columbus council is involved with three local Masonic lodges in civic improvement efforts and charitable work. These discussions are also aimed at understanding each other's beliefs. Is this allowed? — D.B., Wisconsin

A. As we have noted before, the Sacred Congregation for the Doctrine of the Faith stated in 1983 that Catholics are not permitted to join the Masons. But what about contributing financially to a Masonic charity such as the Shriners, or accepting assistance from them, or cooperating with them in civic or charitable endeavors? In none of these cases are the Catholic questioners expressing agreement with Masonic principles, taking an active role in Masonic rituals, or promoting a naturalistic religion that is incompatible with Catholic faith and practice.

Therefore, we see nothing wrong with contributing to the work the Shriners are doing for crippled children or those suffering from burns, with accepting financial assistance for one's own handicapped children, or with jointly participating with local Masonic lodges in community service projects. The same would be true for ecumenical cooperation with other groups or denominations with whom we differ on religious and moral beliefs.

It would not be right, however, for K of C councils to enter into discussions with Masonic lodges that are aimed at "understanding each other's beliefs" unless the local bishop has approved such interreligious dialogue and established proper safeguards. Otherwise, there is the risk of indifferentism and of thinking that the Church must be wrong in warning Catholics against getting involved with the "nice people" in this naturalistic religion.

Q. What can you tell me about the Mormon Church and its beliefs? — J.P.D., Massachusetts

A. The Mormon Church, whose official name is the Church of Jesus Christ of Latter-Day Saints, was founded in 1829 by Joseph Smith, who said that an angel led him to golden plates buried near Palmyra, New York. He said that the angel gave him magic spectacles which enabled him to decipher the hieroglyphics on the plates and dictate the *Book of Mormon.*

According to Smith, the Christian church fell into error shortly after the death of the last Apostle, but was restored when God the Father and Jesus appeared to him in 1829. He moved his new church to Ohio, Missouri, and then to Illinois, where he was murdered in 1844. Smith's place was taken by Brigham Young, who led the Saints west to what is now Utah. The Mormon community flourished there and today has more than seven million members worldwide.

Mormon beliefs can be found in the Bible "as correctly translated," in the *Book of Mormon,* and in *Doctrines and Covenants.* While they claim to be a Christian religion, Mormons reject some fundamental Christian beliefs. For instance, Mormons say that there are many gods for many worlds, that God was once a man, and that faithful Mormons will becomes gods themselves after death. It was Brigham Young who said: "What God was once, we are now; what God is now, we shall be."

While Christians describe the Trinity as three distinct Persons (Father, Son, and Holy Spirit) but only one God, Mormons say that the Trinity involves three separate Gods.

Mormons forbid the use of alcohol, tobacco, and caffeine; tithe 10 percent of their income to the church; encourage large families; and require all young men to spend a year or two as unpaid missionaries trying to win converts. These missionaries have a memorized conversion talk as well as selected Bible texts and prepared answers to objections raised by non-Mormons. Unless you are well versed in the Bible and the teachings of the Catholic Church, you would be wise not to invite them into your home or to try to debate them.

For more information on the Mormons, see William J. Whalen's *Faiths for the Few* (Our Sunday Visitor), Fr. Albert J. Nevins' *Strangers at your Door* (Our Sunday Visitor), and "A Catholic/Mormon Dialogue," a videotaped debate between Patrick Madrid and Gary Coleman available from Catholic Answers, P.O. Box 17490, San Diego, California 92177.

Q. Can you tell me something about the Jehovah's Witnesses? — M.K., Vermont

A. The cult known as the Jehovah's Witnesses was founded over 100 years ago by a man named Charles Russell. Also known as the Watchtower Society, it has more than two million members worldwide, with about half a million in the United States. Individual witnesses spend 16 to 20 hours a week knocking on doors, studying the group's publications (*Watchtower* and *Awake!*), and attending Bible classes at their local Kingdom Hall. The typical Kingdom Hall has about 75 members.

Jehovah's Witnesses believe that we are living in the last days before the final battle of Armageddon between Christ and Satan. Even though their predictions that Armageddon would occur in 1914, 1925, and 1975 did not come true, they still insist that it is just around the corner. They consider themselves citizens not of any country but of Jehovah's New World Society. Therefore, Witnesses refuse to salute the flag, stand for the national anthem, serve in the military, vote, or hold public office.

They believe that the only God is God the Father (Jehovah), that Jesus is not God, that He became man and died for our sins on a torture stake, not a cross, and that He is a spirit-creature who serves as God's executive officer in Heaven, where He is also known as Michael the Archangel. The Witnesses believe that only 144,000 people will eventually live in Heaven, that other Jehovah's Witnesses will live forever in a paradise on earth, and that the rest of humanity will be destroyed.

Witnesses also believe in a strict sexual morality, including opposition to adultery, fornication, abortion, and homosexuality. They condemn gambling, blood transfusions, observance of Christmas and Easter, the Catholic and Protestant churches, and the celebration of birthdays.

Most Jehovah's Witnesses are former Catholics or Protestants. They are very skilled in presenting their views and in using selective quotations from the Bible, so don't attempt to engage them in debate unless you are well-versed in Scripture and the teachings of the Catholic Church.

For more information on the Witnesses, see William J. Whalen's *Faiths for the Few* (Our Sunday Visitor) and *Strange Gods* (OSV), Fr. Albert J. Nevins' *Strangers at Your Door*, and *Index of Watchtower Errors*, edited by David A. Reed.

Q. The Jehovah's Witnesses claim that Christ died, not on a cross, but on a "torture stake," which they depict as a straight-up tree trunk with the Savior's hands impaled above His head rather than stretched out on a crossbeam. Is there any basis in Scripture or elsewhere for this claim? — C.F., Pennsylvania

A. In the October 1991 issue of *This Rock* magazine, there is an excellent article by Clayton F. Bower Jr. debunking this claim of the Jehovah's Witnesses. Bower points out that the traditional posture of a man crucified under Roman rule — with arms outstretched on a crosspiece — is confirmed by second-century graffiti scratched into the wall of a Roman palace, by ancient non-Christian literature, by early Christian writings, and by the discovery in Jerusalem in 1968 of the bones of a man who had been crucified around 70 A.D.

There were nail scratches on the arms of the executed man, indicating that the arms had been stretched out and nailed through the wrists; the nail that had fixed the victim's feet to the cross was still imbedded in his ankle bones; and his legs had been deliberately broken to hasten his death.

Bower also cites the habit we have of making the Sign of the Cross as evidence of the traditional Christian belief that Jesus was crucified on a T-shaped cross. This manner of signing ourselves, which goes back to the earliest years of the Church, would make no sense unless it duplicated the posture of our crucified Lord.

Chapter 5

Catholic Prayers and Practices

Q. Are lay ministers permitted to distribute ashes on Ash Wednesday? — R.J.S., Kentucky

Q. Are lay people permitted to bless throats on the feast of St. Blaise? — A.E.F., New York; J.H., Florida; and M.R., Texas

A. On March 22, 1988, the Administrative Committee of the National Conference of Catholic Bishops approved the *Book of Blessings* for use in the United States. That approval was confirmed by the Apostolic See by decree of the Congregation for Divine Worship on January 27, 1989.

In Chapter 51 of the *Book of Blessings*, which is entitled "Order for the Blessing of Throats on the Feast of Saint Blaise," it says that "the blessing of throats may be given by a priest, deacon, or a lay minister who follows the rites and prayers designated for a lay minister" (n. 1626).

The same holds true for distribution of ashes by lay ministers. In Chapter 52 of the *Book of Blessings*, which is entitled "Order for the Blessing and Distribution of Ashes," it says that "this rite may be celebrated by a priest or deacon who may be assisted by lay ministers in the distribution of the ashes. The blessing of the ashes, however, is reserved to a priest or deacon" (n. 1659).

Q. Why and when were the holy days of obligation established? Our pastor told a high school CCD class that they were instituted to provide another Mass at which a collection could be taken up because the Church needed money to refurbish St. Peter's. — M.R., South Dakota

A. There are 10 holy days celebrated by the universal Church, six of which are commemorated in the United States. Those six holy days are the Solemnity of Mary, Mother of God (January 1st), which in 1970 replaced the Circumcision, which dated back to the sixth century; the Ascension of the Lord (40 days after Easter), which can be documented in the fifth century but goes back farther than that; the Assumption of Our Lady into Heaven (August 15th), which was celebrated in Jerusalem and Rome as early as the seventh century; All Saints (November 1st), which dates to the fourth century and was fixed on its present day by Pope Gregory IV in 835; the Immaculate Conception of Mary (December 8th), which dates in its present form to 1854, when

Pope Pius IX proclaimed the dogma of the Immaculate Conception, but was celebrated in the East as early as the eighth century; and the Birth of Our Lord (December 25th), which was observed on that date at least by the year 354.

These special days were singled out in different places and at different times not to increase Church revenues, but to call to the attention of the faithful important events in the life of Jesus, the Blessed Mother, and the saints.

Q. Are Catholics still supposed to abstain from meat on Fridays? — F.G., California, and D.M., Iowa

Q. When were meatless Fridays instituted? — J.S., Florida

Q. Is it a sin to allow any Friday of the year to pass without an act of penance? — W.F.H., Rhode Island

Q. Are the fast and abstinence rules for Lent binding under pain of sin? — A.M.P., Michigan

Q. What is the official Church teaching on abstaining from meat every Friday? What other foods could we abstain from? — K.M.D., Massachusetts

A. The custom of abstaining from meat on Friday goes back to the first century A.D. According to the *Didache*, a second-century collection of the teachings of the Apostles, the early Christians fasted on Wednesdays and Fridays. This included abstaining from meat on Friday in commemoration of the Passion and death of Jesus on Good Friday. Saturday replaced Wednesday as a day of fast in the Western Church around the year 400, and abstinence without fast was generally observed on all Fridays and Saturdays throughout the year until the 19th century, when the bishops of the United States obtained from Rome dispensations from the Saturday abstinence.

While there were other changes in the laws and customs in this century, it was not until 1966 that Pope Paul VI issued an *Apostolic Constitution on Penance* that completely reorganized the discipline of fasting and abstinence. After declaring that "by divine law all the faithful are required to do penance," the Holy Father said that Ash Wednesday and all the Fridays of Lent would be days of penance and that "their substantial observance binds gravely." He also said that abstinence from meat is to be observed on every Friday throughout the year which does not fall on a holy day of obligation, and he gave the bishops' conferences in each country the authority to "transfer for just cause the days of penitence" and to "substitute abstinence and fast wholly or in part with other forms of penitence and especially works of charity and the exercises of piety."

On November 18, 1966, the U.S. Catholic Bishops said that "Catholics in the United States are obliged to abstain from the eating of meat on Ash Wednesday and on all Fridays during the season of Lent. They are also obliged to fast on Ash Wednesday and on Good Friday. Self-imposed observance of fasting on all weekdays of Lent is strongly recommended. Abstinence from flesh meat on all Fridays of the year is especially recommended to individuals and to the Catholic community as a whole."

The key to determining whether serious sin is involved in these matters is whether the fasting and abstinence are prescribed or only recommended and whether an individual "substantially" observes these laws. Thus, a person can fail to abstain from meat on a Friday of Lent without committing a serious sin, but that person would sin gravely if he or she totally disregarded the Church's norms during the entire penitential season, assuming of course that the person fully understood the serious nature of the laws on abstinence.

While the Lenten regulations are prescribed and "bind gravely" all Catholics, the Friday abstinence from meat is only "especially recommended." Therefore, no serious sin is involved in failing to abstain from meat on Fridays throughout the year, or in neglecting to substitute works of charity and exercises of piety for abstinence.

It should be emphasized, however, that even though Friday abstinence is no longer required by law, the U.S. Bishops said in their 1983 statement *The Challenge of Peace* that Catholics should continue to observe this custom "out of love for Christ crucified," as a reminder that "we must preserve a saving and necessary difference from the spirit of the world," and as "an outward sign of the spiritual values that we cherish."

As for other foods that we could abstain from, it could be any food that we particularly like. It's no sacrifice for a person who is a vegetarian to abstain from meat on Friday, so that person should stay away from a favorite food of another kind that day. But people who do enjoy meat should try to abstain every Friday of the year. And if that is not possible, then they should perform some work of charity (any corporal work of mercy) or engage in some exercise of piety (attend Mass, pray before the Blessed Sacrament, make the Stations, say the rosary, or read the Bible).

Q. Some months ago, you mentioned the November 1966 document of the U.S. Catholic bishops on Friday abstinence

from meat and then claimed the 1983 canon law regarding abstinence is not binding under pain of sin. So please reexamine your answer that it is okay to be outside the current 1983 canon law. The 1983 canon law replaced the 1966 document, not the other way around. — **D.M., Iowa**

A. We never said that it is okay to be outside canon 1251, which reads as follows: "Abstinence from eating meat or another food *according to the prescriptions of the conference of bishops* is to be observed on Fridays throughout the year unless they are solemnities; abstinence and fast are to be observed on Ash Wednesday and on the Friday of the Passion and Death of Our Lord Jesus Christ."

What we did say was that the bishops in each country (note the portion of the canon italicized by us) have the authority to modify that canon. Thus, the U.S. bishops, while obliging Catholics in this country to abstain from meat on Ash Wednesday and the Fridays of Lent, imposed no such obligation on the other Fridays of the year. What they said was that "abstinence from flesh meat on all Fridays of the year is *especially recommended* to individuals and to the Catholic community as a whole" (emphasis ours).

Canon 1251 codifies the decision of Pope Paul VI, in his 1966 *Apostolic Constitution on Penance*, to give the bishops' conferences the authority to make the rules about the days of abstinence.

Q. Can you give me some information on the origin of holy water, why we use it, etc.? — C.B., Florida

A. According to the *Catholic Encyclopedia* edited by Fr. Peter Stravinskas, water was used in many Old Testament Jewish religious ceremonies (Exodus 29:4 and 30:17-21, Leviticus 8:6, Numbers 8:7). "The Church, by the command of Christ," the *Encyclopedia* says, "has always used water as the essential matter for the sacrament of Baptism (John 3:5), and in imitation of His example, maintains the devotional practice of the washing of feet with water on Holy Thursday (John 13:5).

"Through His Baptism by St. John the Baptist in the Jordan, Christ sanctified water for the Christian sacrament of Baptism, and confirmed this symbolically when water and blood flowed from His pierced Heart."

A symbol of cleansing and purification, holy water blessed by a priest is a sacramental that is used in blessings of persons and objects, during exorcisms, and in times of spiritual and even physical danger. It is used for sprinklings during Mass and for washing the priest's hands, and a tiny amount is mingled with the wine used by the priest at the Consecration of the Mass.

Q. I have always felt that wearing a veil or hat was something a woman should do at Mass to show respect to our Lord. I am always the only one that seems to do this. I don't mind the stares if I am right, but I would certainly feel more comfortable not entering church with a head covering if I don't have to. — G.R., Tennessee

Q. Some people at the Latin Tridentine Mass here wear head coverings, and some do not. Is the rule for head covers still in effect? — B.T., Wisconsin

A. There was a provision in the 1917 Code of Canon Law requiring women to wear a veil or hat to cover their heads in church. It was based on St. Paul's comments on the conduct of men and women at public worship services (1 Corinthians 11:2-16), and may have reflected the fact that women wore hats at all public gatherings at the time that Code was written. However, there is no such provision in the 1983 Code. A woman can still wear a head covering in the Real Presence of our Lord if she wishes, but it is no longer mandatory to do so.

Q. Have the vigil rites for funerals been changed in the Catholic Church to a Scripture service in place of the rosary? The rosary is such a beautiful service for a wake that taking it away seems to be just another example of shoving the Blessed Mother and her rosary into the background. — J.B., Colorado

Q. Is it true that Vatican II said that the rosary should no longer be said at the vigil of a funeral? Can the family decide whether to have the rosary said? What if the parish priest refuses to say the rosary? — M.A.F., Colorado

A. Yes, the vigil rite for the deceased has been changed to a Scripture service. In centuries past, liturgical vigils were held for clergy, monks, and nuns, as well as for nobility in the Middle Ages, since these literate classes were able to participate in the appropriate hours of the Office of the Dead. The rosary was popularized as the poor man's psalter, with the 150 Hail Marys replacing the 150 psalms and the prayers between the decades representing other features of the Office.

Now the liturgical vigil has been extended to everyone, and it is not optional; it is the Church's official prayer for the deceased, and the priest is obligated to celebrate it, either in the form of the

Liturgy of the Word (the vigil service we encounter) or the appropriate hour of the Office of the Dead. Since the ordained minister's job is to celebrate the official rites of the Church, and a very long period of prayer (Liturgy of the Word and rosary) at a crowded wake probably would cause considerable congestion, and even extension of visiting hours well beyond their scheduled time, the rosary is not being said as much these days.

This should not be seen, however, as a downgrading of the rosary, which remains an honored and popular non-liturgical prayer. Vatican II never prohibited the rosary at wakes, and it may always be recited at vigils for the deceased. But since the shortage of priests, and the increasing demands on their time, make it difficult for them to spend an extended period of time at a wake, it may fall to a family member to lead the rosary if a priest is not available or not willing to do so.

The rosary could even be said before visiting hours begin. This is sometimes necessary when a large number of people is expected at the funeral home. In fact, we have been to wakes that were so crowded that the funeral director removed the kneelers in front of the casket to speed up the line of mourners and keep the visiting hours within reasonable limits.

Q. What do you think about having a wake service in church? I attended one for an 84-year-old person that was very loud and disrespectful. Maybe the Blessed Sacrament should be removed. — W.F., Missouri

A. The *Order of Christian Funerals*, which has been mandated in the United States since November 2, 1989, permits a wake service or vigil for the deceased in church, "but at a time well before the funeral liturgy so that the funeral liturgy will not be lengthy and the liturgy of the word repetitious" (n. 55). The vigil in church is to consist of introductory rites (greeting, opening song, silent prayer, and an opening prayer), liturgy of the word (first reading, responsorial psalm, Gospel reading, and homily), prayer of intercession (litany, Lord's Prayer, and concluding prayer), and concluding rite (blessing, song, and/or silent prayer).

Wakes are often noisy because they are attended by people who haven't seen each other for a long time, and there are effusive greetings and sometimes boisterous conversations. We don't pay much attention to this at a funeral home, but such behavior seems out of place to those who still believe in showing respect for the Blessed Sacrament.

The only wakes we have attended in church were for priests who had served in a particular parish, and those services were conducted with the proper decorum. W.F. didn't mention whether the person in her church was a priest or not, but if the vigil followed the structure recommended in the *Order of Christian Funerals*, that should have precluded loud and unseemly behavior. Such misbehavior in church, unfortunately, has become all too commonplace in recent years as people have lost their sense of the sacred.

Q. My wife and I have two young daughters and we have made a decision to tithe, which we understand to be ten percent of my gross income. My income is modest and our possessions few, and we hope some day to have a home of our own and to fill it with children. At times, however, things get pretty tight, and we wonder if we will ever get ahead and if tithing would be unfair to our family. Can you comment and also recommend further reading on the subject? — D.J.M., Ohio

A. First of all, congratulations on your desire to contribute generously to the support of the Church. There is an old saying that God will not be outdone in generosity, and we are confident that He will bless the efforts of you and your wife.

The practice of tithing, giving usually one-tenth of one's income to church and charity, is mentioned 46 times in the Bible. For instance, Abram gave Melchizedek, the king of Salem, a tenth of everything he owned (Genesis 14:18-20). And the obligation to pay tithes in crops and animals is spelled out in Leviticus 27:30-33. This practice was continued by the early Christians, and the first positive Church law on tithing was enacted in 567.

Catholics have a serious obligation (it is a precept of the Church) to contribute to the support of the Church, not only in their own parish but also the worldwide Church and the Holy Father, but there is no amount fixed by law. The idea of tithing as a way of fulfilling this obligation has become more widespread in recent years in the United States, and those doing so are quite enthusiastic about it. Teams of priests and laity are going into parishes to explain the merits of tithing. There are different ways of carrying this out, including gross vs. net income (after taxes), with five percent going to church and five percent to charity.

For more information, you should read Fr. Joseph Champlin's book, *Sharing Time, Treasure and Talent* (Liturgical Press).

Q. How can Catholics gain indulgences? Have the regulations for obtaining a plenary indulgence for the souls in Purgatory changed in recent years? — M.K.V., Texas, and S.N., California

Q. Some time ago, you had an article about indulgences. Could you send me a copy of it? — L.A.N., Minnesota

A. Instead of doing that, let's review the Church's teaching on indulgences, using as a guide paragraphs 1471-1479 of the *Catechism of the Catholic Church.*

An indulgence is a remission of the temporal punishment due to sins that have already been forgiven in the sacrament of Penance. This temporal punishment exists because every sin, even venial, "entails an unhealthy attachment to creatures, which must be purified either here on earth, or after death in the state called Purgatory" (n. 1472). Indulgences are obtained through the Church, which opens to us the treasury of the merits of Christ and the saints. The remission can be plenary or partial, depending upon whether it removes all or only some of the temporal punishment attached to sin. The indulgence can be applied to the person performing the works of devotion, penance, and charity or to a soul in Purgatory.

According to Pope Paul VI's 1967 *Apostolic Constitution on the Revision of Indulgences*, the following are the conditions for obtaining a plenary indulgence: the person must be free from all attachment to sin, even venial sin; must perform the indulgenced work as perfectly as possible; and, within several days before or after doing so, must receive sacramental Confession and Eucharistic Communion, and offer prayers for the intentions of the Holy Father. One Our Father and one Hail Mary would satisfy the latter requirement.

A plenary indulgence can be gained only once a day and, if each condition is not fulfilled perfectly, the indulgence gained will only be partial. The number of indulgenced works and prayers was reduced by Paul VI in his 1968 *Enchiridion Indulgentarium* to about 70. Some of these are good works, such as acts of charity for those in need, but most of them are traditional prayers and devotions. The previous practice of attaching a certain number of days or years to a specific task is no longer in effect.

Q. How and where can I obtain a copy of Pope Paul VI's *Enchiridion Indulgentarium*, or a list of some of the works and prayers now required to obtain indulgences? — F.M.N., Connecticut

A. The best place to get a copy of the Holy Father's 1968 listing of prayers and works to gain indulgences would be your nearest Catholic bookstore. If they don't have a copy, they should be able to order one for you.

Q. Each month I try to secure spiritual benefits for others through Mass stipends or through enrollments in the Union of Masses. Is a person likely to derive greater spiritual benefit from an individual Mass or from being enrolled in a Union of Masses? — W.A.D., Massachusetts

A. By a Union of Masses, W.A.D. is referring to 500 Masses said annually for members of the Union who support the Church's missionary activities in Africa with prayers and financial contributions. Since each Mass is of potentially great spiritual benefit to those for whom it is celebrated, the spiritual benefits would be multiplied considerably if individuals were prayed for in 500 Masses over the course of a year. W.A.D. is simultaneously performing two works of charity by aiding the missions and by arranging for prayers for family and friends.

Q. My priest says that you can't do penance for other people unless they are dead. This seems to contradict some things I have read about people being converted because of the suffering of invalids or being saved from Hell because of the sacrifices and penances of others. Which of us is right? — W.A., Kentucky

A. You are. In his apostolic letter on the Christian meaning of human suffering, Pope John Paul II said: "In the Body of Christ, which is ceaselessly born of the cross of the Redeemer, it is precisely suffering permeated by the spirit of Christ's sacrifice that is the irreplaceable mediator and author of the good things which are indispensable for the world's salvation. It is suffering, more than anything else, which clears the way for the grace which transforms human souls. Suffering, more than anything else, makes present in the history of humanity the powers of the Redemption. In that 'cosmic' struggle between the spiritual powers of good and evil, spoken of in the letter to the Ephesians, human sufferings, united to the redemptive suffering of Christ, constitute a special support for the powers of good, and open the way to the victory of these salvific powers" (*Salvifici Doloris*, n. 27).

Q. As a non-Catholic who has been drawn to Roman Catholicism, I am very disturbed about ads promoting the

St. Michael scapular as something magical. Isn't it superstitious to believe a piece of cloth has the power to ward off
the devil? — D.E.W., New York

Q. Must brown scapulars be wool to be valid or has this
rule changed? Is it all right to wear a scapular medal on a
ring instead of around my neck? Please give the exact
promises of our Lady about those who wear the scapular?
— M.A.W., Ohio; E.V., New Brunswick; and L.A.O.,
Montana

A. In the beginning, scapulars were part of the habit of
religious orders. Resembling an apron, they were originally
shoulder-wide strips of cloth worn over the tunic and reaching
almost to the feet in front and behind. They came to symbolize
the cross and yoke of Christ. They now consist of two small
squares of cloth joined by strings and worn about the neck by
laypersons as a sign of their association with a religious order
and for devotional purposes.

The Catholic Church has approved the scapular as a
sacramental, i.e., a holy object that can bring spiritual benefits
to its user. Unlike the Sacraments, which produce grace by
virtue of the rite itself, the efficacy of sacramentals depends on
the devotion, faith, and love of those who use them. Wearing a
scapular will not keep a person out of Hell or ward off the
power of the devil unless that person sincerely tries to lead a
holy life and seeks God's mercy and forgiveness if he falls into
sin. No one can wear a scapular while deliberately leading a
sinful life and expect to be saved.

The Church recognizes nearly 20 scapulars for devotional
use, with the five major ones being those of Our Lady of
Mount Carmel (brown), the Passion (red), the Seven Dolors
(black), the Immaculate Conception (blue), and the Holy
Trinity (white). In 1910, Pope St. Pius X authorized the substitution of a scapular medal for the cloth scapular. It may be
worn about the neck or made part of a ring.

There are certain promises attached to wearing a scapular
and living at the same time as a faithful follower of Christ,
including the intercession of the Blessed Mother at the hour of
death, which by the way is something we pray for every time
we say the Hail Mary ("pray for us sinners now and at the hour
of our death"). If one believed that the piece of cloth itself was
a guarantee of Heaven, that would be superstitious. But that is
not what Catholics believe.

Just as a person might wear a mother's ring or a father's
watch as a reminder of a loved one, so one can wear a scapular

or other religious object as a reminder of our eternal destination in Heaven, and our responsibility to live in such a way as to reach that destination.

Appearing in 1251 to St. Simon Stock, the Prior General of the Carmelite Order, the Blessed Mother promised that all those who wear the brown Carmelite scapular "shall not suffer eternal fire; and, if wearing it they die, they shall be saved." This does not mean, of course, that one could deliberately lead a sinful life and expect to benefit from the scapular promise since that would constitute a sin of presumption.

Seven centuries after the appearance to St. Simon Stock, Pope Pius XI put the promise in perspective when he warned the faithful that, "although it is very true that the Blessed Virgin loves all who love her, nevertheless those who wish to have the Blessed Mother as a helper at the hour of death must in life merit such a signal favor by abstaining from sin and laboring in her honor."

The other promise, which is called the Sabbatine Privilege, was approved in 1613 by Pope Paul V, who stated:

"It is permitted to the Carmelite Fathers to preach that the Christian people may believe that the Blessed Virgin will help by her continued assistance and her merits, particularly on Saturdays, the souls of the members of the Scapular Fraternity who have died in the grace of God, if in life they had worn the scapular, observed chastity according to their state of life, and recited the Office of the Blessed Virgin or observed the fasts of the Church, practicing abstinence on Wednesdays and Saturdays."

An earlier papal statement, allegedly made by Pope John XXII in 1322, had the Pope saying that faithful wearers of the scapular would be released from Purgatory on the Saturday after their death. In his *Modern Catholic Dictionary*, Fr. John Hardon considers this version of the Sabbatine Privilege to be "certainly erroneous." The commonly accepted version, the one stated by Paul V, is that the intercession of the Blessed Virgin will occur "particularly on Saturdays," but not on a particular Saturday.

Q. I would like to learn about the Little Office of the Blessed Virgin Mary, its significance, history, spiritual value, and relation to the Divine Office. — R.L., Michigan

A. According to Fr. Jovian P. Lang's *Dictionary of the Liturgy* (Catholic Book Publishing Company), the Little Office of the Blessed Virgin Mary developed as a private devotion in the 11th century, was later adopted by several congregations of religious women in place of the Divine Office after the Council of Trent in the 16th century, is considered part of the public prayer of the Church by decision of the Second Vatican Council, and was revised in English as recently as 1988. Patterned after the Liturgy of the Hours, the Little Office is comprised of seven hours and features biblical texts referring directly or indirectly to Mary, as well as variable Psalms with proper antiphons, responsories, intercessions, and prayers — all in a Marian vein.

"Its originality," says the *Dictionary of the Liturgy*, "lies precisely in this emphasis given to the person of Mary, who nonetheless never appears in isolated fashion. She is always portrayed as part of the history of salvation, as the admirable fruit of the Divine Power, as the Mother of the Lord, or as the image of the Church. Hence, the Little Office is a way of living — in praise and reflection — the principal moments of each day with Mary, who spent her life alongside her Son in ardent love, in joyous praise, and in deep faith."

Q. I have placed the enclosed St. Jude novena in my parish church, but my pastor said the instruction at the end of the prayer is superstitious, and he asked me not to leave copies in the church in the future. Can you explain why my pastor said this? — L.G., New Jersey

Q. Would you please clarify why "chain letter novenas" are wrong? I have seen these novenas in church pews with the promise that if a person follows the directions, their prayers will be answered because this particular novena is "never known to fail." Could you give some guidelines on this? — L.M.C., Texas

A. A novena, which usually involves nine successive days of public or private prayer for some special intention or in preparation for a feast, can be a wonderful devotional experience and a source of many graces. This longstanding tradition recalls the nine days that Mary and the Apostles spent together in prayer between the Ascension and Pentecost.

The St. Jude novena is a very popular devotion among Catholics, and many Catholics, L.G. included, have said that a particular request was granted after saying the prayers. The novena includes recitation of the Our Father and Hail Mary, praise for the Sacred Heart of Jesus and the Immaculate Heart of Mary, and a request for St. Jude's assistance in obtaining a favorable answer to a prayer.

Petitioning Jesus, His mother, and the saints for help with our needs is an ancient and venerable tradition of the Catholic

Church, and there is nothing superstitious about making requests to those who do indeed have the power to fulfill them.

However, L.G.'s pastor may be concerned about the instruction: "Make 81 copies and leave nine copies in church for each consecutive day. You will receive your intention before the nine days are over, no matter how impossible it may seem."

God answers every prayer, but sometimes the answer is "no." People who have been led to believe that this novena will always and unfailingly produce a favorable answer, whatever the request, can suffer a crisis of faith when the desired answer is not forthcoming.

Also, if the novena is treated like a chain letter, or if there is more emphasis on the distribution of copies — exactly nine each day, not eight one day and 10 the next — than on the prayers themselves, then some people's understanding of the novena can border on superstition. The St. Jude novena is a good and pious practice, but efforts must be made to avoid abuses in the way it is understood and carried out.

Q. How are we to understand our Lord's words that whatever we ask for we will receive? I have prayed for a number of things in my life and my petitions were not granted. — A.P.S., New York

A. God answers every prayer and petition that we voice, but not always in the way that we want. Because He knows what is best for us, He does not grant every request. Perhaps the thing we seek, e.g., winning the lottery, would not be good for us or would not help us along the road to Heaven. Or while we would welcome the return to good health of a dying family member or friend, maybe that would not be the best thing for the person near death. Only God knows what is best for all concerned, and we will not fully understand this until we see Him in Heaven.

Q. Why do Catholics pray to the saints? Why not pray directly to God? — L.R., Kansas

A. Many Catholics do pray directly to God and that's fine. But there is nothing wrong with praying to the saints and asking them to intercede for us with God. The saints once experienced the same problems and temptations we face, and they overcame them with lives of great holiness. They give us a good example to follow and we take their names at Baptism and Confirmation so that they will help us in our daily lives.

A person seeking a job can always go directly to the head of the company, or he or she could ask a friend to speak to the boss first. Either approach is perfectly acceptable in this situation or in our relationship with God and the saints. Just as it can be beneficial to have a friend who knows the head of the company, so also it can be helpful to have friends in Heaven who can speak to God on our behalf.

Q. Our priest said that we should never pray to the saints or to the Blessed Virgin because it would diminish God. He said that we should pray only to God and that it was useless to ask the intercession of Mary and the saints. I think the priest was wrong. What do you think? — E.A., Florida

A. We think the priest was wrong, too. Praying to God is the most important thing we can do, and we cannot neglect this obligation. But praying to the Blessed Mother and the saints does not diminish God. In fact, God must be pleased that we would seek the intercession of those persons in Heaven who are close to Him and who got to Heaven by conforming their lives to His will. We not only venerate the saints; we also try to imitate their lives of holiness. Why would the Church set aside all those feast days during the year if it doesn't want us to honor the saints?

Q. On what does the Church base its teaching that the Blessed Mother and the saints can hear our prayers and respond to them? — M.A.S., Michigan

A. The Church's teaching on prayers to the saints and the Blessed Mother is based on the doctrine of the Communion of Saints, which we profess to believe each time we say the Apostles' Creed or the Nicene Creed. The Communion of Saints refers to the Pilgrim Church on earth, the Triumphant Church in Heaven, and the Suffering Church in Purgatory.

We are all part of this spiritual community, and we try to help each other with our prayers. Just because someone has died does not mean that they are beyond our reach. The saints in Heaven are alive (1 Corinthians 15:22) and are just as interested in our well-being as when they were on earth.

Over a century ago, Orestes Brownson responded this way to the charge that the saints cannot hear our prayers:

"But wherefore can they not hear us? Are they not living men and women — even more living than when they tabernacled with us? ... There can be no communion where there is no medium of communication. We who live have a medium of communication with those who have gone to their reward and therefore form one communion with them. That medium is Christ Himself, who is the head of every man, and whose life is the life of all who have been begotten anew by the Holy Ghost....

"There being a medium of communication between us and the saints, and they and we forming only one communion, one Body of our Lord, being members of Him and members of one another, nothing can be more reasonable, more natural even, than that we should invoke their prayers, and that they should intercede for us."

Q. How do you answer those who say that Catholics worship statues and holy pictures? — H.M., Georgia

A. You tell them that Catholics only worship God. The attention that we pay to the Blessed Mother and the saints is not worship but rather veneration or honor for the holy lives they led. When we kneel before a painting of Mary or a statue of St. Joseph, we are not praying to the object, but rather to the person represented.

We would not accuse a man of worshiping his wife and children because he keeps a picture of them in his wallet. Or a woman of worshiping her parents because she keeps a photograph of them on the mantelpiece. Just as these pictures help us to remember our loved ones, so religious statues and art aid us in honoring and imitating those who are closest to God.

Q. It has been my impression that Bishop Sheen spent an hour in prayer before the Blessed Sacrament each morning before beginning his daily work. Can you confirm this? — K.B., Texas

A. You will find confirmation of this in chapter 12 ("The Hour That Makes My Day") of Fulton J. Sheen's autobiography, *Treasure in Clay*. The book should be available at your local library.

Q. I have a number of broken religious statues, pictures, rosaries, etc., which are beyond repair. How can I dispose of them? Would it be wrong to throw in the trash mail solicitations with images of Jesus, Mary, and the saints? — J.M.Z., Virginia

A. There is nothing wrong with throwing away mail solicitations bearing the images of Jesus, His mother, or the saints. If one kept all the religious pictures that come unsolicited through the mail, a huge pile of material would be accumulated in a very short time.

As for disposing of religious articles that are beyond repair, there is nothing wrong with that either. While these articles once were blessed, they are not holy in themselves and can be thrown away. However, there are religious societies and organizations that repair religious articles and make them available to the missions. You can find the names of these groups in Catholic newspapers or magazines or by contacting your local chancery office

Q. Is there any specific regulation on how relics should be treated. I have acquired a relic of my patron saint and wear it around my neck on a chain. Is that all right? — A.C.G., Illinois

A. Like any holy objects, relics should be treated with reverence since they are either the physical remains (bones) or the personal effects (clothing or other articles) of the saints, or objects that were touched to a part of a saint's body. They may not be sold and should be "honored with great veneration" (Canon 1190). There is nothing wrong with wearing a relic on a chain as long as you treat it with the proper respect.

Q. I sometimes pray at work, but obviously not vocally. Do prayers said silently have any value? — M.D.H., Iowa

A. They sure do. All prayer is talking to God and is of value in that we are praising Him, thanking Him, asking Him for what we need, or making reparation for sin. There are two kinds of prayer: vocal prayer, in which the words are recited out loud either in a group or privately, and mental prayer, in which we silently tell God what is in our minds and hearts. Silent prayer is an excellent way to keep ourselves close to God while in the middle of our daily activities. Keep up this wonderful habit.

Q. Is it correct when blessing yourself to say, "In the name of the Father, the Son, and their Holy Spirit"? — D.M., Massachusetts

A. It is Catholic teaching that the Holy Spirit is the Third Person of the Blessed Trinity, distinct from the Father and the Son but coequal and coeternal with them. He "proceeds from the Father and the Son," in the words of the Nicene Creed, and is the perfect expression of the mutual love of the Father and Son.

It may be this procession from Father and Son that prompts some people to say "their" Holy Spirit, but that implies the

Holy Spirit is not a distinct Person and is not equal to the Father and Son. It would be much better to use the Church's traditional formulation: "In the name of the Father, and of the Son, and of the Holy Spirit."

Q. Is it permitted to say "you" instead of "thee" when reciting the Hail Mary? — A.W., Pennsylvania

Q. Why do we say "hallowed be *thy* name" and "*thy* kingdom come" during the Lord's Prayer at Mass and then switch to "the kingdom, the power, and the glory are *yours*"? — F.J.C., Massachusetts

A. Since we no longer talk or write the way people did centuries ago, there is a trend toward using modern pronouns in the Hail Mary, although many people prefer to say the prayer the way they learned it as children. The same is true of the Our Father. "Thy" has been retained because we are most familiar with that pronoun, while "thine" has been changed to "yours" in the less familiar (to Catholics) doxology that follows recitation of the Our Father at Mass.

In his *Catholic Answer Book*, Fr. Peter Stravinskas said that "no permission has been granted for such a switch [to modern pronouns]. As a matter of fact, some years back the International Commission on English in the Liturgy had proposed a whole series of such updatings to the National Conference of Catholic Bishops (the only body authorized to make such changes), and the project was defeated. Simply put, then, whoever is inserting such changes is doing so on his/her own authority and is infringing on the rights of the rest of the community in so doing" (p. 120).

Q. Why does the prayer "Glory be to the Father ..." end with "world without end. Amen"? Surely Catholics believe that the world will end, so why does this prayer indicate the contrary? — J.R.L., New York

A. The words "world without end" do not mean that the world will never end. It is a poetic way of saying forever and ever. In Latin it is *per omnia saecula saeculorum* ("through all the ages of ages"). Consider the entire prayer: "Glory be to the Father, and to the Son, and to the Holy Spirit. As it was in the beginning, is now, and ever shall be, world without end. Amen." This prayer to the Trinity is saying that the Father, Son, and Holy Spirit will never change and will forever be praised — just as They were in the beginning, as They are now, and as They will be for all eternity.

Q. Fundamentalists have told me that repetitive prayer, such as the Our Father and the Hail Mary in the rosary, was forbidden by Jesus. How do I respond? — V.F.M., Minnesota

Q. Well-meaning Protestants say that the rosary is too repetitious. Since they have only the Bible for their teachings, can you show me where in the Bible we can prove the authenticity of saying the rosary? — M.M.R., Minnesota

A. There is no mention of the rosary in the Bible and no Scripture passage that would authenticate this devotion, although the events in the life of our Lord and the Blessed Mother that we meditate upon while saying the prayers of the rosary, as well as the Our Father and the Hail Mary themselves, are biblically based. This devotion was popularized by St. Dominic (1170-1221) at the time of the Albigensian heresy in France, and it became the "poor man's breviary," as those who were unable to read the 150 psalms could recite 150 Hail Marys instead while meditating on the 15 Joyful, Sorrowful, and Glorious Mysteries of the rosary.

As for the charge that the rosary is repetitious, and therefore a violation of Jesus' warning in Matthew 6:7 against "the sheer multiplication of words" (New American Bible) or "vain repetitions" (King James Bible), Jesus was talking about "the hypocrites who love to stand and pray in synagogues or on street corners in order to be noticed" (Matthew 6:5), not about sincere people who engage in repetitive prayer.

Our Lord Himself repeated the same prayer over and over again during His agony in the Garden of Gethsemani (Matthew 26:39, 42, 44), and He told us that the humble tax collector, who kept repeating, "O God, be merciful to me, a sinner," went home from the temple "justified," while the proud and self-righteous Pharisee did not (Luke 18:9-14).

Q. In saying the Rosary, I do not include after each decade the prayer, "O my Jesus, forgive us our sins. Save us from the fire of Hell. Lead all souls to Heaven, especially those in most need of your mercy." I realize this prayer comes from the Fatima revelations, but since I have never seen any official Vatican approval of the prayer, I don't say it. Is it official or not? — B.T.F., Ohio

A. The Fatima apparitions and message of the Blessed Virgin Mary were declared worthy of belief by the bishop of the area in 1930, and papal approval has been given through the visits to the shrine by Pope Paul VI in 1967 and by Pope John Paul II in 1982. As for the special prayer after each decade of the rosary, that was authorized by the Vatican's Sacred Apostolic Penitentiary on February 4, 1956.

Q. After seeing a cousin wearing an oversized ankh cross, I informed her that I had seen a documentary showing that it figured centrally on satanic altars. She told me that the Christian Coptic Church has integrated this symbol as one of its own. Who is right? — L.M., Idaho

A. All we know about the ankh cross is what the dictionary tells us, namely, that it is "a cross having a loop for its upper vertical arm and serving especially in ancient Egypt as a symbol of life." It would seem inappropriate for a Catholic to wear such a cross, but perhaps one of our readers could provide additional information.

Q. In a recent column, you asked for additional information about the ankh cross. The enclosed fact sheet may be of help. — A.L.M., West Virginia

A. Our thanks to A.L.M., who said that "the origin of the ankh is not Christian. It was in use for many centuries before Christ, specifically in Egypt. Therefore, in no way does it derive from the cross on which Jesus was crucified and which is, therefore, symbolic of the means of our salvation and a sign or symbol of His redemptive love. The original meaning of the ankh (and the meaning at present for most people) is not Christian. Perhaps a quotation from J.C. Cooper's *An Illustrated Encyclopedia of Traditional Symbols* (London, Thames and Hudson, 1978) will make this clear:

"'**Ankh.** An Egyptian symbol of life; the universe; all life both human and divine; the key of knowledge of the mysteries and hidden wisdom; power; authority; covenant. The ankh is formed of the combined male and female symbols of Osiris and Isis, the union of the two generative principles, of heaven and earth. It also signifies immortality. "Life to come," "time that is to come."... Maat, Goddess of Truth (pre-Christian Egyptian), holds the ankh in her hand.'"

Editor's Note: Regarding a recent reply about the origins of the ankh cross in ancient Egypt and its use by Catholics today, William J. Grimm, M.M., of the Maryknoll Social Communications Department sent along the following comments:

"The ankh cross is commonly used in the Coptic Rite of the Church (both Catholic and Orthodox). Coptic Christians are descendants of the ancient Egyptians, and as part of the inculturation of the Church into their culture, the hieroglyph for 'life,' which resembles the Cross, was taken over to be the symbol of the Cross of Christ, the source of true life. This sort of cultural and aesthetic adaptation has been common in the Church, as can be seen in the Celtic, tau, Maltese, Jerusalem, and other crosses with which we have commemorated the death of Christ."

Chapter 6

Mary, Angels, and Saints

Q. If the Gospels say that Jesus had brothers and sisters, how can Mary be called a virgin? Can you confirm that she had no other biological children? — J.B.O., Massachusetts

A. In Hebrew and Aramaic (the language spoken by Jesus and His followers), there was no specific word for "cousin," so the word for "brother" was sometimes used for brother, cousin, or other relatives. But we know, for example, that the James and Joses mentioned in Mark 6:3 as the brothers of Jesus were in fact the sons of Mary, the wife of Clopas (Matthew 27:56). Since the Gospels also tell us that Mary of Clopas was the Blessed Mother's sister (John 19:25), that means she was Jesus' aunt and her sons were Jesus' cousins.

Search the Scriptures all you want, and you will not find Mary identified as the mother of anyone but Jesus. Her perpetual virginity has been taught by the Church from the beginning and has been reaffirmed in the *Catechism of the Catholic Church*, nos. 499-501. Our belief today is the same as it was in the fifth century when St. Augustine described the Blessed Mother as "a virgin who conceives, a virgin who gives birth, a virgin with child, a virgin delivered of child — a virgin ever virgin."

Q. I always thought that Mary was a virgin from her birth to her death, but Matthew 1:25 says that Joseph "had no intercourse with her *until* her son was born. And he named the child Jesus." Can you explain this? — M.P.M., Illinois

A. In his excellent book *Catholicism and Fundamentalism*, Karl Keating explains that the word "until" (or "till") in the Bible "means only that some action did not happen up to a certain point; it does not imply that the action did happen later, which is the modern sense of the term. In fact, if the modern sense is forced on the Bible, some ridiculous meanings result."

He mentions such examples as "Michal the daughter of Saul had no children until the day of her death" (2 Samuel 6:23). Does this mean that she had children *after* her death? Also, "And they went up to mount Sion with joy and gladness, and offered holocausts, because not one of them was slain till they had returned in peace" (1 Maccabees 5:54). Is it likely that these soldiers were slain *after* they had returned from battle?

Q. What proof is given that the Blessed Virgin Mary was 14 years of age when the angel Gabriel announced to her that she was to be the mother of Christ, that she was 15 years of age when Christ was born, and that she traveled 80 miles to visit her cousin Elizabeth, at which time John the Baptist leaped in Elizabeth's womb? — T.F.O., Florida

A. There is no "proof" that Mary was 14 or 15 when Jesus was conceived by the Holy Spirit and born in Bethlehem. The tradition that Mary was in her early teens is based on a knowledge of Jewish marriage customs. Girls at that time were usually betrothed at the age of 12 or 13 and married a year later. Men were usually betrothed between the ages of 18 to 24.

By the way, betrothal was not just a promise to marry, as it is today, but a legal marriage contract. Though married, the husband and wife continued to live with their respective families for one year if the bride was a virgin, and one month if she was a widow. The wedding ceremony at the end of this period of time involved the welcoming of the wife into the husband's home.

As for Mary's journey to the house of her cousin Elizabeth in a town in Judah, we have the word of St. Luke, who tells us that he is reporting precisely events that were "transmitted to us by the original eyewitnesses and ministers of the word" (Luke 1:2). It is not unreasonable to assume that the Blessed Mother herself may have given this information to Luke. If the town in Judah is Ain Karim, as many scholars think, it was about four days' journey from Nazareth.

Q. I learned long ago that the Jewish people had no word for relatives and so all were called "brothers" and "sisters." How is it, then, that the angel Gabriel said to Mary, "And behold, your cousin Elizabeth has conceived a son in her old age ..."? — M.K., Colorado

A. Since there was no specific Aramaic word for "cousin," and the word for "brother" had to be used for a variety of relatives, the only way to determine which meaning was intended in a particular verse was to consider the context. So translators of Luke 1:36 have described Elizabeth variously as Mary's cousin (King James), kinswoman (Confraternity of Christian Doctrine, Jerusalem Bible, and 1970 New American Bible), and relative (1986 New American Bible).

Q. When the angel Gabriel appeared first to Zechariah (Luke 1:5-20) and then to the Virgin Mary (Luke 1:16-38),

both seemed to have the same doubts, but Zechariah was struck dumb and Mary was not. Why were they treated differently? Also, why do the newer Bible translations quote Gabriel as saying that Mary found "favor" with God, while the older translations say that she found "grace" with God? Many patriarchs, prophets, and saints found favor with God. How is Mary distinguished from them? — J.F.M., Rhode Island

A. Regarding the second question, the newer translations use "favor" instead of "grace" not only in Luke 1:30 ("You have found favor with God") but also in Luke 1:28 ("Rejoice, O highly favored daughter!" instead of "Hail, full of grace" in the older translations) because it is a literal rendering of the Greek.

It seems to us that being "full of grace" says much more about Mary than her being a "highly favored daughter," a description that could be applied to many women in the Bible. If Mary was full of grace, then she was completely free from sin and must have been free from original sin from the moment of her conception in her mother's womb (the Immaculate Conception).

As J.F.M. suggests, Mary did more than just find favor with God; she found grace, which means a complete sharing in the life of God, something we would expect of the person who had been chosen to be the Mother of God.

As for the first question, Zechariah was punished because he doubted ("How am I to know this?") that God could give his elderly wife a child, while Mary was unpunished because she did not doubt God but only wanted to know the manner in which she would conceive a child since she had taken a vow of virginity ("How can this be since I do not know man?"). Another reader, P.D.F. of New York, has summed the matter up so well that we would like to share his comments with you:

"It seems to me the difference in phrasing is crucial. Zechariah, in asking how he could know, expresses doubt about the possibility of a miracle, and so Gabriel understands him. Mary, in asking how the divine maternity might be ... in the circumstances of the Annunciation, is not expressing a doubt about the possibility of a miracle, but is inquiring (according to the Fathers of the Church, such as St. Ambrose) about (1) her freedom to assent to such an offer because she is a virgin and not free any longer to opt for a maternal vocation, and (2) the credentials of the angel to make so stupendous an offer — to be Mother of God — to her.

"And so the angel interprets her query, not as a doubt about the omnipotence of God, but as a necessary inquiry bearing on the prudence of her involvement in something still future. Gabriel confirms his credentials in the process of explaining how God will permit our Lady to be a mother without loss of her virginity and how in fact virginal maternity will be a divine maternity by the power of the same Holy Spirit by whom she had been perfectly consecrated as a virgin, full of grace."

Q. Our priest said in a homily that it was his personal opinion that Mary was not the only woman asked to be the Mother of God. Is it possible that there were others? — J.C., Michigan

A. We can't imagine what would prompt such speculation from your priest, but there is nothing in Scripture or the Church's teaching to support such an opinion. On the contrary, St. Paul says that "when the designated time had come, God sent forth his Son born of a woman, born under the law, to deliver from the law those who were subjected to it, so that we might receive our status as adopted sons" (Galatians 4:4-5). That "designated time," Pope John Paul has said, "indicates the moment fixed from all eternity when the Father sent his Son 'that whoever believes in him should not perish but have eternal life'" (*Mother of the Redeemer*, n. 1).

In the same encyclical letter, John Paul also said that when the "designated time" was drawing near, "she who was from eternity destined to be his Mother already existed on earth" (n. 3). Thus, Mary was chosen to be the Mother of Jesus long before time began, and no other woman was ever extended that divine invitation.

Q. What do we mean by the Immaculate Conception of Mary? — R.J.S., New York

A. Because even some Catholics are confused about this dogma, let us say first that the Immaculate Conception *does not* refer to the virginal conception of Jesus in Mary's womb through the power of the Holy Spirit. That is the doctrine of Mary's divine maternity.

What the Immaculate Conception *does mean* is that Mary, from the first instant of her conception in the womb of her mother, St. Ann, was preserved from all stain of original sin. This doctrine is implied in the greeting of the angel Gabriel to the young Jewish girl (Confraternity Version): "Hail, full of grace, the Lord is with thee" (Luke 1:28). If Mary was full of grace, then she was completely free from sin.

In other words, Mary was redeemed from the moment of her

conception. Here is the pertinent section of Pope Pius IX's infallible pronouncement in 1854 on the Immaculate Conception (see also section 491 of the *Catechism*):

"The Most Blessed Virgin Mary was, from the first moment of her conception, by a singular grace and privilege of almighty God and by virtue of the merits of Jesus Christ, Savior of the human race, preserved immune from all stain of original sin."

It is also the teaching of the Church, as reiterated in the *Catechism* (n. 493), that by the grace of God Mary remained free of every personal sin during her entire life.

Q. Why does the Church teach that Mary is our mother when Jesus only mentioned her as John's Mother? — M.A.S., Michigan

A. The teaching that Mary is our mother is based on Jesus' words from the cross: "Seeing his mother there with the disciple whom he loved, Jesus said to his mother, 'Woman, there is your son.' In turn he said to the disciple, 'There is your mother.' From that hour onward, the disciple took her into his care" (John 19:26-27).

John is seen here as representing us at the foot of the cross and, when Jesus told him that Mary was to be his mother, our Lord was implying that she was also to be the mother of us all. "This maternity will last without interruption until the eternal fulfillment of all the elect," said Vatican II's *Dogmatic Constitution on the Church*. "For, taken up to heaven, she did not lay aside this saving role, but by her manifold acts of intercession, continues to win for us gifts of eternal salvation. By her maternal charity, Mary cares for the brethren of her Son who still journey on earth surrounded by dangers and difficulties, until they are led to their happy fatherland" (n. 62).

For additional insights into this teaching, see paragraphs 967-970 of the *Catechism of the Catholic Church*.

Q. A dear Catholic friend of mine told me it is her sincere feeling that the Virgin Mary is divine. I am only a convert, but I cannot see how this could be possible. Would it be wrong to believe in Mary's divinity? — M.A.D., Missouri

Q. Please discuss Mary as co-redemptrix. What precisely are we to believe? — M.J.O., Minnesota

A. Yes, it would be wrong to believe that Mary is divine. What we are to believe is that Jesus is the one Mediator and the sole Redeemer, but that His mother has been given a share in the saving role of her Son. While we give Mary the highest place in the Church after Jesus Himself, we do not consider her to be God's equal.

The Blessed Mother is "invoked by the Church under the titles Advocate, Auxiliatrix, Adjutrix, and Mediatrix," said the Second Vatican Council. "These, however, are to be so understood that they neither take away from nor add anything to the dignity and efficacy of Christ the one Mediator. For no creature could ever be classed with the Incarnate Word and Redeemer .... The Church does not hesitate to profess this subordinate role of Mary. She experiences it continuously and commends it to the hearts of the faithful, so that encouraged by this maternal help they may more closely adhere to the Mediator and Redeemer" (*Dogmatic Constitution on the Church*, n. 62).

For a correct understanding of the Virgin Mary's unique place in the Church and the special veneration (the Greeks call it *hyperdulia*) that we pay to her, one can also read Chapter VIII of Vatican II's *Constitution on the Church*, Pope John Paul's encyclical letter *Mother of the Redeemer*, and paragraphs 963-975 of the *Catechism of the Catholic Church*.

Q. Where do Catholics get the idea that Mary was taken bodily into Heaven? Did she die first? — Name Withheld, Washington

A. The publicly stated belief in Mary's bodily Assumption into Heaven goes back at least to the sixth century, when St. Gregory of Tours wrote that the Lord Jesus came to earth at the end of Mary's life and commanded that her holy body "be taken in a cloud into Paradise where now, rejoined to the soul, it rejoices with the Lord's chosen ones, and is in the enjoyment of the good of an eternity that will never end."

The dogma of the Assumption was never in doubt, but after Pope Pius IX defined the Immaculate Conception in 1854, Rome was inundated over many decades with literally millions of requests for a similar definition of the Assumption. Pope Pius XII answered those petitions on November 1, 1950, when he solemnly declared it to be "a dogma divinely revealed: that the Immaculate Mother of God, Mary ever Virgin, on the completion of her earthly life, was taken up to heavenly glory both in body and soul."

The reasoning behind the Church's belief is that since Mary was free from all sin, and the corruption of the body is a consequence of sin, she did not suffer the decay of the grave. Furthermore, since it was Mary's body that brought the Savior into the world, her body should share in His bodily glorification.

The Church has never formally stated whether Mary died. St. John Damascene, in the eighth century, referred to an "ancient and most truthful tradition" that Mary did die and was placed in a coffin in the Garden of Gethsemani. After three days of singing and chanting by angels, the coffin was opened, but the Apostles "were unable anywhere to find her most lauded body."

It is striking, too, that there have never been any bodily relics of Mary, nor any attempt to identify her tomb. This seems to be a case where Tradition was from the beginning consistent and unanimous.

Pius XII did not address the issue of her death in his proclamation of her Assumption, saying only that the Blessed Mother was taken up to Heaven "on the completion of her earthly life." The Eastern Church celebrates the Feast of the Dormition (Falling Asleep) of Mary on August 14th, the day before the Feast of the Assumption.

Q. Why was the feast celebrated on January 1st changed from the Circumcision of Our Lord to the Solemnity of Mary? — F.A.S., Maryland

A. Since at least the sixth century, the Church had commemorated January 1st, the Octave of Christmas, as the Circumcision of Our Lord. The feast recalled the initiation of Jesus into Judaism (Luke 2:21) and foreshadowed our initiation into the Church through the sacrament of Baptism. In 1970, the Church decided to reemphasize Mary's role in the Incarnation by changing the name of the feast to the Solemnity of Mary, Mother of God. This holy day of obligation takes the place of the former feast of the Maternity of Mary, which was observed on October 11th.

Q. What is the process for an apparition to receive Church approval? Does the process go beyond the confines of the local diocese where the apparition happens? — J.M., New York

A. When there are reports of an apparition, say by the Blessed Mother, in a particular diocese, the bishop of that diocese will send a representative to gather information about the reported appearances. If there seems to be some substance to the reports, the bishop may appoint a commission to conduct a thorough investigation, and his conclusions about whether the reported apparitions are authentic and worthy of belief by the faithful will be based on the commission's findings. The process is usually confined to a particular diocese since the bishop is the primary teacher of the faithful in that geographical sector of the Catholic Church.

For an illustration of how the process works, see chapter 5 of Fr. Robert Fox's book, *Fatima Today* (Christendom Publications), which summarizes the procedures set in motion by the bishop of Leiria-Fatima following the events in the Portuguese village in 1917. The chapter also includes excerpts from the bishop's pastoral letter of October 1, 1930, declaring the visions of the three shepherd children "worthy of belief."

Q. What is the story of Fatima and the "dancing of the sun" all about? — P.S., Minnesota

A. From May to October of 1917, the Blessed Mother appeared six times to three shepherd children in the Portuguese village of Fatima. She showed them a vision of Hell, predicted World War II and the rise of Communism in Russia, and promised the conversion of Russia to her Immaculate Heart if people would pray, do penance, and make reparation for sin.

On October 13, 1917, our Lady gave the children her promised miracle in order to convince the tens of thousands of onlookers that she had indeed been appearing to the children and that people should heed her message. What happened that day was described in detail by an atheistic reporter for the Lisbon newspaper *O Seculo*. He had come to Fatima to prove the childrens' claims a hoax, but could not ignore what he witnessed with his own eyes.

On the front page of the October 15th edition of *O Seculo* was a picture of the children and a headline that read: "Bewildering Happenings! How the Sun Danced at Midday at Fatima." According to the story, and the testimony of eyewitnesses, a heavy rain stopped at noon and the sun came out. The people were able to look directly at the sun without hurting their eyes. As they gazed upward, the sun began to spin on its axis, sending out rays of multicolored light like a giant pinwheel.

The sun then seemed to tear itself loose from the sky and began a mad, zigzag plunge toward earth. People cried out in terror, thinking they were about to die, and begged God for forgiveness. But then the sun halted its descent and returned to its place in the sky, resuming a normal brightness that prevented people from looking directly at it.

The solar phenomenon was witnessed by over 70,000 persons and reported in Portuguese publications at the time. For additional details, one can read *The Sun Danced at Fatima*

(Image Books) by Fr. Joseph A. Pelletier or *Fatima Today* by Fr. Robert Fox.

Q. Has the third secret of Fatima ever been made public? — T.A., Massachusetts

A. During her appearance to the three children on July 13, 1917, the Blessed Mother revealed three secrets. Two of them — the vision of Hell and devotion to the Immaculate Heart of Mary — were later made public by Lucia, one of the visionaries. She put the third secret in a letter that was not opened until 1960 by Pope John XXIII. Neither John nor his successors have made that secret public.

This has led to all kinds of apocalyptic speculation as to the nature of the secret. Rather than join in that speculation, however, it would be prudent to focus instead on the clear message of Fatima, which is a call to conversion and prayer. We must reform our lives, make reparation for sin, and pray the rosary every day, said Our Lady of Fatima. Then, she promised, Russia will be converted and "a period of peace will be granted to the world."

Q. Has the Church given approval to our Lady's appearance at Beauraing, and what was her message there? — E.B., New York

A. Yes, the Church has given its approval of the apparitions at Beauraing, a village in Belgium where the Blessed Mother appeared 33 times to five children from November 29, 1932, to January 3, 1933. Ten years later, on February 2, 1943, Bishop Andre-Marie Charue authorized public devotion to "Our Lady of Beauraing."

On July 2, 1949, the Bishop sent a letter to all the priests in his diocese in which he said: "We are able in all serenity and prudence to affirm that the Queen of Heaven appeared to the children of Beauraing during the winter of 1932-1933 especially to show us in her maternal Heart the anxious appeal for prayer and the promise of her powerful mediation for the conversion of sinners."

Our Lady of Beauraing is known as the "Virgin with the Golden Heart" because she showed the children a heart of gold. Her messages included an admonition that the children "always be good" and that they "pray, pray very much." She also identified herself as the "Immaculate Virgin," the "Mother of God," and the "Queen of Heaven," and she promised that "I will convert sinners."

Q. An old religion text refers to "Our Lady of the Pillar at Saragossa," but gives no further information. Can you shed some light on this? — P.O., Washington

A. According to Joan Carroll Cruz's book *Relics* (pages 97-99), tradition has it that while the Apostle James was in Spain around the year 40 A.D., the Blessed Virgin appeared to him and seven of his disciples to encourage them in their missionary work in Spain. She requested that a chapel be built and, as evidence of her appearance, left them a column made of jasper upon which stood a small statue of her. The chapel built over the place of the apparition was eventually destroyed, as were several replacements, but the column or pillar has survived to this day.

The 15-inch-high statue atop the six-foot-tall pillar can be found today in the Church of the Virgin of the Pillar in Zaragoza, Spain. The 17th century church was declared a national museum in 1904 and is visited by many thousands of pilgrims each year. Pope John Paul II stopped at this ancient shrine during a tour of Spain in 1982.

Q. Can you please tell me something about Our Lady's appearances in Betania, Venezuela? Are they approved? — D.G., Pennsylvania

A. According to Rene Laurentin's book *The Apparitions of the Blessed Virgin Mary Today* (Veritas), the Blessed Mother appeared a number of times from 1976 to 1984 to a Venezuelan woman, Maria Esperanza Medrano de Bianchini, at her farm two hours outside the capital city of Caracas. The bishop of the area, Monsignor Pio Ricardo, after interviewing nearly 500 witnesses and compiling a file of almost 400 written statements, declared in a pastoral intruction dated November 21, 1987:

"Having studied the apparitions of the Virgin Mary at Finca Betania and having prayed assiduously to God for spiritual discernment, I declare that in my judgment the aforementioned apparitions are authentic and are supernatural in character.

"I therefore officially approve that the place where they occurred be considered a sacred place. May it become a place of pilgrimage, a place of prayer, reflection, and cult; (it is my wish) that liturgical rites be celebrated there, above all the celebration of Mass and the administration of the sacraments of Reconciliation and the Eucharist, in accordance with the laws of the Church and the diocesan norms for overall pastoral ministry."

Q. I have recently received by mail some literature on the work of Rosa Mystica. Is this an approved devotion? — Name Withheld, Manitoba

A. During a series of reported apparitions to an Italian woman named Pierina Gilli, the Blessed Mother asked that she be known as "Rosa Mystica" (or Mystical Rose), that an "Hour of Grace" be observed every year at noon on December 8th, that the 13th of July be celebrated in honor of Rosa Mystica, and that prayers, sacrifices, and penances be offered for the salvation of mankind. The seven reported appearances, three in 1947 and four in 1966, took place near the northern Italian towns of Montichiari and Fontanelle.

Miraculous healings and other extraordinary events have been reported in connection with the apparitions, and statues of the Pilgrim Rosa Mystica sent to other countries for veneration have reportedly shed tears of blood and water. According to the literature sent to us, the Church has been investigating these reports to determine whether Catholics may take part in devotion to Rosa Mystica.

Q. I am told that our Lady seems to have visited Akita, Japan, in 1973 and that the reported visits enjoy some kind of approval in the person of the local ordinary. Can you confirm this? — R.P., New Hampshire

A. On August 18, 1993, Franciscus Keiichi Sato, O.F.M., the bishop of Niigata, issued the following statement on the reported occurrences in Akita:

"1. Even today opinions differ about whether the statue of Our Lady at Yuzawadai, Akita (the statue which shed tears) should be venerated or not. While pilgrims continue to increase, there are also many priests who are against it.

"2. The fact that the wooden statue of Our Lady shed tears is undeniable. It is something that occurred over and over (101 times) between 1975 and 1981, with a great number of eyewitnesses.

"3. The first investigating commission, set up at the request of Bishop Ito (Ordinary of Niigata at the time), found that: 'The supernatural nature of the events cannot be proved.' Bishop Ito, however, was not satisfied with this conclusion and, after consulting with Rome, established a second investigating commission.

"4. The findings of the second investigating commission were reported in 1984 in a pastoral letter of Bishop Ito: 'It is not possible to make a negative statement that there is no supernaturality. Also, nothing can be found that is opposed to faith or morals. Consequently, until a final judgment is handed down by the Holy See, I will not forbid the showing of veneration within this diocese towards the holy statue of Akita.'

"5. In 1985 Bishop Ito resigned and I, Bishop Sato, succeeded him. I have not passed any subsequent judgment, and therefore the report of Bishop Ito is still valid.

"6. At present Yuzawadai in Akita appears to be taking hold as a place of prayer. It cannot be compared with Lourdes or Fatima, but it definitely has an atmosphere of prayer, and many pilgrims visit both from within the country and from overseas.

"7. I believe that time will clarify whether this is the work of God or of human beings. In [the] future it is my intention to neither especially encourage veneration and pilgrimages to the aforesaid statue of Our Lady, nor to forbid them."

Q. Where does the Church stand on the claim of miracles at Medjugorje, Yugoslavia? Has the Holy See issued an official and final decision on the alleged apparitions there? — R.P.G., Indiana, and A.Z, New York

A. The Holy See does not usually issue decisions on reported apparitions. That responsibility belongs to the bishop in the region where the alleged appearances have taken place. In 1991, the Yugoslavian Bishops' Conference declared by a vote of 19 to 1: "On the basis of inquiries conducted up to the present time, one cannot affirm that we are dealing here with supernatural apparitions or revelations." In October 1993, the bishop of the region, the Most Reverend Ratko Peric, gave this judgment on Medjugorje:

"The Church recommends prayer, fast, penance, reconciliation, and conversion to each of its members. I do not want to forbid anyone to go wherever he wants to pray to God. But I cannot approve that from the altar of the church in Medjugorje the priests themselves advertise 'pilgrimages to the place of apparitions,' despite the fact they have simply not been recognized as supernatural by the Church.

"If, after serious, solid, and professional investigation, our Bishops' Conference had the courage to declare that Medjugorje's apparitions are not supernatural, in spite of massive stories and convictions to the contrary, then that is a sign that the Church, even in the 20th century, 'upholds the truth and keeps it safe' (1 Tim. 3:15). I affirm this unequivocally and I answer it publicly to all those who have written either anonymous or signed letters to me with contrary advice...."

Q. Should I distribute the enclosed pamphlet containing prophecies by the Blessed Mother to Veronica Lueken at Bayside, New York? — L.T. and P.S., Wisconsin, and A.L., Michigan

A. The alleged apparitions of the Blessed Mother at Bayside, New York, have been going on since 1970. After an investigation of them in 1973, the Diocese of Brooklyn (where Bayside is located) declared them not worthy of belief and said that nothing miraculous was occurring there. This warning was repeated in 1986 when the Bishop of Brooklyn, Francis J. Mugavero, after consulting with the Sacred Congregation for the Doctrine of the Faith in Rome, said that "no credibility can be given to the so-called 'apparitions' reported by Veronica Lueken and her followers."

Bishop Mugavero went on to say that "the 'messages' and other related propaganda contain statements which, among other things, are contrary to the teachings of the Catholic Church, undermine the legitimate authority of bishops and councils, and instill doubts in the minds of the faithful, for example, by claiming that, for years, an 'imposter Pope' governed the Catholic Church in place of Paul VI."

He also said that "members of Christ's faithful are hereby directed to refrain from participating in the 'vigils' and from disseminating any propaganda related to the 'Bayside apparitions.' They are also discouraged from reading any such literature. Anyone promoting this devotion in any way, be it by participating in the 'vigils,' organizing pilgrimages, publishing or disseminating the literature related to it, is contributing to the confusion which is being created in the faith of God's people, as well as encouraging them to act against the determinations made by the legitimate pastor of this particular Church."

Despite this conclusion, many well-meaning Catholics continue to believe in Veronica Lueken and the statements she attributes to our Lady. Mary's messages in those appearances approved by the Church have always focused on prayer, penance, and reparation for sin. But Mrs. Lueken has her getting into specifics that one cannot imagine coming from the Blessed Mother.

For example, our Lady is supposed to have said in 1973 that the late Jesuit paleontologist Teilhard de Chardin "is in Hell," in 1976 that Freemasonry is "a synagogue of Satan," in 1977 that "Satan has full control" of the Church, in 1981 that altar railings should be restored in Catholic churches, and in 1985 that "Jesus wishes that the Old Mass be returned to wipe out many of the errors that have crept in since the New Mass has started."

While some people may want to believe some of these statements that the Blessed Mother is alleged to have made, it is highly improbable that she actually made them. In any case, Catholics ought not to distribute any of the literature that emanates from Bayside since the Church in that diocese has officially warned Catholics to stay away from the vigils there.

Q. In a recent column, you quoted Bishop Mugavero of Brooklyn as having said that the messages allegedly received from the Blessed Mother at Bayside "are contrary to the teachings of the Catholic Church." Could you please give a few examples that I could use to speak out against these so-called apparitions? — M.H.C., Washington, DC

A. In a letter to us dated March 30, 1993, Monsignor Otto L. Garcia, Chancellor of the Diocese of Brooklyn, said that Bishop Thomas V. Daily "has endorsed the contents" of the statement on the Bayside Movement that was issued by his predecessor, Bishop Mugavero, in 1986. Monsignor Garcia also enclosed an information packet on Bayside to help answer future questions on the alleged apparitions.

One of the enclosures in that packet, a special report on Bayside that appeared in the December 8, 1986 issue of *The Archangel Press*, listed several doctrinal errors contained in statements attributed to the Blessed Mother:

Item: The Blessed Virgin is reported to have said on June 18, 1986: "My children: but I, as your Mother, must treat you at this time as adults, being able to reason with the God-given reasoning that Heaven gave unto you when you were conceived by the Holy Ghost."

Comment: Only Jesus was conceived by the Holy Ghost. All other human beings were conceived in the normal human fashion.

Item: On August 14, 1979, the Blessed Mother was quoted as saying: "Do not judge your brothers and sisters who have not been converted. For my Father's house, my Son has repeated over and over, remember always that my Father's house — there are many rooms in the mansion, signifying faith and creeds. However, the Eternal Father, the Beatific Vision, is reserved for the Roman Catholic following. This — it has been deemed by the Eternal Father since the beginning of time."

Comment: The idea that in heaven there will be certain rooms for those of other faiths and creeds, and a special room for Roman Catholics, is not a part of Church teaching. The meaning of our Lord's words, "In my Father's house there are many dwelling places [or mansions]" (John 14:2), is that there will be plenty of room in Heaven for the disciples of the Lord. Jesus is telling them not to worry about a place in Heaven, that "I am indeed going to prepare a place for you, and then I shall come back to take you with me, that where I am you also may be" (John 14:3).

Item: On May 30, 1978, the Blessed Mother is reported to have said: "The Church of my Son, that is being stripped of all holiness, shall emerge with the world and the world's leaders to be directed for a short time by Satan."

Comment: To suggest that at some point in time, Satan will direct the Church of Christ is to contradict two explicit promises of our Lord: the "jaws of death," or gates of Hell, will not prevail against His Church (Matthew 16:18), and that He will be with His Church "always, until the end of the world" (Matthew 28:20).

Q. Are Catholics permitted to visit Our Lady of the Roses Shrine in Bayside, New York? What about the claim of the Baysiders that no ecclesiastical permission is required to publish books dealing with revelations, visions, and miracles, and that Catholics are permitted "to frequent places of apparitions, even those not recognized by the Ordinaries of the dioceses or by the Holy Father"? — A.B., Illinois

Q. Would you be willing to print, on behalf of Bayside, the truth that Bishop Thomas Daily is receiving hundreds of testimonies of spiritual conversions and physical cures through Our Lady of the Roses at Bayside and that these are being dismissed without scrutiny or any investigation? Your lack of professionalism in replying to the Bayside question reduces the credibility of your answers to other questions. Letters like this one are not published by you. We challenge you to print letters that present an informed perspective so that readers can have an opportunity to know the facts. — J.S. and C.B., Pennsylvania

A. Replying to questions about Bayside is no easy task. To those who abide by the Church's judgment on Bayside, no explanation is necessary. To those who reject the Church's disapproval of the reported apparitions, no explanation is acceptable. Devotees of Bayside may be the most sincere and well-meaning people in the world, but we believe that they are sincerely wrong in defending events that the Bishop of Brooklyn, after a thorough investigation, deemed to be completely lacking in authenticity. But not even Bishop Muga-vero's 1986 declaration, nor Bishop Daily's endorsement of that declaration, nor statements issued by the Brooklyn Chancery listing doctrinal errors contained in "messages" attributed to the Blessed Mother have been able to dissuade certain people from supporting Bayside.

These supporters contend that no ecclesiastical permission is required to publish information about Bayside because Pope Paul VI abrogated canons 1399 and 2218 of the 1917 Code of Canon Law. The Holy Father did abolish those canons in 1966, but that does not mean that one can cavalierly publish or disseminate religious material that might endanger the faith of Catholics.

The key point to remember is that those who do publish and spread the "messages" of Bayside are acting against the judgment of legitimate Church authority. They are giving to Veronica Lueken, and not to the bishop, an authority and a credibility that she does not possess. It is inconceivable to think that the Blessed Mother, the model of obedience and the Queen of the Apostles, would be handing on "messages" that would cause Catholics to disobey Church authority and to reject the considered judgment of a successor of the Apostles.

In assessing the Bayside materials, one must also use prudence and common sense. The claim that Pope Paul VI was replaced by an imposter Pope is not supported by any credible evidence. And the claim takes on the aura of a "Twilight Zone" episode when one wades through a 40-page tabloid-size newspaper containing more than 120 photographs of Pope Paul and his alleged imposter and purporting to prove that they are two different men by pointing out differences in the size and shape of the Pontiff's nose and ears. The pictures were taken over a period of 15 years, and they were taken from different angles and in different lights, which explains why the Pope doesn't always look exactly the same. But to suggest that the photos show two different persons is ludicrous.

Speaking of photographs, Baysiders have sent us pictures reportedly taken at various vigils over the years and allegedly showing miraculous figures and forms on the ground and in the sky. Without the accompanying suggestive captions for the pictures, one would be hard-pressed to see anything miraculous in them. Photographic experts at the Polaroid Corporation have suggested ways that such pictures could have been fabricated to achieve the effects shown.

Another thing that casts considerable doubt on the Bayside

messages is the content of the statements attributed to the Blessed Mother. As we noted before, in her many Church-approved appearances over the centuries, including Guadalupe, LaSalette, Lourdes, and Fatima, our Lady's messages have been of a general nature and have emphasized the need for prayer, penance, and reparation for sin. Even the famous July 13, 1917 appearance in Fatima, with the vision of Hell and the prediction of World War II and the rise of Russia, did not contain the kind of specific details that have come out of Bayside.

It is completely out of character for the Blessed Virgin to call Boris Yeltsin "the man of sin" and Yeltsin and Gorbachev "Satan's consorts," or to say that Lenin and Stalin are in Hell, or that there is no life on other planets and that those things called flying saucers are "transports from hell." These things could be true, but our point is that we have no way of knowing with certainty if they are true (only God knows who is in Hell), and the chances of the Blessed Mother handing on "messages" like these are slim and none.

To suggest that Bishop Daily, who has a great devotion to our Lady, would dismiss without investigation "hundreds" of reported conversions and cures, is absurd. If the Mother of God were truly appearing at Bayside, the Bishop would be leading pilgrimages there himself. But Bishop Daily wants Catholics to stay away from Bayside because the alleged apparitions are not believable and the "messages" are confusing and contrary to the teachings of the Catholic Church.

Q. Would you please give me a clear answer as to individuals making pilgrimages to Conyers, Georgia? Also, I would like a reply regarding Theresa Lopez in Denver, Colorado. — J.N.H., Connecticut

A. First of all, we contacted the office of Archbishop J. Francis Stafford in Denver for his statement on the alleged visions there. Here is what Archbishop Stafford said after an investigation that took more than two years:

"On December 9, 1991, I appointed a commission to investigate alleged apparitions of the Blessed Virgin Mary at Mother Cabrini Shrine and other places within the Archdiocese of Denver to Theresa Antonia Lopez. On February 22, 1994, the commission completed its investigation and presented its findings to me.

"As Archbishop of Denver, I have concluded that the alleged apparitions of the Blessed Virgin Mary to Theresa Antonia Lopez are devoid of any supernatural origin. Because of my concern for the spiritual welfare of the People of God, I direct the faithful to refrain from participating in or promoting paraliturgical or liturgical services related to the alleged apparitions.

"Furthermore, anyone encouraging devotion to these alleged apparitions in any way is acting contrary to my wishes as Archbishop of Denver. It remains my constant hope that all the faithful will promote devotion to our Blessed Lady in the many forms which have been approved by the Catholic Church."

As for reported apparitions in Conyers, Georgia, Archbishop James P. Lyke, now deceased, declared on March 9, 1992, that "the authenticity of these alleged apparitions is in grave doubt." The present Archbishop of Atlanta, John F. Donoghue, has expressed his agreement with the conclusion of Archbishop Lyke.

Editor's Note: To a recent question about the Marian Movement of Priests (MMP) and the messages published by Fr. Stefano Gobbi, we replied by quoting from Archbishop Agostino Cacciavillan, the apostolic pro-nuncio and representative of the Pope to the Church in the United States, who said on October 31, 1994: "As to the writings of Fr. Gobbi, competent authorities have advised that they are not the words of our Blessed Mother, but his private meditations for which he assumes all the theological, spiritual, and pastoral responsibility."

Since that time, we have been criticized by a number of readers and particularly by the Reverend Albert G. Roux, national director of the Marian Movement of Priests, whose American headquarters are located in St. Francis, Maine. In a four-page letter to us, the bulk of which became the MMP's official statement on the matter, Fr. Roux devoted nearly two pages to a summary of Fr. Gobbi's two-month visit to the United States in the fall of 1994, during which he reportedly spoke to nearly 2,000 priests and more than 65,000 men and women religious and laypeople in 30 states.

According to Fr. Roux, "Fr. Gobbi spoke on the spirituality and the three commitments of the Marian Movement of Priests. They are as follows:

1. Consecration to the Immaculate Heart of Mary (making, living, and fostering it).

2. Unity with the Pope, his Magisterium, and all the bishops united to him.

3. Leading the faithful to entrustment to Our Lady, inspiring

in them a love and devotion to her."

Fr. Roux also noted in his letter that Fr. Gobbi celebrated Mass with Pope John Paul in his private chapel on December 19, 1994, that he meets with the Holy Father at least once a year, and that the MMP is made up of people who "are loyal to the Holy Father and work to defend the faith."

We do not dispute any of this, since we know bishops, priests, and laypeople who are members of this Movement, and they are indeed loyal to the Holy Father and the Catholic Faith.

However, Fr. Roux made some other statements in his letter that we do dispute. For example:

* He said that the "alleged letter from Archbishop Cacciavillan" is not authentic and that "it is being used to try to undermine the mission of the Marian Movement of Priests." We would point out that the phrase "competent authorities" is code for the Vatican without specifying the congregation. It is an unofficial advisory from an official source and more than just Cacciavillan's opinion. We did not quote from the letter to undermine the MMP, but only as a cautionary note to our readers.

* He said that "you chose to denounce Fr. Gobbi before you even researched the facts and in the process you have caused irreparable harm to his mission. By your lack of true journalism and lack of discernment, you have joined forces with the enemies of the Church." We did not denounce Fr. Gobbi in any way, but merely said that Catholics should not consider the messages as statements coming directly from the Blessed Mother.

* He said that we portrayed Fr. Gobbi as a "dissident priest." We did no such thing.

* He said that we are out to silence Fr. Gobbi, "or at least make him out to be a fool." Not true.

* He said that "the issue concerning the nature of the messages received by Fr. Gobbi was resolved in 1986. At that time, the Sacred Congregation for the Doctrine of the Faith asked Fr. Gobbi to write a preface to his book which would explain the origin of the messages. He did so, thoroughly explaining that these words were received, not directly as with the apparitions at Fatima or Lourdes, but interiorly through the mystical phenomenon well known in the Church as interior locution. The Holy See approved and accepted the preface and they never stated that the messages were the product of Fr. Gobbi's own private meditations."

The preface in question, which can be found in the collection of messages entitled *To the Priests, Our Lady's Beloved Sons*, reads as follows:

"It is hereby stated that the messages contained in this book must be understood not as words spoken directly by Our Lady, but received, in the form of interior locutions, by Don Stefano Gobbi."

Despite this caveat, however, it must be noted that the messages in the main part of the book are clearly presented as the exact words of our Lady, with direct quotes at the beginning and end of each message and with our Lady speaking in the first person ("I am your Mother and Queen ... I urge you ... I announce to you ... This is my plan ... Pray with me").

How many readers of these books will even notice the caveat? And of those who do, how many will quickly forget all about it when they see page after page of direct quotes attributed to the Blessed Mother?

The books do carry an imprimatur ("There is nothing contrary to faith or morals in this manuscript"), but that does not guarantee the reliability of predictions that the Great Chastisement will arrive soon. There is also much good advice in the books. Readers are urged to pray constantly, turn away from sin, get ready for the coming of Christ, etc. But there are also apocalyptic statements about the end times that should be read with caution since they are open to varied interpretations. For example:

* "The Church will know the hour of its greatest apostasy. The man of iniquity will penetrate into its interior and will sit in the very Temple of God, while the little remnant which will remain faithful will be subjected to the greatest trials and persecutions. Humanity will live through the moment of its great chastisement and thus will be made ready to receive the Lord Jesus who will return to you in glory. For this reason, especially today, I am coming down again from heaven ... to prepare the minds and hearts of all to receive Jesus at the closely approaching moment of his glorious return" (May 13, 1990).

* "The glorious reign of Christ, which will be established in your midst, with the second coming of Jesus in the world, is close at hand. This is his return in glory .... I reveal my secret only to the hearts of the little, the simple, and the poor, because it is being accepted and believed by them .... With a small number of these children, the Lord will soon restore on earth his glorious reign of love, of holiness, and of peace" (October 13, 1990).

* "There is in preparation a true schism which could soon become open and proclaimed. And then, there will remain only a small faithful remnant, over which I will keep watch in the garden of my Immaculate Heart. The great trial has arrived for all humanity. The chastisement, predicted by me at Fatima and contained in that part of the secret which has not yet been revealed, is about to take place. The great moment of divine justice and of mercy has come upon the world" (November 15, 1990).

Reasonable people cannot help but see these statements as direct warnings from our Lady, since that is how they are presented, and we see no need to apologize for holding up a caution sign. It also concerns us that some readers of these messages have withdrawn from the battle for souls. They have little interest in fighting the good fight and running the race to the end. They seem content to wait expectantly for a chastisement that they believe is just around the corner.

But we know not the hour or the day of the Second Coming of our Lord and, while we should indeed pray as if everything depended on God, we must also work, as St. Augustine suggested, as if everything depended on ourselves. Christians in the first century also thought that the Parousia was imminent, but they were wrong.

The purpose of our reply was simply to urge Christians in the 20th century to exercise more prudence in these matters than did our ancestors in the early Church. It is unfair and inaccurate to label this cautionary note of ours as a personal attack on Fr. Gobbi and an attempt to harm his reputation and his mission.

Q. Two teachers in the Catholic school my children attend said that guardian angels are something taught to little children and do not really exist. Are guardian angels for real? — M.T., Pennsylvania

A. Yes, guardian angels are for real. The Church sets aside a special day every year, October 2nd, to honor these angelic beings who protect us from spiritual and physical harm and inspire us to do good. In the Old Testament, God told Moses: "I am sending an angel before you, to guard you on the way and bring you to the place I have prepared. Be attentive to him and heed his voice. Do not rebel against him, for he will not forgive your sin. My authority resides in him" (Exodus 23:20-21).

The Church's longstanding belief in guardian angels is based on Matthew 18:10, where Jesus, after warning against scandalizing little children, said: "See that you never despise one of these little ones. I assure you, their angels in heaven constantly behold my heavenly Father's face." Recall, too, that when Peter was miraculously released from prison, his friends said, "It must be his angel" (Acts 12:15).

For some fascinating accounts of modern-day life-saving angelic visitations, see three books by Joan Wester Anderson: *Where Angels Walk* (Barton & Brett), *Where Miracles Happen* (Brett Books), and *An Angel to Watch Over Me* (Ballantine Books).

It is a good thing to pray every day to our guardian angel, either by simply saying, "Holy Guardian Angel, watch over me," or by reciting the prayer many of us learned as children: "Angel of God, my guardian dear, to whom God's love commits me here, ever this day be at my side, to light and guard, to rule and guide. Amen."

Q. Can you explain how the angels Michael, Raphael, and Gabriel can be called saints when they never lived on earth as the canonized saints did? — L.W.W., Florida

A. According to the dictionary, the word "saint" comes from the Latin *sanctus*, which means holy or sacred. The word usually refers to those persons, now presumed to be in Heaven, whose lives of extraordinary holiness and heroic virtue while on earth have been recognized by the Church, usually by the process called canonization.

However, another dictionary meaning for saint is "angel," which makes sense since these purely spiritual beings are also noted for their great holiness. Thus, it is appropriate to call Michael a saint because he remained faithful to God and led the heavenly hosts to victory in the battle against the fallen angels (Revelation 12:7-9), as well as Gabriel, who announced to Mary that she was to be the Mother of the Savior (Luke 1:26-38), and Raphael, who identified himself as "one of the seven angels who enter and serve before the Glory of the Lord" (Tobit 12:15).

Q. How do angels do battle? Can an angel die or be wounded? Can angels endure physical pain? Isn't it far-fetched to depict Saint Michael with a sword? — R.N.M., Massachusetts

A. Angels are purely spiritual beings with intelligence and free will. Since they have no bodies, they cannot die, be wounded, or suffer physical pain. They usually take on human form when they intervene in human affairs, but they are not subject to human limitations. They exert power on our world through an act of the will.

For scriptural examples of angelic power, see chapter 19 of Genesis (the destruction of Sodom and Gomorrah), chapter 24 of 2 Samuel (the beginning of the destruction of Jerusalem), and chapter 19 of 2 Kings (the destruction of 185,000 Assyrians).

St. Michael is usually depicted in art with a sword to symbolize his driving the bad angels from Heaven (Revelation 12:7-9), but this is only an artist's conception. Michael is a spiritual being with no hand in which to carry a sword and no need for such a weapon.

Q. Why did the Fathers of Vatican II change the feasts of so many saints on the Church calendar? — S.C., Maine

A. The Second Vatican Council's *Constitution on the Sacred Liturgy* said that to prevent the feasts of the saints from taking "precedence over the feasts which commemorate the very mysteries of salvation, many of them should be left to be celebrated by a particular church, or nation, or family of Religious. Only those should be extended to the Universal Church which commemorate saints who are truly of universal importance" (n. 111).

In 1969, Pope Paul VI ordered a reorganization of the calendar of saints which led to the removal of more than 200 saints from the calendar and shifting of the feast days of many others, most commonly to mark the date of the saint's death, if known. For those who were dropped from the universal calendar, it is obvious that with thousands of saints and only some 300 days in the year, it would not be possible to give each saint his or her day. Some were removed because their feast was on the same day as a greater saint, others because they lacked universal significance, and still others because there was insufficient information about them.

This latter criterion caused great anguish among Catholics when such popular saints as Christopher were dropped. This was not a declaration that Christopher never existed, or that he did not attain great holiness. It was simply a judgment that the only thing certain about him was his name, so he couldn't be presented as a model of heroic virtue. Nor did it mean that one could not still have a devotion to a particular saint; only that the saint would no longer be listed on the universal calendar.

Q. What happened to all the saints? There are so many blank spaces on each month's page of the Church calendar.

And some have been shifted around in a kind of ecclesial musical chairs. My own patron, St. Monica, was moved from May 4th to August 27th. Why? — M.M.T., Australia

A. In the booklet *Norms Governing Liturgical Calendars*, published originally by the Vatican in 1969 and by the U.S. Catholic Conference in 1984, it says that the date of St. Monica's death is unknown and that her feast was first assigned to May 4th because the Augustinians celebrated the conversion of St. Augustine (Monica's son) on May 5th. Her day was changed to August 27th because that is the day before the feast of Augustine.

It should be noted, too, that there are not really blank days because there are a variety of options, such as celebrating Votive Masses and Masses for Various Occasions.

Q. Who was the first saint canonized, and what is the background? — R.D.H., Maine

A. The first official canonization by a Pope was of St. Ulrich by Pope John XV in 993. Prior to that time, cults developed around certain holy individuals, particularly martyrs, and those cults grew until the persons were proclaimed saints by popular acclamation. The current process of beatification and canonization, which is handled by the Vatican Congregation for the Causes of Saints, stems back to 1588, when Pope Sixtus V established the Sacred Congregation of Rites. For more information, see the introduction to the *Dictionary of Saints* (Doubleday) edited by John J. Delaney and *The Making of Saints* (Our Sunday Visitor) by Michael Freze, S.F.O.

Q. Is it true that John the Baptist was freed from original sin before his birth? — B.M., Ontario

A. There is a tradition in the Church that John the Baptist was freed from original sin while in the womb of his mother Elizabeth during the visitation of Mary. The tradition is supported by the words of the angel Gabriel, who told Zechariah that his son's name would be John and that "he will be filled with the Holy Spirit from his mother's womb" (Luke 1:15). A person still in original sin could not be filled with the Holy Spirit.

The angel's prediction came true during Mary's visit to her cousin. "When Elizabeth heard Mary's greeting," the Gospel tells us, "the baby leapt in her womb. Elizabeth was filled with the Holy Spirit and cried out in a loud voice: 'Blest are you among women and blest is the fruit of your womb. But who am

I that the mother of my Lord should come to me? The moment your greeting sounded in my ears, the baby leapt in my womb for joy'" (Luke 1:41-44).

This leaping of John in his mother's womb is thought to signify the Baptist's release from original sin. It is not to be confused with Mary, who was *conceived* without original sin.

Q. You have said that when John the Baptist leapt in the womb of his mother during the Visitation of Mary, it may have meant that he was freed from original sin. If this is true, then how do you explain the passage from Luke 7:28? Wouldn't you have to assume that John did not have sanctifying grace for Jesus to say this? — C.G., California

A. The passage in question reads: "I assure you, there is no man born of woman greater than John. Yet the least born into the kingdom of God is greater than he." In saying this, Jesus was not implying anything about the state of John's soul. What our Lord was saying was that while the Baptist was the greatest of all the prophets, he lived and preached before the reign of Jesus and did not have the benefit of the Gospel or of the sacramental life of the Church founded by Christ. Those who come after our Lord, even the least in His kingdom, will be able to accomplish more than John the Baptist, Jesus is saying, because He has showed them the way, the truth, and the life.

Q. Was St. Maria Goretti required to give up her life rather than submit to her attacker, or was she offering God a heroic act of chastity? — H.B., Washington

A. We would assume the latter explanation. Maria Goretti was a 12-year-old Italian girl when she was stabbed to death on July 6, 1902, while resisting the sexual advances of a young man. Her killer, Alexander Serenelli, completely changed his life after receiving a vision of Maria and attended her canonization in Rome in 1950.

Rather than submit to her attacker, Maria chose the path of heroic chastity. "She did not flee from the Spirit's voice, from the voice of her conscience," Pope John Paul has said of the youthful martyr. "She did not give in. She rather chose death. Through the gift of fortitude, the Holy Spirit helped her to 'judge' — and to choose with her young spirit. She chose death when there was no other way to defend her virginal purity."

Q. In all my years as a Catholic, including 16 years of Catholic schools, I had never heard until recently that Mary

Magdalene was the same Mary mentioned as the sister of Lazarus. How could Mary Magdalene have sat at Jesus' feet so often and yet fall so far from the kind of life Jesus taught? Is there a Scripture reference to validate this? — H.C., South Carolina

A. There is no clear scriptural evidence that Mary Magdalene was the sister of Martha and Lazarus. Some have identified her as that Mary, and as the repentant sinner who washed Jesus' feet with her tears in the house of Simon the Pharisee (Luke 7:36-50), but the proof of these identifications is lacking in the Gospels.

What we do know about Mary Magdalen is that she had seven devils cast out of her by Jesus (Mark 16:9), that she helped Jesus in His ministry in Galilee (Luke 8:2), that she was one of the women at the crucifixion (Matt. 27:56, Mark 15:40, John 19:25), and that she was the first person to see Jesus after His resurrection (Mark 16:9, John 20:14-18).

Q. I read recently that St. Nicholas of Tolentino is the patron saint of the holy souls in Purgatory. Is this true? If so, what did he especially do for them during his life? — E.M.L., California

A. Yes, Nicholas of Tolentino is a patron saint of the souls in Purgatory, but we don't know what he did during his life to earn this designation. According to John J. Delaney's *Dictionary of Saints*, Nicholas was born in Italy in 1245, was professed in the Augustinian order in 1263, and was ordained about 1270. He was sent in 1274 to Tolentino, where he became famous as a preacher and a confessor, converting hardened sinners and ministering to the poor, the sick, criminals, and the needy. He died in Tolentino in 1305, was venerated for the many miracles he is reported to have performed, and was canonized in 1446.

Q. Who are the canonized saints from the United States? Who in the United States has been designated as "blessed"? — P.Z., New Jersey

A. At the time this book goes to press, those Americans canonized as saints include Elizabeth Ann Seton (1774-1821), the first American-born saint; Frances Xavier Cabrini (1850-1917), who was born in Italy but became the first American citizen to be honored with sainthood; John Neumann (1811-1860), who was born in Bohemia but was canonized as an American citizen; Rose Philippine Duchesne (1759-1852), who was born in France but who worked as a missionary in the United States for 34 years.

We should also mention the eight Jesuit missionaries who were martyred between 1642 and 1649 in what is now upstate New York and southeastern Canada and were canonized in 1930 by Pope Pius XI. These North American martyrs are Saints Isaac Jogues, Rene Goupil, John Lalande, Jean de Brebeuf, Antoine Daniel, Gabriel Lalemant, Charles Garnier, and Noel Chabanel.

Those Americans declared blessed include Kateri Tekakwitha, the Indian maiden who was born in what is now upstate New York in 1656 and died in 1680; Junipero Serra (1713-1784), the Spanish priest who established nine Franciscan missions in California between 1769 and 1782; Katharine Drexel (1858-1955), a wealthy Philadelphian who used her $12 million inheritance for the work of the order she founded, the Sisters of the Blessed Sacrament for Indians and Colored People; and Fr. Damien de Veuster (1840-1889), who was born in Belgium but ministered to lepers in Hawaii and whose statue stands under the dome of the U.S. Capitol building in Washington, D.C.

For those interested in more details about these and other holy persons, there are such books as *Sanctity in America* by Amleto Cardinal Cigognani, *Saints of the Americas* by Fr. Marion Habig, *American Martyrs from 1542* by Fr. Albert Nevins, *The Martyrs of the United States of America* by Monsignor James Powers, and *Portraits in American Sanctity* by Fr. Joseph Tylenda.

Q. Has any person, other than a Catholic, been given the stigmata? — P.T., Pennsylvania

A. We are not aware of a complete or comprehensive list of those persons who have been stigmatized, i.e., received on their bodies and suffered terribly from some or all of the wounds of Christ during His Passion and death. So we don't know the religion of all those who have visibly borne the stigmata. According to the *Encyclopedia of Catholic History* (Our Sunday Visitor), however, there have been throughout history some 330 cases of the stigmata appearing on some persons, 60 of whom have been canonized or declared blessed. Two of the best-known stigmatists are St. Francis of Assisi in the 13th century and Padre Pio in the 20th century.

Q. A friend of mine who is a fallen-away Catholic is reading *Meditations With Hildegard of Bingen* by Gabriele Uhlein. Can you comment on this? — J.B.C., New Jersey

A. We have heard of Hildegard of Bingen, but not of Gabriele Uhlein's book. Hildegard was a Benedictine nun and visionary who lived in Germany in the 12th century. A versatile writer, musician, and artist, Hildegard wrote poetry and hymns, works of medicine and natural history, lives of the saints, and commentaries on the Gospels, the Athanasian Creed, and the Rule of St. Benedict. She also reformed several convents and reproved by letter several rulers of her time, including Henry II of England, the Emperor Frederick Barbarossa, and Pope Eugenius III.

Although miracles were attributed to her intercession both during her life and after her death at the age of 80, attempts to have Hildegard canonized a saint in the 13th and 14th centuries were unsuccessful. Her name was added to the Roman Martyrology in the 15th century, and her feast day is celebrated in German dioceses on September 17th.

Q. I am interested in learning about the philosophy of St. Thomas Aquinas. Are there any books that deal with his philosophy at the layman's level? — J.M., California

A. You might try Frederick Copleston's *Thomas Aquinas*, James Weisheipl's *Friar Thomas d'Aquino*, David Knowles' *The Evolution of Medieval Thought*, and Peter Kreeft's *A Summa of the Summa: The Essential Philosophical Passages of St. Thomas Aquinas' Summa Theologica*. The latter book is published by Ignatius Press.

Chapter 7

The Last Things

Q. Could you please explain what will happen to us at the time of the particular and the general judgments? — M.H., Nevada

A. It is the teaching of the Church that every person will face two judgments following death. Immediately after we die comes the particular judgment, when Christ will judge each one of us on how well we loved and served God and neighbor while on earth. "It is appointed that men die once, and after death be judged," said St. Paul (Hebrews 9:27), which rules out the possibility of reincarnation.

According to the *Catechism of the Catholic Church* (n. 1022), each one of us will receive eternal retribution at the moment of our death, in a particular judgment before Christ Himself. Then will come either entrance into Heaven — immediately or after purification in Purgatory — or immediate and everlasting damnation in Hell.

At the end of the world comes the general judgment, when all members of the human race will be judged on the basis of how they responded to those in need — the hungry, the thirsty, the sick, the imprisoned. This social judgment will not change the verdict rendered at the particular judgment, but it will reveal to the whole world God's mercy toward those who are saved and His justice toward those who are condemned.

In the presence of Christ, who is Truth itself, says the *Catechism* (n. 1039), the truth of each person's relationship with God will be laid bare. The Last Judgment will reveal once and for all the good that each person did or failed to do during his life on earth.

When Christ returns in glory at the Last Judgment, the *Catechism* (n.1040) continues, God the Father, through Jesus Christ, will pronounce the final word on all history. Then we shall know the ultimate meaning of the whole work of creation and of the entire economy of salvation and understand the marvelous ways by which the Providence of God led everything toward its final end. The Last Judgment will reveal that God's justice triumphs over all the injustices committed by His creatures and that God's love is stronger than death.

Following that judgment, our Lord will say to the just, "Come. You have my Father's blessing! Inherit the kingdom prepared for you from the creation of the world" (Matthew 25:34). To the wicked Jesus will say, "Out of my sight, you condemned, into that everlasting fire prepared for the devil and his angels" (Matthew 25:41).

Q. I have heard it said that when we are judged by our Lord after our death, we must account for every thought, word, or action of our lives. Why is this so when God has said that our forgiven sins and iniquity will be remembered no more (Isaiah 43:25, Jeremiah 31:34, Ezekiel 18:22)? — A.E.L., Michigan

A. Even though God forgives our sins through the sacrament of Penance and wipes the slate clean, it is still necessary to heal by prayer or penance the damage inflicted by those sins — here or after death. This will be true for those of us who did not do enough good works to atone for the sins we committed. There may be no unforgiven mortal sins that would keep us out of Heaven, but we are not ready to see God face to face. We must undergo a period of purification before we can attain the Beatific Vision.

Perhaps then, when we meet Jesus at the particular judgment, He will show us all the times in our lives when we failed to love God and neighbor as much as we should have, when we left undone those things which God expected us to do. We will then see clearly that we could have been much better followers of Christ. And this may be part of the suffering in Purgatory — the knowledge that we would already be enjoying unimaginable happiness in Heaven if only we had tried harder to do God's will while we lived on earth.

Q. Considering the enormous number of people who have lived on planet earth, how will the earth hold all the people at the Last Judgment? Or will it even take place on earth? — M.D.H., Iowa

A. Where and how and when the Last Judgment will take place is known only to God. It does boggle our finite minds to think about how God can gather together at one time all the billions of people who will have lived on earth by the time the world ends. But we can't imagine it being a problem for God. If He could create the universe out of nothing, He shouldn't have any trouble assembling the entire human race for the Last Judgment. If Jesus could multiply five loaves of bread and two fish to feed over 5,000 people, what is to prevent Him from multiplying the area of the earth, if that is where the Last

Judgment is to take place, to accommodate billions of people? Nothing is impossible for God.

Q. What is the Church's stand on the rapture mentioned in 1 Thessalonians 4:17? — D.A., Missouri

Q. A sister of mine attends a Fundamentalist church and believes that all religions and churches are the same and that someday she will be taken up bodily into Heaven. I would appreciate your comments. — S.J., California

A. The idea that some believers will be snatched up to Heaven is called the rapture, and it is based on a passage in St. Paul: "The Lord himself will come down from heaven at the word of command, at the sound of the archangel's voice and God's trumpet; and those who have died in Christ will rise first. Then we, the living, the survivors, will be caught up with them in the clouds to meet the Lord in the air" (1 Thessalonians 4:16-17).

Over the centuries, many have read these and other passages in Scripture, such as chapter 24 of Matthew and chapter 21 of Luke, and tried to fit the language and imagery to their own time. They have assigned a particular date to the rapture or to the end of the world, but have always been wrong because no one but God knows the hour or the day of the Second Coming.

If people insist on getting caught up (pardon the pun) in these speculations, they will inevitably be disappointed and disillusioned when the predicted events do not occur. Better to live as if every day and hour were our last on earth so that we may be prepared to meet the divine Judge and to be deemed worthy of enjoying eternity with Him.

Q. I once heard a priest say in a homily that we will know the end of the world is imminent when many thousands of Jews recognize Jesus as God. Is this true? — S.D., New York

A. Chapter 11 of St. Paul's Letter to the Romans is the ultimate source of the theory that the conversion of the Jews will herald the Second Coming. This theory flourished in the Middle Ages but has never been granted official status by the Church and has no substantial foundation. Paul may have been expressing a "wouldn't it be wonderful if" scenario, not supplementing the Lord's teaching on the signs of the end times. "The exact time is not yours to know," Jesus told the Apostles. "The Father has reserved that to himself" (Acts 1:7).

Q. What is the teaching of the Catholic Church on cremation? — M.C., Minnesota

Q. If a Catholic has his body cremated, can the ashes be brought to church for the funeral Mass? — L.M.Z., Iowa

A. The Church has always earnestly recommended that the deceased be buried rather than cremated (Canon 1176) because it wishes to honor the body, which was once a temple of the Holy Spirit, and to follow the example of Christ. However, the Church does permit cremation provided it has not been chosen for reasons contrary to Christian teaching, such as hatred of the Catholic Church or denial of the doctrine of the resurrection of the body.

If cremation has been chosen, the Church prefers that the body be brought to church for the funeral Mass and then taken to the crematorium. If it is physically or morally impossible for the body to be present, it is permitted to celebrate the funeral service. Some dioceses in regions of the world where cremation is part of a long cultural tradition have obtained permission from Rome to conduct the full rites over the ashes, and the practice seems to be spreading.

Q. What is the importance of a Catholic burial in a Catholic cemetery? And can a Catholic be buried in a national cemetery for veterans? — C.M.B., Massachusetts

A. The Catholic Church has over the centuries established its own cemeteries to provide sacred places for the burial of its deceased members. Canon 1240 of the 1983 Code of Canon Law states that "the Church is to have its own cemeteries wherever this can be done, or at least space in civil cemeteries destined for the faithful departed and properly blessed." If this is not possible, the canon goes on to say, then "individual graves are to be properly blessed as often as needed."

The ideal situation would be burial in a Catholic cemetery, but this is not possible for many Catholics. Therefore, the faithful departed can be buried in civil cemeteries, including those set aside for war veterans, and a priest should bless the grave just as he would in a Catholic cemetery.

Q. After the birth of our stillborn child seven years ago, he was buried in a civil cemetery. We were not present and have not visited his grave. Should we try to find the grave and have a priest bless it? — M. and L. W., Michigan

A. Although you don't indicate whether a priest buried your child, it is customary for a priest to bless the grave of the deceased at the time of burial in a civil cemetery (Canon 1240.2). If a priest was at the cemetery, you could ask him if the grave was blessed. If not, the cemetery office could tell you where the grave is located and you could arrange for a priest to bless it.

Q. What happens to the souls of aborted babies? Do they go to Limbo? — R.J.D., Massachusetts

Q. I have been told that the true doctrine of the Church on the fate of unbaptized babies is not that of Limbo, but actually that of eternal damnation in Hell. Is this a rebirth of an ancient heresy? — M.M., New Hampshire

A. We don't know about an ancient heresy, but the official teaching of the Church on the fate of unbaptized babies, including those who die at the hands of abortionists, can be found in the *Catechism of the Catholic Church* (n. 1261), which says that the Church can only entrust them to the mercy of God. The *Catechism* reminds us of the great mercy of God, who wants all of us to be saved (1 Timothy 2:4), as well as the tenderness of Jesus toward children, which prompted Him to say, "Let the children come to me and do not hinder them" (Mark 10:14).

These passages allow us to hope that there is a way of salvation for children who have died without Baptism. They also remind us not to prevent little children from coming to Christ through the gift of Baptism.

Q. Our pastor and his assistant tell us that there is no Purgatory. Five of our children are religious education teachers in the Madison, Wisconsin, area, and they are told to "cool it about Purgatory" when they're teaching the students. For Heaven's sake, will you please set these people straight! — D.R., Illinois

A. If there is no Purgatory, then anniversary Masses for the dead are a waste of time, we can abolish All Souls Day, and we can reduce the Communion of Saints to the Church Triumphant in Heaven and the Church Militant on earth.

The existence of Purgatory is a defined dogma of the Catholic Faith. The basis for this belief can be traced to Second Maccabees 12:46 (Confraternity Version), which says, "It is therefore a holy and wholesome thought to pray for the dead, that they may be loosed from sins," and it has been affirmed by the Second Council of Lyons (1274), the Council of Florence (1439), the Council of Trent (1545-1563), Vatican Council II (1964), and the *Catechism of the Catholic Church* (1994).

According to the *Catechism* (n. 1031), the Church gives the name Purgatory to the final purification of the elect, which is entirely different from the punishment of the damned. The Church formulated her doctrine on Purgatory especially at the Councils of Florence and Trent, the *Catechism* says, and relies on certain Scriptural texts (cf. 1 Corinthians 3:15 and 1 Peter 1:7) in speaking of a cleansing fire.

The *Catechism* says (n. 1032) that this teaching is also based on the practice of prayer for the dead described in Second Maccabees 12:46, and emphasizes that from the beginning the Church has honored the memory of the dead and offered prayers in suffrage for them, especially at the Holy Sacrifice of the Mass, so that, once purified, they may see God. The Church also recommends that almsgiving, indulgences, and works of penance be undertaken on behalf of the dead.

Q. What does the Church tell us about the sufferings in Purgatory? Is the punishment there measured by time? — N.Y., Colorado; J.D., New York; and E.J.M., Florida

A. The Church has never defined the exact nature of Purgatory, whether our punishment there is measured by the passage of time, or what kind of pain the souls there experience. The sufferings in Purgatory are thought to be of two kinds: the pain of sense and the pain of loss because the souls of the just love God, but they must remain apart from Him and deprived of Him until they have completed their purification. Unlike the souls of the damned in Hell, who know that their pain will never cease, the pain of the souls in Purgatory is mitigated by the knowledge that they will attain Heaven and experience everlasting joy and happiness there. For some interesting insights into the nature of Purgatory, see Peter Kreeft's book *Everything You Ever Wanted to Know About Heaven* (Ignatius Press).

Q. At a funeral Mass recently, the celebrant said that the deceased was in Heaven. Was this a slip of the tongue or is it the new theology? Doesn't this discourage prayers for the souls in Purgatory? — M.F.S., Pennsylvania, and M.A., Ohio

A. It may be comforting to the family and friends of the deceased to hear the priest say that their loved one is in Heaven, but the priest has no way of knowing such a thing and has no business saying it. Such a remark also contradicts the prayers at the funeral Mass, which ask God to be merciful to the deceased and to welcome him or her into Heaven but which do not assume that he or she is already there.

The *Order of Christian Funerals* says that "a brief homily based on the readings should always be given at the funeral liturgy, but never any kind of eulogy. The homilist should dwell on God's compassionate love and on the paschal mystery of the Lord as proclaimed in the Scripture readings. Through the homily, the community should receive the consolation and strength to face the death of one of its members with a hope that has been nourished by the proclamation of the saving word of God" (n. 141).

The canonization of the deceased from the pulpit can also harm the credibility of the priest and the Church with those in the congregation who may know that the person being extolled was far from being a saint.

Q. At a funeral recently, the priest asked the congregation to pray *to* the deceased. I was taught that you couldn't pray to anyone unless the Holy Father had declared them blessed. Have I missed something? — H.J.B., Oregon

A. No, you haven't missed anything. What you were taught is still true; the only persons that we can be sure are in Heaven are those declared blessed or saints by the Church. The beatification and canonization process is long and involved because the Church wants to make sure of the extraordinary holiness of a person before declaring them worthy of imitation and veneration. And even after a lengthy and careful investigation, the Church requires a sign from God, in the form of one or more authenticated miracles, that the person is truly in Heaven.

So inviting the congregation to pray *to* the deceased is theologically unsound since we have no way of knowing whether the deceased is in Heaven. Better that we should pray *for* the deceased, and for all the souls in Purgatory, that they will soon be with God.

Q. In a previous reply, you said that praying to the uncanonized deceased was theologically unsound. True enough, but in admitting that authentic miracles are required before beatification and canonization, aren't you saying that these miracles are the results of prayers to that saint-to-be? Isn't that in itself praying to the uncanonized deceased? — E.M., Ohio

A. The first step in the process of declaring a person blessed and then saint is a thorough investigation of the person's life for evidence of heroic virtue and extraordinary holiness. Once that has been officially established, the Servant of God is given the title "Venerable," which allows private prayers to the deceased. The next title is "Blessed," which requires at least one miracle and allows public prayers to the deceased. The final step is sainthood, which requires an additional miracle and confers a seven-fold honor on the person: (1) inscription of name in the Catalogue of Saints and reception of public veneration; (2) invocation in the public prayers of the Church; (3) dedication of churches in the saint's honor; (4) celebration of Mass and the Divine Office; (5) assignment of a feast day on the liturgical calendar; (6) pictorial representation with the heavenly light of glory; and (7) public veneration of the saint's relics.

The priest who advised prayers to the deceased at a funeral was premature since the Church does not approve private prayers to a person until he or she has been declared Venerable, and public prayers only after a person has been beatified.

Q. Regarding prayers to the uncanonized deceased, I was always taught that a person in Purgatory cannot help himself but can help us if we ask for help. Is that true? — H.M., Minnesota

Q. The doctrine of the Communion of Saints says that the Church Militant can pray for the Church Suffering. Even though the souls in Purgatory cannot help themselves, they can pray for the Church Militant since they are "friends of God." Fr. John Hardon in his *Question and Answer Catholic Catechism* says that the souls in Purgatory can pray and obtain blessings for those on earth. — D.C.H., South Carolina

Q. In speaking of the souls in Purgatory in *The Catholic Catechism*, Fr. John Hardon says that "they can pray and obtain blessings for those living on earth. They are united, as the Second Vatican Council teaches, with the pilgrim Church in the Communion of Saints." If we can pray to the poor souls and invoke their aid, certainly we can pray to those we feel sure are in Heaven, even if they have never been called venerable — or anything else — by the Catholic Church. — E.M., Texas

Q. I disagree with your statement about prayers to the deceased. My wife and I had a premature child who lived about eight hours after birth and was baptized before death. My pastor told us that since the child was baptized and had committed no sins, he went straight to Heaven. Therefore, he could be considered a saint and we could pray to him. — J.M., Florida

A. We do not disagree with anything these questioners have said, although the situation referred to by J.M. is actually different from the other three since his child, having been baptized shortly after birth, is certainly in Heaven.

Perhaps the confusion stems from a misunderstanding of our original reply. The question then had to do with the priest's advice at a funeral Mass to pray to the deceased as if he were already in Heaven. We said at the time that such advice was theologically unsound since the only persons that we can be sure have reached Heaven are those who have been beatified or canonized or, in the case of newborn babies, those who have been baptized immediately after birth.

The first three questioners above are talking about something different, i.e., praying for the souls in Purgatory and asking them to pray for us. We agree with Fr. Hardon, whose books we often consult, that both practices are sound and we wholeheartedly encourage them. We also agree that individuals may pray to deceased loved ones as if they were in Heaven, but we think that a priest at a funeral Mass is being imprudent when he implies or categorically states that the deceased is already enjoying heavenly glory.

Q. What will Heaven be like? Will we see friends and family there? — E.O., Massachusetts

A. Although we don't know precisely what Heaven will be like, Scripture and Church teaching give us an inkling of the great joy that awaits us. St. Paul said it this way: "Eye has not seen, ear has not heard, nor has it so much as dawned on man what God has prepared for those who love him" (1 Corinthians 2:9).

The happiness of Heaven consists primarily in the Beatific Vision, which means seeing God as He really is and sharing intensely in the life of the Trinity. "Now we see indistinctly, as in a mirror; then we shall see face to face," said St. Paul (1 Corinthians 13:12).

This direct gaze on God will of itself produce incredible happiness, but we will also be able to enjoy and communicate with Christ in His humanity, with the Blessed Mother and the saints, and with family and friends we had on earth. We will never grow tired or bored. We are "strangers and foreigners" on earth, said Paul (Hebrews 11:13), and will not reach our true home until we are in Heaven.

This mystery of blessed communion with God and all who are in Christ is beyond all understanding and description, says the

Catechism of the Catholic Church, adding that "Scripture speaks of it in images: life, light, peace, wedding feast, wine of the kingdom, the Father's house, the heavenly Jerusalem, paradise" (n. 1027).

Peter Kreeft offers an intriguing look at what Heaven might be like in his book *Everything You Ever Wanted to Know About Heaven.*

Q. Will married people be united with their spouses in Heaven? — J.K., Illinois

A. Jesus was asked this very question by the Sadducees, who posed the elaborate scenario of a woman whose husband died and she eventually married his six brothers in succession. "At the resurrection, whose wife will she be?" the Sadducees asked our Lord. "Remember, seven married her."

Jesus replied that there would be no marriage in Heaven. "The children of this age marry and are given in marriage," He said, "but those judged worthy of a place in the age to come and of resurrection from the dead do not. They become like angels and are no longer liable to death. Sons of the resurrection, they are sons of God" (Luke 20:33-36).

This does not mean that those who were married in this life will not know or enjoy the company of their spouses in Heaven, but they will not be married there.

Q. Will there be dogs in Heaven. Say it isn't so! I would like to see a nice, quiet Heaven, not with barking dogs like my neighbor's. — R.R., Colorado

A. We are not aware of any Church teaching on whether there will be animals in Heaven, but Peter Kreeft, in his book on Heaven, says, "Why not? How irrational is the prejudice that would allow plants (green fields and flowers) but not animals into Heaven! Much more reasonable is C.S. Lewis' speculation that we will be 'between the angels who are our elder brothers and the beasts who are our jesters, servants, and playfellows.' Scripture seems to confirm this: 'Thy judgments are like the great deep; man and beast thou savest, O Lord.' [Psalm 36:6]. Animals belong in the 'new earth' as much as trees."

If there are dogs in Heaven, we presume that they will be well-behaved and will not disturb others with their barking.

Q. Is it superstitious or old-fashioned to believe in the devil? — C.A., California

A. The pseudo-sophisticates of the day would have you think so, even as there is an increase in satanic activity all around them. But the constant teaching of the Catholic Church is that Satan really exists and has greatly influenced the course of human history. "A monumental struggle against the powers of darkness pervades the whole history of man," said Vatican II's *Constitution on the Church in the Modern World.* "The battle was joined from the very origins of the world and will continue until the last day, as the Lord has attested" (n. 37).

The Church teaches that Satan and the other demons were at first good angels, beings created naturally good by God, who became evil by their own doing, says the *Catechism of the Catholic Church* (n. 391). It says that there is abundant evidence in Scripture of the disastrous influence of the one whom Jesus said "brought death to man from the beginning" (John 8:44) and who even tried to divert Jesus from the mission received from His Father (cf. Matthew 4:1-11). "It was to destroy the devil's works," the evangelist tells us, "that the Son of God revealed himself" (1 John 3:8).

At a general audience on November 15, 1972, Pope Paul VI described the devil as "a living, spiritual being, perverted and perverting. A terrible reality. Mysterious and frightening .... He is the enemy number one, a tempter par excellence. So we know that this dark and disturbing spirit really exists, and that he still acts with treacherous cunning; he is the secret enemy that sows errors and misfortunes in human history."

Paul VI was echoed on August 13, 1986 by Pope John Paul II, who said that "the action of Satan consists primarily in tempting men to evil, by influencing their imaginations and higher faculties, to turn them away from the law of God."

It needs to be stressed, however, that the power of Satan is not infinite, the *Catechism* (n. 395) says, noting that he is only a creature, powerful from the fact that he is pure spirit, but still a creature, incapable of preventing the building up of God's reign.

While Satan may act in the world out of hatred for God and His kingdom, and although his actions may cause grave injuries of a spiritual nature and, indirectly, sometimes even of a physical nature to persons and to society, the *Catechism* says, these actions are mysteriously permitted by the same Divine Providence which guides human and cosmic history with strength and gentleness. We don't know why God permits diabolical activity, but we believe that in everything God works for good with those who love Him.

For more on the devil, one can read the 1975 document of the

Sacred Congregation for Divine Worship entitled *Christian Faith and Demonology*, or Corrado Balducci's book *The Devil: ... Alive and Active in Our World* (Alba House).

Q. I've heard two monsignors mention a vision by the Holy Father which referred to "the smoke of Satan entering the Church." What exactly was this vision and when did it occur? — K.S., Minnesota

A. Pope Paul VI delivered a homily on June 29, 1972 in which he said that the confusion and problems in the Church in the wake of the Second Vatican Council had given him the feeling that the smoke of Satan had entered the temple of God through a crack in the wall.

Asking how this uncertainty had come about, the Holy Father said: "We believe that some preternatural power has come into the world to upset and stifle the fruits of the Ecumenical Council and to prevent the Church from breaking out into a hymn of joy for having regained a full awareness of itself. Precisely because of this, we would like to be able, now more than ever, to exercise the function assigned by God to St. Peter, namely, to confirm our brethren in the faith."

Q. Do we know the reason for Satan's fall? I have read that it was because he was asked to accept the Incarnation. — E.R., New Jersey

A. We know from Scripture that a "war broke out in heaven: Michael and his angels battled against the dragon. Although the dragon and his angels fought back, they were overpowered and lost their place in heaven. The huge dragon, the ancient serpent known as the Devil or Satan, the seducer of the whole world, was driven out; he was hurled down to earth and his minions with him" (Revelation 12:7-9).

In *Christian Faith and Demonology*, the Vatican said that a majority of the early Church Fathers "saw the angels' pride as the reason for their fall. The 'pride' of the angels was manifested in their desire to exalt themselves above their condition, to maintain complete independence, and to make themselves divine. Many Fathers, however, emphasized not only the pride of the angels but also their malice toward men. For St. Irenaeus the Devil's apostasy began when he became jealous of man and sought to make him rebel against his Creator."

Q. Is there such a thing as diabolical possession, and are there priests who perform exorcisms? — K.D., Oregon

A. Yes, there are many well-documented cases of diabolical possession of human beings. Even the much-exaggerated movie *The Exorcist* was based on an actual case. Further information can be found in such books as Corrado Balducci's *The Devil*, Fr. Jeffrey J. Steffon's *Satanism: Is It Real* (Servant Publications), and Msgr. Leon Cristiani's *Satan in the Modern World* (Roman Catholic Books).

An exorcism is a ritual of the Catholic Church in which evil spirits are commanded on the authority of Jesus (Mark 16:17) and with the prayer of the Church to depart from a person or to cease causing harm to someone suffering from diabolical possession. The ritual is a sacramental that is officially administered by a priest who is "endowed with piety, knowledge, prudence, and integrity of life" and who is acting with the "special and express permission" of the local bishop (canon 1172).

The elements of the rite include the Litany of the Saints; recitation of the Our Father, one or more creeds, and other prayers; specific prayers of exorcism; reading of Gospel passages; and use of holy water and the Sign of the Cross.

The bishop will not order an exorcism without a careful investigation to establish that the person is truly possessed by a demon and not just suffering from some mental or emotional illness. Some of the signs that point to diabolical possession are speaking in a language that one could not possibly know, having knowledge of hidden things, and manifesting a strength that far exceeds one's age or physical condition.

One priest who performed exorcisms in Rome for more than 25 years said that "it is a terrible strain, both physically and mentally." He said that the devils use such "unbelievably obscene" language that "you have to steel yourself and remember that the Church is behind you, although I have been afraid on occasion."

Q. With the Church's approval of the Fatima appearances, during which the Blessed Mother showed the three children a vision of Hell, can we now be certain that there are human souls in Hell? — M.T., Michigan

A. That Hell exists, and that souls who deliberately and obstinately reject God and His grace will spend all eternity there, have been certain teachings of the Church since the time of Christ. Our Lord warned us that we would be separated from Him if we failed to meet the serious needs of the poor because failure to help others, He said, would be the same as failure to help Him (cf. Matthew 25:31-46).

According to the *Catechism of the Catholic Church*, one who dies in mortal sin without repenting and accepting God's merciful love will be separated from God forever by one's own free choice. The *Catechism* calls this state of definitive self-exclusion from communion with God "hell" (n. 1033).

The *Catechism* goes on to say that the constant teaching of the Church affirms the existence of Hell and its eternity. It says that immediately after death, the souls of those who die in a state of mortal sin descend into Hell, where they suffer the punishments of that infernal region, including eternal fire. The chief punishment of Hell, the Church teaches, is eternal separation from God, in whom alone we can possess the life and happiness for which we were created and for which we long (n. 1035).

Q. Priests have told me that Jesus' statements in Matthew 7:14 and 22:14, and in Luke 13:23-24, are just hyperbole. Are these statements about the number of people who might wind up in Hell to be taken literally? — M.G.L., Florida

A. It may be comforting to think that very few people will end up in Hell, but there is much evidence in Scripture, and in history, to indicate that Hell will not be lacking in occupants. What we cannot determine from the Gospel passages mentioned, however, is the precise meaning of "many" and "few," as when Jesus says:

"Enter through the narrow gate. The gate that leads to damnation is wide, the road is clear, and many choose to travel it. But how narrow is the gate that leads to life, how rough the road, and how few there are who find it" (Matthew 7:13-14).

Instead of speculating about these matters, we should take the advice of the *Catechism* and consider the affirmations of Scripture on the subject of Hell as a call to make use of our freedom with a view to our eternal destiny and as an urgent call to conversion (n. 1036).

Bear in mind, as we noted in chapter 1, that God predestines no one to go to Hell. For this to happen, the *Catechism* (n. 1037) says, there must be a willful turning away from God (a mortal sin) and persistence in it until the end. That is why the Church, in her Masses and in the daily prayers of her faithful, constantly beseeches the mercy of God, who "wants none to perish but all to come to repentance" (2 Peter 3:9).

Chapter 8

The Sacraments

Q. I can understand the connection of sanctifying grace with Baptism and the Eucharist because in Scripture "life" is connected with each. How do Matrimony and the other sacraments give sanctifying grace? — J.M., California

A. The seven sacraments, as many of us have been taught since childhood, are "efficacious signs of grace, instituted by Christ and entrusted to the Church, by which divine life is dispensed to us," says the *Catechism of the Catholic Church*. It adds that the visible rites by which the sacraments are celebrated signify and make present the graces proper to each sacrament, and they bear fruit in those who receive them with the required dispositions (n. 1131).

If the sacraments are celebrated worthily, says the *Catechism*, they "confer the grace that they signify. They are efficacious because in them Christ himself is at work: it is he who baptizes, he who acts in his sacraments in order to communicate the grace that each sacrament signifies .... As fire transforms into itself everything it touches, so the Holy Spirit transforms into the divine life whatever is subjected to his power" (n. 1127).

The *Catechism* has divided the seven sacraments into three categories:

Sacraments of Initiation — The faithful are born anew by Baptism, strengthened by the sacrament of Confirmation, and receive in the Eucharist the food of eternal life. By means of these sacraments of Christian initiation, they thus receive in increasing measure the treasures of the divine life and advance toward the perfection of charity (n. 1212).

Sacraments of Healing — The Lord Jesus Christ, physician of our souls and bodies, who forgave the sins of the paralytic and restored him to bodily health, has willed that His Church continue, in the power of the Holy Spirit, His work of healing and salvation, even among her own members. This is the purpose of the two sacraments of healing: the sacrament of Penance and the sacrament of the Anointing of the Sick (n. 1421).

Sacraments of Service — Two other sacraments, Holy Orders and Matrimony, are directed toward the salvation of others; if they contribute as well to personal salvation, it is through service to others that they do so. They confer a particular mission in the Church and serve to build up the people of God (n. 1534).

Q. When did the Roman Catholic Church start to baptize babies? Did the Apostles do this, or did the Church start much later, as some of her enemies claim? — D.J.B., Texas

A. Baptism of infants is implied in the Acts of the Apostles when Paul baptized Lydia "and her household" (16:15) and Paul and Silas baptized their jailer "and his whole household" (16:33). One's whole household presumably encompasses parents and children, including infants. There is also evidence that infant baptism was practiced in the early Church.

In the third century, for example, Origen (185-255) wrote that "the Church received from the apostles the tradition of giving baptism also to infants." In the fourth century, St. John Chrysostom (347-407) said: "For this reason we baptize even infants, though they do not have sins [of their own]: so that there may be given to them holiness, righteousness, adoption, inheritance, brotherhood with Christ, and that they may be his members."

This immemorial tradition of the Church is surely based on the statement of our Lord that "no one can enter into God's kingdom without being begotten of water and Spirit" (John 3:5), and His plea to "let the children come to me. Do not hinder them. The kingdom of God belongs to such as these" (Matthew 19:14). For if Baptism is required for entry into the kingdom, and the kingdom belongs to children, then it is reasonable to conclude that Baptism should be available to them.

Q. A Pentecostal friend says that the Catholic form of Baptism ("In the name of the Father, and of the Son, and of the Holy Spirit") taken from Matthew 28:19 is not what Jesus intended. He says that the formula of Baptism should be in the name of Jesus since that is what is called for in the Acts of Apostles (verses 2:38, 8:16, and 10:48, for example). What can I say to him? — T.G.A., Louisiana

A. For one thing, you could say that Jesus made His intention quite clear in Matthew 28:19 when He told the Apostles to "go, therefore, and make disciples of all the nations. Baptize them in the name of the Father, and of the Son, and of the Holy Spirit." He didn't say, "Baptize them in my name alone," but rather in the name of the Trinity. Whatever your friend wants to make of the verses in Acts, Jesus' command in Matthew is unequivocal.

Furthermore, it is an historical fact that the Trinitarian formula was used in the early centuries of the Church. For example, in the *Didache*, the first-century collection of the teachings of the Apostles, it says: "In regard to Baptism, baptize thus: After the foregoing instructions, baptize in the name of the Father, and of the Son, and of the Holy Spirit in living water."

In a treatise on Baptism written between 200 and 206 A.D., Tertullian said: "The law of washing has been imposed, and the form has been prescribed: 'Go,' He says, 'teach the nations, washing them in the name of the Father and of the Son and of the Holy Spirit.'"

The Catholic form of Baptism is based on the words of Jesus Himself and on 2,000 years of tradition; it is also the form used by all the classic Protestant denominations, and by the Orthodox Church.

Q. Four years ago, my infant grandson was baptized by a priest who, instead of pouring water on my grandson's head, wet his hand in a bowl of water and rubbed his hand on the baby's head. I have been tormented by the thought that my grandson was not validly baptized, but another priest told me that the Church would supply for any defects in the sacrament. Would it be all right for me to baptize my grandson conditionally myself when no one else is around? — L.G.S., Arkansas

A. Canon 854 of the Code of Canon Law says that "Baptism is to be conferred either by immersion or by pouring" of water, and what was done to L.G.S.'s grandson does not seem to comply fully with either requirement. However, since water and the Trinitarian formula were used, it is probable that the boy was validly baptized. The principle of *ecclesia supplet* ("let the Church supply for the defects") could reasonably be applied here.

Q. What is the official Vatican position on "full immersion" baptismal fonts in Catholic churches replacing existing smaller baptismal fonts? — J.B.J., Ontario

A. According to the *Catechism of the Catholic Church* (n. 1239), Baptism can be performed in the most expressive way by triple immersion in the baptismal water. However, from ancient times the sacrament has also been able to be conferred by pouring the water three times over the candidate's head. So parishes that are able to construct full-immersion fonts in their baptisteries are permitted to do so.

Q. The *Baltimore Catechism* **says that children should be baptized as soon as possible after birth and that parents who put off for a long time or neglect the baptism of their children commit a mortal sin. But under present diocesan regulations, parents must satisfy pre-baptismal requirements that delay the reception of the sacrament by months. How is this regulation justified? — J.H., New Jersey**

A. Canon 867.1 says that "parents are obliged to see to it that infants are baptized within the first weeks after birth; as soon as possible after the birth or even before it parents are to go to the pastor to request the sacrament for their child and to be prepared for it properly."

This canon is echoed in the *Catechism of the Catholic Church*, which says that because children also have need of a new birth in Baptism to be freed from the power of darkness and brought into the realm of the freedom of the chidren of God, to which all persons are called, the Church and the parents would deny a child the priceless grace of becoming a child of God were they not to confer Baptism "shortly after birth" (n. 1250).

If there are regulations in some dioceses that delay the reception of Baptism for months (which sounds unlikely), those regulations are contrary to canon law and the practice of the Church. Parents who recognize their responsibility to have their child baptized within the first weeks after birth often attend classes on the sacrament, and fill out the necessary forms, *prior* to the birth of the baby, so that all they have to do once the joyous event has taken place is to bring the child to their parish church on whatever Sunday baptisms are performed in that particular parish. It is usually lax and neglectful parents, not parishes or dioceses, that delay the baptism of children for months or even years.

Q. In a reply some time ago, you blamed "lax and neglectful parents, not parishes or dioceses," for delaying the baptism of infants for months and even years. The circled section from my parish bulletin lists regulations for Baptism that could delay reception of the sacrament for months. Please don't blame the parents alone; it's the regulations. — R.H., Texas

A. The regulations cited by R.H. state that parents "must be registered, attending Mass, and contributing to the support of your parish for at least three months before you can register for the Baptism class." Furthermore, the classes are held only on the second Wednesday of the month, and the Baptisms are scheduled on the first and third Sundays of the month. To someone moving into the parish after the birth of a child elsewhere, said R.H., this could mean no Baptism for months.

R.H. has a point, but the circumstance he cites of a family moving into a parish with a newborn unbaptized child is not one that happens with great frequency. And those who might find themselves in such a situation could have their child baptized in a private ceremony at the parish they are leaving if they expect a long delay in their new parish.

Experience tells us, however, that the blame for delayed Baptism is much more often the fault of careless parents than parish regulations. For practicing Catholics, there need be no delay since, typically, the classes can be taken before the birth. The regulations clearly apply to non-practicing Catholics and are an attempt to meet the requirement that there be some assurance the child will be raised in the Faith — otherwise the baptism is illicit (canon 868.2).

We see the same carelessness with children in fifth and sixth grade, and even ninth and tenth grade, whose parents suddenly want them registered for parish religious education programs so they can receive their First Communion or Confirmation.

R.H. also wondered about the requirement that those seeking Baptism be registered financial contributors for three months. It's too bad this is necessary, but how else does a pastor deal with people who only show up when a sacrament is needed? It's not "extortion"; it's an attempt to get people to recognize their obligation to be active and supportive members of a parish.

Q. Is it necessary that a sponsor for infant Baptism attend classes? — R.H., Illinois

A. Canon 851.2 of the Code of Canon Law says that "the parents of an infant who is to be baptized and likewise those who are to undertake the office of sponsor are to be properly instructed in the meaning of this sacrament and the obligations which are attached to it; personally or through others the pastor is to see to it that the parents are properly formed by pastoral directions and by common prayer, gathering several families together and where possible visiting them." One way of properly instructing parents and sponsors would be attendance at classes prior to the Baptism of a child.

Q. Does the Church permit the use of two godfathers at a Baptism? We are expecting our eighth child and have run

out of practicing Catholics to invite to be godparents. —
V.M.L., Massachusetts

A. First of all, congratulations on your generous cooperation
with God in bringing new life into the world. The Second
Vatican Council singled out for "special mention" couples like
you and your husband, "who with wise and common delib-
eration, and with a gallant heart, undertake to bring up suitably
even a relatively large family" (*Constitution on the Church in
the Modern World*, n. 50).

As for your question, the Church does not permit two male
godparents at Baptism, but it does allow only one godparent,
either male or female. Canon 873 of the Code of Canon Law
reads: "Only one male or one female sponsor or one of each
sex is to be employed." So you may have just a godfather for
the Baptism of your child. Or you could ask a previous godmother to act as a sponsor again.

**Q. Is it required that a child be given a Christian or a
saint's name at Baptism? If a married couple serves as
godparents and only one of them is a baptized Catholic,
can they both be considered as godparents to the child? —
J.M.T., California**

A. (1) Canon 855 says that "parents, sponsors, and the pastor
are to see that a name foreign to a Christian mentality is not
given." Thus, there is no specific requirement that the name of
a saint be given to the child, although one should be so the
child will have another advocate in Heaven to imitate and
venerate. The canon says only that the child not be given a
name that would be offensive to the Faith, e.g., Judas, Lucifer,
Hitler.

(2) Canon 874 says that to be a godparent, or sponsor, one
must have completed the 16th year and "be a Catholic who has
been confirmed and has already received the sacrament of the
Most Holy Eucharist and leads a life in harmony with the faith
and the role to be undertaken." Paragraph 2 of the same canon
says that "a baptized person who belongs to a non-Catholic
ecclesial community may not be admitted except as a witness
to baptism and together with a Catholic sponsor." Thus, the
baptized Catholic spouse would be the godparent of the child,
and the other spouse would be a witness.

**Q. Why would a priest allow non-Catholics or non-
practicing Catholics to be godparents at a Baptism or the
best man at a wedding? — P.D.F., Maryland**

A. We don't know why a priest would allow anyone but practicing Catholics to be godparents, but he is wrong if he does so knowingly. The point of having godparents is so they will help the baptized to lead a good life and to follow faithfully the teachings of the Catholic Church. How can one who is not a Catholic, or who does not faithfully practice the Catholic religion, fulfill this responsibility?

As for the best man at a wedding, he does not have to be a practicing Catholic or even a Catholic, for that matter. The Church's official witness at a marriage is the priest, whose responsibility is to ask for and receive the consent of both parties. The function of the other two witnesses — usually a maid of honor and a best man — is simply to attest that the marriage took place. They don't have to make any promises that they will assist the married couple in living up to the marriage laws of the Church, so there are not the same requirements as for baptismal sponsors.

Q. My six-year-old nephew was baptized in the Episcopalian Church as a baby. His three-year-old sister was recently baptized in the Catholic Church. I was godmother to the girl, but the man chosen as godfather was an atheist. I was shocked at this and also when the priest said that the Episcopalian child could receive all the Catholic sacraments. Are the two different churches one and the same? When I baptized my own children eight and ten years ago, I had to show proof that I was a practicing Catholic. Have the rules changed? — B.L., New York

A. No, the rules for the baptism of infants and young children haven't changed. Those rules, as spelled out in the Code of Canon Law, state that the parents and sponsors (godparents) "are to be properly instructed in the meaning of this sacrament and the obligations which are attached to it" (canon 851.2); that "there be a founded hope that the infant will be brought up in the Catholic religion" (canon 868.2); that "only one male or female sponsor or one of each sex is to be employed" (canon 873); and that a sponsor must be designated by the parents or one who takes their place, have completed the sixteenth year, "be a Catholic who has been confirmed and has already received the sacrament of the Most Holy Eucharist and leads a life in harmony with the faith and the role to be undertaken," and not be bound by any canonical penalties (canon 874).

Applying these rules to the situation you described, having an atheist as a godfather was a violation of canon 874 since he was not a practicing Catholic who was leading a life in harmony with the faith. If the priest was aware of this and still permitted it, he was wrong. He was also wrong in saying that an Episcopalian child could receive the same sacraments as his Catholic sister. The two churches are not one and the same and do not share exactly the same understanding of the sacraments. While baptism in the Episcopal Church is recognized as valid by the Catholic Church, the two churches do not share the same understanding of the other sacraments, and to suggest that sacraments in both churches are of equal value smacks of indifferentism, the fallacious theory that one religion is as good or true as another.

Q. My grandson is to be baptized soon. His parents were told the Baptism is merely a celebration of the child becoming a Christian. What happened to original sin? — C.E., California

Q. At the recent baptism of my grandchild, the priest said that "the Church has grown and no longer believes a child is born with original sin." Is this what is being taught in seminaries now? — M.B., New Jersey

A. Nothing happened to original sin except that some people don't talk about it anymore. However, it is an ancient teaching of the Church that infants should be baptized for the forgiveness of sins. The rite itself makes this clear in the following words from the prayer before the first anointing: "Set him/her free from original sin ...." That this is one of the effects of the sacrament is a teaching that was first stated by the Council of Carthage in the fifth century and then by the Council of Trent in the 16th century.

And as paragraphs 388-421 of the *Catechism of the Catholic Church* clearly demonstrate, the belief that every person is born with original sin is an essential truth of the Catholic Faith. Thus, the *Catechism* says that the Church, which has the mind of Christ, knows very well that it cannot tamper with the revelation of original sin without undermining the mystery of Christ (n. 389).

The *Catechism* (n. 403) also follows the lead of St. Paul in teaching that the overwhelming misery which oppresses us, and our inclination toward evil and death, cannot be understood apart from our connection with Adam's sin and the fact that he has transmitted to us a sin with which we are all born afflicted, a sin which is the death of our soul. Because of this certainty of faith, the Church baptizes for the remission of sins even tiny infants who have not yet committed any personal sin.

Q. Do I have any responsibility toward two infant grandchildren who may never be baptized because my sons have abandoned their Catholic Faith? Would it be all right for me to baptize them myself? — P.M., Florida

Q. My daughter, who goes to church regularly, has refused to have my granddaughter, who is almost four, baptized on the grounds that she knows of no suitable practicing Catholics (except me) to serve as sponsors. What can I say to change her mind? — D.J.M., Illinois

A. Other than the "gentle reminders" that she mentioned in her letter, and lots of prayers, there isn't much that P.M. can do. She cannot force her sons to recognize their duty if the Church means nothing to them. The only time that she would be justified in baptizing the grandchildren herself would be if they were in danger of death.

D.J.M.'s situation is more amenable to solution since his daughter goes to church regularly. Perhaps if she were to read the *Instruction on Infant Baptism*, which not only treats the origins and reasons for infant baptism, but also offers pastoral directives for some of the difficulties being raised today, she might be more receptive to having her child baptized. The document can be found in volume II of Austin Flannery's collection of post-conciliar documents entitled *Vatican Council II* (St. Paul Editions).

Regarding the daughter's feeling that there are no suitable sponsors or godparents, D.J.M. himself would seem to be a worthy candidate. Or the pastor of the parish could be asked to supply a sponsor. This sometimes happens in the case of a convert who doesn't know any local Catholics, but it can also happen with an infant or child whose parents have only recently arrived in the parish.

Q. The underlined paragraph in the enclosed parish bulletin about no baptisms during Lent is confusing. Can you check this out? — C.M.K., New York

A. The paragraph in question reads: "The Church discourages Baptism during Lent. The proper time for Baptism would be Easter Sunday or some date within the Easter season. Except for serious reasons, such as medical emergencies, we will not baptize until Lent is over. Lent is our desert experience, a time for retreat and reform, a time for longing for the renewing and life-giving waters which immerse us in the mystery of the Resurrection. Lent is the traditional time for baptismal preparation."

The Church does not discourage baptisms during Lent. It says in the Code of Canon Law that "parents are obliged to see to it that infants are baptized within the first weeks after birth" (c. 867.1). Delaying Baptism for the six-plus weeks of Lent would contradict the sense of that canon. As for the day or time for Baptism, the Code says: "Although baptism may be celebrated on any day, it is recommended that ordinarily it be celebrated on a Sunday or if possible at the Easter Vigil" (c. 856). There is no provision excluding the Sundays of Lent.

Q. Is it possible to baptize a baby in the womb if the mother were planning to abort the child? May confessions be made over the telephone? I have no access to an "orthodox" priest. — A.J.M., Colorado

A. No to both questions. In the first case, the water of Baptism has to be poured on the baby's head, and this would not be possible while the child is still in the womb. As for the second question, sins must be confessed in person to a priest for the sacrament to be valid. A moral presence between priest and penitent is an important part of the sacrament of Penance. The proper place for the sacrament is in a church or an oratory, although confessions may be heard elsewhere, such as a hospital, a nursing home, or one's own home, for "a just cause" (Canon 964).

Q. Can a person who is an active homosexual be baptized into the Catholic Church? — P.A., New York

A. Yes, if the person sincerely intends to stop his homosexual activity. This intention can be reaffirmed in the baptismal ceremony when the candidate is asked to respond "I do" to the following questions: "Do you reject sin so as to live in the freedom of God's children? Do you reject the glamour of evil, and refuse to be mastered by sin? Do you reject Satan, father of sin and prince of darkness?"

Q. When a baby is baptized, it does not give its assent to the sacrament or to any Christian doctrines. Can an unbaptized adult who believes in God but does not accept Church teaching about Christ and the sacraments nevertheless be validly baptized by a layman? The person I speak of, my wife, an unbaptized non-Catholic, knows my concern and is willing to let me baptize her. — J.A.J., Arizona

A. If your wife does not accept Church teaching about Christ or the sacraments (including Baptism?), then she should not be baptized. In the case of an infant, the assent to the sacrament and to Christian doctrines is given by the parents and godparents of the child, who are charged with seeing that he or she is raised in the Catholic Faith. However, the requirements for an adult are different: "To be baptized, it is required that an adult have manifested the will to receive baptism, be sufficiently instructed in the truths of the faith and in Christian obligations, and be tested in the Christian life by means of the catechumenate; the adult is also to be exhorted to have sorrow for personal sins" (canon 865.1).

We appreciate your concern for your wife's salvation, and we pray that your example and your discussions with her will lead her to seek Baptism after she has been "sufficiently instructed in the truths of the faith and in Christian obligations" and accepted them wholeheartedly.

Q. When I was confirmed thirteen years ago, I did not choose a biblical name or a saint's name. Was this wrong? If so, is there any way that I can change my Confirmation name? — M.K., Wisconsin

A. There is no requirement that one choose a biblical name or a saint's name for Confirmation, although it is certainly a good idea to do so since it gives the person another patron saint in Heaven to imitate and to call upon for assistance. What you did was not wrong, but you cannot change the name you chose.

Q. The Holy Thursday liturgy in our parish included the introduction to the parish of adults and younger people who were candidates for Baptism and Confirmation or just for Confirmation. Those that required Baptism were baptized by the celebrant, our pastor, and he then confirmed those requiring Confirmation, using the holy oils that had been blessed by our bishop. I thought that the sacrament of Confirmation was reserved to bishops. — B.H.H., Illinois

Q. We have been advised that the bishop won't be at our parish to confirm our children. We have also learned that for many of the parishes around us the bishop has given the priest this duty. Is this corrrect? — M.W., Iowa

A. Before answering these questions, we are puzzled that the welcoming of new people into the Church took place on Holy Thursday in B.H.H.'s parish. This is supposed to occur at the Easter Vigil on Holy Saturday.

Regarding the queries, canon 882 says that "the ordinary minister of confirmation is the bishop; a presbyter [priest] who has this faculty by virtue of either the universal law or a special concession of competent authority also confers this sacrament validly." The bishop may give this faculty to a pastor who baptizes an adult or admits a baptized adult into full communion (canon 883.2) or to a priest "if necessity requires" (canon 884.1). Cases of necessity would include the illness of the bishop, his unavoidable absence from the diocese for a long period of time, or the need for Confirmation in a large number of parishes.

With at most half a dozen bishops even in big dioceses, and Confirmations taking place in scores of parishes at the Easter Vigil, it is obvious that the bishop would have to give pastors permission to confer the sacrament on that occasion. We suspect that M.W.'s bishop has also delegated the responsibility for Confirmation because his schedule does not allow him be there.

Q. In our diocese, the bishop is implementing the reception of Confirmation at the same age as First Holy Communion (age 7 or 8), and Confirmation will be administered by a priest instead of the bishop. It is my understanding that the reason Confirmation is separated from Baptism is to allow ample opportunity for the bishop to administer the sacrament. In addition, the bishop is not to delegate the responsibility readily. If I allow my child to be confirmed by my priest, am I guilty of assisting my bishop in defiance of Rome? — J.P., Pennsylvania

A. Regarding the bishop delegating Confirmation to a priest, see the previous reply. As for the age of the confirmandi, the Code of Canon Law says that "the sacrament of Confirmation is to be conferred on the faithful at about the age of discretion unless the conference of bishops determines another age or there is danger of death or in the judgment of the minister a grave cause urges otherwise" (c. 891).

The age of discretion is about seven, but the bishops of the United States have since 1984 left the age of Confirmation up to the individual bishop in his diocese, and the age for the sacrament has ranged from seven to 18. On February 8, 1994, the Vatican's Congregation for Bishops ratified that range of ages for the United States and gave the U.S. bishops five years, until July 1, 1999, to come up with a more specific age for the ordinary reception of the sacrament.

So J.P.'s bishop is following canon law and the policy of the American bishops in permitting reception of Confirmation at the same age as reception of First Communion.

Q. In a recent column, you expressed surprise that the sacraments of Baptism and Confirmation were administered in an Illinois parish on Holy Thursday. I too am puzzled as this has become the practice in my parish. I find nothing in the rubrics of Holy Thursday which give rise to this possibility. Please determine if authority exists for this. — J.E.W., South Carolina

A. We can't find any authority for this practice. According to the *Rite of Christian Initiation of Adults*, "the celebration of the sacraments of Christian initiation should take place at the Easter Vigil itself" (n. 23). However, "it is permissible, but only for serious pastoral needs (for example, if there are a great many people to be baptized), to choose a day other than the Easter Vigil or Easter Sunday, but preferably one during the Easter season, to celebrate the sacraments of initiation" (n. 26).

The purification and enlightenment phase of the RCIA process, including the Rite of Election and the Scrutinies, is specifically targeted for Lent so as to culminate at the Easter Vigil. It makes no sense to celebrate the sacraments of initiation on Holy Thursday. Why not wait two more nights and do it at the proper time?

Q. You recently treated a case where a pastor refused Confirmation to a child taught at home. What about a case where the bishop refuses to confirm the child taught at home by the parents under the guidance of the pastor simply because the child did not take the diocesan program? What can the parents do? What can the pastor do? — Name Withheld, Bermuda

A. It is difficult for us to answer this question without knowing all the circumstances. Every baptized person not yet confirmed can and should receive the sacrament of Confirmation so as to complete the process of Christian initiation, says the *Catechism of the Catholic Church* (n. 1306), so a bishop would have to have a very good reason to refuse the sacrament. Why was the child in question not prepared in the diocesan program? Is that program defective in some way? You say that the preparation was done under the pastor's guidance. Why wouldn't that be sufficient for the bishop? Is there some conflict between the bishop and the pastor?

If the preparation was done according to the rules of the Church, but the bishop insists that all confirmandi come through the diocesan program, then you will have to abide by his decision or seek Confirmation through another bishop, which may be difficult to do.

Q. We are looking for some good books for a ninth and tenth grade Confirmation program. Can you recommend any? — R.L.K., Rhode Island

A. Yes, we can. We have had very good results with *Catholicism and Reason* (Prow Books) by Hayes, Hayes, and Drummey in the ninth grade, and *One Faith, One Lord* (Sadlier) by Msgr. John F. Barry in the tenth grade. *Catholicism and Reason* deals with the Creed and features a special emphasis on apologetics. It presents in popular language the essential beliefs of the Catholic Faith and the reasons why we hold those beliefs. The material in the book is fun to teach, and it is suitable for high school and college students, as well as for adult education.

One Faith, One Lord offers an excellent survey of Catholicism, beginning with the Bible, Creation, and the Fall and covering the Incarnation, the Redemption, and the Holy Spirit; the Church, the Sacraments, and the Mass; the Ten Commandments, the Beatitudes, the works of mercy, and the laws of the Church; the last things (death, judgment, Purgatory, Heaven, and Hell); and the Blessed Virgin.

Q. Why do we confess our sins to a priest? Why not confess them directly to God? — P.M., Wisconsin

A. There are several reasons. First, because that is what Jesus wants us to do. On Easter Sunday night, our Lord told the Apostles, His first priests: "Receive the Holy Spirit. If you forgive men's sins, they are forgiven them; if you hold them bound, they are held bound" (John 20:22-23). Since "hold them bound" means not to forgive them, the Apostles, and their successors, could not know what sins to forgive or not to forgive unless they were first told the sins by the penitent.

Second, telling our sins to a priest teaches us humility, something we would not learn if we confessed our sins privately to God. Third, we receive graces from the sacrament of Penance. Fourth, by absolving us of our sins, the priest, who is representing Christ, gives us the assurance that our sins have been forgiven. And fifth, the priest can give us some sound advice on how to avoid sin in the future, while the person praying in private receives no helpful instructions or necessary counsel.

In his 1984 statement on *Reconciliation and Penance*, Pope John Paul II urged Catholics to confess their sins often to a priest, saying that it would be "foolish ... to disregard the means of grace and salvation which the Lord has provided and ... to claim to receive forgiveness while doing without the sacrament which was instituted by Christ precisely for forgiveness."

Q. With First Communions coming up soon, could you give some references for the Church teaching that First Confession should precede First Communion? — R.S., Illinois

A. Around 1970, parishes in different parts of the country began delaying First Penance until fourth grade or later on the grounds that too early Confession could be psychologically disturbing to young children. On April 11, 1971, the Sacred Congregation for the Clergy, which was headed by John Cardinal Wright, called for a return to the traditional practice of putting Confession before First Communion. In the Appendix to the *General Catechetical Directory*, the SCC said that any concern about psychological disturbance could be alleviated "by a humane and prudent catechetical preparation."

Because some parishes were still delaying First Penance in 1973, the Vatican on May 24, 1973, issued a *Declaration on First Confession and First Communion*. The final paragraph of that brief document said:

"After mature consideration and having taken account of the views of the Bishops, the Sacred Congregation for the Discipline of the Sacraments and for the Clergy declares by this present document, with the approval of the Sovereign Pontiff, Paul VI, that these experiments, which have lasted for two years up to the end of the school year 1972-1973, should cease and that everybody everywhere should conform to the decree *Quam Singulari*." (*Quam Singulari* was the document issued by Pope St. Pius X in 1910 that said children might receive the sacraments of Penance and the Eucharist as soon as they had attained the age of reason, which was considered to be about the age of seven.)

In *Sharing the Light of Faith*, the National Catechetical Directory for Catholics of the United States published in 1979, the bishops of this country said that "the sacrament of Reconciliation normally should be celebrated prior to the reception of First Communion" (n. 126). The *Catechism of the Catholic Church* reiterated this view: "Children must go to the sacrament of Penance before receiving Holy Communion for the first time" (n. 1457). One exception to the norm would be some special-needs children.

Q. My son's school has First Communion in 2nd grade, but First Confession is anywhere between 2nd and 4th grade (and it's a communal Penance service). I wrote to our archdiocesan education center and inquired about canon 914 — First Eucharist is to be "preceded by sacramental confession." They responded by quoting *The Code of Canon Law: A Text and Commentary*, which says that Confession is not necessary before First Communion, but it should be available to those who need or desire it. Is their response correct? Does the *Commentary* book they quote from have an imprimatur? Am I worrying needlessly that First Confession is a communal Penance service with no individual penances? — D.L.O., Minnesota

A. As noted above, two Vatican congregations and four Church documents have since 1971 reiterated that children should normally receive the Sacrament of Penance/Reconciliation before receiving their First Communion. A possible exception to this rule would be special-needs children whose sense of right and wrong will develop more slowly than usual.

Technically speaking, second-graders do not need First Penance before receiving First Communion since they are not capable of committing mortal sins. With proper instruction, however, they are capable of understanding sin and forgiveness (just as they are capable of understanding that Jesus is present in the Holy Eucharist), and it is the mind of the Church to have First Penance precede First Communion. It makes good pastoral sense to introduce children to the sacrament of Penance when their sins are not serious rather than to wait until they are older and more reluctant to confess more serious sins.

As for a communal service for First Penance, we have no problem with that if it means communal prayers and examination of conscience, followed by individual confession and absolution for the children and then a communal prayer for their penance. That appears to be what your archdiocesan education center is talking about.

The *Code of Canon Law: A Text and Commentary* has an imprimatur from Archbishop Peter L. Gerety of Newark. The 1,152-page book contains the entire revised Code, along with a commentary on each of the 1,752 canons by 23 scholars who were chosen by the Canon Law Society of America. The comments on canon 914 are those of Fr. John M. Huels, O.S.M., with whom we sometimes agree and sometimes disagree. In this case, we disagree with his statement that the right of children to the sacrament of Penance can be served best when the opportunity for Penance before First Communion is provided only "for those children who need or desire the sacrament."

Q. Does the Church still require that we receive the sacrament of Penance at least once a year? Can we receive absolution from the priest if we have committed no sins since our last Confession? — D.B., California

A. It is one of the commandments or precepts of the Church that Catholics must receive the sacrament of Penance at least once a year if they have committed a mortal sin. But if a person is not conscious of having committed a mortal sin, then annual Confession is not mandatory. Canon 989 of the Code of Canon Law makes this clear by saying that "after having attained the age of discretion, each of the faithful is bound by an obligation faithfully to confess *serious* sins at least once a year" (emphasis added). It should be noted, however, that the Church has long encouraged the faithful to frequent the sacrament of Penance even when only venial sins have been committed.

"Though the Church knows and teaches that venial sins are forgiven in other ways too — for instance, by acts of sorrow, works of charity, prayer, penitential rites — she does not cease to remind everyone of the special usefulness of the sacramental moment for these sins too," Pope John Paul said in his 1984 apostolic exhortation *Reconciliation and Penance.* "The frequent use of the sacrament — to which some categories of the faithful are in fact held — strengthens the awareness that even minor sins offend God and harm the Church, the Body of Christ" (n. 32).

This also answers D.B.'s second question. All of us commit at least venial sins from one Confession to the next. If we tell these minor sins to the priest, he can give us absolution for them.

Q. Is it true that canon law states that venial sins are to be confessed? — A.D.H., New York

A. No, the Code of Canon Law does not say this. While canon 988.1 says that Catholics are "obliged" to confess all serious sins committed after Baptism, section 2 of that canon says only that "it is to be recommended to the Christian faithful that venial sins also be confessed."

The *Rite of Penance* makes this same distinction, saying first that "the faithful must confess to a priest each and every grave sin that they remember after an examination of conscience," but going on to say that "the frequent and careful celebration of this sacrament is also very useful as a remedy for venial sins. This is not a mere ritual repetition or psychological exercise, but a serious striving to perfect the grace of baptism so that, as we bear in our body the death of Jesus Christ, his life may be seen in us ever more clearly" (n. 7).

Q. What is meant by a Confession of Devotion? — K.C., New York

A. Technically speaking, Catholics are obliged to receive the sacrament of Penance or Reconciliation only if they are conscious of having committed a mortal sin (canon 988.1). However, the Church also encourages Catholics to confess venial sins, too (canon 988.2), and this is what is known as a devotional Confession.

Without being strictly necessary, says the *Catechism of the Catholic Church* (n. 1458), confession of everyday faults (venial sins) is nevertheless strongly recommended by the Church. Indeed, the *Catechism* says, the regular confession of our venial sins helps us to form our conscience, fight against evil tendencies, let ourselves be healed by Christ, and progress in the life of the Spirit. By receiving more frequently through this sacrament the gift of the Father's mercy, it says, we are spurred to be merciful as He is merciful.

Q. If a person confesses what he or she believes to be a serious or mortal sin, and the priest in turn says that the matter confessed is no longer considered a sin, is that a valid Confession? — W.B., California

A. Without knowing the specific sin confessed, it is difficult to answer this question. We can understand a priest telling a penitent that some thought, word, action or omission is not grave matter, or that it was not a mortal sin for the person involved because he or she did not have sufficient knowledge of the gravity of the matter or did not fully consent to it, but we wonder what sin is no longer considered a sin.

There are priests today who do claim, erroneously, that certain acts — artificial contraception, homosexual behavior, fornication, even abortion — are not always gravely sinful, but this is contrary to the law of God as taught by the Church. We don't know of anything once considered to be a serious sin that is no longer a sin, except perhaps eating meat on Friday. If an action has long been against the law of God, and the law of God never changes, then how can an evil action suddenly become not evil anymore?

In any case, if a penitent has doubts about advice received in the sacrament of Penance, he or she should compare what the priest said with what the Church teaches through the Pope and those bishops and priests loyal to him, as well as through the *Catechism of the Catholic Church*, and, if that confessor's advice is out of line with what the Church is teaching, then the penitent should consult another priest.

Q. Many years ago, I received Communion while in the state of mortal sin. I have since then been to Confession many times and have at least twice said that I had received Communion unworthily. Am I in trouble or have I taken care of that unworthy Communion? — M.B., New Jersey

A. If you have twice confessed that you once received Communion while in the state of mortal sin, and received absolution from a priest, then you are not in any trouble with God. You have expressed sorrow for the unworthy Communion and have received God's forgiveness through the priest. There is no need for any further concern on your part. Once past sins have been forgiven, there is no need for us to dwell on them anymore. Put this behind you and continue to perform the good works you mentioned in your letter.

Q. I frequently suffer from scruples and have been avoiding the Sacrament of Penance because I don't know how to deal with a long list of possible mortal sins. What do I need to tell the priest so I can be certain of walking out of the confessional in the state of grace? — Name and State Withheld

A. The conditions for a mortal sin are grave matter, sufficient reflection or understanding, and full consent of the will. If one of these three conditions is lacking, there is no mortal sin. What you need to do is to tell the priest of your scruples and then tell him the sins you think you have committed and the circumstances surrounding them. He will help you determine whether they were mortal sins or not. Once you have stated your sins candidly and expressed sorrow for them, listened to the advice of the priest and his words of absolution, and performed the required penance, then you can be certain that you are leaving the church in the state of grace.

Q. I was taught in a Jesuit college that a mortal sin honestly forgotten in Confession was forgiven but had to be confessed in one's next Confession. In the enclosed column from *Our Sunday Visitor*, however, it says that "such sins that are not called to mind at the time of Confession are forgiven in the absolution the priest bestows and do not have to be confessed at a later date." I would welcome your comments on this very practical problem. — B.J.S., Missouri

A. What you learned many years ago in college is still true: honestly forgotten mortal sins are forgiven, but they should be confessed the next time a person goes to the sacrament of Penance in order to submit them directly to "the keys" or the power of the Church. Canon 988.1 of the 1983 Code of Canon Law has this to say on the subject: "A member of the Christian faithful is obliged to confess in kind and in number all serious sins committed after Baptism and not yet directly remitted through the keys of the Church nor acknowledged in individual Confession, of which one is conscious after diligent examination of conscience."

The following excerpt from the commentary on Canons 988 and 989 in the 1983 Code makes clear the obligation to confess honestly forgotten mortal sins:

"The reference, unchanged from Canon 902 of the former [1917] law, to sins 'not yet directly remitted through the keys of the Church,' i.e., through the power and ministry of the Church, indicates the precise nature of the confessional obligation. The divine forgiveness may indeed have taken place, and the contrition of the penitent may have been such that he or she has indeed been pardoned by God. Nevertheless, the obligation remains to submit oneself to the power and ministry of the Church in the sacrament of Reconciliation. Moreover, although grave sins forgotten in Confession are indirectly remitted, the canon indicates that these must be confessed when remembered and thus be submitted for 'direct remission.'"

Q. I am in the habit of attending daily Mass and, in the event of a mortal sin, say on a Monday, I make an act of perfect contrition, assign myself an interim penance which I perform until Saturday Reconciliation, and continue to receive Communion daily. Is this an acceptable practice? Please recommend an act of perfect contrition. — R.J.F., New York

A. While it is good practice to say an Act of Contrition after having committed a mortal sin and before one has a chance for sacramental Confession, it is not acceptable to assign oneself an interim penance and continue to receive Communion daily until Saturday. Not even the Pope can forgive his own sins on an interim basis. There are two possible options here. The first is to refrain from receiving Holy Communion until Saturday. The second is to ask the priest to hear your Confession before Mass any weekday morning or at some other time during the day. You don't have to wait until Saturday for the sacrament of Penance.

Any Act of Contrition would suffice as an act of perfect contrition. It is not so much the words that matter as the sincerity of our sorrow for having offended God. We must be sorry for our sins because of our love for God, not because of our fear of punishment, in order to make an act of perfect contrition. It should be noted, however, that making an act of perfect contrition is not that easy since it includes a certain detachment from all sin.

Q. Why is the Act of Contrition omitted from Confession? I have had the door slammed in my face whenever I try to say it. — C.J., Wisconsin

Q. When I go to Confession, my pastor gives me the penance and goes immediately into absolution without giving me a chance to say an Act of Contrition. I am sorry for my sins. Does that mean that all of those Confessions were invalid and the sins not forgiven? — F.Z., Ohio

Q. In our diocese, some priests do not require an Act of Contrition when receiving the sacrament of Penance. Is the confession invalid if there is no Act of Contrition? What can I do if the priest won't go along with me saying an Act of Contrition? — M.D.H., Iowa

A. According to the revised *Rite of Penance*, after the person has confessed his sins and the priest has imposed an act of penance or satisfaction, "the penitent manifests his contrition and resolution to begin a new life by means of a prayer for God's pardon. It is desirable that this prayer should be based on the words of Scripture."

Later in the same document, under the headline "Prayer of the Penitent and Absolution," the rite suggests several prayers by which the penitent can express his sorrow. The first prayer resembles the traditional Act of Contrition that many of us learned as children and that is posted on the walls of some confessionals, and the other prayers are excerpts from Scripture.

In answer to the specific questions, an act of sorrow is necessary for one's confession to be valid, and that sorrow can be manifested in various ways, including an Act of Contrition. But a prayer of some kind must be said, according to the *Rite of Penance*, and it is wrong for a priest to shut off a penitent before that prayer is said. If the priest won't listen, the penitent can recite the Act of Contrition after leaving the confessional and before performing the penance prescribed, thus preserving the "moral unity" of the sacrament.

Q. During Confession a priest gave me absolution in his own words. Does he have to say the correct absolution prayer for the sacrament to be valid? — M..C., Kentucky

A. Every sacrament has a specific matter and form that must be observed if the sacrament is to be valid. One cannot, for example, use Coke instead of water in Baptism, or baptize someone only in the name of Jesus. In the sacrament of Penance, the correct formula for absolution is:

"God, the Father of mercies, through the death and resurrection of his Son has reconciled the world to himself and sent the Holy Spirit among us for the forgiveness of sins; through the ministry of the Church may God give you pardon and peace, and I absolve you from your sins, in the name of the Father, and of the Son, and of the Holy Spirit."

If a priest adds some words to this formula, that would not affect the validity of the sacrament. But if he uses some other words instead of this formula, then the validity of the sacrament would be in doubt. As Fr. Peter Stravinskas has said, "Tampering with sacramental formulas is foolish, prideful, and dangerous."

Q. Once in a while the priest at Mass gives general absolution with no mention of confessing any mortal sins privately. Is this a valid Confession? — I.M., California

Q. In my parish, which is within six miles of three other parishes, we had a Penance service with the readings, prayers and examination of conscience. My pastor said that because there were so many people present, he would give us general absolution. Was the absolution valid, or does a person with serious sins have to go to Confession privately? — J.H., Ohio

A. No, the confessions were not valid in either case. Canon 960 of the Code of Canon Law says that "individual and integral confession and absolution constitute the only ordinary way by which the faithful person who is aware of serious sin is reconciled with God and with the Church." General absolution can be given only in cases of grave necessity. Canon 961 says that would be when "the danger of death is imminent and there is not time for the priest or priests to hear the confession of individual penitents" (e.g., soldiers going into battle), or when "in the light of the number of penitents a supply of confessors is not readily available rightly to hear the confessions of individuals within a suitable time so that the penitents are forced to be deprived of sacramental grace or Holy Communion for a long time through no fault of their own." (See also paragraphs 1483 and 1484 of the *Catechism of the Catholic Church.*)

J.H's pastor was wrong to give general absolution not only because there was no grave necessity involved (he could have invited priests from neighboring parishes to help with his Penance service), but also because it is up to the diocesan bishop to decide whether the conditions are present for the use of general absolution.

In order for the general absolution to be valid (although illicit), any person in serious sin would have had to be sorry for his sins, make an Act of Contrition prior to the general absolution, and intend to confess individually his serious sins "as soon as there is an opportunity to do so before receiving another general absolution unless a just cause intervenes" (Canon 963). A pastor who had permission from his bishop to give general absolution would be required to instruct the penitents present about these conditions for valid absolution.

Q. Recently we attended a Penance service that had at least 10 priests participating and about 800 people in the church. The pastor instructed the congregation to line up in each of the aisles and, when they got to the priest hearing confessions at the end of the aisle, to tell him our worst fault. It was like an assembly line without any privacy. No one knelt down; both priest and penitent stood up. Was this legitimate or was the pastor breaking or bending the rules? — J.R.B., New Jersey

A. The pastor may not have broken any rules — he didn't, for example, give general absolution with no individual confession of sins — but he sure bent them a bit. There is nothing wrong with Penance services, particularly around Christmas and Easter, if they are properly conducted, but it was not right to rush people through the sacrament in assembly-line fashion. Nor was it right for the pastor to say that since most of those in the congregation were not really big sinners, it would be enough for them to state only their worst fault. Confession should be integral, i.e., all serious sins must be confessed.

The pastor had no way of knowing the condition of each of the 800 souls in the church. Some may indeed have had only one bad fault to confess, but surely there were others with perhaps many serious sins; and there may have been still others who had not received the sacrament in years and who needed more time with the priest than was made available under that format. Persons in the latter situation probably should not come to a Penance service for that very reason.

This is all part of an unfortunate trend in recent years toward a trivialization of sin and of the ordinary means provided by Christ and His Church to have our sins forgiven. There is very little talk from the pulpit about sin, or about the importance of receiving the sacrament of Penance frequently, even though the Holy Father has urged a strong emphasis on both. With evil so rampant in society today, there is a need for more preaching about sin and for more priests like St. John Vianney, who spent 16 to 18 hours a day in the confessional. He, too, had long lines of penitents, but he did not suggest that each person state only his or her worst fault and then be on their way.

Q. What is your opinion of the "Communal Reconciliation Service" mentioned in the enclosed article from our church bulletin? — A.U., Illinois

A. The article says in part that "the communal service allows us to celebrate together God's generous forgiveness and healing together in song, in readings from Scripture, in homily reflection, and with a mutual awareness of our common sinfulness and need of the Lord's healing. We, together in prayer, express our sorrow for our sin and our purpose of amendment — our desire to really put our best efforts at changing for the better." So far, so good.

Problems arise, however, when the article goes on to say: "Then, the service allows for the persons desiring to receive the sacrament to approach the priests individually but in a much simplified manner. They, ever so briefly, name their primary sins, and the priest simply extends absolution over each individual. (The homily and communal reflection take the place of any individual counsel the priest might give.) The individual penitent then returns to his place for prayer. We walk away feeling closer to the Lord and to one another in the reconciling love of Jesus."

According to the *Rite of Reconciliation of Several Penitents with Individual Confession and Absolution,* the singing, praying, reading from Scripture, homily, and examination of conscience are to be followed by individual confession, where each penitent tells his or her sins to a priest and "receives and accepts a fitting act of satisfaction and is absolved. After hearing the confession and offering suitable counsel, the priest extends his hands over the penitent's head (or at least extends his right hand) and gives him absolution. Everything else which is customary in individual confession is omitted" (n. 55).

This is quite different from stating one's primary sins "ever so briefly" and missing out on the individual counsel that some penitents may need very badly if they have been away from the sacrament for a long time. Communal Penance services are fine, but they must be conducted according to the norms of the Church.

Q. What are the benefits of receiving Extreme Unction and is there an obligation to receive it? — A.D., New Jersey

A. The sacrament formerly known as Extreme Unction is now called the Anointing of the Sick to indicate that it is not just for those in immediate danger of death, but for any one of the faithful who "begins to be in danger of death from sickness or old age (Vatican II, *Constitution on the Sacred Liturgy,* n. 73). It may be celebrated individually or communally.

Those to be anointed, according to *Hominum Dolores,* the 1972 instruction on the sacrament by the Sacred Congregation for Divine Worship, include persons facing surgery necessitated by a dangerous illness, elderly people who are weak but not dangerously ill, and sick children who are mature enough to be comforted by the sacrament. A sick person may be anointed more than once if he recovers and then becomes ill again, or if the danger becomes greater in the course of the illness.

A Catholic is not obliged to receive the Anointing of the Sick, but it would be foolish for a sick person not to take advantage of this special source of God's grace and help given to us by Jesus Himself (Mark 6:13 and James 5:14-16). Even if the anointing does not restore the sick person to health, it can have many good effects.

Those effects or benefits of the sacrament were enumerated in the *Catechism of the Catholic Church* (n. 1532):

— the uniting of the sick person to the passion of Christ, for his own good and that of the whole Church;

— the strengthening, peace, and courage to endure in a Chris-

tian manner the sufferings of illness or old age;
— the forgiveness of sins, if the sick person was not able to obtain it through the sacrament of Penance;
— the restoration of health, if it is conducive to the salvation of his soul;
— the preparation for passing over to eternal life.

Q. Would you comment on the enclosed clipping from a parish bulletin on the Anointing of the Sick? It seems that this is an abuse of the sacrament. — F.V.K., Connecticut
A. The item in the parish bulletin invited parishioners to a "special Mass of Healing and Anointing of the Sick" on a Sunday morning. It said that "any parishioner age 65 and over should receive this anointing. Any parishioner of any age experiencing a chronic illness that may be physical, mental, or spiritual in nature may receive the Sacrament of the Sick. Any parishioners who are preparing for surgery may also receive this sacrament. The Mass of Healing and Anointing of the Sick would be a very good opportunity to bring to church any and all shut-ins or homebound parishioners."

The Church document *Pastoral Care of the Sick: Rites of Anointing and Viaticum*, which was approved in 1982 by the National Conference of Catholic Bishops and confirmed that same year by the Sacred Congregation for the Sacraments and Divine Worship, provides for the sacrament of Anointing to be celebrated within Mass (nos. 131-148). It says that "this rite may be used to anoint a number of people within the same celebration (see nos. 108-110). It is especially appropriate for large gatherings of a diocese, parish, or society for the sick, or for pilgrimages" (n. 132).

There is, however, a note of caution in paragraph 108, which says that the diocesan bishop or his delegate "should ensure that all disciplinary norms concerning anointing are observed, as well as the norms for pastoral preparation and liturgical celebration. In particular, the practice of indiscriminately anointing numbers of people on these occasions simply because they are ill or have reached an advanced age is to be avoided. Only those whose health is seriously impaired by sickness or old age are proper subjects for the sacrament."

We can see a possible abuse of this paragraph in the section of the bulletin notice that says any parishioner over 65, or anyone suffering from a chronic illness, ought to be anointed. That seems to us to constitute the practice of indiscriminate anointing that the document says should be avoided.

Q. I am a 26-year-old male who would like to know what the procedure is to become a priest. — S.C., Massachusetts

A. You can start the procedure yourself by telling a priest whom you know and respect that you think you might have a religious vocation. Ask him for assistance and advice on how best to pursue this call from God.

If you are a high school graduate, you will need a college degree to apply to a major seminary. The diocese in which you live, and most large religious orders, can provide a college education at a modest cost, or you could undertake college studies yourself, preferably at a reliable Catholic institution.

If you are a college graduate, you must first try to discern where you think God is leading you, i.e., to a parish-centered/educational apostolate or to a community-oriented vocation. Then, you should contact the vocation director for the diocese or for whatever religious order interests you. You do not have to attend a seminary in your own diocese.

Typically, the director will want to see your baptismal record, your parents' marriage certificate, an evaluation of you by your pastor, and the results of psychological tests the diocese or order will administer. There is also an interview process.

As for the qualifications to become a priest, you must want to dedicate your life wholeheartedly to Christ, you must be a morally sound person with no evil habits or nasty character traits, you must enjoy normal good health, and you must possess average intelligence and a willingness to study.

We applaud your openness to God's call, and we pray that you will attain your vocation to the priesthood.

Q. As a conservative Catholic who is interested in the priesthood, I'm nervous that I might be sent to a liberal seminary. How are seminarians placed? Does the seminarian have any say on the matter? — D.W.W., Kentucky

A. Placement of seminarians may vary from diocese to diocese, but it is usually the bishop's decision, with advice from his vocations director. Most bishops have one or two seminaries where they habitually send candidates for the priesthood, either in their own diocese, if there is a seminary, or elsewhere. The bishop's preference can be discovered in advance by talking to the vocations director or to priests in the diocese. D.W.W. should seek the advice of a priest in whom he has confidence.

Q. I have heard that if the deceased parents of a young Catholic man were not married in the Church, that man can

never be ordained a Catholic priest. Is this true? — L.V., New York

A. No, it is not true. There are certain irregularities or impediments that can prevent a man from receiving Holy Orders, but the marital situation of his parents is not one of them. According to canon 1041 of the Code of Canon Law, reception of Orders is prohibited to a person who suffers from insanity or some other psychic defect; who has committed apostasy, heresy, or schism; who has attempted marriage when he was impeded from doing so; who has committed voluntary homicide or procured an effective abortion; who has mutilated himself or another person or has attempted suicide; or who has abused sacred Orders.

These are perpetual impediments to ordination. Simple impediments that would bar a man from receiving Orders (canon 1042) include marriage, holding public office or certain administrative positions (see canons 285 and 286), and being only a recent convert to the Catholic Church. These latter impediments can be dispensed (1) if the wife consents, seeks admission to a religious institute, or promises not to interfere with her husband's priestly vocation; (2) if the candidate gives up the forbidden offices or duties; or (3) if the candidate practices his Catholic Faith for a period of time, say, several years.

Q. Is it true that canon law prohibits males born out of wedlock from becoming Catholic priests? — P.R.D., Virginia, and B.E.D., Texas

A. Canon 1363 of the 1917 Code of Canon Law forbade the entry into the seminary of illegitimate males, but there is no such canon in the 1983 Code. So being born out of wedlock is no longer an impediment to ordination.

Q. Can someone with a homosexual orientation become a priest or Religious provided that they are willing to live a celibate life? — S.G., Pennsylvania

Q. Does the Catholic Church knowingly ordain homo-sexuals? My reading of Pope Paul VI's encyclical on priestly celibacy (*Sacerdotalis Caelibatus*) seems to rule out such ordinations. — P.A.R., Virginia

A. Let us quote two sentences from the encyclical on priestly celibacy that were underlined by P.A.R. They appear in section 64 of the document, which bears the subhead "Unsuitable Candidates for the Priesthood." The sentences read: "Those who are discovered to be unfit — either for physical, psychological, or moral reasons — should be quickly removed from the path to the priesthood .... The life of the celibate priest, which engages the whole man so totally and so delicately, excludes in fact those of insufficient pyschophysical and moral balance. Nor should anyone pretend that grace supplies for the defects of nature in such a man."

The sentences do not mention homosexuality and therefore cannot be said to rule out the ordination of homosexuals. Of course there has to be a distinction made between men with a homosexual orientation, but who are living chaste and celibate lives, and men who are engaging in genital sexual activity with other men. People in the latter group could not be ordained because they are taking part in acts that the Church has condemned as "intrinsically disordered" (*Declaration on Certain Problems of Sexual Ethics*, n. 8).

We know that there is great concern about active homosexuals in the priesthood, and we would never advocate the ordination of a practicing homosexual. We also doubt if more than a few persons with a homosexual orientation, who are living celibate lives, could pass a thorough and honest psychological screening process for the priesthood. But Fr. John Harvey, the founder of Courage, who has worked wonders with homosexuals seeking to lead a chaste life, makes clear in his book, *The Homosexual Person* (Ignatius Press), that men and women can overcome the slavery of homosexual practice and lead vibrant spiritual lives.

Q. Why doesn't the Pope change the Church's rule on mandatory celibacy and let there be married priests to solve the lack of vocations? Other churches have married clergy. — M.C., New York

A. If you look at churches that allow married priests, you will find that their vocations are not increasing either. So letting priests marry is not the answer to the clergy shortage. Priestly celibacy, which Pope Paul VI called "a brilliant jewel," has been practiced in the Catholic Church since the fourth century for a number of reasons.

First, it follows the example of Christ Himself, who promised great rewards to those who have "given up home, brothers or sisters, father or mother, wife or children or property for my sake" (Matthew 19:29). Second, it allows priests to focus exclusively on serving Christ and the Church, without at the same time worrying about wives and children. They are called to a higher fatherhood and have many more "spiritual children" than in an ordinary family. Married clergy in other religions, torn between their own families and their congregations, have expressed appreciation for the celibacy required of Catholic priests.

Third, it provides space and time for serious prayer and development of a deep bond with Christ, whom the priest is called to share with the world. Fourth, it is a foreshadowing of Heaven where there will be no marriage. And fifth, it is a wonderful example of commitment and sacrifice under difficult circumstances; it gives credibility to priests who ask their people also to make great sacrifices for God.

It is important to remember that no one is required to become a priest; that celibacy is not forced on priests but is freely chosen by them after years of training, reflection, and prayer; that celibacy is no more responsible for unfaithful priests than marriage is responsible for unfaithful husbands and wives; and that a great number of priests, Religious, and laity all over the world are today living inspiring lives of voluntary and consecrated celibacy.

Q. A deacon in my parish gave a homily about the possibility of married priests. When I spoke to him after Mass, he said that St. Peter was married, that there are married priests now, and that there is a lot of discussion on this matter, so maybe the Church will permit married priests. Would you please comment? — M.J., Virginia

A. Yes, St. Peter was married, but celibacy has been partially observed since the fourth century and generally practiced by priests of the Western Church since the 12th century. Those Catholic priests who are married today received a special dispensation because they came into the Church, with their wives, mostly from the Episcopal Church. This exception to the rule of celibacy, the Sacred Congregation for the Doctrine of the Faith said in April 1981, "should not be understood as implying any change in the Church's conviction of the value of priestly celibacy, which will remain the rule for future candidates for the priesthood from this group."

There may be a lot of discussion of married priests today, but it is idle and divisive chatter since two Holy Fathers have clearly stated that the matter is closed. The pertinent statements are those of Pope Paul VI (*On Priestly Celibacy*), dated June 24, 1967, and Pope John Paul II in his letter to the priests of the world, dated April 6, 1979.

Q. We read of priests leaving the ministry and getting married. Just what is their status? Do they still have the power to change bread and wine into the Body and Blood of Christ? — J.L.N., New Jersey

A. A man who receives the sacrament of Holy Orders is a priest forever, but he may go through a process called laicization, which removes him from the clerical state and restores him to the lay state. Accomplished only for the most serious reasons by means of a rescript from the Apostolic See, this process means that while the man still has the powers of the priesthood, he can no longer function as a priest, except in an emergency situation, such as hearing the Confession of a person who is dying. If the man wants to return to the clerical state, he must obtain the permission of the Apostolic See.

The permanent character of Holy Orders has been summarized by the *Catechism of the Catholic Church.* According to the *Catechism* (n. 1583), someone validly ordained can, for a just reason, be discharged from the obligations and functions linked to ordination, or can even be forbidden to exercise them. But this man cannot become a layperson again in the strict sense because the character imprinted by ordination is for ever. He is marked permanently by the vocation and mission received on the day of his ordination.

Q. Is there a canon law which forbids ex-priests to teach theology at a Catholic institution? If so, why was a university in the Midwest allowed to hire such a person to head its Theology Department? — J.A.Z., Indiana

A. Technically speaking, there is no such thing as an "ex-priest." The power of Holy Orders can never be taken away, but the priest who has been returned to the lay state is prohibited from using that power to celebrate Mass or to confect the sacraments.

There is no canon that specifically prohibits a laicized priest from teaching theology at a Catholic institution. Canon 292 says that "a cleric who loses the clerical state ... is deprived of all offices, functions, and any delegated power," but teaching is not an activity that is proper to the clerical state.

Canon 812 says: "It is necessary that those who teach theological disciplines in any institute of higher studies have a mandate from the competent ecclesiastical authority." Such authorities would include the Holy See, the diocesan bishop, and possibly the superior of a major religious congregation involved in higher Catholic education.

If a priest was not properly dispensed from the clerical state, he certainly should not teach theology. But approval of these situations ought to come from "competent ecclesiastical authority," although the heads of many so-called Catholic institutions have vigorously resisted attempts by bishops to exert control.

Q. *Catholic Replies* on laicization might usefully have added two points [about laicized priests and whether they can teach theology in Catholic institutions]. — D.G., State Unknown
A. We welcome the comments of D.G., a canon lawyer, and pass them along to our readers:

"1. Canons 1708-1712 provide a procedure for invalidating holy orders. This could happen if the minister of the sacrament were incapable of conferring it (c. 1012), if the ordinand were incapable of receiving it (c. 124, 849, 1024), if there were defect of form, matter, or intent (c. 1009), or other invalidating cause (c. 125, 1026).

"2. A validly ordained priest can be laicized by papal rescript. This papal favor renders the man canonically a lay man while not affecting the validity of the sacrament. These rescripts always contain a prohibition on holding certain offices and exercising certain functions.

"He may not give a homily, be an extraordinary minister of Holy Communion, nor hold any directive office in the pastoral field. Further, he may not discharge any functions in seminaries, nor teach in a Church-related university. In non-Church-related universities, he may not teach one of the ecclesiastical disciplines. An Ordinary may permit him to teach in a Catholic primary or secondary school if the danger of scandal is avoided. See *Canon Law Digest*, IX, p. 100."

Q. What are the Church laws or regulations concerning laicized priests participating in parish ministries and apostolates? Are laicized priests allowed to teach and lead RCIA classes, teach other religion classes, serve on and/or lead liturgy committees, and so forth? Can they function as lectors and cantors? — J.W., Georgia
A. In 1980, the Sacred Congregation for the Doctrine of the Faith issued along with Norms for Laicization of Priests (*Per Litteras ad Universos*) a sample list of restrictions on former priests. The sample rescript said that a dispensed cleric could not give a homily at Mass or function as an extraordinary

minister of the Eucharist, and could not exercise a leadership role in any pastoral activity, such as heading a Catholic school or directing a parish religious education program.

One dispensed from priestly celibacy was originally forbidden to exercise any liturgical functions, or even to live, in a parish where his former status was known lest it cause confusion among the faithful as to whether he was functioning as a priest or as a lay man. However, present policy permits the local Ordinary to dispense from some of these restrictions if no scandal is foreseen, and some former priests have been allowed to function as lectors at Mass (but they are still not supposed to distribute Holy Communion) and to teach in Catholic schools and religious education classes (but they are still not supposed to be the principal of the school or the director of the CCD program).

Q. In a recent column, you made mention of an instruction from the Sacred Congregation for the Doctrine of the Faith pertaining to the laicization of priests and certain restrictions which apply to them. The U.S. Catholic Conference catalogue of publications does not list this as being available through them. Could you inform me where I could acquire a copy of this instruction? — E.P., Washington

A. The Norms for Laicization of Priests (*Per Litteras ad Universos*) can be found in volume 2 of *Vatican Council II: More Post Conciliar Documents* (Daughters of St. Paul), edited by Austin Flannery, O.P., pages 382-386.

Q. Priests are ordained by the order of Melchizedek. Who is Melchizedek, and why are priests ordained by this order? — J.F.E., Florida

A. Melchizedek was the king of Salem (later Jerusalem) and a priest of God who offered bread and wine as an unbloody sacrifice in thanksgiving for Abraham's victory over the four eastern kings (Genesis 14:18-20). Because he was a type of Christ (both are kings and priests who offer bread and wine to God), an antiphon in the rite of ordination for a priest reads: "Christ the Lord, a priest forever in the line of Melchizedek, offered bread and wine." See also chapter 7 of St. Paul's Letter to the Hebrews for his comments on the link between Melchizedek and Jesus.

In the first Eucharistic Prayer of the Mass, the priest prays that God will accept his offerings just as He once accepted "the bread and wine offered by your priest Melchizedek."

Q. Our parish priest seldom wears the traditional black shirt and black pants of a priest. He usually wears shirts and pants of many different colors, and you would never know that he was a priest. Is this allowed? — M.A.F., Colorado

A. Canon 284 of the 1983 Code of Canon Law says that "clerics are to wear suitable ecclesiastical garb in accord with the norms issued by the conference of bishops and in accord with legitimate local custom." This means that priests should certainly wear clerical garb when functioning as a priest, but may wear sports clothes while engaging in recreational activities or even in other situations, such as traveling or attending classes.

But what must not be overlooked is the distinctive sign value that clerical garb can have in today's world. This sign, Pope John Paul wrote to the papal vicar of Rome in 1982, is valuable "not only because it contributes to the propriety of the priest in his external behavior or in the exercise of his ministry, but above all because it gives evidence within the ecclesiastical community of the public witness that each priest is held to give of his own identity and special belonging to God."

The Holy Father emphasized that in our modern secular society, where "the sense of the sacred is so frighteningly weak," there is a need for the sign value that is given by the wearing of religious attire.

Q. Is there any evidence that women were ordained priests and bishops in the early Church? — A.B., Massachusetts, and D.B.M., New York

Q. An article in a local newspaper said that "up to the fifth century, women were priests in Italy, Sicily, and Gaul. Their names were Leta, Martia, Flavia, Vitalia, Olybrius, and Nepos. Information about them was unearthed in papal letters and on tombstones by Professor Georgio Otranto, an Italian scholar." Can you explain this? — A.I., West Virginia, and E.D., California

Q. Is there any official statement in an encyclical or apostolic exhortation that clearly states that women cannot be ordained priests in the Catholic Church? — Name and State Withheld and W.B., New York

Q. I have been told that there is evidence in the writings of the early Church Fathers of women having been ordained priests and bishops. And what about deaconesses in the early Church? — J.Z., New Jersey

A. Just because some women claimed to be priests in the early centuries of the Church, as some women claim to be priests today, does not mean that they were lawfully ordained to the Catholic priesthood. Women played important roles in the early Church, supporting Jesus during His ministry and working closely with St. Paul and the other Apostles, but there is no evidence that women were ever ordained as priests or bishops or that they served as deaconesses. There were some heretical sects in the early centuries that elevated women to the priesthood, but these innovations were condemned by the Church Fathers.

For instance, Tertullian, in his *Demurrer Against the Heretics*, which was written around 200 A.D., denounced the "shameless" conduct of "the heretical women themselves," saying that "they make bold to teach, to debate, to work exorcisms, to undertake cures, and perhaps even to baptize. Their ordinations are casual, capricious, and changeable."

In the disciplinary canons of the First Council of Nicaea (325), Canon 19 says that although deaconesses have been enrolled in the register of the clergy, they have not been "in any way ordained," and "they are certainly to be numbered among the laity."

As for official statements against women's ordination, the Sacred Congregation for the Doctrine of the Faith said on October 15, 1976 that "the Church, in fidelity to the example of the Lord, does not consider herself authorized to admit women to priestly ordination" (*Declaration on the Admission of Women to the Ministerial Priesthood*). In 1983, Canon 1024 of the revised Code of Canon Law stated: "Only a baptized male validly receives sacred ordination." And on May 22, 1994, Pope John Paul II made this unequivocal, and possibly infallible, statement in an apostolic letter entitled *Ordinatio Sacerdotalis*:

"Wherefore, in order that all doubts may be removed regarding a matter of great importance, a matter which pertains to the Church's divine constitution itself, in virtue of my ministry of confirming the brethren (cf. Lk. 22:32), I declare that the Church has no authority whatsoever to confer priestly ordination on women and that this judgment is to be definitively held by all the Church's faithful" (n. 4).

Q. The enclosed article by Dolores Curran disturbed me. Is what she said true? — R.E., Minnesota

A. In her syndicated column, Dolores Curran said, among other things, that in the early Church, priests were allowed to marry until the fourth century (that's true); that bishops were sometimes chosen by the acclamation of the crowd to whom they were presented (also true); that local priests were not well-educated and seldom gave instructions about the faith to the laity (that was true in some ages, e.g., the seventh and tenth centuries, but in general priests were more knowledgeable than the ordinary layperson); and that "in the year 584 in Lyons, France, 43 bishops and twenty men representing other bishops took a vote on the question, 'Are women human?' After a lengthy debate, the results came in: 32, yes and 31, no. Women were declared human by one vote."

Regarding the last item, we want to thank G.J.K. of Nebraska for sending us the following excerpt, which is taken from pages 534-535 of volume 1 of *A History of Private Life: From Pagan Rome to Byzantium*, edited by Paul Veyne and published by Harvard University Press in 1987:

"The change in mental outlook did not occur overnight. Violence perpetuated male superiority, as did a linguistic phenomenon about which little is known: the shift from vulgar Latin to proto-French. Although Carolingian councils such as the Council of Compiegne (757) proclaimed 'a single law for men and women,' people were slow to accept the idea. Evidence for this assertion can be found in the words of one bishop to the Synod of Macon in 585, words that are all too well known:

"'He rose to say that a woman cannot be called man (*homo*), but he calmed down when the bishops explained to him that the Old Testament says: "Male and female created He them," and called them Adam, which means man (*homo*) made of earth; at the same time He named the woman Eve [the living]. In other words, he said that both were men.'

"This text, responsible for the legend that a council denied that women have souls, actually reveals a linguistic mutation from which modern French still suffers. When the bishop raised the question, he was thinking of *homo* in the sense of *vir*, the male, rather than 'humankind in general.' His question was perfectly logical, but his Latin was already French, and French, which had dropped the term *vir*, still lacks a specific word for man in the sense of male (whereas German distinguishes between *der Mann* and *der Mensch*).

"The dual meaning of 'man' (human being and male) perpetuated the conviction that one sex was superior to the other, whereas the biblical text implied strict equality. Here the gap between the pagan and Christian mentality is patent, and because of the power of the signifier to obscure the signified, the distinction remains irremediable even today."

Q. If American bishops ordained women into the priesthood in defiance of the Pope, would Masses said by them be valid? If invalid, would a parishioner be obligated to attend? — G.M., Iowa

A. If the exclusion of women from the priesthood is contrary to the will of Christ, as the historical evidence and the mind of the Church make clear, then such ordinations would be invalid, and parishioners would not be obligated to attend the correspondingly invalid Masses celebrated by priestesses.

Q. I was under the impression that the Holy Father had forbidden priests to hold public office, and this led to Fr. Drinan leaving his seat in Congress. So why was a priest, Fr. Bertrand Aristide, an extremely leftist person, allowed to be President of Haiti? — J.T.W., Maryland

A. To his credit, Fr. Robert Drinan obeyed the Holy Father and did not seek re-election to the U.S. House of Representatives in 1980. But other priests, such as Aristide, who was ousted in a military coup in September 1991, have chosen to ignore the Pope. Recall when John Paul II visited Nicaragua in March of 1983, after having ordered five priests to resign from the Communist-controlled government there. When one of those disobedient priests, the Reverend Ernesto Cardenal, knelt and attempted to kiss the Pope's ring, the Holy Father withheld his hand, shook his finger at the rebellious priest, and told him, "You must straighten out your position with the Church."

Q. What is the status of Jean-Bertrand Aristide of Haiti? Some news reports refer to him as "Father" Aristide. Is he still a priest? Has he been defrocked? Has he been excommunicated? — Name Withheld, New Jersey

A. Aristide, who was born in Haiti in 1953, was ordained to the priesthood in 1982 as a member of the Society of St. Francis de Sales, or the Salesians. His fiery sermons against the Duvalier regime (he called them "voracious and insatiable dogs who go their own way, each one looking out for himself"), his leftist politics, and his support for the violent activities of those known as *dechoukaj* brought him public notoriety and warnings from his Salesian superiors. Finally, on December 15, 1988, the Salesians expelled Aristide from their order on the grounds that his "incitement to hate and violence [and] the exaltation of class struggle go directly against that fidelity to the [teachings] of the

Church that forms a living part of the Salesian spirit."

In October 1990, Aristide announced his candidacy for president of Haiti, and he was elected two months later, capturing nearly 70 percent of the vote. He took office on February 7, 1991, but was overthrown on October 1st of that year. Shortly before being deposed, Aristide endorsed the horrible punishment known as "necklacing," where a tire soaked in gasoline is placed around the victim's neck and set on fire, causing an agonizing death. In an address at the National Palace on September 27, 1991, Aristide said:

"If I speak to you this way, it does not mean that I am unaware of my power to unleash public vindication .... What a nice tool! What a nice instrument! What a nice device! It is a pretty one. It is elegant, attractive, splendorous, graceful, dazzling. It smells good. Wherever you go, you feel like smelling it. It is provided for by the constitution, which bans Macoutes [security forces] from the political scene .... Whatever happens to them is their problem."

According to canon 701 of the Code of Canon Law, when a priest is dismissed from a religious order, "he cannot exercise sacred Orders until he finds a bishop who receives him after a suitable probationary period in the diocese according to can. 693 or at least allows him to exercise sacred Orders." We are not aware of any bishop who has accepted Aristide into his diocese, so we believe that he no longer has the faculties to celebrate Mass and hear confessions. Since he no longer functions as a priest, he should not be called "Father." He has not been excommunicated as far as we know.

Q. Jean-Bertrand Aristide was a Salesian, yes, but the Salesians were founded by Don Bosco, not St. Francis de Sales, as you mentioned in your reply. — J.F., Indiana, and R.D., Massachusetts

A. We did not say that the Salesians of St. Don Bosco were founded by St. Francis de Sales, only that another name for the order is the Society of St. Francis de Sales.

Q. In a recent reply, you pointed out that Haiti's Jean-Bertrand Aristide has been expelled from the Salesians, no longer functions as a priest, and should not be called "Father." You also said that "he has not been excommunicated, as far as we know." Didn't Pope Pius XII issue an edict still in effect which provides that any Catholic that joins the Communist Party automatically excommunicates

himself from the Catholic Church? Hasn't Mr. Aristide excommunicated himself? — J.S., Michigan

A. While Aristide has engaged in leftist politics, incited people to hate and violence, and preached the Communist notion of class struggle, we have not seen any evidence that he ever joined the Communist Party. We don't believe that Pope Pius XII's edict is still in effect, and we know that the 1983 Code of Canon Law does not list Communist Party membership as an excommunicable offense.

Q. A local movie theater owner has asked people to come to his two theaters and vote on whether he should show the movie *Priest*. Do you think I should vote on something like this? What can I tell my friends who think it's okay to see this movie? — S.P., Massachusetts

A. There is a story about a priest who lived during the French Revolution and was summoned secretly one night by the family of a man who was known for his fierce hatred of the Catholic Church. When the dying man realized who his visitor was, he cursed and raged and said to the priest, "Don't you know who I am? I hate priests. I have strangled a dozen of them with my bare hands."

"No," the priest replied, opening his collar and showing the man the marks on his throat, "you only killed eleven. I survived your attack and now I'm here to prepare you for death." The man was so moved by the priest's courage that he repented of his sins and asked for God's mercy and forgiveness.

All of us during our lives have known some wonderful and holy priests. The priests who baptized us and our children, heard our first Confession and gave us our first Communion, prepared us for marriage and performed the ceremony, visited us in hospitals and in our homes, consoled us in times of tragedy and trouble, and anointed our loved ones in the final moments of their lives.

These priests were not perfect. Like the rest of us who make up the human race, they were and are sinners, too. But as someone once said, a saint is a sinner who kept on trying. And we all know, admire, and love those priests who kept on trying, who truly acted as ambassadors of Christ, as shepherds, as spiritual fathers, as physicians of the soul, as instruments that Jesus uses to bring us to God and God to us, especially in the Holy Eucharist. They are indeed a bridge between Heaven and earth.

At the same time, we must admit that we have known or read about priests who were weak, who were mean and tyrannical, and who were even evil men. But these men were not typical of the priesthood, any more than dishonest doctors or lawyers, bad teachers or police officers, and corrupt politicians or businessmen are typical of their professions. There are aberrant people in every walk of life. Recall, for instance, that one of the twelve Apostles was a traitor.

Relating this to the Disney/Miramax movie *Priest*, the problem with the movie is not that it puts some priests in a bad light, but that it portrays all five priests in the film as twisted, tortured, and dysfunctional characters. One is a homosexual, another is a fornicator, and a third is a drunk. Of the remaining two, one is obviously crazy and the bishop is just plain wicked. There is not one normal, well-balanced, faithful priest in the movie.

Not only are all the priests seriously flawed, but the thrust of the film is to blame the Catholic Church for the unsavory lives of these men. They are not portrayed as persons who have consciously made sinful choices, but rather as victims of a Church that oppresses its members by telling them that certain sexual activities are always and everywhere wrong and sinful. Of course, the Catholic Church didn't make up these rules; they come from God Himself, but the clergy in *Priest* don't have much connection with God.

Why this animus toward the Catholic Church? Well, the writer of the movie, Jimmy McGovern, has called the priests of his youth "reactionary bastards." And the director, Antonia Bird, who told the *Los Angeles Times* that she "seethes with rage" over the Catholic Church's opposition to birth control, said that the movie's central message is opposition to "a hierarchy adhering to old-fashioned rules without looking at the way the world's changed." Another indicator of Bird's bias is that she wanted *Priest* to open on Good Friday, the most solemn day of the year for Catholics.

As for the theater owner who asked people to vote on whether he should show the film or not, we wonder why, if the movie displays such deep hostility toward the Catholic Church, he would want to show such callous disregard for the sensibilities of a large segment of his potential patrons? Would he have put to a vote the question of whether to screen a movie about five depraved rabbis, or five deranged blacks, or five evil theater owners? Don't bet on it. Catholic bashing is one of the country's leading spectator sports, primarily because too many Catholics sit back and let it happen.

What should be the Catholic response to *Priest*? Well, Catholics who love their Church and their priests certainly should not put money in the pockets of those who have so viciously disparaged both. Of course, there are some who will patronize the movie out of curiosity, or to show how "broadminded" they are, or perhaps because they themselves have an ax to grind against the Church, some disagreement with a teaching of the Church or a memory of some priest who treated them unfairly.

But people of good will should stay away from *Priest*, not only because the film attempts to tear down an important moral and spiritual force in our society, but also because the movie is part of a widespread assault on religion and religious values. We will never bring about the much-needed return of morality and religion to our culture by supporting those who have helped to undermine these essential pillars of society.

Q. I am considering becoming a contemplative religious and would like your opinion of the current state of the Carthusian order. Are the Carthusians strict? Are they obedient to the Holy Father? — J.W., Illinois

A. "Yes, the Carthusians are strict," a reader informs us. "Yes, they are faithful to the *Magisterium*. A vocation to the Carthusian life is not common; they are a small order, by deliberate choice. The reader can write to the Carthusians at the Charterhouse of the Transfiguration, R.R. 2, Box 2411, Arlington, Vermont 05250. They are experienced in dealing with inquiries. They receive hundreds each year, but only a few persevere."

Our correspondent also recommended two books about the order: *Halfway to Heaven: The Hidden Life of the Sublime Carthusians* by Robin Bruce Lockhart (Vanguard Press) and *The Way of Silent Love: Carthusian Novice Conferences* by a Carthusian (Cistercian Publications).

Q. During a recent visit with my mother in California, she said she knew of several married ministers who, after converting to Catholicism, were allowed to bring their wives and families with them. This means that there are married priests in the Catholic Church. Have you heard of this? — F.H., Oklahoma

A. Yes, we have heard of this. Acting on a request from the bishops of the United States, the Holy See in June 1980 gave permission for some clergy and laity from the Episcopal (Anglican) Church to enter into full communion with the Catholic Church. In April 1981, the Sacred Congregation for the Doctrine of the Faith issued the following statement about allowing married Episcopalian clergy into the priesthood:

"In accepting former Episcopalian clergy who are married into the Catholic priesthood, the Holy See has specified that this exception to the rule of celibacy is granted in favor of these individual persons, and should not be understood as implying any change in the Church's conviction of the value of priestly celibacy, which will remain the rule for future candidates for the priesthood from this group."

The SCDF at that time named then-Bishop Bernard F. Law of Springfield-Cape Girardeau, Missouri, as the Ecclesiastical Delegate in this matter, with the responsibility for developing and implementing the pastoral provision that would govern the admission of former Episcopalian clergy into the Catholic priesthood.

Q. Is it my imagination or has the quality of the priests ordained in the past five years or so greatly improved? — G.P., Florida

A. There have always been many high-quality and holy priests serving the faithful and, despite some well-publicized failures, there are many fine priests of all ages today, including those recently ordained in such fast-growing orders as the Legionaries of Christ. Unfortunately, we usually hear more about priests who are involved in dissent from Church teachings, or liturgical aberrations, or sinful and scandalous lifestyles. All priests need our prayers and we can help them by reciting daily this prayer for priests:

"Sacred Heart of Jesus, hear my humble prayer on behalf of your priests. I pray for your faithful and fervent priests; for your unfaithful and tepid priests; for your priests who labor at home and abroad; for your tempted priests; for your lonely and desolate priests; for your young priests; for your dying priests; and for the souls of your priests in Purgatory.

"Merciful Heart of Jesus, remembering that they are but weak and frail human beings, give them a deep faith, a bright and firm hope, and a burning love. I ask that, in their loneliness, you comfort them; in their sorrow, you strengthen them; in their frustrations, you show them that it is through suffering that the soul is purified.

"Loving Heart of Jesus, keep them close to your Sacred Heart and bless them abundantly, in time and in eternity. Amen."

Chapter 9

The Holy Eucharist

Q. How can we be sure that Jesus is really present in the Holy Eucharist? — G.F.E., Massachusetts

A. Around the year 700 A.D., a priest in Italy who had begun to doubt the presence of Jesus in the Eucharist held up the Host during Mass one day and saw it change into flesh, while the liquid in the chalice became clots of blood.

This treasure was guarded by monks until 1970 when Church authorities gave a team of scientists permission to study the substances. After taking samples and putting them through a variety of tests, the scientific team concluded that the flesh was really human flesh and the clots were human blood. The team found no trace of any preservative, yet the flesh and blood were just as fresh then as they were 13 centuries earlier.

Very few of us will ever have the privilege of witnessing such a miracle. Most of us accept the Real Presence of Christ on faith, i.e., we believe it because Jesus, the Son of God, revealed it to us. At the Last Supper, when our Lord said the first Mass and gave us the Holy Eucharist, He took bread and said, "This is my body." He did not say, "This represents my body," but rather, "This *is* my body."

Our Lord also took a cup of wine and said, "This is my blood." He did not say, "This is a symbol of my blood," but rather, "This *is* my blood." And for nearly 2,000 years the Catholic Church has faithfully taught that Jesus is really and truly present, Body and Blood, Soul and Divinity, in the Eucharist.

Further evidence of this marvelous truth can be found in chapter 6 of John's Gospel. "If you do not eat the flesh of the Son of Man and drink his blood, you have no life in you," Jesus said. "He who feeds on my flesh and drinks my blood has life eternal and I will raise him up on the last day. For my flesh is real food and my blood real drink."

That Jesus' listeners took Him literally is indicated by the fact that many of His disciples found His words disturbing and "would not remain in his company any longer." Our Lord did not call them back and say, "Wait a minute, you misunderstood me; that wasn't what I meant." He let them go.

When Jesus asked the Apostles if they were going to leave Him, too, St. Peter answered for the Twelve:

"Lord, to whom shall we go? You have the words of eternal

life. We have come to believe; we are convinced that you are God's holy one" (John 6:67-69).

Q. Why does the Apostles' Creed not contain a statement of our belief in the true Presence of Jesus in the Eucharist? — M.R., Washington

A. A creed is a brief summary of religious beliefs and is not meant to cover all the doctrines of a particular church or denomination. During the time when the Apostles' Creed was compiled in the last half of the first century, the Church was in its infancy and its statement of beliefs was rather brief.

That creed more than doubled in length at the Councils of Nicaea (325) and Constantinople (381) primarily because of heresies surrounding the human and divine natures of Jesus. Thus, while the Apostles' Creed said simply that Jesus was God's only Son and our Lord, the Nicene Creed described Him as "eternally begotten of the Father, God from God, Light from Light, true God from true God, begotten, not made, one in being with the Father."

In 1968, Pope Paul VI felt compelled to issue a lengthy and comprehensive statement of Catholic beliefs because certain doctrines were being disputed, some Catholics were "allowing themselves to be seized by a kind of passion for change and novelty," and there was "disturbance and perplexity in many faithful souls."

The Holy Father's Credo of the People of God, which ought to be read frequently by Catholics, does speak at some length about the Real Presence because that was one of the doctrines being disputed by certain people in the Church. Among other things, Paul VI declared that "the bread and wine consecrated by the priest are changed into the Body and Blood of Christ enthroned gloriously in Heaven, and we believe that the mysterious Presence of our Lord, under what continues to appear to our senses as before, is a true, real, and substantial Presence."

Q. When Christ instituted the Eucharist, He made two distinct statements: "Take and eat, this is my Body .... Take and drink, this is my Blood." When and why did the Church make it a one-species offering to the faithful? What are the terms used to describe the condition of the remnants of Christ's Blood when it is mixed with water after Communion, and can it then be disposed of properly? What did Christ mean when He said: "I will not drink this

fruit of the vine from now until the day when I drink it new with you in my Father's reign" (Matthew 26:29)? — W.A.L., Michigan

A. Taking the questions in reverse order, Christ was telling the Apostles that this would be His last cup of wine with them until they would be together again at the Messianic banquet in the kingdom of Heaven. After Communion, the priest is to consume any Precious Blood remaining in the chalice, pour water into the chalice to purify the vessel, and then drink from the chalice again so that no traces of the Precious Blood remain. For more on this, see paragraphs 120 and 238 of the *General Instruction of the Roman Missal* and the clarifications that appear in Appendix 2 of that document. See also paragraph 14 of *Inuestimabile Donum*, which was issued in 1980 by the Sacred Congregation for the Sacraments and Divine Worship.

As for the first question about when Communion was first given under one species, it seems that frequent Communion under both species declined in the fifth and sixth centuries as awe for reception of the Eucharist increased, and that in the 12th century the laity gradually ceased to communicate from the cup. So from the 13th century on, lay communicants received only the Host, and this practice was reaffirmed by the Council of Constance in 1415, which forbade lay Communion from the cup to "avoid any abuse and scandal."

Q. How should one answer the accusation that Catholics are practicing cannibalism when they consume the actual Body and Blood of Christ? — R.D.S., Ohio

Q. A priest told us about his nephew who was afraid to make his First Communion because it would be like engaging in cannibalism. The priest reassured him that this was not true because the Host was not really the Body of Christ but only a symbol, that Christ was present spiritually but not physically. Was the priest right or wrong? — E.J.M., Florida

A. The priest was wrong. As Pope Paul VI declared in his Credo of the People of God, "Every theological explanation which seeks some understanding of this mystery must, in order to be in accord with Catholic faith, maintain that in the reality itself, independently of our mind, the bread and wine have ceased to exist after the Consecration, so that it is the adorable Body and Blood of the Lord Jesus that from then on are really before us under the sacramental species of bread and wine, as the Lord willed it, in order to give himself to us as food and associate us with the unity of his Mystical Body."

Regarding the accusation of cannibalism, that goes all the way back to the time of Christ, when He shocked some of His followers by telling them that "if you do not eat the flesh of the Son of Man and drink his blood, you have no life in you" (John 6:53). Some disciples, as noted above, found this statement so hard to accept that they no longer followed Jesus.

But they were thinking on the natural plane of the horrible act of eating human flesh and drinking human blood. Jesus was talking on the supernatural plane. Yes, His flesh is "real food" and His blood "real drink" (John 6:55), but it is present to us supernaturally. We do eat the actual Body and Blood of Jesus, but we chew or consume the accidents of bread and wine, thus refuting the charge of cannibalism.

"Man cannot understand this, cannot perceive it," said St. Thomas Aquinas, "but a lively faith affirms that the change, which is outside the natural course of things, takes place. Under the different species, which are now signs only and not their own reality, there lie hidden wonderful realities. His Body is our food, His blood our drink."

Q. How can the Eucharist be what Roman Catholics say it is when both the Old and New Testaments forbid the eating of blood? — J.L., Maryland

A. The biblical prohibition against drinking blood (Genesis 9:4, Deuteronomy 12:16, and Acts 15:20) refers to the blood of animals. It is not to be confused with our Lord's command to drink His Blood (John 6:53-57 and 1 Corinthians 11:25). Jesus would not have commanded us to do something that had been forbidden elsewhere in the Bible.

Q. Our pastor, who is a very good priest, told a group of Eucharistic ministers that we do not have to believe in transubstantiation, that it is not a dogma, and that the more appropriate term to use is transignification. How can I show him that he is incorrect? — D.C.D., California

A. You can begin by telling your pastor that any doctrine promulgated by the Church to the faithful over many centuries is most certainly a dogma. You can tell him that the term "transubstantiation" was incorporated into the creed of the Fourth Lateran Council in the 13th century and was reaffirmed in the 16th century by the Council of Trent, which defined transubstantiation as the "wonderful and singular conversion of the whole substance of the bread into the Body, and the whole substance of the wine into the Blood" of Christ.

In his Credo of the People of God, Pope Paul VI said that "this hidden conversion is appropriately and justly called by the Church *transubstantiation*." And the *Catechism of the Catholic Church* repeats the Council of Trent's summary of this miraculous change, a change that "the holy Catholic Church has fittingly and properly called transubstantiation" (n. 1376).

In his 1965 encyclical letter *Mysterium Fidei*, Pope Paul condemned the theory of transignification if it was understood to deny transubstantiation by holding that only the meaning or significance of the bread and wine, not the substances themselves, was changed by the words of consecration. He said that it was not allowable "to discuss the mystery of transubstantiation without mentioning what the Council of Trent stated about the marvelous conversion of the whole substance of the bread into the Body and of the whole substance of the wine into the Blood of Christ, speaking rather only of what is called 'transignification' and 'transfinalization.' ... Everyone can see that the spread of these and similar opinions does great harm to the faith and devotion to the Divine Eucharist."

Q. What exactly is meant by "valid matter" in regard to the Holy Eucharist? — D.G.S., Alabama

A. The matter of the Holy Eucharist is specified in canon 924 of the Code of Canon Law: "1. The Most Sacred Eucharistic Sacrifice must be offered with bread and wine, with which a small quantity of water is to be mixed. 2. The bread must be made of wheat alone and recently made so that there is no danger of corruption. 3. The wine must be natural wine of the grape and not corrupt."

In its 1980 Instruction on Certain Norms Concerning the Worship of the Eucharistic Mystery (*Inaestimabile Donum*), the Sacred Congregation for the Sacraments and Divine Worship said that the bread must be made solely of wheat, must be unleavened, must have no other ingredients added to the wheaten flour and water, and "should appear as actual food." The wine must be of "'the fruit of the vine' (Luke 22:18) and be natural and genuine, that is to say, not mixed with other substances" (n. 8).

In the early centuries, leavened bread (with yeast) was used for the Eucharist in both the Eastern and Western Churches. The Church in the West began using unleavened bread in the eighth and ninth centuries, but the Church in the East has continued to use leavened bread to this day.

Q. A university near me has "Holy Communion" in cake-like form that contains wheat and baking soda. I know this because the woman who bakes it told me so. Is this a valid Eucharist? Is Christ really present, or are we just receiving bread and not Jesus? — P.K., Illinois

Q. The bread used at Mass recently was a dark, raised bread that resembled an ordinary rye or whole wheat bread and appeared to have been made with yeast. Is this practice illicit or invalid? — R.E.W., Texas

Q. The ladies in our parish take turns baking the bread for the Eucharist. I have made this and it does contain honey. It is cake-like and sheds crumbs easily. Are those hosts valid? — M.W., Michigan

A. Quoting again from *Inaestimabile Donum*:

"The bread for the celebration of the Eucharist, in accordance with the tradition of the whole Church, must be made solely of wheat and, in accordance with the tradition proper to the Latin Church, it must be unleavened. By reason of the sign, the matter of the Eucharist celebration 'should appear as actual food.' This is to be understood as linked to the consistency of the bread, and not to its form, which remains the traditional one. No other ingredients are to be added to the wheaten flour and water" (n. 8).

The addition of baking soda or honey to the recipe for the Eucharistic bread is illicit, that is, contrary to the laws of the Church, and is a serious abuse that should be reported to your bishop. It does not, however, make the bread invalid matter; Christ still would be present after the words of consecration, but no one should knowingly receive the illicit Communion, except in grave necessity. Using bread made of any substance other than wheat would constitute invalid matter, as would bread to which had been added such a great quantity of another substance that it was no longer recognizable as wheat bread.

Q. Is a Mass valid if the altar wine contains sulfites, which are chemicals added to wine to protect the flavor and color? — J.K., Pennsylvania

Q. I find it impossible to believe that the Sacred Congregation for the Doctrine of the Faith authorized bishops in the United States to permit priests who are recovering alcoholics to use unfermented grape juice in place of wine. — J.D.H., Illinois

Q. I thought the permission to allow alcoholic priests to use grape juice had been abrogated. — W.G.S., Delaware

Q. Wouldn't the use of unfermented grape juice affect the validity of the Mass? — F.A., Texas

A. The wine used at Mass must be a natural product from the juice of grapes and not mixed with any foreign substance. It would become invalid matter if it corrupted (turned into vinegar) or if so much water was added that it lost the qualities of wine. We are not sure about sulfites.

Priests who are recovering alcoholics can obtain permission to use mustum in place of wine at Mass. Mustum is defined as the freshly squeezed juice of grapes in which the natural process of fermentation has been suspended by freezing or other methods that do not alter its nature. According to a letter sent to the bishops' conferences by the Congregation for the Doctrine of the Faith on June 19, 1995, "the permission to use mustum can be granted by Ordinaries to priests affected by alcoholism or other conditions which prevent the ingestion of even the smallest quantity of alcohol, after presentation of a medical certificate."

Q. Regarding your recent columns, it is my understanding that yeast does not affect the validity of the bread used for the Holy Eucharist, but only the liceity. Regarding sulfites, it is my understanding that they occur naturally in wine. They are not added any more than the alcohol is. The government requires that they be mentioned on the label on all wine because some people have a proven allergy to sulfites. — M.M.D., Virginia

Q. Yeast makes the bread for the Eucharist illicit but not invalid since in the Eastern liturgies yeast is compulsory. — T.P., Tasmania

A. Our two correspondents are correct. Fr. John Huels, in *The Pastoral Companion*, his commentary on the Code of Canon Law, says that "for validity, the bread must be made substantially of wheat flour. If there are any additives in it, they cannot be such that the bread would no longer be considered wheat bread *according to the common estimation* .... Thus, knowing the composition of the bread, if the common estimation of persons would judge that it is wheat bread, it would be valid matter even if there are other additives. However, the use of any additives at all other than wheat flour and water is illicit." It should be noted that liceity binds under pain of sin. It would be seriously sinful deliberately to use illicit matter under normal conditions.

As for sulfites, we quote from a letter dated January 15, 1988, that was sent to all distributors, agents, and brokers of the Mont La Salle altar wines by Brother Timothy Diener, F.S.C., vice president and cellar-master of the Christian Brothers Winery in St. Helena, California:

"In answer to questions you may have about the sulfite statement you now find on wine labels, I can assure you that sulfites in wine are nothing new because yeast cells naturally produce a small amount of sulfites during fermentation. And, for many centuries, the better winemakers have made tiny additions of sulfite as an anti-oxidant and wild yeast inhibitor. This preserves the natural good condition of the wine and retards spoilage.

"For the information and protection of those few people who are extremely sensitive or allergic to sulfites, U.S. federal law now requires that wine containing 10 or more parts per million of sulfites be labelled 'contains sulfites.' The labelling is new, but the wines are the same as they were before such labelling was required.

"Substances that assist in making a sound wine and that remain in the wine in minute traces, such as sulfites, have been and are considered by canonists and theologians to be acceptable for the Eucharist. One such approval, as reported in the *Sacramentary*, was the Holy Office Decree of 2nd August, 1922."

Q. What is the proper size of the consecrating host that the priest uses at Mass? One of our priests has been using a host that is approximately the size of a dish, or about eight inches in diameter. Is it permitted to use a host this large? — L.B.B., Ohio

A. According to a priest we consulted, there is no authorized size. The host should be large enough to be visible to the congregation when shown to them, and large enough to be broken into pieces so that at least a few people can communicate it. The size you describe, often scored for easier fractioning, is within the norms.

Until the 11th century, large flat breads were used and broken for the congregation at the fractioning. Small hosts were a German invention and were long resisted as unliturgical. They won out because of practicality.

With today's liturgical consciousness, however, the priest should not communicate the entire large host (traditional size), but half or a quarter of it, using the rest to communicate two or three minor ministers or congregants. With a very small congregation, the best practice would be to communicate all from a large host.

Q. Is it permissible for the priest to dip the Host into the Precious Blood and place it on the communicant's tongue? I am concerned that some of the Precious Blood might be spilled. — R.L.W., Texas

A. This method of giving out Communion is called intinction, and it stems back at least to the third century. It has long been a regular method of distributing Communion in the Eastern Catholic Churches, and was revived after the Second Vatican Council in the Western Churches.

Two cautions: (1) If the Host is dipped into the chalice, Communion may not be received in the hand. (2) Persons coming to Communion may not take the Host from the priest and then dip it into the Precious Blood themselves. This would be the same as self-communication, and only the priest may do that.

Q. My understanding of *Inaestimabile Donum* is that Communion under both kinds is not to be an every-Sunday occurrence, but only for special occasions. Has that been changed? — J.A., North Carolina; T.H., Kentucky; and J.V.C., Michigan

A. Receiving Holy Communion under the appearances of both bread and wine was authorized by Pope Paul VI in 1965 and has been reaffirmed several times since then, notably in the documents *Ecclesiae Semper* (1965), *Eucharisticum Mysterium* (1967), *Sacramentali Communione* (1970), the *General Instruction of the Roman Missal* (1970), and *Inaestimabile Donum* (1980).

In the last-named document, the Sacred Congregation for the Sacraments and Divine Worship said that "the granting of permission for Communion under both kinds is not to be indiscriminate, and the celebrations in question are to be clearly defined, well-disciplined, and homogeneous" (n. 12). A footnote refers the reader to the *General Instruction of the Roman Missal*, n. 242.

That section lists 14 cases where Communion can be received from the chalice, e.g., at Masses where adults are baptized, confirmed, or received into full communion in the Church; weddings, ordinations, professions of vows, and jubilees; and concelebrations. It also says that "the conferences of bishops have the power to decide to what extent and under what considerations and conditions Ordinaries may allow Communion under both kinds in other instances that are of special significance in the spiritual life of any community or group of the faithful."

According to Appendix 1 of the *General Instruction*, the

National Conference of Catholic Bishops added five more categories in 1970, including funeral Masses, Holy Thursday and Easter Vigil Masses, and weekday Masses. Then, in 1978, the NCCB approved a motion that Communion under both kinds may be given to the faithful at Masses on Sundays and holy days if, "in the judgment of the Ordinary, Communion may be given in an orderly and reverent manner."

Q. What are the requirements for fasting before Communion? Do chewing gum or breath mints break the fast? — M.P., Colorado

Q. I have seen people chew gum during Mass and then go to Communion, choir members use cough drops before going to Communion, and a friend take a breath mint before receiving our Lord. Don't all of these things break the one-hour fast? — H.S.S., Texas

A. Canon 919 of the Code of Canon Law states that "one who is to receive the Most Holy Eucharist is to abstain from any food or drink, with the exception of water and medicine, for at least the period of one hour before Holy Communion." The canon also says that "those who are advanced in age or who suffer from any infirmity, as well as those who take care of them, can receive the Most Holy Eucharist even if they have taken something during the previous hour." A person who has reached the age of 60 is considered to be "advanced in age."

While eating a breath mint or other type of candy would certainly break the fast, cough drops used for medicinal purposes by a choir member probably would not, and it is doubtful whether gum (either with or without sugar) would break the fast since the gum is not swallowed and the sweeteners in it are of such minute quantities that they are neutralized by the saliva in the person's mouth.

But even if gum does not break the fast, it is highly inappropriate and irreverent to chew gum at Mass since it shows a deplorable lack of appreciation for the sacredness of the liturgy and considerable disrespect for the Lord and Savior whom we are to receive in Holy Communion.

Q. When we receive the Eucharist, we respond with the word "Amen." What does this "Amen" signify? — M.M., Massachusetts

A. The word "Amen," which has Latin, Greek, and Hebrew roots, is an acclamation of fervent assent or hearty approval of something a person has just said or of what is in the mind of the speaker. Thus, when we say "Amen" after the priest or extraordinary minister says "Body of Christ," we are solemnly confirming our belief that the Host we are about to receive is indeed the Body of Christ.

Q. As a recent convert to Catholicism, I have to ask whose idea it was to make us consume the Body of our Lord while walking. I do not eat anything while walking, much less the Host that has been placed in my hand. Is it acceptable to wait and communicate at my place in the pew? This problem is an impediment to my awareness and reverence of the Eucharist. — H.W., Massachusetts

A. First of all, Catholics who receive the Host on the tongue, as millions have for many centuries, begin consuming the Body of the Lord as they walk back to their pews, so there is nothing new or startling about that. And we would suggest that you can notice great reverence and awareness on the faces of many who receive Communion in this manner.

Second, those who receive the Host in their hand are supposed to take one step to the side and place the Host in their mouth before going back to their pews. These people also begin consuming the Host as they return to their seats, and many of them are clearly aware of the wonderful sacrament they have just received.

Third, it is not acceptable to wait and communicate at your place in the pew. Such a practice is not only contrary to liturgical law but, in our opinion, would show less reverence for the Body of Christ than placing the Host in one's mouth immediately. Can't you picture people who have little respect or reverence for the Eucharist carrying the Host in their hand to the back of the church, or even outside, if there were not a rule to place the Host in one's mouth upon receiving it from the priest, deacon, or extraordinary minister?

Fourth, you are to be commended for the awe and reverence you have for the Eucharist. May you never lose either. But we see no reason why this awe and reverence should be diminished by beginning to consume the Host as you walk back to your seat.

As for never eating anything while walking, have you never eaten a hot dog or an ice cream cone or a candy bar while strolling along?

Q. When in the history of the Catholic Church has permission ever been given to receive Holy Communion in the hand? — R.W.S., Florida

Q. We know Satanists steal Holy Communion for sacrilegious rites. Since Communion in the hand makes it easier for them to do this, why is it allowed? — G.A., Indiana

A. The current practice of giving people the option of receiving Communion in the hand has its origins in the early centuries of the Church. In its 1969 instruction on the manner of distributing Holy Communion (*Memoriale Domini*), the Sacred Congregation for Divine Worship said "it is certainly true that ancient usage once allowed the faithful to take this divine food in their hands and to place it in their mouths themselves. It is also true that in very ancient times they were allowed to take the Blessed Sacrament with them from the place where the Holy Sacrifice was celebrated. This was principally so as to be able to give themselves Viaticum in case they had to face death for their faith."

By the ninth or tenth centuries, however, the practice of receiving the Host on the tongue was mandated. This was partly because of abuses and partly because "there came a greater feeling of reverence towards this sacrament and a deeper humility was felt to be demanded when receiving it. Thus the custom was established of the minister placing a particle of consecrated Bread on the tongue of the communicant" (*Memoriale Domini*).

This method of receiving our Lord remained the norm until recent times, when certain countries began experimenting with Communion in the hand. Pope Paul VI wanted the traditional practice of receiving on the tongue continued, but he said that Communion in the hand could be permitted in countries where two-thirds of the bishops petitioned Rome for permission. Authorization for Communion in the hand in the United States was given in 1977.

The danger of abuses, and even of sacrilegious uses of the Holy Eucharist, is greater of course with Communion in the hand, although determined Satanists did manage to supply themselves with Hosts when Communion was received only on the tongue. In a 1980 letter on the Eucharist (*Dominicae Cenae*), Pope John Paul II noted that "cases of a deplorable lack of respect toward the Eucharistic species" had been reported to him. He traced the blame for this "not only to the individuals guilty of such behavior but also to the pastors of the Church who have not been vigilant enough regarding the attitude of the faithful toward the Eucharist" (n. 11).

The Holy Father went on to say that many Catholics who receive Communion in the hand "do so with profound reverence and devotion." But it is up to priests and pastors to make sure that all of their parishioners are constantly reminded that profound reverence and devotion are due to the Holy Eucharist every time we receive the Body and Blood of our Lord, whether in the hand or on the tongue.

Q. How many times can a person receive Communion in one day? — M.A., Ohio

Q. Our assistant pastor said that we may receive Communion as many times during a day as we wish. Is he correct? — T.R.E., Texas

Q. Canon 917 states that "a person who has received the Most Holy Eucharist may receive it again on the same day only during the celebration of the Eucharist in which the person participates, with due regard for the prescription of can. 921.2." My parish priest says that this means receiving only once a day unless you are participating in a special additional Mass, such as a funeral. Is he right? — J.G., Connecticut

A. Canon 921.2 says that those in danger of death may receive the Eucharist more than once a day. A Catholic not in danger of death may receive Communion at two Masses in one day (regular or special Masses) provided that he or she is physically present at each Mass. One cannot, for instance, come into the church only in time to receive Communion.

Saturday Vigils are a distinct category, so one may communicate at a Mass on Saturday morning and again on Saturday evening at the Vigil Mass for Sunday. It is the same calendar day, but a different liturgical day.

The reason for prohibiting multiple Communions in one day is to discourage a superstitious or misguided attitude toward the Body and Blood of our Lord. We mean an attitude that assumes if one reception of the Eucharist is good, many receptions on the same day will be better. Every Host is of infinite value, and one does not collect them like stamps.

Editor's Note: Two readers, D.A.H. of Virginia and J.H.P.O. of Pennsylvania, have written seeking clarification of a recent reply about the number of times a Catholic may receive Holy Communion in one day. They suggested another interpretation of canon 917 based on their own personal experience. Both were in the habit of receiving at home when Communion was brought to a sick relative on a Sunday. If they had received the Eucharist at home in the morning, they believed that they could receive a second time only at a Mass. If they had already received at Mass that day when the Eucharist was brought to the sick person, both would refrain from receiving a second time to remain in conformity with canon 917.

It seems reasonable, therefore, to interpret canon 917 as meaning that a person may attend Mass twice in one day and receive Communion at both Masses. However, if one has already received the Eucharist outside of Mass, as in the situations noted above, then a second reception is permitted only within the context of a Mass.

Q. My copy of the *Baltimore Catechism* states that "we are bound to receive Communion, under pain of mortal sin, during the Easter time." Does this mean every Sunday, or just once during Easter time? — D.J.B., State Unknown

A. Canon 920 of the Code of Canon Law says that "all the faithful, after they have been initiated into the Most Holy Eucharist, are bound by the obligation of receiving Communion at least once a year. This precept must be fulfilled during the Easter season unless it is fulfilled for a just cause at some other time during the year." The Easter season (Lent is a separate season) is from Easter Sunday to the Vigil of Pentecost, and the canon means receiving Holy Communion once during that season, not on each of the Sundays during the fifty-day period.

Again, canon law specifies the absolute minimum. Catholics who understand and appreciate the great gift of Jesus in the Eucharist will want to receive Him at least weekly, if not more often.

Q. It is my recollection that extraordinary ministers can be used only under certain conditions. Can you tell me what the conditions are? — A.S., Montana

Q. We have noticed recently in our parish the "modern methods" of the extraordinary ministers of Communion. Where can we procure the specific directives for extraordinary ministers? — E.O., Georgia

A. You can consult *Immensae Caritatis*, the document on the Eucharist that was issued by the Sacred Congregation for the Discipline of the Sacraments on January 25, 1973. This should be available at any Catholic bookstore, either as a single document or as part of a collection, such as in volume 1 of *Vatican Council II: The Conciliar and Post Conciliar Documents*, edited by Austin Flannery, O.P.

In *Inaestimabile Donum*, the document on the Eucharist issued by the Sacred Congregation for the Sacraments and Divine Worship on April 3, 1980, there is this brief summary of what is expected of extraordinary ministers:

"The faithful, whether religious or lay, who are authorized as extraordinary ministers of the Eucharist can distribute Communion only when there is no priest, deacon, or acolyte, when the priest is impeded by illness or advanced age, or when the number of the faithful going to Communion is so large as to make the celebration of Mass excessively long. Accordingly, a reprehensible attitude is shown by those priests who, though present at the celebration, refrain from distributing Communion and leave this task to the laity" (n. 10).

The problem in the United States is the use of extraordinary ministers in parishes and at Masses where there is no extraordinary need for them. In his apostolic exhortation *Christifideles Laici*, Pope John Paul alluded to this problem when he urged pastors to "guard against a facile yet abusive recourse to a presumed 'situation of emergency,' or to 'supply by necessity,' where objectively this does not exist or where alternative possibilities could exist through better pastoral planning" (n. 23).

Q. Are Eucharistic ministers allowed to go to the tabernacle to get the consecrated Hosts for distribution at Mass or to bring to the sick, or must a priest do this for them? — F.D., New York

Q. Is it permissible for the Eucharistic ministers to talk with their friends while opening the tabernacle door after Mass each morning to obtain the Body of Christ to bring to the sick? What about visiting with their friends, and even going out to breakfast, before distributing Communion to the sick? — L.G., Arizona

A. Extraordinary ministers of the Eucharist are allowed to bring ciboria containing the consecrated Hosts from the tabernacle to the altar for distribution at Mass, and they are allowed to obtain Hosts after Mass to bring to the sick. But the way they conduct themselves ought to give some indication of the extraordinary privilege they have been given.

Chatting with friends in front of the tabernacle shows a lack of respect and reverence for the Eucharist. Visiting with friends or going out to breakfast while carrying the Blessed Sacrament is not appropriate behavior either. Both abuses are evidence of an increasing loss of the sense of the sacred.

Older readers can remember bowing or even kneeling when a

priest carrying the Blessed Sacrament passed by outside the church. And how many were taught as children to venerate and imitate St. Tarcisius, the third-century Roman boy who suffered death by stoning rather than reveal the Host he was taking to Christians in prison? We've come a long way since then, and in the wrong direction.

Q. I have seen Eucharistic ministers after Communion consume the remaining Hosts and drink the left-over Precious Blood. I thought lay people could receive Communion only once during a particular Mass. — A.E.N., Ontario

Q. We celebrate Mass in the chapel of a cemetery. If there are any Hosts left over, the priest usually consumes them. This Sunday, however, there were so many that the priest started feeding them to the five servers until they balked. Isn't this highly irregular? — Name Withheld, California

A. If there are Hosts or Precious Blood left over after Mass, either the celebrant of the Mass or the extraordinary ministers should consume the sacred remains. Feeding the Hosts to the servers was indeed highly irregular. If the priest was unable to consume them himself, could he not at least have taken them to a place of reservation?

Q. My pastor gives a parishioner (who is not a Eucharistic minister) two Hosts at Communion time so she can take one home to her husband, who is a shut-in and does not like visitors. What is your view of this practice? — J.E.C., Pennsylvania

A. There is a right way and a wrong way to bring Communion to shut-ins. Why not do things the proper way, i.e., train the woman to be an extraordinary minister and have her get the Host after Mass to bring home to her husband?

Q. While receiving Communion, I observed a man before me ask for and be given a fistful of Hosts. Upon communicating my dismay to a deacon after Mass, I was told that the person was probably a lay distributor who needed the Hosts for a home visit. Is it acceptable for a lay distributor to carry around in his coat pocket a supply of Hosts? — G.T.C., Ohio

A. Of course not. Such lack of reverence and respect for the Blessed Sacrament is shameful. Extraordinary ministers who have been deputed to bring the Eucharist to the sick or to shut-ins should obtain the consecrated Hosts after Communion or after Mass and transport the Body of the Lord in a small metal case known as a pyx.

Q. One of the extraordinary ministers in our parish fills a small plastic medicine bottle with the Precious Blood for the residents in a nursing home. Can you tell me what the regulations are on this? — G.C.B., Wisconsin
A. Here are the regulations for the Archdiocese of Boston:

"Sick people who are unable to receive Communion under the form of bread may receive it under the form of wine alone. If the wine is consecrated at a Mass not celebrated in the presence of the sick person, the Blood of the Lord is kept in a properly covered vessel and is placed in the tabernacle after Communion. The Precious Blood should be carried to the sick in a vessel which is closed in such a way as to eliminate all danger of spilling. If some of the Precious Blood remains, it should be consumed by the minister, who should also see to it that the vessel is properly purified."

Q. Can a divorced man who is living with a divorced woman (they are not married to each other) give out Communion at Mass on Sundays? — G.A.H., Minnesota
A. One of the conditions for being an extraordinary minister of the Eucharist is that a person be a practicing Catholic who is living up to the teachings of the faith. If the situation in your parish is as you have described it, the man is living in adultery and should certainly not be distributing Communion.

Q. As a nurse working in a psychiatric unit of a general hospital, I am deeply troubled by the manner in which lay Eucharistic ministers distribute Communion to patients here. I have seen them give Communion to non-Catholics, lapsed Catholics openly living in sin, and non-believers. I heard one lay minister tell a man who asked about Confession that it was no longer necessary to receive the sacrament of Penance before receiving Communion if you were sick and in the hospital. Can something be done about this? — J.M.F., New Jersey
A. You are right to be troubled since these Eucharistic ministers are going about their solemn and important apostolate in a careless and frivolous manner. First, there ought to be an effort to identify which patients are Catholics. Second, if the patients

are lucid, they ought to be given the opportunity to go to Confession if they think they have serious sins to be forgiven. J.M.F. mentioned that there is no longer a chaplain in residence at the hospital, but the lay ministers ought to make arrangements for a priest to come to the hospital for the sacrament of Penance.

Third, the pastor of the parish from which the Eucharistic ministers come ought to sit them down and explain proper procedures to them. He should also tell them that the sacrament of Penance is just as necessary for those in mortal sin in hospitals — if not more necessary since the person may be in danger of death — as anywhere else.

Q. Why are we forbidden to kneel for Holy Communion? — G.A., Indiana

Q. A priest told the son of a friend of mine that he would not give him Communion in the future if he genuflected beforehand. My friend complained to the bishop, who said that since we kneel from the Sanctus through Communion, that serves as our personal reverence; therefore, bowing or genuflecting is redundant. Is the bishop right about this? — D.A.H., Virginia

Q. Recently a priest refused to give me Communion because I knelt for the Eucharist. He told me that if I came to his church again and chose to kneel for Communion, he would have me arrested on a charge of disturbing the Mass. Can he do such a thing? — N.W., New York

Q. Do we lay people genuflect when we go to Communion? — D.W., Colorado

A. In its 1980 instruction on the Eucharist, the Sacred Congregation for the Sacraments and Divine Worship said the following:

"With regard to the manner of going to Communion, the faithful can receive it either kneeling or standing, in accordance with the norms laid down by the Episcopal Conference. When the faithful communicate kneeling, no other sign of reverence towards the Blessed Sacrament is required since kneeling is itself a sign of adoration. When they receive Communion standing, it is strongly recommended that, coming up in procession, they should make a sign of reverence before receiving the Sacrament. This should be done at the right time and place so that the order of people going to and from Communion is not disrupted" (*Inaestimabile Donum*, n. 11).

That sign of reverence is also recommended in paragraphs

244c, 246b, and 247b of the *General Instruction of the Roman Missal.*

So there is nothing wrong with kneeling to receive the Eucharist, and any priest who refuses Communion to a kneeling communicant, or who threatens to have a communicant arrested for kneeling, is very wrong. In the interests of not disrupting the Communion line, however, one who plans to kneel ought to alert the person behind them or perhaps come up to Communion last.

Should we genuflect before receiving the Host? This would certainly be a sign of reverence, and it would follow the example of the priest, who genuflects before he receives Communion. In the *Ceremonial of Bishops*, it says that when priests concelebrate Mass with a bishop, "one by one the concelebrants approach the bishop, genuflect, and reverently receive from him the Body of Christ."

It is not illogical to contend that if it is proper for priests to genuflect before receiving Communion from the bishop, it should also be proper for the laity to do likewise when receiving our Lord from the priest or extraordinary minister. For a good discussion of this matter, and of the current campaign to require Catholics to stand during the entire Eucharistic Prayer, including the Consecration, see the article ("Kneeling and Faith in the Eucharist") by Regis Scanlon, O.F.M. Cap., in the August-September 1994 issue of *Homiletic & Pastoral Review*.

Fr. Scanlon argues that "when Catholics 'worship' by 'bending the knee' in Eucharistic adoration, they strengthen belief in the doctrine of the Real Presence of Christ in the Eucharist, for themselves and for the entire Church. And when they can and do not, they weaken it."

Q. In one of our local parishes, the priest presents a ciborium filled with Hosts to a member of the congregation (not an extraordinary minister of the Eucharist). The ciborium is then passed around the church with each person giving Communion to his or her neighbor. Is this not an abuse? — E.L.M., Minnesota

Q. If there is no eucharistic minister available, our priest leaves the chalice on the altar and invites each communicant to drink from the chalice and hand it on to someone else while he distributes the Host. Is this proper? — G.T.C., Indiana

A. Both methods of distributing Communion are improper. Here is the relevant section of *Inaestimabile Donum*:

"Communion is a gift of the Lord, given to the faithful through the minister appointed for this purpose. It is not permitted that the faithful themselves pick up the consecrated Hosts and the sacred chalice; still less that they should hand them from one to another" (n. 9).

With no extraordinary minister available, the priest should distribute Communion under only one species. However, if the priest had consecrated a large quantity of the Precious Blood and then found himself without the expected extraordinary minister, Appendix V at the back of the *Sacramentary* gives him the authority to designate a minister of the Eucharist for that single occasion only. He would then be showing "the reverence due to the Sacrament" and would be acting "for the good of those receiving the Eucharist" (n. 12).

Q. In a local church, the women of the parish bake the Communion bread and lay ministers assist the celebrant in breaking the Bread prior to Communion. This leaves a plateful of crumbs after Communion, and I don't know what disposition is made of these fragments. This would seem to violate paragraph 8 of *Inaestimabile Donum*. Am I correct? — J.R.B., Ohio

A. Since we are apparently talking about loaves of bread and not traditional Hosts, J.R.B. is correct in objecting to the careless manner in which the Eucharist is broken. The paragraph from the 1980 document on the Eucharist says in part: "The preparation of the bread requires attentive care to ensure that the product does not detract from the dignity due to the Eucharistic bread, can be broken in a dignified way, does not give rise to excessive fragments, and does not offend the sensibilities of the faithful when they eat it."

Q. I recently found a Host in the pew in our parish church. There was a priest in the confessional, so I told him about it and he consumed the Host. The priest told me that if it happened again, I should consume the Host myself. Is this permitted? — T.G., Florida

A. We wouldn't be so quick to give such permission. In most parishes, it is unlikely that no priest would be available to whom the Host could be given within a reasonable amount of time. Therefore, a person who finds a Host would be obliged to make every effort to locate a priest, a deacon, or an extraordinary minister of the Eucharist. But if none of them were available, then it would be all right for you to consume the Host, provided that you were in the state of grace.

Q. In my travels around the United States I have noticed large amounts of the Precious Blood left in vessels after Communion under both species. There doesn't seem to be an attempt to purify the vessels and the Precious Blood is disposed of in the sacrarium. Is this an outrage, a sacrilege, or an indifference? — T.G., Florida

A. Whatever word you want to use, the actions are wrong on two counts, according to *Inaestimabile Donum*, which said that the Precious Blood "is to be consumed immediately after Communion and may not be kept. Care must be taken to consecrate only the amount of wine needed for Communion" (n. 14).

The document also said that the sacred vessels that contained the Eucharistic species must be purified according to directives contained in the *General Instruction of the Roman Missal*. There is no excuse for any carelessness in handling the Body and Blood of the Lord.

Q. I have seen the Eucharist dropped several times and no washing procedure was applied. Has this procedure been eliminated? — D.G.C., Maryland

A. There was a time when great care was taken to wash the spot on which the Host was accidentally dropped to make sure that all the sacred particles were recovered, but there is today no required purification of the spot. However, any visible particles must still be recovered reverently and disposed of properly. And there is no reason why a priest, deacon, or extraordinary minister should not purify the spot anyway as a sign of the special reverence called for by Pope John Paul in his 1980 letter to the priests of the world, On the Mystery and Worship of the Eucharist (*Dominicae Cenae*):

"It is necessary for all of us who are ministers of the Eucharist to examine carefully our actions at the altar, in particular the way in which we handle that Food and Drink which are the Body and Blood of the Lord our God in our hands; the way in which we distribute Holy Communion; the way in which we perform the purification.

"All these actions have a meaning of their own. Naturally, scrupulosity must be avoided, but God preserve us from behaving in a way that lacks respect, from undue hurry, from an impatience that causes scandal" (n. 11).

Q. I recently attended a funeral Mass where everybody lined up to receive Holy Communion. Assuming that some had neither gone to Confession nor were they in a state of

grace, were these valid administrations of the Eucharist?
— R.H., Arizona

A. There is no question that the number of people going to Confession has gone way down in recent years while at the same time the number of those going to Communion has gone way up. Since there is also considerable evidence of widespread sinful activity in the world around us, it is not unusual to wonder whether there are many sacrilegious receptions of the Eucharist these days. But it would be idle for us to speculate on these matters because only God knows who is receiving Communion worthily or unworthily. Instead of wasting time trying to judge others, let us pray that people will recognize their sinfulness, seek forgiveness through the sacrament of Penance, and approach the altar in a state of grace.

Q. Is it permissible for a priest to invite non-Catholics to receive the Blessed Eucharist by saying, "Feel free to approach the table of the Lord"? Is it allowed for a priest to say Mass sitting down if he does not have some infirmity or illness? Our parish priest (not always vested) seats himself at a coffee table arranged between the sanctuary and the front pews and says Mass. He sometimes has a dozen or more children clustered around the altar at the Consecration saying the words with him. — M.M.T., Australia

A. All of these actions are highly improper and contrary to the Church's liturgical regulations. Your priest should be suspended for such blatant disobedience and for the scandal he is giving.

Regarding reception of Communion by non-Catholic Christians, the U.S. Bishops have issued this guideline, which should be just as true in Australia: "Catholics believe that the Eucharist is an action of the celebrating community, signifying a oneness in faith, life, and worship of the community. Reception of the Eucharist by Christians not fully united with us would imply a oneness which does not yet exist, and for which we must all pray."

Q. Is it permitted for a sister to expose and repose the Blessed Sacrament in the monstrance for a day of adoration for retired sisters? — W.B., Missouri

A. Paragraph 91 of the Roman Ritual says that "the ordinary minister for exposition of the Eucharist is a priest or deacon."

It goes on to say, however, that "in the absence of a priest or deacon or if they are lawfully impeded, the following persons may publicly expose and later repose the Holy Eucharist for the adoration of the faithful:

a) an acolyte or special minister of Communion;

b) a member of a religious community or of a lay association of men or women which is devoted to Eucharistic adoration, upon appointment by the local Ordinary.

Such ministers may open the tabernacle and also, if suitable, place the ciborium on the altar or place the Host in the monstrance. At the end of the period of adoration, they replace the Blessed Sacrament in the tabernacle. It is not lawful, however, for them to give the blessing with the Sacrament."

Q. What is the proper procedure to be followed when the Blessed Sacrament is exposed for perpetual adoration? We need to know the proper location, furnishings, container, behavior of those in close proximity to the sacred Host, and method of handling the Host to and from the tabernacle. — J.M.P., Pennsylvania

A. The proper procedures to be followed can be found in paragraphs 82-92 of the *Roman Ritual*, in the section entitled "Exposition of the Holy Eucharist." This material is contained in volume 1 of *The Rites of the Catholic Church* (Pueblo Publishing Company), pp. 671-674.

In summary, the regulations state that exposition takes place in the body of a church or in a chapel; that genuflection in the presence of the Blessed Sacrament is on one knee; that four to six candles are lighted and incense is used for exposition in a monstrance; that lengthy exposition may take place only if a sufficient number of worshipers will be present; that shorter periods of exposition must be preceded by readings from Scripture, songs, prayers, and silent prayer; that the ordinary minister of exposition is a priest or deacon; that in the absence of a priest or deacon, an acolyte, another special minister of Communion, or a person appointed by the local bishop may expose and repose the Eucharist, but may not give the blessing with the Sacrament; that the priest or deacon should vest in an alb, or a surplice over a cassock, and a stole; and that the priest or deacon should wear a white cope and humeral veil to give the blessing at the end of adoration.

Q. Our pastor does not use the humeral veil during Benediction, places the monstrance on top of the altar, and

changes the words in some parts of the Mass. When I asked him why, he invited me to leave the confessional. When I said I would write to the bishop, he asked me if I wanted his address. Please advise how to handle this? — J.E.C., Pennsylvania

A. While these points might better have been raised outside the confessional, let us say first that there is nothing wrong with placing the monstrance on top of the altar. However, the Rite of Eucharistic Exposition and Benediction does say that "after the prayer the priest or deacon puts on the humeral veil, genuflects, and takes the monstrance or ciborium. He makes the sign of the cross over the people with the monstrance or ciborium, in silence" (n. 99).

As we have noted in the past, no priest is allowed to change the words spoken at Mass. Pray for your pastor and for all those who do not follow the liturgical directives of the Church.

Chapter 10

The Sacred Liturgy

Q. Isn't it mandatory that a crucifix be displayed in the sanctuary of a Catholic Church? — J.R.H., Wyoming

A. Yes, it is mandatory. The *General Instruction of the Roman Missal* states: "There is also to be a cross, clearly visible to the congregation, either on the altar or near it" (n. 270).

Q. In answer to my question about a crucifix being mandatory in the sanctuary of a Catholic church, be advised that a cross is not a crucifix. Our church has a cross but not a crucifix, as do most Protestant churches. Is there any other source which indicates that a crucifix is mandatory? — J.R.H., Wyoming

Q. In your answer about whether a crucifix should be displayed in the sanctuary of a Catholic Church, you quoted the *General Instruction of the Roman Missal*. The questioner asks about a crucifix; you answer about a cross. A cross is not a crucifix, so would you please clarify the situation. — F.&H.F., Arizona

A. While Protestants may consider a cross and a crucifix to be two different things, Catholics have for centuries used the words interchangeably in referring to the object carrying the body of the crucified Savior. The liturgical directive cited in the *General Instruction of the Roman Missal* uses the word "cross" (in Latin *crux*) and not the word "crucifix," but there is no evidence that the *GIRM* is referring to anything but the traditional representation of our Lord. Crosses on or near the altar in Catholic churches ought to have the body of Christ on them.

Q. Several churches where we have recently attended Mass display the risen Christ instead of the crucified Christ. What is the significance of this change. Am I old-fashioned to prefer Christ crucified as a reminder that He died for our sins? — R.H.H., Oregon

A. In the first 1,000 or so years after Christ, crosses represented a resurrected and glorious Jesus. Then, as the emphasis shifted towards the Passion and death of our Lord, crucifixes began to portray a dead or suffering Christ, and that portrayal has been the most common one down to the present day.

Good arguments can be advanced for both representations of our Lord — there is much we can learn from meditating on His terrible suffering for our sins, as well as on His glorious resurrection that foreshadows our resurrection at the end of the world. But the crucified Christ might be more appropriate today in a world that has lost its sense of sin. The body of our crucified Lord is as stark a reminder as one could imagine of the horror of sin.

As Archbishop Fulton J. Sheen once noted, Christ's blood is the ink and His skin the parchment on which was written the awful litany of sin. The crown of thorns reminds us of all our evil thoughts and desires — the sins of pride, lust, envy, hatred, anger, prejudice, betrayal; the open wounds from the scourging of the numerous sins of the flesh — impurity, drunkenness, drug abuse, gluttony, sloth; the nails in the hands and feet of the times when those bodily members have led us to sins of theft, murder, violence, reckless driving, vandalism; and the stab wound that pierced His heart of the many times that we have turned our hearts away from Him.

Q. A new young priest in our parish did not allow decorations in church during ordinary time, saying that such was too festive in a "pre-Lenten period." Yet with the arrival of Ash Wednesday, the church was wild with ornaments and decorations, including banners, streamers, grapevines and ribbons around the columns and arches, and manzanita branches everywhere, including behind the head of Jesus on the cross. This seems very contradictory and out of place. — L.O., California

A. Such decorations certainly are out of place, particularly during Lent. The *General Instruction of the Roman Missal* says that "the choice of materials for church appointments must be marked by concern for genuineness and by the intent to foster instruction of the faithful and the dignity of the place of worship" (n. 279). We would think that any decorations in church would have to meet the same standard.

Q. Our pastor has indicated that he wants to abolish all use of flowers on the altar except for such special occasions as weddings. Are there any norms regarding flowers on the altar? — E.V.S., Ohio

A. The *Order of Prayer for 1992* repeats (p. 63) the traditional discipline: "In Lent the altar should not be decorated with flowers ... [excluding Laetare Sunday, solemnities, and feasts]." This makes no sense unless flowers are appropriate during the rest of the year. Furthermore, there are 22 days (in addition to the Sundays of Advent and Lent) when the Mass of the Day must be used for weddings rather than the Nuptial Mass. If these celebrations are more important than weddings, then any decoration appropriate for weddings is certainly appropriate on these 22 days.

Q. When I asked the pastor why none of the statues or the crucifix were covered for Lent, he replied, "It is not necessary." Was he correct? — J.R., Ontario

A. They were never covered for Lent, but only for Passiontide (from the fifth Sunday of Lent). This is still an option if the episcopal conference so decides. The National Conference of Catholic Bishops in the United States has not decided one way or the other, so a parish is free to cover, or not to cover, the crucifixes from the vigil of the fifth Sunday of Lent until the end of the Lord's Passion on Good Friday, and images from the fifth Sunday until the beginning of the Easter Vigil on Holy Saturday.

Q. Last winter, our parish priest allowed an Arts and Environment Committee to remove the holy water from the fonts throughout the whole season of Lent. Is this a permissible practice? — E.G.C., Louisiana

A. No, it is not a permissible practice. The Church-approved practice is to remove holy water from the fonts during the Paschal Triduum (Holy Thursday through Easter Sunday) until the new holy water can be blessed at the Easter Vigil. But some so-called liturgists feel compelled to go to extremes; you know, if the Church says three days, why don't we make it 40 days? This liturgical silliness can lead to situations like the one experienced by a priest we know. While visiting an out-of-state parish to celebrate a funeral Mass during Lent, he was told not to sprinkle the casket because the rule in that parish was "no holy water in Lent." All the stoups near the doors of the church had been filled with sand.

Q. Please verify if it is all right to have a 4' x 8' picture of Martin Luther King behind the altar. — F.F., California

A. The *General Instruction of the Roman Missal* says that "in keeping with the Church's very ancient tradition, it is lawful to set up in places of worship images of Christ, Mary, and the saints for veneration by the faithful" (n. 278). Since Martin Luther King is not a canonized saint of the Catholic Church, it is not appropriate to have a picture of him behind the altar in a Catholic place of worship.

Q. The sanctuary lamps in both our upper and lower churches are seldom lighted. I wrote to the pastor about it, but he never responded. Isn't a sanctuary lamp required when the Holy Eucharist is present in the tabernacle? And how can I persuade the pastor to relight the lamps? — R.F.G., Pennsylvania

A. Yes, a sanctuary lamp is required, according to the 1967 instruction *Eucharisticum Mysterium*, n. 57; the 1980 instruction *Inaestimabile Donum*, n. 25; and the 1983 Code of Canon Law. Canon 940 states: "A special lamp to indicate and honor the presence of Christ is to burn at all times before the tabernacle in which the Most Holy Eucharist is reserved."

Bring these citations to the attention of your pastor and politely suggest to him that the sanctuary lamps ought to be lit. If he refuses to do so, then you should contact your bishop.

Q. Is it permissible to use another light source, for example an electric light, instead of a candle to indicate the Real Presence of Christ in the sanctuary? — W.F.H., Rhode Island

A. According to the Appendix 2 of the *General Instruction of the Roman Missal*, "Candles intended for liturgical use should be made of material that can provide a living flame without being smoky or noxious and that does not stain the altar cloths or coverings. Electric bulbs are banned in the interest of safeguarding authenticity and the full symbolism of light" (n. 269). Except for the altar candles, however, oil lamps can be used.

Q. Regarding the location of the tabernacle, is it true that St. Charles Borromeo convinced the Council of Trent to situate the tabernacle at the center of the high altar? — P.M., Florida

Q. What would be the appropriate response to the enclosed column that says the placement of the tabernacle close to the main altar is "symbolically confusing?" — S.D., New York

Q. Is it okay for the tabernacle to be other than center altar? What about separate Eucharistic chapels? — R.M., Kentucky

A. According to Klauser's *Short History of Western Liturgy*, the central tabernacle appeared at Rome in the 16th century and was mandated in the Ritual of 1614. St. Charles Borromeo played a leading role at the Council of Trent and may have been part of this movement. He died in 1584, thirty years before it became a matter of law.

Let us review what the Church has said about location of the tabernacle since the end of the Second Vatican Council. In 1967, the document *Eucharisticum Mysterium* said that "the Blessed Sacrament should be reserved in a solid, inviolable tabernacle in the middle of the main altar or on a side altar, but in a truly prominent place. Alternatively, according to legitimate customs and in individual cases decided by the local Ordinary, it may be placed in some other part of the church which is really worthy and properly equipped" (n. 54).

In 1980, the document *Inaestimabile Donum* said that "the tabernacle in which the Eucharist is kept can be located on an altar, or away from it, in a spot in the church which is very prominent, truly noble, and duly decorated, or in a chapel suitable for private prayer and for adoration by the faithful" (n. 24).

In its second edition (1982), the *General Instruction of the Roman Missal* said that "every encouragement should be given to the practice of Eucharistic reservation in a chapel suited to the faithful's private adoration and prayer. If this is impossible because of the structure of the church, the sacrament should be reserved at an altar or elsewhere, in keeping with local custom, and in a part of the church that is worthy and properly adorned" (n. 276).

In the 1983 Code of Canon Law, section 2 of canon 938 says: "The tabernacle in which the Most Holy Eucharist is reserved should be placed in a part of the church that is prominent, conspicuous, beautifully decorated, and suitable for prayer."

Commenting on this matter, Fr. Peter Stravinskas of *The Catholic Answer* has said that canon 938 takes precedence over previous Church legislation; that a separate chapel would make sense in a cathedral or historic church where there were many tourists, but not in the average parish church; and that a "prominent" position for the tabernacle does not necessarily mean "dead-center," but would "certainly imply visibility from the central axis of the church."

What about the statement that having the tabernacle on or near the main altar would be "symbolically confusing?" It is true that at Mass the focus of the congregation should be on what is happening at the altar; that is, where Jesus becomes present when the priest recites the words of the institution of the

Eucharist. And that is where the Hosts are consecrated for later reservation in the tabernacle.

There may be some people who would find the close proximity of the altar and the tabernacle confusing, but we would say from personal experience that those in the congregation who are paying attention are focused on the actions of the priest at the altar. If there is a problem of divided attention, says Fr. Stravinskas, "the simplest solution is to situate the tabernacle in such a way that a grille or drape can be drawn before it whenever the Eucharistic Sacrifice is being offered, while leaving it open to view at other times."

Q. Our pastor wants to move the tabernacle because he says canon law prohibits him from turning his back to it. Is this true? — W.R., Wisconsin.

Q. How can a priest or bishop, who stands with his back turned on God while he is offering the Holy Sacrifice of the Mass, expect to convince anyone that he believes Jesus is truly present in the Blessed Sacrament? — R.J.K., Ohio

A. There is nothing in canon law that prohibits a priest from turning his back to the tabernacle. There have always been times during the Mass, even in the Tridentine Mass, when the priest turned his back on the tabernacle, such as when proclaiming the Word of God or when distributing Communion. There is no sign of disrespect or irreverence involved, any more than when members of the congregation walk out of church with their backs turned to the tabernacle. A priest or bishop who celebrates Mass in a reverent and holy manner, particularly when he is consecrating the bread and wine, gives the clearest evidence for his belief in the Real Presence.

Q. In our church, the tabernacle is in a separate chapel and not visible to those in the pews. No one genuflects when passing through the sanctuary prior to the beginning of Mass. Is there any reason why we should genuflect in the main chamber of the church? — M.S., Michigan

A. No, there isn't. If there is no tabernacle in the main church, there is no point in genuflecting before Mass since Jesus is not present there. One could, however, make the traditional sign of reverence, a bow, to the altar.

Q. I will be getting married soon and I am concerned about the traditional music for a Nuptial Mass. I understand that both the processional and the recessional have

been frowned on because of their secular/pagan origins. Can you enlighten me about this? — G.J.E., New Jersey

A. The processional and recessional refer to the music played before and after the Nuptial Mass, and both are standard at weddings. While the traditional wedding marches are not of liturgical origin (Mendelssohn and Wagner composed the two pieces most often heard), they are generally permitted. Music within the wedding ceremony should be strictly liturgical.

Q. Some of the strange innovations going on these days makes one wonder whether the Mass is valid. What would constitute an invalid Mass? — G.M., Iowa

Q. Can you give me absolute and indisputable proof that the "New Mass" is valid? — E.P.R., California

A. For a Mass to be valid, the celebrant must be a validly ordained priest (canon 900) and he must use valid matter (see the previous chapter for a discussion of what constitutes valid matter). The *Ordo Missae* promulgated by Pope Paul VI is valid because he was the Vicar of Christ on earth and had the same authority over the Mass as his papal predecessors. To say that the Mass celebrated throughout the Universal Church today is not valid is to say that the gates of Hell have prevailed against the Church, which Jesus promised would never happen (Matthew 16:18).

Q. Would the following words, which were said after the Breaking of the Bread at Mass, make the Mass invalid? And what is the difference between an invalid and an illicit Mass? The words were: "Whoever comes to this table and eats of this Bread, that person is saying: I believe in a new world, a world where bread is for everyone — for the poor as much as for the rich. And everyone here who will share this cup shares too a covenant with the brokenhearted and with all those who are yearning for justice. So let us eat and drink then as He taught us, and may this Bread and Wine provoke a new hunger in us that will never be satisfied until we taste his kingdom." — C.B., Pennsylvania

A. An invalid Mass would be one where something essential was left out, e.g., the proper matter (bread and wine) or key words ("This is my Body"). An illicit (but not invalid) Mass would be one where certain prescribed words or actions were omitted or changed, but not enough to alter the meaning of those parts of the Mass.

The words which C.B.'s priest added to the liturgy, while profoundly inappropriate and contrary to the discipline of the Church, would not invalidate the Mass because they did not change the meaning of that section of the Communion Rite. If the priest really wanted to make a point along those lines, he should have included those sentiments in his homily.

We reiterate the admonition of the Second Vatican Council, that no priest "may add, remove, or change anything in the liturgy on his own authority" (*Constitution on the Sacred Liturgy*, n. 22). We find the same admonition in the *Catechism of the Catholic Church* (n. 1125), which says that no sacramental rite may be modified or manipulated at the will of the minister or the community. It says that even the supreme authority in the Church may not change the liturgy arbitrarily, but only in the obedience of faith and with religious respect for the mystery of the liturgy.

Q. Can you explain what the Church means by licit and illicit, valid and invalid? — D.M., Massachusetts
A. These words are usually used in connection with the celebration of Mass or the administration of the sacraments. Licit means something that is permitted by Church law, while illicit means something that is unlawful or contrary to the rules and regulations of the Church. Valid refers to some element that is necessary for a sacrament to be efficacious, while invalid means that the necessary element was missing and that the sacrament was null and void or ineffective.

Thus, if the required matter and form are not used when administering a sacrament, the sacrament is invalid. If the priest uses the prescribed matter and form, but adds some extra words of his own, the sacrament is valid but not licit since he has acted contrary to what the Church requires in that instance.

This question frequently arises in connection with the Consecration at Mass. If the priest were to use a substance other than wine, or a wine that had turned to vinegar, the Consecration would not be valid since a necessary element was missing. If the priest were to change the words of institution and say, for example, "This is a symbol of my Body," that would make the Consecration invalid. If, on the other hand, the priest were to use the correct words ("This is my Body which will be given up for you"), but were to add something like "whether you are rich or poor, young or old, Christian or non-Christian," the Consecration would be valid, but it would not be licit since he had acted contrary to the rubrics required by the *Sacramentary*.

Q. If a priest does not believe in transubstantiation, is his Mass valid? — W.A.D., Massachusetts

Q. Is there a danger that Jesus may no longer come to us in Communion if some of our priests no longer accept Catholic beliefs? — R.V.S., Arkansas

A. According to the Council of Trent and many orthodox theologians, a priest's belief in transubstantiation is not necessary for a valid consecration of the Eucharist. If the priest says the proper words over the bread and wine, and has the intention of doing what the Church intends, then a valid Consecration has taken place, even if the priest is in mortal sin and no longer believes in transubstantiation. A habitual intention, i.e., a presumed intention based on his ordination, would be sufficient for validity.

For the security of the faithful, the Church would also insist that any objective sins consequent upon the failings of a celebrant are not imputed to the congregation (e.g., participating in the simulation of a sacrament by a fraudulent celebrant) unless they know what is going on.

Q. I accept that a priest says a valid Mass if he has the intention of doing what the Church intends and says the proper words at the Consecration. But with so many shocking revelations of homosexuality in the seminaries and ordained priests committing homosexual acts, I cannot help but wonder if these priests have received valid orders and if the Masses they say are valid. — J.R., Ontario

A. Prior to ordination, canon 1051.1 requires the rector of the seminary or house of formation to issue testimonial letters "concerning the qualities required for the reception of orders; that is, the candidate's correct doctrine, genuine piety, good morals and his suitability for exercising the ministry; and, after a duly executed inquiry, the state of his physical and psychological health."

If this inquiry fails to screen out unworthy candidates (we are not talking here about those prohibited from receiving orders due to the irregularities and impediments listed in canons 1041 and 1042), their ordination would still be valid, and the Masses they celebrated would be valid, even though these priests may be in the state of sin, whether because of homosexual, heterosexual, or any other sinful actions. They would not receive the graces from the sacrament of Holy Orders, or from Masses celebrated, until their sins had been forgiven in the sacrament of Penance.

In other words, the state of a priest's soul does not affect the validity of his sacramental actions. This may strike us as odd, but it is the Church's way of eliminating doubt in the minds of the faithful about whether they are participating in a valid Mass or receiving valid sacraments. Otherwise, one could never be sure.

Q. Why did the Church call the new Mass the *Novus Ordo*? — F.K., Texas

A. The Church did not call the Mass that we now celebrate the *Novus Ordo* (New Order), but only the *Ordo Missae* (Order of Mass).

Q. Is there a publication called the *Order of Mass*? If so, where could I obtain a copy? — F.J.S., Ohio

Q. What is the *Roman Missal*? How much authority does it have? — S.N., Pennsylvania

Q. Please define the *Sacramentary* used at Mass. Can priests alter the wording of Eucharistic Prayers? Is the wording of the Consecration the same in all nine Eucharistic Prayers? — J.J., Michigan

A. The *Roman Missal*, which was revised by decree of the Second Vatican Council and published by the authority of Pope Paul VI in 1970, is the authoritative book that contains the prayers and rites for the celebration of the Holy Sacrifice of the Mass throughout the world. It is actually divided into two parts: the *Sacramentary*, which contains the complete Order of the Mass (the rites and prayers, as well as instructions on what to say and do and what options are available) and the *Lectionary*, which contains the readings from Scripture for each day of the week and for Sunday, as well as readings for special feasts and occasions. In 1984, the Vatican gave permission for priests, under certain conditions, to celebrate Mass using the 1962 edition of the *Roman Missal* promulgated by Pope St. Pius V in 1570.

A copy of the *Sacramentary*, the large red-covered book that you see on the altar, would be very expensive, but perhaps one of your priests would let you look at it.

The preface to the *Roman Missal* is known as the *General Instruction of the Roman Missal*. It gives the regulations for celebrating Mass, explains the functions and duties of each participant, and describes the material things, furnishings, and arrangements required to celebrate Mass properly. It has been published as a separate, 118-page document by the U.S. Catholic Conference and should be available through any Catholic bookstore or from the USCC's Office of Publishing and Promotion Services in Washington, D.C. (Tel. 202-541-3000). Ask for No. 852-5 in the Liturgy Documentary Series.

In answer to J.J., a priest is forbidden to change the wording of the Eucharistic Prayers, and the words of Consecration are the same in all nine Eucharistic Prayers approved for use in the United States.

Q. My child's CCD book doesn't mention the "sacrifice" of the Mass. Has that term been dropped? — A.G., Oregon

A. No, it has not been dropped. The sacrificial character of the Mass has been clearly taught by the Second Vatican Council, recent Popes, and the *Catechism of the Catholic Church*. It is also reiterated at every Mass when the priest asks us to "pray, brethren, that our sacrifice may be acceptable to God, the Almighty Father."

Vatican II's *Constitution on the Sacred Liturgy* put it this way: "At the Last Supper, on the night when He was betrayed, our Savior instituted the Eucharistic Sacrifice of His Body and Blood. He did this in order to perpetuate the sacrifice of the Cross throughout the centuries until He should come again, and to entrust to His beloved spouse, the Church, a memorial of His death and resurrection: a sacrament of love, a sign of unity, a bond of charity, a paschal banquet in which Christ is consumed, the mind is filled with grace, and a pledge of future glory is given to us" (n. 47).

And the *Catechism* devotes a whole section (nos. 1362-1372) to the sacrificial memorial of Christ and His Body, the Church. In paragraph 1365 in particular, the *Catechism* says that because the Eucharist is the memorial of Christ's passover, it is also a sacrifice. It says that the sacrificial character of the Eucharist is manifested in the very words of institution: "This is my body which is given for you" and "This cup which is poured out for you is the New Covenant in my blood." In the Eucharist, says the *Catechism*, Christ gives us the very body which He gave up for us on the cross, the very blood which He "poured out in behalf of many for the forgiveness of sins" (Matthew 26:28).

Q. How was the Mass celebrated before the reforms of the Council of Trent in the 16th century? — Name Withheld, Pennsylvania

A. In the appendix to his *Dictionary of the Liturgy*, Fr. Jovian P. Lang offers some valuable background information on the origins and history of the Mass. This appendix includes a useful

"Chronological Table of Mass Prayers" (a century-by-century listing of when certain prayers and actions became part of the Mass), a comparison of the Latin/Roman rite of Pius V (1570) with that of Paul VI (1970), and a "Select Chronology of Major Events in the History of the Liturgy."

Relying on Fr. Lang's chronology, which should be read in its entirety, here are a few highlights of the first 1570 years of the Mass.

— 30-100: Liturgy is first called the "Breaking of the Bread" (Acts 2:42) or the "Lord's Supper" (1 Corinthians 11:20) and then the "Eucharist" toward the end of the 1st century. The principal parts of the Liturgy are the Opening Prayer, readings from the Old Testament, accounts of the Lord's Passion, miracles, and teachings (Gospel), a sermon, Prayer over the Gifts, Preface, Sanctus, Eucharistic Prayer, and reception of His Body and Blood. Jewish Christians celebrate the Liturgy in Aramaic, and Hellenistic Christians in the Greek of the people, known as "Koine."

— 150: St. Justin Martyr describes the Eucharist as consisting of a Liturgy of the Word, Prayer of the Faithful, Preparation of the Gifts, Liturgy of the Eucharist, and a collection for the poor.

— c. 300: Various liturgies arise in the major cities of the Empire — Alexandria, Antioch, Constantinople, and Rome.

— 366-384: The changeover of the language of the Mass from Greek to Latin is completed under Pope Leo the Great.

— 401-417: The Eucharistic Prayer becomes one fixed formula or canon during the reign of Pope Innocent I.

— 428: Special vestments begin to be used at Mass.

— 492-496: Pope Gelasius I gathers the prayers of the Mass into three books of a *Sacramentary* — a Proper of the Season, a Proper of the Saints, and a Book of Votive Masses.

— 590-604: Pope Gregory the Great condenses the three books of Gelasius into a forerunner of our *Roman Missal*.

— 850: Pope Leo IV prescribes the amice, alb, stole, maniple, and chasuble for Mass.

— 1198-1216: Pope Innocent III brings forth a *Missal* that is a forerunner of the *Missal* of Pius V.

— 1570: The *Roman Missal* is promulgated by Pius V.

Q. Can you give some brief definitions of the following Masses: Traditional Latin, Tridentine, *Ordo Missae, Novus Ordo* of Paul VI? Which Masses can be said in private and which ones in public? Which are licit and illicit? What are

rites? Are "Tridentine" and "English" rites? — P.W.V., North Carolina

A. The Traditional Latin and the Tridentine Mass are the same thing — the liturgy promulgated by Pope St. Pius V in 1570 and celebrated in Latin as the official Mass in the Western Church for 400 years. The *Ordo Missae* ("Order of the Mass") and the *Novus Ordo* ("New Order") are the same thing — the liturgy promulgated by Pope Paul VI in 1970 and now celebrated in the language of each country as the official liturgy of the Western Church.

Both the Tridentine Mass and the *Ordo Missae* are licit, although permission must be obtained from a bishop to celebrate the Tridentine Mass. Both may also be celebrated in private or in public, although the *General Instruction of the Roman Missal* says that "Mass should not be celebrated without a server or the participation of at least one of the faithful, except for some legitimate and reasonable cause" (n. 211).

A rite is the words and actions used in celebrating the Mass. Tridentine is the mode of the Roman rite which stemmed from the reforms of the Council of Trent and was mandated in the *Roman Missal* of Pius V; English is not a rite, but rather the language in which the rite of the Mass is celebrated in the United States and some other countries, according to the *Roman Missal* of Paul VI.

Q. If Pope Pius V said that the Tridentine Mass could never be changed, how could Pope Paul VI change it? — G.B., Minnesota, and D.J.S., Rhode Island

A. Pope Paul VI, a successor of St. Peter like Pius V, had the same authority over the Mass as his predecessor four centuries earlier. Both men had the power of "binding and loosing" that our Lord promised to St. Peter and his successors. Just as Pius V promulgated the *Roman Missal* at the instruction of the Council of Trent, so Paul VI promulgated the *Ordo Missae* at the instruction of the Second Vatican Council.

The reasons for the changes were spelled out by Pope Paul in his *Apostolic Constitution on the Roman Missal*, dated April 3, 1969. He said that the revisions in the Mass were based on centuries of study of ancient manuscripts and liturgical texts and were intended to bring about a more active and devout participation by the people. He also expressed the hope that the *Missal* "will be received by the faithful as an aid whereby all can witness to each other and strengthen the one faith common to all."

Finally, the Holy Father said: "It is our will that these decisions and ordinances should be firm and effective now and in the future, notwithstanding any constitutions and apostolic ordinances made by our predecessors, and all other decrees, including those deserving of special mention, no matter of what kind."

Some have suggested that because Paul VI's language was not as forceful as that of Pius V in 1570, it is somehow less binding on Catholics. That is not true. Granted, Pius V was more forceful, but he was speaking at the height of the Protestant Reformation, when all Catholic teaching, and especially the Mass, was under attack. But Paul VI was just as much the Vicar of Christ as Pius V and had the same authority as each of his predecessors to change the manner of celebrating the Holy Sacrifice of the Mass.

Furthermore, the technical formulas used by the Popes have their own history; a prohibition against changing a decree is meant to inhibit the activities of the Roman Curia (the administrative arm of the Church), not of future Pontiffs. Pius V did in fact authorize minor changes after the decree of 1570, and Benedict XIV and Pius X carried out more significant changes.

Q. From whom must a priest obtain a celebret to say the Tridentine Mass? Does the Tridentine Mass follow the old (pre-Vatican II) liturgical calendar? — J.M., California, and J.F.D., Colorado

A. A celebret, or permission for a priest to say Mass, must be obtained from a bishop or the superior of a religious congregation. Since the Roman documents do not explicitly answer the question of which liturgical calendar to use, the practice in many dioceses is to follow the calendar of Trent because the Missal of Trent cannot be simply applied to the new calendar.

Q. In my diocese, the bishop has denied people the Latin Mass. Can you give me a reason why some bishops will not allow a Latin Mass in their diocese? — J.J., Washington

A. The reason might vary with each bishop, but no bishop would find support at the Vatican for refusing a legitimate request for something that has the approval of the Holy Father and is being done in over 50 dioceses in the United States. It is being done because Pope John Paul II said in 1988 that "respect must everywhere be shown for the feelings of all those who are attached to the Latin liturgical tradition, by a wide and generous application of directives already issued some time ago by the Apostolic See, for the use of the *Roman Missal* according to the typical edition of 1962" (*Ecclesia Dei*).

According to the directives mentioned by the Holy Father, which were issued in 1984 by the Congregation for Divine Worship, the local bishop may give permission for public celebration of the Tridentine Mass provided that it answers a spiritual need of the faithful in his diocese and that those who request it do not question the legitimacy of the new Order of Mass.

For more information on the traditional Latin Mass — Vatican support for it, where it is being said, and how to get it into your area — you can write to the Coalition in Support of Ecclesia Dei, P.O. Box 2071, Glenview, Illinois 60025.

Q. There is a new church in our neighborhood which has been encouraging Catholics to attend its Latin Mass. I would love to go, but I have learned that is not affiliated with our archdiocese and that it does not recognize Vatican II or the *Magisterium* of Pope John Paul II or Pope John XXIII. Would its Mass be valid? — A.M., Michigan

A. If the priest celebrating the Mass was validly ordained and used valid matter, then the Mass and Eucharist would be valid but illicit since the new church in your neighborhood is not in communion with the local bishop or with the Pope, and has rejected the legitimate teaching authority of the Catholic Church. To attend Mass at this church would be an act of disobedience to the lawful authority of the Church and a sin. The seriousness of the sin would depend on one's understanding of the situation and whether the disobedience was motivated by a sincere desire for the Latin Mass or by a knowing and obstinate rejection of the Church's authority.

Q. Is it permissible to attend a Mass offered by priests of the Society of St. Pius X? — T.K., Oregon; A.J.L., California; and J.G., New York

A. No, it is not. The Society of St. Pius X was founded in 1970 by the late Archbishop Marcel Lefebvre, who was excommunicated from the Catholic Church by Pope John Paul II on July 1, 1988 because he had consecrated four bishops against the will of the Pope. The Society is a schismatic group that has cut itself off from the Church, and no faithful Catholic can attend one of its services without becoming a cooperator in the schism.

Q. Upon what canonical authority do you base your statement that the Society of St. Pius X is a schismatic group

that has cut itself off from the Church and that no faithful Catholic can attend one of its services without becoming a cooperator in the schism? — E.W.K., New York

Q. The excommunication of Archbishop Lefevbre was not an infallible statement and never was applied to the priests or faithful. It is impossible to understand why the Pope was so opposed to the Society having bishops. — L.J.G., Kansas

Q. You did not do not your homework. Write the Vatican and you will see that these Society of St. Pius X Masses are valid. This error should be corrected in your column. — D.F.C., California, and E.F.S., South Carolina

Q. Is it better to suffer a mutilated Mass than to assist at one which, while possibly illicit, is certainly valid and, I might add, reverently done? — K.E.M., Colorado

Q. Any Catholic would agree that in normal times to consecrate bishops against papal orders is schismatic. I think, however, that we would all agree that these are far from normal times. I believe that attendance at Society of St. Pius X Masses is permissible and is also an attempt to maintain communion with the Roman Catholic Church. — J.J.B., New Jersey

Q. I must admit that Archbishop Lefebvre did wrong by ordaining four bishops without permission from the Pope. But other bishops are also disobeying the Pope. It's my conviction that if the bishops obeyed the directives of Pope John Paul as expressed in *Ecclesia Dei*, there would be no reason for our people to have to attend Mass celebrated by a priest of the Society of St. Pius X. — V.Y., Arizona

Q. Archbishop Marcel Lefebvre was not excommunicated. He is in Heaven with our Lord. St. Pius X Society is the true church. *Novus Ordo* is the Mass of Satan. — P.R., California

A. Before taking up the specific questions, let us note for the record that on July 1, 1988, Bernardin Cardinal Gantin, Prefect of the Congregation for Bishops, issued a decree excommunicating Marcel Lefebvre for performing "a schismatical act by the episcopal consecration of four priests, without pontifical mandate and contrary to the will of the Supreme Pontiff." In also announcing the excommunications of Bernard Fellay, Bernard Tissier de Mallerais, Richard Williamson, Alfonso de Galarreta, and Monsignor Antonio de Castro Mayer, Cardinal Gantin cited the penalties contained in canons 1364.1 and 1382 of the Code of Canon Law.

Canon 1364.1 says that "an apostate from the faith, a heretic, or a schismatic incurs automatic (*latae sententiae*) excommunication." Canon 1382 states: "A bishop who consecrates someone a bishop and the bishop who receives such a consecration from a bishop without a pontifical mandate incur an automatic (*latae sententiae*) excommunication reserved to the Holy See."

In the decree, Cardinal Gantin also said that "the priests and faithful are warned not to support the schism of Monsignor Lefebvre, otherwise they shall incur ipso facto the very grave penalty of excommunication."

In the apostolic letter *Ecclesia Dei,* issued on July 11, 1988, Pope John Paul II reaffirmed what Cardinal Gantin had said and cited in the footnotes canons 1364, 1382, and 751. The latter provision defines schism as "the refusal of submission to the Roman Pontiff or of communion with the members of the Church subject to him."

The Holy Father made a solemn appeal "to all those who until now have been linked in various ways to the movement of Archbishop Lefebvre, that they may fulfill the grave duty of remaining united to the Vicar of Christ in the unity of the Catholic Church, and of ceasing their support in any way for that movement. Everyone should be aware that formal adherence to the schism is a grave offense against God and carries the penalty of excommunication decreed by the Church's law."

To E.W.K.: Canon law and the authoritative statement of the Pope make clear that the Society of St. Pius X is in schism and that anyone who knowingly and deliberately takes part in its services is guilty of "a grave offense against God."

To L.J.G.: Excommunication is an ecclesiastical censure, not a matter of faith and morals requiring the Holy Father to exercise the charism of infallibility, and it most certainly was applied to priests or faithful who cooperate in the schism. Pope John Paul was not opposed to the Society having bishops, but only to it having bishops that had not been approved by him. The Pontiff was concerned because, in his own words, it is through "the ordination of bishops whereby the apostolic succession is sacramentally perpetuated. Hence such disobedience — which implies in practice the rejection of the Roman primacy — constitutes a schismatic act."

To D.F.C. and E.F.S.: We never said that the Masses of the Society of St. Pius X were not valid. They are indeed valid if celebrated by validly ordained priests. These Masses, however, are illicit, that is, contrary to Church law, and one who attends them is at best disobedient and at worst guilty of grave sin.

To K.E.M.: You will find more criticisms of "mutilated Masses" in these pages than perhaps in any other Catholic publication. Our heart goes out to the faithful who are subjected to bizarre liturgical abuses week in and week out, but how can you object to one group acting contrary to the Church's laws, while supporting another group that is doing the same thing?

To J.J.B.: Living in abnormal times is no excuse for performing schismatic acts and separating oneself from the one, true Church founded by Jesus Christ on Peter and his successors. One cannot attend the Masses of a schismatic group and still claim to be in communion with the Church that declared the group to be schismatic.

To V.Y.: Bishops who disobey the Pope are wrong whether their disobedience involves consecrating bishops without a papal mandate or rejecting the Church's teaching on artificial contraception. It is not logical to invoke the violation of Church law by a bishop with whom we disagree in order to justify violation of Church law by a prelate with whom we agree. You may be right that fewer people would attend St. Pius X Masses if more bishops followed the Pope's wishes in allowing celebration of Latin Masses in their dioceses, but that is still not a good reason for risking one's eternal salvation by joining in schismatic actions.

To P.R.: We send our prayers that you will recognize the truth and not separate yourself from the only Church that Jesus established to carry out His mission in the world. The Church whose leader, the Pope, has the same authority given to St. Peter — "Whatever you declare bound on earth shall be bound in heaven" (Matthew 16:19). The Church that Christ promised would never be overcome by the forces of Hell (Matthew 16:18).

This is the Church that has survived 20 centuries of Roman persecution, barbarian invasions, the Protestant Reformation, Communist persecution, and heresies and scandals. It has survived over nearly two millenia, said Fr. Joseph Manton, "not because it is physically powerful, not because it is financially wealthy, not because it is intellectually brilliant, not because it is incredibly lucky, but simply and solely because it was founded by Jesus Christ, the Son of God. The Son of God who once spread His arms in majestic benediction over the little band of Apostles and promised He would be with them all days, even to the end of time."

Q. The Pope excommunicated Archbishop Lefebvre for disobeying him, so why are other bishops, priests, and presidents of "Catholic" universities allowed to defy the Holy Father and to undermine the Catholic Church and its faithful? — D.M., Massachusetts

A. This is a common question voiced by faithful Catholics today and one that is not easily answered. Pope Paul VI was once asked the same question, and he responded by citing the biblical parable of the wheat and the weeds (Matthew 13:24-30). In that parable, Jesus said that when the farmer's helpers asked for permission to pull up the weeds that had grown among the wheat, the farmer told them to let them grow together and he would separate them at harvest time.

Jesus explained that the wheat represented the good people, the weeds the followers of the Evil One, and the harvest the end of the world. He said that at the end of the world He would "dispatch his angels to collect from his kingdom all who draw others to apostasy, and all evildoers. The angels will hurl them into the fiery furnace where they will wail and grind their teeth. Then the saints will shine like the sun in their Father's kingdom" (Matthew 13:36-43).

Q. Enclosed is a recent decision from Cardinal Ratzinger about the Society of St. Pius X being a schismatic group. You may wish to print this reply from the office of the Prefect of the Congregation for the Doctrine of the Faith. — M.D., Pennsylvania

Q. Are you aware of the ruling received from Rome, reversing a formal canonical warning of excommunication issued by Bishop Joseph Ferrario of Hawaii? I think in fairness to your readers, especially those who would attend a Mass celebrated by a priest of the Society of St. Pius X, you would retreat from your previous answer. — L.L., Delaware

Q. I can't wait to see what sort of response you confect when next somebody writes to ask you your opinion about their attending the Pius X Mass. — J.K., Arizona

A. Our three correspondents are referring first to a previous column in which we quoted canon law and authoritative statements by Pope John Paul II and Bernardin Cardinal Gantin, Prefect of the Congregation for Bishops, to the effect that the Society of St. Pius X is in schism and that "everyone should be aware that formal adherence to the schism is a grave offense against God and carries the penalty of excommunication decreed by the Church's law" (Pope John Paul).

These correspondents sent us information indicating that on May 1, 1991, Bishop Ferrario excommunicated Patricia Morley and five other members of the Society of St. Pius X for establishing a chapel, for hosting a radio program "through which you have caused grave and serious harm, namely, confusion, scandal, and heresy, impugning the lawfulness and doctrinal soundness of the *Roman Missal* (1970) and further aligning yourselves with the Pius X schismatic movement," and for "procuring the services of an excommunicated Lefebvre bishop, Richard Williamson, who performed *contra iure* illicit Confirmation in your chapel."

The six persons appealed the decision to Rome and, on June 28, 1993, U.S. Apostolic Pro-Nuncio Archbishop Agostino Cacciavillan, acting upon the instructions of Cardinal Ratzinger, sent Mrs. Morley a letter stating that an examination of the case showed that they had not engaged in "formal schismatic acts in the strict sense" and that the decree of excommunication "lacks foundation and hence validity."

Does this mean, as our correspondents suggest, that the Society of St. Pius X is no longer in schism, and that it is permissible for Catholics to attend Masses celebrated by priests of the Society? Certainly not. All that the decision by the Congregation for the Doctrine of the Faith means is that in this particular case, "formal schismatic acts in the strict sense" were lacking. If the Hawaii Six had committed such acts, the excommunication would have stood.

That this decision was not a green light for Society adherents is made clear elsewhere in Archbishop Cacciavillan's letter. According to the Pro-Nuncio, "the Congregation for the Doctrine of the Faith holds that those same facts referred to in the decree on the whole do not conform to the liturgical and canonical norms; the five petitioners with their behavior cause grave nuisance, putting in danger the common good of the local Church; and therefore the local bishop can avail himself of Canon 1373 of the Code of Canon Law, imposing upon them the foreseen punishment of interdict or other penalties, either medicinal or expiatory."

Canon 1373 says: "One who publicly either stirs up hostilities or hatred among subjects against the Apostolic See or against an Ordinary on account of some act of ecclesiastical power or ministry or incites subjects to disobey them is to be punished by an interdict or by other just penalties." An interdict does not separate a person from the Church, as an excommunication does; it is a censure forbidding attendance at liturgical services, reception of some of the sacraments, and Christian burial.

Contrary to what our correspondents seem to think, the *Magisterium* of the Church has not changed its mind on the schismatic nature of the Society of St. Pius X. There has been no retreat.

Q. During these summer months people arc coming to Mass in short shorts and other indecent clothing. The church is air-conditioned. Is it not appropriate for the parishioners to be told that this is improper attire for Mass? I have also noticed a lot more gum chewing during Mass and have even found a candy wrapper. Should not the pastor discourage people from this crude behavior? — S.F., New York

Q. I am in my eighties and am shocked when I see the immodest and careless attire of those who attend Mass and receive Holy Communion. It is my understanding that the Vatican has strict rules regarding the dress of those who attend Mass at St. Peter's Basilica. Is this true? — E.A.N., Pennsylvania

A. Both readers are entirely correct that short shorts and other indecent clothing do not belong at Mass, and chewing gum and eating candy is indeed crude and inappropriate behavior for those attending the Eucharistic Sacrifice of the Body and Blood of our Lord. But we can count on one hand the number of times we have heard priests in the pulpit say something about these matters.

While no one we know condones chewing gum or eating candy in church, some priests and parish councils feel that as long as people are coming to Mass, it doesn't matter what they wear. We disagree. The way we dress and the way we act are an outward sign of our interior disposition. Not only does indecent or provocative clothing show great disrespect for God and His house, it also distracts attention from the holy action taking place at the altar and can even cause impure thoughts in the minds of those at Mass.

The irony of this situation is that those who dress so casually or even crudely for their Lord and Savior would not think of dressing that way for dinner at a fancy restaurant. Restaurants have dress codes. Why not churches? The time is long past for priests to remind those in church that they are at a Eucharistic Banquet far above any earthly meal they will ever attend, and they should act and dress accordingly.

"Bodily demeanor (gestures, clothing) ought to convey the respect, solemnity, and joy of this moment when Christ becomes our guest," says the *Catechism of the Catholic Church* (n.1387).

At St. Peter's Basilica, the dress code is no shorts (for men or women) and no bare shoulders, i.e., men without shirts, women with halter tops or sleeveless dresses.

Q. Is there anything wrong with saying the rosary during Mass? — P.G., Ohio

A. The rosary is one of the greatest devotions a Catholic can practice, but it should not be said during Mass because one's concentration would be divided between the prayers of the rosary and the sacrifice being offered on the altar. We go to Mass to hear the Word of God and how to apply it to our lives today, and to receive our Lord in the Holy Eucharist to strengthen us for the struggles of daily living. That should be our only focus. There is plenty of opportunity to say the rosary before or after Mass, either in church or at home or even on the way to and from church.

Q. Are home Masses valid? If so, what are the rules and regulations and under what circumstances are they allowed? — M.K., Illinois

A. Although Mass should normally be celebrated in a "sacred place," such as a church or oratory, it may be celebrated elsewhere if necessity demands it in a particular case (canon 932.1). Cases of necessity might include sickness, old age, or distance from a church. Thus, a Mass could be said at home to mark the anniversary or birthday of a person or persons who were unable for reasons of age or health to get to a church. Some dioceses require the permission of the local bishop for a home Mass.

If the Eucharistic Sacrifice is performed in the home, a "suitable table" can be used as the altar and an altar cloth and corporal must be used (canon 932.2).

Q. In your reply about home Masses, you said that they are not permissible except in cases of necessity, such as sickness, old age, or distance from a church. What about Masses celebrated with the Home Enthronement of the Sacred Heart? — E.M.K., California

A. As we said in our previous reply, Mass should normally be celebrated in a "sacred place" (canon 932.1), such as a church or oratory, but we see no reason why one could not be offered in conjunction with a ceremony as special as the Home Enthronement of the Sacred Heart. However, since some dioceses require the permission of the local bishop for a home Mass, why not check with your bishop first.

Q. Is there a guideline in canon law or elsewhere regarding whether or not Mass can be offered on a beach, in a field, in the woods, etc.? We live in a beachfront community, with a beautiful church just two miles from the nearest beach, but a proposal has been made for a "Beach Mass" during the summer because some people think it would be "fun." — C.P., Connecticut

A. Canon 932 says that "the celebration of the Eucharist is to be performed in a sacred place, unless in a particular case necessity demands otherwise; in such a case the celebration must be done in a respectable place."

Cases of necessity might include sickness and old age (hospitals and nursing homes), distance from a church (ships at sea or military outposts), or when there is some pastoral advantage (occasional Masses for children or other groups).

But even in cases of particular need, the place of celebration must be respectable and worthy of the holy action that is to occur, and there must not be undesirable distractions that would prevent those in attendance from paying attention to the Mass.

We can't imagine a "Beach Mass" satisfying the conditions of necessity and respectability, let alone being free of undesirable distractions.

Q. Before Vatican II, we were taught that we had attended Mass if we were present for the Offertory, the Consecration, and the Priest's Communion. Today we talk about two parts of the Mass — the Liturgy of the Word and the Liturgy of the Eucharist. If we came in at the end of the Gospel, would we have to attend a second Mass? — V.K., Ohio

Q. In his 1980 encyclical on the Eucharist (*Dominicae Cenae*), Pope John Paul II described the Liturgy of the Word as "the first part of the Sacred Mystery" (n. 10). Regarding Sunday Mass, does this mean that people who carelessly arrive at Mass after the readings have begun must assist at another Mass? — E.M., Texas

A. It goes without saying that one ought to attend the entire Mass, from the entrance prayer to the final blessing, since this is the most important act of worship in which a Catholic can take part. The old rule was that one must be present "when the chalice veil comes off," that is, when the Liturgy of the Eucharist begins. There is no stated rule today, but we would think that the absolute minimum necessary to satisfy one's obligation to participate in the Mass would include being present for the Liturgy of the Word and the Liturgy of the Eucharist. It's a sad commentary that those to whom God gives 168 hours a week can't find it in their hearts to spend even one of those hours giving adoration, thanksgiving, petition, and reparation to their generous and loving Lord.

Q. Are liturgical dances allowed at any time during the Mass? — W.J.P., New York
A. While dancing may be part of liturgical celebrations in countries like Africa, where dancing is an important part of the culture, it is not permitted during Mass in the United States. "The faithful have a right to a true liturgy, which means the liturgy desired and laid down by the Church, which has in fact indicated where adaptations may be made as called for by pastoral requirements in different places, or by different groups of people," said the foreword to *Inaestimabile Donum*. The document noted that "undue experimentation, changes, and creativity bewilder the faithful."

Paraliturgies, such as prayer services that are not strictly liturgical acts, are not as tightly regulated. They are usually composed at the local level and dancing at them probably would be considered licit, although still in questionable taste.

Q. Our parish has a nun serving as a Pastoral Administrator, and a priest from a neighboring parish says Mass on Sunday. Recently, the priest became ill early on Sunday morning and could not say Mass. A Liturgy of the Word was conducted by a layperson, the parishioners were told that this would fulfill their Sunday obligation, and the times of Masses in neighboring parishes were announced. We were able to drive to one of those parishes for Mass, but wonder if we would have been obliged to stay for the Liturgy of the Word if it had been too late to drive to Mass in another parish. — T.G., Minnesota
A. The situation of priestless parishes is becoming more common due to the shortage of clergy and the lack of vocations, and more and more faithful Catholics are experiencing the heartache of not being able to attend Mass on a regular

basis. But if the only worship service in your parish on a Sunday is the aforementioned Liturgy of the Word, then you should attend that service as part of your Catholic obligation to keep holy the Lord's Day.

Q. Would a person be obligated to attend Sunday Mass when there are blatant liturgical abuses or when a priest is absent and a Communion service is conducted by a nun or by a layperson? — L.D.B., Minnesota

A. The Sunday Mass obligation still binds regardless of liturgical abuses. Such abuses, while a violation of Church discipline, do not affect the validity of the Mass, and you should not stay away for that reason. Jesus still becomes present on that altar and you should not deprive yourself of the Eucharist. Perhaps you could offer up your Communions for a return to a liturgically correct Mass, and for more vocations to the priesthood so that nuns and laypeople will not have to conduct Communion services in place of the Holy Sacrifice of the Mass.

If there is no priest to celebrate Mass, then the next best thing would be a service where we could receive Jesus in the Holy Eucharist. When you think of the millions of people who risked their lives over the past 20 centuries to go to Mass or to receive the Body of Christ in lands where religious practice was banned, we should be grateful to God for the freedom and the opportunity to receive Him in the Eucharist, whether it's at Mass or at a Communion service.

Q. My college-age daughter claims that missing Mass on Sunday is no longer a mortal sin. Can you comment? — P.B., Massachusetts

A. Answering this question requires more than a simple yes or no. We know that Jesus died on the cross to save us from our sins. We also know that He asked us at the Last Supper to "do this in memory of Me." So the Church set aside Sunday as a special day to honor Him by attending a memorial service that recalls His death and resurrection.

Because the Mass is the central act of worship for Catholics, because it is such a powerful prayer to God, because it is such a tremendous fountain of graces, the Church since the 4th century has had a commandment requiring Catholics to participate actively at Mass on Sunday and holy days. The Church adopted this law not to make things difficult for us (how difficult is it to give God one hour out of the 168 hours He gives us each week?) but because going to Mass is good for us.

The Catholic bishops of the United States have said that "it is both a privilege and a serious duty of the individual Catholic, as well as the Catholic faith community, to assemble on Sunday in order to recall the Lord Jesus and His acts, hear the word of God, and offer the sacrifice of His Body and Blood in the Eucharistic celebration. This is, in fact, a precept of the Church following the commandment of God" (*Sharing the Light of Faith*, n. 105a). And the *Catechism of the Catholic Church*, in paragraphs 1389, 2042, and 2180, restated the obligation of every Catholic to attend Mass each Sunday.

Wouldn't it be ungrateful of us to stay away from Mass and refuse the chance to thank Jesus publicly for all He has done for us? Or to turn down the opportunity to hear the word of God and how it applies to our lives today? Or to miss out on the wonderful gift of our Lord in Holy Communion?

With this as background, is it a sin to miss Mass deliberately on Sunday? The traditional conditions for a mortal sin are (1) grave matter, (2) sufficient reflection or understanding of the grave action or omission, and (3) full and deliberate consent to the sinful act.

It should be obvious from the Church's teachings that attendance at Mass is a "serious duty" for every Catholic. Therefore, missing Mass on Sunday without a good reason (illness, great difficulty in getting to Mass, or such urgent duties as caring for a sick or dying person) is a grave wrong. So a person who deliberately stays away from Mass, knowing that it is a grave wrong to do so, has committed a mortal sin.

Q. In my parish, the children are marched out of Mass by grade just before the Scripture readings, brought to the Activity Center, where they discuss the lessons they read at home during the week, and then returned to Mass after the homily. Is this correct? — J.T.D., New Hampshire

A. There is a Church-approved practice of removing young children from Mass after the opening prayer and taking them elsewhere for a Liturgy of the Word that has readings from the *Lectionary* for children, a homily geared to their mentality, the Apostles' Creed, and petitions adapted to their understanding. But they must be returned to the church in time for the Eucharistic Prayer or they have not heard Mass.

There have undoubtedly been abuses of this practice, so it would be important to make sure that the readings, homily, and petitions conform to the Mass of the day and that the children be able to recognize a continuity in the liturgical celebration.

Q. Can you give me your opinion of the enclosed prayer service? I am bothered most by the people saying the words of consecration and distributing the "bread." Since there was no priest, there was no Mass, but this service seems almost like a mock Mass. Am I overreacting? — M.S., Virginia

A. The service was entitled "Fifth Grade Breaking of Bread," and it featured children sprinkling holy water on the group and reading the Gospel; families sharing reflections on the readings as the homily; adults leading a Eucharistic Prayer of sorts; everyone pronouncing the words, "Take and eat this bread. This is my Body which will be given up for you" ("Body" was capitalized); all joining in a paraphrase of the doxology; and catechists coming to the altar to break bread and distribute the "Bread of Life" to the families.

Those who arranged the prayer service were probably trying to make the Mass more understandable to the children and may have had the best of intentions. But they sure must have confused the fifth graders, and probably the families too, by having lay people perform rites that are restricted to priests. Capitalizing words like "bread" and "body" implies that lay people were able to effect transubstantiation. The whole thing seems highly inappropriate and foolish to us.

Q. Does the Church approve of women reading Scripture at Mass and giving out Communion? — J.R.W., Virginia

Q. Is it against Church law for a female Eucharistic minister to conduct a Communion service? — J.A.J., Arizona

Q. What about high school students doing the readings at Mass and distributing Communion? — G.R., New York

A. While women once were prohibited from being in the sanctuary, they can now serve as lectors and extraordinary ministers of the Eucharist. The relevant documents are the 1970 Third Instruction on the Correct Implementation of the Constitution on the Sacred Liturgy (*Liturgiae Instaurationes*, n. 7) and *Inaestimabile Donum* (n. 18).

Assuming that no priest is available, a Eucharistic minister, male or female, may conduct a Communion service. Such a service consists of the Liturgy of the Word, the Our Father, distribution of Communion, and a final prayer.

There is nothing wrong with having responsible and mature high school students read from Scripture at Mass. In fact, it's a good idea because it helps to train and prepare the younger generation to serve their Church in the future. As for giving out

Communion, one must normally be 18 years of age, according to the National Conference of Catholic Bishops, although a pastor, for good reason, can install 16-year-olds.

Q. When a stipend is offered to celebrate Mass for a deceased person, does each stipend merit one Mass, or can one Mass cover all the stipends received for the deceased? — M.G., Ontario

A. The Code of Canon Law contains 14 canons governing Mass offerings. The word "offering," which signifies a freewill donation by the faithful, is now used instead of "stipend," which some felt suggested a commercial exchange of money for services rendered.

In answer to the question, canon 948 says that "separate Masses are to be applied for the intentions for which an individual offering, even if small, has been made and accepted." Canon 950 says that "if the sum of money is offered for the application of Masses without an indication of the number of Masses to be celebrated, the number is to be computed in view of the offering established in the place where the donor resides unless the donor's intention must be lawfully presumed to have been different."

In other words, if a priest accepts a $50 offering from a parishioner, and the usual Mass offering in that parish is $10, then the priest is obligated to say five Masses for the intention requested. If, however, the person making the donation wishes to give a larger amount than the customary donation, it would not be wrong for the priest to accept the larger offering and to say just one Mass for the donor's intention (canon 952). On the other hand, it would be unlawful for a priest to accept more offerings for Mass intentions than he could reasonably be able to satisfy personally in one year (canon 953).

Q. Can a Mass stipend for one person's intention be combined with another stipend for someone else's intention so that one Mass is offered for two intentions and two stipends are accepted for that one Mass? — C.J.O., California, and I.A., Minnesota

A. Once a priest has accepted a stipend or Mass offering to say Mass for a certain intention, he is obliged to say a specific Mass for the intention of the person who gave the individual offering. There can be no more than one offering combined with the intention accepted by a priest for a single Mass. However, the intention may include more than one person. So the listing of more than one person for one Mass is all right provided that multiple offerings were not accepted for the one Mass.

Q. What is the purpose of a concelebrated Mass? Do all participating priests satisfy their individual Mass intentions, or is the intention for the Mass solely that of the primary celebrant? — R.L.M., California

A. A concelebrated Mass is the celebration of Mass by many bishops and/or priests who associate themselves with the sacrifice of the principal celebrant, consecrating the same bread and wine. Concelebration has been revived since Vatican II, says the *General Instruction of the Roman Missal*, because it "effectively brings out the unity of the priesthood, of the sacrifice, and of the whole people of God" (n. 153).

Regarding the second question, canon 945.1 of the Code of Canon Law says that "it is lawful for any priest who celebrates or concelebrates Mass to receive an offering to apply the Mass according to a definite intention." So each concelebrant may offer Mass for his own intention, bearing in mind that "a priest who concelebrates a second Mass on the same day may not take an offering for it under any title" (canon 951.2).

Q. In your reply regarding more than one intention for one Mass celebration, did you perhaps omit the fact that this is permitted when a Mass is concelebrated? — L.A.S., Indiana

Q. In your answer about Mass intentions, you indicated that a single Mass could not be celebrated for multiple intentions. Enclosed please find a copy of a church bulletin in which you will notice that each daily Mass and two Sunday Masses are being said for more than one intention. Does canon 957 give the local Ordinary the authority to permit this practice, or would you still take the position that a priest cannot accept several offerings and celebrate only one Mass for all of them? — B.E.D., Texas

A. In answer first to B.E.D., (1) we said that a single Mass could be celebrated for multiple intentions, provided that the celebrant took only one offering; (2) we still take the position stated in canon 948 that a priest cannot accept several offerings and celebrate only one Mass for all of them; and (3) we do not believe that canon 957 gives the local Ordinary any authority to permit a contrary practice. That canon says that the local bishop has "the duty and right of seeing to it that Mass obligations are fulfilled." Canon 958.2 says that the bishop also has the obligagation to examine the special book kept in each parish, "in which they list accurately the number of Masses to be celebrated, the intention, the stipend given, and their celebration."

The purpose of all this is spelled out in canon 947: "Any appearance of trafficking or commerce is to be entirely excluded from Mass offerings."

Regarding the question posed by L.A.S., if five priests were concelebrating a Mass, they each could apply the Mass for some intention for which they had accepted an offering. Otherwise, canon 951 says that a priest who celebrates or concelebrates two Masses on the same day may retain the offering from only one Mass, except for Christmas Day, when a priest is permitted to celebrate up to three Masses and keep the three offerings. If a priest presides at two Masses on the same day, say a regular parish Mass and a funeral Mass, he may receive offerings for each Mass, but may keep only one of them. The other must be given to some cause designated by his Ordinary.

Q. When a person pays a stipend to have a Mass offered for a deceased person, is the priest obligated to mention the intention at Mass and, if so, at what part of the Mass? — H.D., Illinois

A. This is a matter of pastoral sensitivity and has become customary only since the liturgy went into the vernacular. Printed bulletins usually carry lists of intentions to be remembered at Masses during the coming week, but accepting a stipend only binds the celebrant to offer a Mass for that intention; it does not bind him to announce the intention.

Over the years, however, we have heard the name of the deceased person for whom the Mass is being offered mentioned at the beginning of Mass, during the General Intercessions, and during the Eucharistic Prayer. The most appropriate time would be during the General Intercessions (prayers of the faithful).

Q. In our parish, the priest will not offer Masses for the parishioners. We have a Book of Intentions at the back of the church, and people write their intentions in it. Please clarify. — G.M., Michigan

A. Canon 945.2 says that "it is strongly recommended that priests celebrate Mass for the intentions of the Christian faithful, especially for the needy, even if no offering has been received." In light of this canon, we can't imagine why your priest won't say Mass for the specific intentions of the parishioners. Has anyone asked him why he won't do this?

Q. When we pray for the faithful departed during the Eucharistic Prayer at Mass, does God animate those individual prayers that we often say for deceased relatives even if we have not reserved the Mass for that special intention? Is a Mass publicly offered for someone who has passed away more effective than these small private prayers we add during the Eucharistic Prayer? — S.C., Massachusetts

A. The Mass is the highest form of public prayer that we can offer, and any intentions prayed for at Mass take on special significance because they are united to the prayers of all the faithful throughout the world. So offering up prayers for a deceased loved one as part of the Mass is a more powerful way of interceding with the Lord than the private prayers of an individual since these private prayers are no longer the prayers of an individual, but rather the prayers of the entire Church community.

Even if we have not reserved a Mass in memory of a departed relative or friend, every Mass is offered for all "our departed brothers and sisters" (those baptized in water and the Holy Spirit), as well as for "all who have left this world in your friendship" and "whose faith is known to you alone" (baptism of desire), whether we are there to whisper their names or not.

Q. Can a pre-Vatican II Catholic request a Requiem Mass for his or her funeral, and without a eulogy but with a sermon maybe on the four last things? What options are available? — E.A.S., Kentucky

A. A Requiem Mass is a Mass celebrated for the dead. The Mass said prior to Vatican II was called by that name because the first words in the opening hymn were *Requiem aeternam dona eis, Domine* ("Eternal rest give unto them, O Lord"). The funeral rites of the Church were revised after Vatican II and, since November 2, 1989, the *Order of Christian Funerals* has been mandated in the dioceses of the United States. However, if your bishop has given permission for a Tridentine Mass in your diocese, you may be able to request such a Mass for yourself.

Q. During a funeral Mass, when should incense be used? I've seen it done at the Offertory, at the end of Mass, and at both times. — W.F.H., Rhode Island

A. After the gifts are brought to the altar, according to the *Rite of Funerals*, the priest may incense the gifts, the altar, and the body of the deceased. The deacon or another minister then incenses the priest and the people. The priest may also incense the body at the final commendation and farewell at the end of the Mass. "If the body was incensed at the preparation of the gifts during Mass," says the *Rite of Funerals*, "the incensation is ordinarily omitted in the rite of commendation."

Q. On Holy Thursday, many parishes are now washing the feet of women and children, as well as men. I feel that a lot of the symbolism of what Christ did for the Apostles at the Last Supper has been lost by this change. What is the Church's current norm regarding this? Would I be acting in good conscience by refusing to partake in this changed ritual if asked to do so? — R.P., Idaho; P.S., New York; J.J.C., Pennsylvania; M.S., Michigan; and M.G.L., Florida

A. According to Fr. Peter Stravinskas, there is a directive from Rome that says the washing of the feet on Holy Thursday is restricted to *viri selecti* (chosen males). We have been told by the Office for Worship in the Boston Archdiocese that this is a "legitimate interpretation" of the Roman directive, and that some bishops do restrict the washing of feet to men.

However, we were also told that the Bishops' Liturgy Committee has interpreted this directive to include women and children, and that is why their feet were washed in the states where our questioners live. Fr. Stravinskas quoted this same contradictory interpretation from a priest at the Bishops' Secretariat for the Liturgy in Washington. On the one hand, the priest said that the directive from Rome "*does not explicitly exclude* women from the footwashing" (emphasis his), but then he stated that "all would honestly have to conclude that to include women in the washing of the feet goes beyond the literal meaning of the text."

No wonder faithful Catholics get so frustrated and upset when even the "literal meaning" of a text can be so easily obfuscated and ignored!

Yes, one can in good conscience refuse to take part in a footwashing ceremony that is contrary to liturgical norms.

Q. May the Liturgy of the Eucharist be celebrated without vestments except for the stole? — E.B., Tennessee

A. According to the *General Instruction*, the vestments worn by the priest while celebrating Mass are the alb, the stole, and the chasuble (n. 81a). Paragraph 161 says that "the principal celebrant always wears the chasuble." In a case of absolute necessity, such as in an underground, persecuted church, only the stole would be required.

Q. Most priests kiss the altar before beginning Mass, but some do not. What does the Church say? — C.A., Florida
A. According to paragraphs 27, 85, and 232 of the *General Instruction of the Roman Missal*, the traditional liturgical practice is for the priest to kiss the altar as a sign of veneration before he begins celebrating Mass.

Q. Our pastor starts Mass by saying "Good Morning" and making a joke, but he does not make the Sign of the Cross. When I asked him about this, he said, "It was eliminated by Vatican II." Is this true? — I.R., Connecticut
A. It is not true. Paragraph 86 of the *General Instruction* says: "After the entrance song, and with all standing, the priest and the faithful make the Sign of the Cross. The priest says: *In the name of the Father, and of the Son, and of the Holy Spirit*; the people answer: *Amen.*" Then, the priest "may give the faithful a very brief introduction to the Mass of the day."

Q. My priest told me that it is no longer proper to genuflect when approaching the altar; he said that bowing is more appropriate. Which do you think is more proper? Many people are also bowing instead of genuflecting. When did all this bowing start? — L.R., New York, and T.M.F., New York
A. It has long been proper to bend one's knee to the floor when in the Real Presence of Jesus in the Blessed Sacrament. The *General Instruction* (n. 233) requires the priest to genuflect after he elevates the Host at the Consecration, after he raises the chalice, and before Communion. The *GIRM* also says: "If there is a tabernacle with the Blessed Sacrament in the sanctuary, a genuflection is made before and after Mass and whenever anyone passes in front of the Blessed Sacrament."

There are also various times during the Mass when bows of the head and the body are appropriate (see *GIRM*, n. 234), but these are separate from the times when genuflection is required, and there is no indication that genuflecting is to be replaced by bowing. One obvious exception would be in the case of a priest who for physical reasons was unable to bend his knee to the floor.

If the Blessed Sacrament is reserved in the sanctuary of your church, then it remains the custom to reverence the Real Presence with a genuflection at the beginning and end of Mass. If it is reserved in a space apart from the sanctuary, then it is appropriate to reverence the altar with a bow at the beginning and end of Mass. The genuflection reverences the Blessed Sacrament, not the altar itself.

Fr. Peter Stravinskas, in *The Catholic Answer Book*, offers some sound comments on this matter:

"Genuflection is a beautiful sign of our belief in the Real Presence of Christ in one Eucharist. If St. Paul says that 'at Jesus' name every knee must bend' (Phil. 2:10), how much more should that be so when one appears directly before the Lord in the Blessed Sacrament?

"Some liturgists have pressed to replace the genuflection with a bow. However, that is not the tradition of the West (although it is in the Eastern churches). In our age and culture, genuflection makes a particularly strong doctrinal statement; after all, people bow to one another all the time — one only bends the knee to God!" (p. 138).

Q. Lately, I have noticed that no processional hymn is sung at the beginning of Mass, but the "Lord, Have Mercy" is sung. Is this correct? I have also noticed that some of our local churches discourage the use of missalettes. We are told that it is better to listen and not to read along. Is there a new Church ruling on this? — M.S., Minnesota

A. There have been no new rules issued on either matter. Singing is highly encouraged at Mass, including the singing of an entrance song and the "Lord, Have Mercy." If there is music at Mass, the entrance song is usually sung, so we can't imagine why there would be no processional hymn at your church unless there was no procession.

As for discouraging the use of missalettes, that is a local decision by the pastor, and we think it is a mistake. Perhaps in a religious community or in a small group that is particularly attentive, missalettes would not be necessary. But for the average person in the pews, having the prayers of the Mass and the Scripture readings right in front of them can only be beneficial. People do not always hear well, especially in large churches, and they may not understand a particular reading at first. Since we retain more of what we see and hear than of what we only hear, it would be a good idea to have the Scripture texts and Mass prayers available for us to read.

Q. Can the priest skip the Gloria and the Credo? — M.J., Minnesota; M.D.G., New York; and T.D., Michigan

A. The *General Instruction* says that "the Gloria is sung or said on Sundays outside of Advent and Lent, on solemnities and feasts, and in special, more solemn celebrations" (n. 31). It is omitted only on the Sundays of Advent and Lent.

Regarding the Credo, it says that "recitation of the profession of faith by the priest together with the people is obligatory on Sundays and solemnities. It may be said also at special, more solemn celebrations" (n. 44).

Q. Can a priest skip making the Sign of the Cross on his forehead, lips, and heart before reading the Gospel? — F.C., Michigan

A. In making these gestures, the priest and the congregation are asking God to open their minds, lips, and hearts to proclaim and put into practice the words of the Gospel. The obligation of the priest to observe faithfully all the rubrics of the Mass has been clearly stated in *Eucharisticum Mysterium* and in the Code of Canon Law.

In the first document, which was issued in 1967 by the Sacred Congregation of Rites, it says:

"In the celebration of the Eucharist above all, no one, not even a priest, may on his own authority add, omit, or change anything in the liturgy. Only the supreme authority of the Church and, according to the provisions of the law, the bishops and episcopal conferences, may do this" (n. 45).

Canon 846 says that "the liturgical books approved by the competent authority are to be faithfully observed in the celebration of the sacraments; therefore no one on personal authority may add, remove, or change anything in them."

Q. Why have the words at the end of the Scripture readings at Mass been changed from "This is the Word of the Lord" and "This is the Gospel of the Lord" to "The Word of the Lord" and "The Gospel of the Lord"? — C.F., Oregon; W.H.B., California; and M.S., Texas

A. Two of the questioners sent along an explanation for the change that appeared in their parish bulletins. According to the explanation, the change was authorized in November 1991 by the National Conference of Catholic Bishops and was implemented in all parishes on the first Sunday in Advent in 1992. The reasons given for the change are that it brings the Liturgy of the Word into harmony with the Liturgy of the Eucharist, where the minister says, "The Body of Christ," not "This is the Body of Christ," and that it emphasizes the presence of Christ at Mass not only in the Eucharist but also in the words of Scripture. The change also aligns the English somewhat more closely to the Latin, which has after all the readings, including the Gospel, the words *Verbum Domini*, or "Word of the Lord."

Q. During a recent Mass, the priest said that we did not have to stand for the Gospel, and then he read a modernized version of the Prodigal Son, which was about a boy who left home with a new car, etc. Was this an allowable practice? — M.J.S., New York

A. Of course not. The priest could just as easily have read the actual Gospel story and then, in his homily, related it to a modern situation. He was also wrong to change the format of the Mass by allowing people to sit for the Gospel. No priest has the right to do that.

Q. For the past two Sundays in our parish, the Gospel reading was presented as a theatrical play, with the two lectors, the priest, and the choir reading and singing the Gospel. The whole drama was acted out without any preassigned roles. The spoken words of Jesus were not always read by the priest. Is this a liturgical abuse and, if so, what can I do about it? — J.H.R., Illinois

Q. Is it permissible during the Good Friday liturgy to have a dramatization of the Way of the Cross and Crucifixion, through the church and sanctuary, by high school students? — J.M., Michigan

Q. My son attends a large state university where the Newman Club has female chaplains who perform various functions. He wants to know if laywomen are prohibited from reading the Gospel at Mass. — J.C.C., Arizona

A. If the dramatization on Good Friday is done with reverence and good taste, we see no reason to object to it. But the only time that the Sunday Gospel is dramatized during the liturgical year, with priest, lectors, and congregation reciting certain parts, is when the account of our Lord's Passion is read on Palm Sunday. Otherwise, the Gospel should be read only by a priest or a deacon (*General Instruction*, n. 34). You should write to your bishop about this abuse.

Q. After the homily at my sister's parish, people newly received into the Church were asked by the pastor to give

witness to their newfound faith. Doesn't canon law forbid anyone other than the priest or deacon to speak at the time of the homily? Shouldn't any witnessing be done at the end of Mass? — K.C.J., Michigan

A. As noted before, canon 767.1 says that preaching the homily "is reserved to a priest or to a deacon." Canon 766 says that "lay persons can be admitted to preach in a church or oratory if it is necessary in certain circumstances or if it is useful in particular cases." This preaching by qualified laypersons might be permitted, for example, when the celebrant or another priest or deacon was physically or morally prevented from giving the homily.

Even in such special circumstances, however, the remarks by the layperson would not be considered a homily, since that is a liturgical function reserved solely to a priest or deacon, but rather a reflection or commentary. This kind of lay reflection could even be given in addition to the priest's or deacon's homily if it seemed useful in a particular situation.

It would seem that the witnessing of the new converts described by K.C.J. would fall into the category of a reflection or commentary, not a homily, and would therefore not be contrary to canon law.

Q. Why are we subjected by priests at Mass only to homilies of the past and not to sermons dealing with the sins of the present? We hear nothing at all about abortion, immorality, divorce and remarriage, drugs, homosexuality. Are such sermons prohibited? — I.R., Connecticut

A. No, they are not prohibited. According to the *General Instruction*, "the homily is an integral part of the liturgy and is strongly recommended: it is necessary for the nurturing of the Christian life. It should develop some point of the readings or of another text from the Ordinary or from the Proper of the Mass of the day, and take into account the mystery being celebrated and the needs proper to the listeners" (n. 41).

Since the readings in the Liturgy of the Word every Sunday cover much of Scripture over a three-year cycle, there are any number of passages that lend themselves to a discussion of the moral issues mentioned by I.R. So there is no reason why those issues should not be mentioned at various times during the year, particularly since the wrong information about them appears almost daily in the media, and those in the pews are in need of the right information.

Some parishes are blessed with priests who give excellent

homilies, while others are stuck with bland and uninspiring talks that spark little fervor and seem unrelated to the world-gone-crazy around us. Why not ask your priest to talk on a certain subject? Look up in a missalette the readings scheduled for future Sundays and suggest to your pastor a homily that would relate the Word of God to modern-day problems.

Many of the priests we know talk about abortion at least twice a year — at the time of the anniversary of *Roe v. Wade* in January and during October, which is supposed to be Pro-Life Month in all dioceses throughout the country. Some priests may not feel comfortable dealing with this subject, so give them encouragement as well as reliable information that they can use in preparing their homilies. Pope John Paul's encyclical on the Gospel of Life (*Evangelium Vitae*) would be an excellent resource.

Q. Today I confronted a woman lector who had changed every reference to "man" to "man and woman," "people," etc. Her defense was that someone had written the substituted words in the margin of the *Lectionary*, that "Father says it's all right," that the new *Lectionary* will have these changes, and that "everybody's doing it." Does she or the parish priest have the authority to change the readings by substituting other words? — C.N.V., Maryland

A. Of course not. But recalling that this same approach worked with regard to Communion in the hand, certain people in the Church are disobeying liturgical laws again on the supposition, or the hope, that what they want will soon become official Church policy. It's a dishonest way to bring about change in the Church, but so far it's been successful.

Q. At the Easter Vigil I attended, the pastor, after many readings, Baptisms, and Confirmations, announced that there would be a "break" before beginning the Liturgy of the Eucharist and that coffee and cookies would be served in the patio area. Is this right, especially with Communion coming up? — R.P.V., California

A. We have heard of celebrants giving the congregation a chance to stand and stretch during a lengthy Easter Vigil Mass, but it's the first time we have heard of refreshments being offered. Unless your pastor was planning to take an hour after the coffee break before distributing Holy Communion, then no one in that church who had something to eat or drink on the patio would be able to receive the Eucharist.

Q. In our parish, a song by Carey Landry that is based on the Creed has been substituted for the Nicene Creed. Do you have some arguments that would support dropping this song? — Name Withheld, Wisconsin

Q. Is it acceptable, when reciting or singing the Our Father during the Mass, to proceed directly into "for the kingdom, the power, and the glory are yours ..." at the end of the prayer and to skip the part that begins, "Deliver us, Lord, from every evil ..."? — F.M.M., New Jersey

Q. A Jesuit priest at my parish has a man and woman join him in reading parts of the Gospel at Mass, he has the congregation sit during the Gospel, and after the Sign of Peace he walks to the back of the Church and says the "Lamb of God" as he walks back down the aisle. Isn't he way off base in these actions? — J.A.W., Massachusetts

Q. My priest says, at the washing of the hands, "Wash away our iniquities, cleanse us from our sins." Shouldn't it be "my" instead of "our"? — F.V.D., California

Q. I attended a Mass at which the priest consecrated the bread and wine at the foot of the altar and, at the usual time, said, "The table has been set and the food prepared." Is this an acceptable change? — R.D., New York

Q. Is it right for the priest to offer the bread and wine together, rather than separately? — D.G.B., New Jersey, and J.W.B., Kentucky

Q. Can the priest mix the water and wine prior to Mass? — K.M., Michigan

Q. Is it allowed for our pastor to use different prayers instead of saying "Lamb of God, you take away the sins of the world, have mercy on us"? — M.L., Wisconsin

Q. Instead of saying, "This is the Lamb of God," now we hear, "This is Jesus, our brother ...." In a Church where all are to call one another "brother," to apply the same label to our Lord and Savior is to treat Him as just one of the gang. — J.H.O., Pennsylvania

A. As we have noted many times, the rite of the Mass has been approved and set forth by the Church in the *Roman Missal* and in the *General Instruction of the Roman Missal.* A spokesman for the U.S. Bishops' Committee on the Liturgy has said that the *GIRM* is, "after the *Constitution on the Sacred Liturgy* itself, the principal liturgical document of the Church dealing with the prayerful celebration of the Eucharist."

All of the examples mentioned by our readers are contrary to the rites and rubrics spelled out in the *Roman Missal* and in the

GIRM, and any priest who engages in these actions is disobedient to the rules of the Church.

To mix the water and wine before Mass is to negate the meaning of the rite. The *GIRM* says that "it is desirable for the faithful to present the bread and wine" because this action "retains the same spiritual value and meaning" as when the faithful brought the bread and wine for the liturgy from their homes. This symbolism would be lost if the priest mixed the water and wine before Mass. They may be mixed at the beginning of the preparation rite, something that is usually done when a deacon is assisting the celebrant.

As for offering the two substances together, the Church decided centuries ago to offer them separately, so the priest has no business structuring the liturgy to suit his own inclinations.

Because Jesus is both God and man, He is our Lord and our brother. But J.H.O. is right in saying that it would be more appropriate (as well as liturgically correct) to refer to Him as the Lamb of God at the same time that the Host is being raised before Communion since it reminds us of His divine nature and of His sacrificial death on the cross for our sins.

Q. You said that the priest should not mix the water and wine before Mass on Sunday, but what about at a daily Mass when there are no altar boys and no bringing up the gifts? Can the priest omit the washing of the hands at daily Mass? Is it wrong for the priest to wash his hands by putting his finger over the cruet, tipping it, and then rubbing his index fingers together? Is it permissible, at the Consecration, to break the Host and elevate it in two pieces? Also, we have another priest who, after the "Lamb of God," says, "We believe" this is the Lamb of God. Am I being overly sensitive, or does this question the divinity of Christ? — J.M.W., Florida

Q. Our parish priest says that the washing of the hands at Mass is optional and only the Scripture readings and the Eucharistic Prayers cannot be changed. Is this true? — P.B.M., California

A. It is not true. During the dozen years after the *General Instruction* was first published in 1969, questions about certain parts of the instruction were directed to the U.S. Bishops' Committee on the Liturgy. One of those questions was: "May the rite of washing the hands be omitted from the celebration of Mass?" Here is the reply that appears in Appendix 2 of the 1982 edition of the *GIRM*:

"In no way. (1) Both the *GIRM* (nos. 52, 106, 222) and the Order of Mass (with a congregation, no. 24; without a congregation, no. 18) show the *Lavabo* to be one of the prescribed rites in the preparation of the gifts. A rite of major importance is clearly not at issue, but it is not to be dropped since its meaning is: 'an expression of the (priest's) desire to be cleansed within' (GIRM, no. 52).

"In the course of the Consilium's work on the Order of Mass, there were a number of debates on the value and place to be assigned to the *Lavabo*, e.g., on whether it should be a rite in silence or with an accompanying text; there was, however, unanimity that it must be retained."

Regarding the other questions, the priest should mix the water and wine at the time of the preparation of the gifts during every Mass, daily or Sunday, and not before Mass begins; it is all right for the priest to wash his fingers in the manner described by J.M.W.; it is not permissible for the priest to break the Host at the Consecration and elevate it in two pieces — the breaking of the Host comes at the time of the "Lamb of God"; we don't know whether the priest has some doubts about the divinity of Christ when he uses the words "we believe" — but we do know that he should follow the directions for the Mass that are found in the *Sacramentary*, and you will not find the words "we believe" in the *Sacramentary*.

Q. There is a priest in my parish who does not genuflect after the Consecration, and I know that he does not have any physical disability. I have written to the pastor and to the bishop, but nothing has been done. What else can I do? — Name Withheld, New York

A. Have you ever approached the priest directly and asked him why he does not genuflect after consecrating the bread and wine? That ought to have been your first step, before contacting the pastor and the bishop. If you have not spoken to the priest, you should do so, pointing out to him paragraph 233 of the *General Instruction*, which says: "Three genuflections are made during Mass: after the showing of the Eucharistic bread, after the showing of the chalice, and before Communion."

If the priest is still not willing to obey the rubrics laid down by the Church, then you can again contact the pastor, and the bishop if necessary. Try to talk to them in person or by phone this time, rather than by letter. If you do not receive any satisfaction, and that may be the case in a time when those in authority have chosen not to correct liturgical abuses, you might get some of your fellow parishioners to join with you in protesting this situation. It will be much more difficult to ignore the concerns of many parishioners than to disregard the complaint of one person.

Q. What is the most important part of the Mass? A priest I know says that Vatican II deemphasized the importance of the Consecration and that the "Great Amen" is the most important part. — L.T., Indiana

A. It is absurd, and false, to say that Vatican II deemphasized the importance of the Consecration. How could any Church council deemphasize that awesome moment when the Second Person of the Blessed Trinity becomes truly present on the altar?

While Vatican II did not specifically use the word "Consecration," it strongly emphasized the centrality of that action when it said in the *Decree on the Ministry and Life of Priests* that "the Eucharistic Action is the very heartbeat of the congregation of the faithful over which the priest presides" (n. 6). The Council further emphasized the importance of the Eucharistic Action in this paragraph:

"At the Last Supper, on the night when He was betrayed, our Savior instituted the Eucharistic Sacrifice of His Body and Blood. He did this in order to perpetuate the sacrifice of the Cross throughout the centuries until He should come again, and so to entrust to His beloved spouse, the Church, a memorial of His death and resurrection: a sacrament of love, a sign of unity, a bond of charity, a paschal banquet in which Christ is consumed, the mind is filled with grace, and a pledge of future glory is given to us" (*Constitution on the Sacred Liturgy*, n. 47).

According to the *General Instruction*, which provides the guidelines for celebrating Mass, Vatican II and other magisterial documents "have reaffirmed in the same sense and as the same teaching that the Council of Trent had proposed as a matter of faith. The Mass does this not only by means of the very words of consecration, by which Christ becomes present through transubstantiation, but also by that spirit and expression of reverence and adoration in which the Eucharistic Liturgy is carried out" (n. 3).

Finally, the *GIRM* calls the Eucharistic Prayer "the center and summit of the entire celebration" (n. 54), and says that among the chief elements of this prayer is "the institution narrative and Consecration" (n. 55d).

The "Great Amen" is listed as another chief element of the Eucharistic Prayer, and the *GIRM* describes it as the people's "assent and a conclusion" to the praise of God that is expressed in the doxology (n. 55h). The people's assent ("Amen") clearly draws its significance as the most important assent of the Mass from the supreme importance of what they are assenting to, i.e., the Real Presence that follows the Consecration.

Q. Would you please comment on the enclosed leaflet from a children's Mass where the word "friends" is substituted for "disciples" at the most important part of the Mass? — D.L.L., Pennsylvania

Q. We have a new priest in our parish. I'm sure he's a good man, but during the Consecration he says that Christ blessed the cup and gave it to His "friends" instead of His "disciples." Since "friend" and "disciple" are not the same meaning, is this okay? — L.B., Michigan

A. The text of the leaflet, which is taken from one of the Eucharistic Prayers for children, says that Jesus, "when he was at supper with his disciples, he took bread, and gave you thanks and praise. Then broke the bread, gave it to his friends, and said: 'Take this, all of you, and eat it: This is my Body which will be given up for you.'"

Unless your parish priest is using one of the Eucharistic prayers for children, or the First Reconciliation Canon, he should not change "disciples" to "friends" because it is wrong to change any of the words in the *Sacramentary*. Also, the words do mean very different things. A friend is an acquaintance or someone for whom we have affection or esteem, but a disciple, according to the dictionary, is "one who accepts and assists in spreading the doctrines of another: as a: APOSTLE b: a convinced adherent of a school or individual." The word comes from the Latin *discipulus*, which the dictionary says refers to "follower of Jesus Christ in his lifetime."

We assume that "friends" is used in the children's canon because the word is more easily understood by youngsters, but it could also be based on Jesus' words in John 15:14-15: "You are my friends if you do what I command you. I no longer speak of you as slaves, for a slave does not know what his master is about. Instead I call you friends."

Q. At the Consecration, the priest holds up the large Host and not the others. Are the smaller hosts consecrated at the same time? — A.C.G., Illinois

A. Yes, all of the hosts on the altar are consecrated at the same time. The intention to consecrate is signaled by the presence of the host on the corporal while the words of institution are pronounced. The elevation of the large Host facilitates the people's adoration, but the transformation of the elements does not depend on it.

Q. At a retreat I attended, the priest at the Consecration held up a small tray full of hosts instead of a single large host while saying, "This is my Body." Was he right to do this? — J.C., New Jersey

A. The *General Instruction* says that "the nature of the sign demands that the material for the Eucharistic celebration truly have the appearance of food. Accordingly, even though unleavened and baked in the traditional shape, the Eucharistic bread should be made in such a way that in a Mass with a congregation the priest is able actually to break the Host into parts and distribute them to at least some of the faithful" (n. 283).

In an effort to clarify the meaning of "Eucharistic bread," Appendix 2 of the *GIRM* (1982 edition) contains the following comments: "The term Eucharistic bread in line 2 is explained by the words of line 4: 'The priest is able actually to break the Host into parts.' Thus line 2 is about this Eucharistic element as to its kind and line 4 as to its shape." The point of using a large host at Mass is so the congregation can see the priest actually break the consecrated Bread. This symbolic action would not be nearly as visible if smaller Hosts were used. Assuming that a large host was available at the retreat you attended, the priest was wrong not to use it. His failure to follow the liturgical rules, however, did not invalidate the Consecration.

Q. Two priests in my parish do not elevate the sacred Species at the Consecration, but only at what used to be called the Minor Elevation (now called the Doxology). They assured me that the new rubrics permit this. They also say that a congregation must be present for the sacrament to be confected. Please tell me: (1) Do the rubrics no longer call for a distinct elevation at the words of institution? (2) Can a priest confect the sacrament without a congregation? (3) Can an unordained imposter ever say a valid Mass and effect transubstantiation? — H.J.B., Massachusetts

A. (1) The *Sacramentary* used by the priest at Mass says after the institution narrative that "he shows the consecrated Host to the people," and "he shows the chalice to the people." It does not specify how distinct the elevations should be, but "show" implies raising the Host and the chalice high enough to be seen clearly by the congregation. Since the priest is calling attention to the miraculous transformation of the bread and wine into the Body and Blood of our Lord, one would expect the elevations to be more than merely pointing the Host and chalice in the direction of the congregation. At the Doxology, the *Sacramentary* says: "He takes the chalice and the paten with the Host and, lifting them up, sings or says ...."

(2) Canon 906 and paragraph 211 of the *General Instruction* both state that a priest may not celebrate Mass without a member of the faithful present, "except for a just and reasonable cause." A just and reasonable cause would be the unavailability of a member of the faithful or the inability of the priest to participate in a communal celebration because of illness, infirmity, or travel. A priest can confect the sacrament without a congregation.

(3) An unordained person posing as a priest could not effect transubstantiation because he had never received Holy Orders and the power that flows from that sacrament to change the bread and wine into the Body and Blood of Christ.

Q. Your answer to the question of whether a congregation need be present for the Holy Eucharist to be confected could be expanded by quoting canon 904. I'm sure that many old priests like myself do not know of this change. — V.O., Ohio

A. Canon 904 reads: "Remembering that the work of redemption is continually accomplished in the mystery of the Eucharistic Sacrifice, priests are to celebrate frequently; indeed daily celebration is strongly recommended, since even if the faithful cannot be present, it is the act of Christ and the Church in which priests fulfill their principal function."

Q. Our bishop has us stand during the Eucharistic Prayer and bow at the Consecration. Does the bishop have authority to do this? — H.M., Colorado

Q. Our pastor says that we should remain standing after the "Our Father" and not kneel when the priest holds up the consecrated Host and says, "This is the Lamb of God ...." He also says that we should sit after Communion rather than kneel down. What are we supposed to do? — R.M.S., California

Q. The people in my brother's church stand at the Consecration. Are we allowed to do this? — R.A.R., New
Jersey

Q. Our parish has been in existence for five years, and
we're scheduled to celebrate the first Mass in our new
church in a few weeks. Until now we have been worshiping
in a local school without kneelers. Please tell me when it is
appropriate to kneel during Mass. — J.L., New Jersey

A. Here is what the *General Instruction* says:

"Unless other provision is made, at every Mass the people
should stand from the beginning of the entrance song or when
the priest enters until the end of the opening prayer or collect;
for the singing of the Alleluia before the Gospel; while the
Gospel is proclaimed; during the Profession of Faith and the
general intercessions; from the prayer over the gifts to the end
of Mass, except at the places indicated later in this paragraph.
"They should sit during the readings before the Gospel and
during the responsorial psalm, for the homily and the presentation of the gifts, and, if this seems helpful, during the period of
silence after Communion. They should kneel at the Consecration unless prevented by the lack of space, the number of
people present, or some other good reason" (n. 21).

At their meeting in November 1969, the U.S. Catholic
bishops voted to adapt paragraph 21 of the *GIRM* "so that the
people kneel beginning after the singing or recitation of the
Sanctus until after the *Amen* of the Eucharistic Prayer, that is,
before the Lord's Prayer."

In the 1982 edition of the *GIRM*, there are a number of
clarifications and explanations of the correct postures at Mass.
After Communion, the appendix says, the faithful "may either
kneel, stand, or sit .... Thus it is a matter of option, not obligation." The appendix reiterates the kneeling posture "from the
epiclesis before the Consecration until the memorial acclamation after it," and says that, where kneelers have been removed
from churches, "there is nothing to prevent the faithful from
kneeling on the floor to show their adoration, no matter how
uncomfortable this may be. In cases where kneeling is not
possible, a deep bow and a respectful bearing are signs of the
reverence and adoration to be shown at the time of the Consecration and Communion."

In 1990, the national meeting of Diocesan Liturgical Com-
missions overwhelmingly approved a proposal to permit
standing during the entire Eucharistic Prayer. This proposal
has not been endorsed by the National Conference of Catholic

Bishops at this writing, but apparently individual bishops have begun to implement it in their dioceses. No bishop should okay such a change until the NCCB gives its approval, but even then we think it would not be wise to impose the posture of bowing on American Catholics because we are not accustomed to the gesture and because it does not dramatize the significance of what is happening on the altar in the same way that kneeling does.

Q. In a video that is part of the DeSales program entitled "Our Celebration of the Eucharist," the priest says that we do not know when the bread and wine change to the Body and Blood of Christ, that it is sometime during the Eucharistic Prayer. Please comment. — G.L., Michigan

A. The bread becomes the Body of Christ when the priest takes the host in his hands and says, "This is my body which will be given up for you." The wine becomes the Blood of Christ when the priest takes the chalice in his hands and says, "This is the cup of my blood, the blood of the new and everlasting covenant."

According to the *Catechism of the Catholic Church*, "the Eucharistic presence of Christ begins at the moment of the Consecration and endures as long as the Eucharistic Species subsist" (n. 1377).

Q. Since I was young I understood that in the bread were present the Body and Blood of Christ. Now we have Communion with wine and, when they give it to you, they say, "The Blood of Christ." Does this mean that people who receive only the Bread at Communion are not receiving the Body and Blood of Christ? — G.R., Louisiana

A. No, anymore than "The Body of Christ" is meant to exclude the Blood. Jesus is completely present, Body and Blood, Soul and Divinity, in both the Host and in the Precious Blood. The phrases are not meant to limit what we are receiving, but to elicit our faith response ("Amen") against the appearances of bread and wine.

In the words of the *Catechism*: "Christ is present whole and entire in each of the Species and whole and entire in each of their parts, in such a way that the breaking of the Bread does not divide Christ" (n. 1377).

Q. Is the singing of the entire Consecration of the Mass permitted? — D.M.D., Washington

A. Singing the Consecration is an option that the priest is permitted to exercise. It can be done in a very reverent and inspirational manner, but it can also be distracting if the celebrant of the Mass does not have a pleasant voice. The option should be exercised with prudence and discretion.

Q. During a recent children's Mass, the teenagers in the sanctuary sang a non-liturgical hymn during the Consecration. Is this permissible? — D.J., Iowa

Q. Is singing a higher or more reverent form of prayer at Mass? — J.M., Indiana

A. Paragraph 19 of the *General Instruction* says this about singing at Mass:

"The faithful who gather together to await the Lord's coming are instructed by the Apostle Paul to sing psalms, hymns, and inspired songs (see Col. 3:16). Song is the sign of the heart's joy (see Acts 2:46). Thus St. Augustine says rightly: 'To sing belongs to lovers.' There is also the ancient proverb: 'One who sings well prays twice.'

"With due consideration for the culture and ability of each congregation, great importance should be attached to the use of singing at Mass; but it is not always necessary to sing all the texts that are of themselves meant to be sung.

"In choosing the parts actually to be sung, however, preference should be given to those that are more significant and especially to those to be sung by the priest or ministers with the congregation responding or by the priest and people together."

Thus, singing has a very special place in the Mass. It is not necessarily more reverent than devout recitation of a prayer, but it can inspire fervor and enthusiasm as we worship the Lord in the Eucharist. One should be an active and joyful participant in the entire Mass, joining in all the hymns, prayers, and responses whether they are said or sung.

As for the congregation, or a group of teenagers, singing during the Consecration, the center and summit of the entire celebration, that is not permissible. "The Eucharistic Prayer calls for all to listen in silent reverence," says the *General Instruction*, "but also to take part through the acclamations for which the rite makes provision" (n. 55).

Q. At a recent daily Mass, the celebrant apparently became distracted and said the words for consecrating the wine over the bread. He then said the proper words over

the wine. Do you think that this was a valid Mass? — B.M.,
Texas

Q. Sometimes at the Consecration of the Mass, the priest,
instead of saying, "Do this in memory of me," says, "When
you do this, remember me." Does this invalidate the Mass?
— F.H.F., Arizona, and T.K., Florida

A. The priest must say the proper words of the Consecration,
as they appear in the *Sacramentary*, for a Mass to be valid. So if
the priest inadvertently said the wrong words over the host, and
never corrected this mistake, then the Mass would be invalid.

As we have noted in the past, a celebrant who adds or subtracts
words from the prayers of the Mass, or changes the words, does
something illicit, but it does not invalidate the Mass unless the
substitutions completely alter the meaning of the action.

Q. In my parish, one of the priests does not ring the bells
at the Consecration. Is this proper and permissible? — J.K.,
New York

A. (1) The main section of the *General Instruction* says that "a
little before the Consecration, the server may ring a bell as a
signal to the faithful. Depending on local custom, he also rings
the bell at the showing of both the Host and the chalice" (n. 109).
Then, in response to questions about this, Appendix 2 of the
GIRM says that while a particular liturgical assembly, such as a
religious community or a small group, "may be able to take part
in the Mass with such attention and awareness that it has no need
of this signal at the central part of the Mass ... the opposite may
be presumed in a parish or public church, where there is a
different level of liturgical and religious education and where
often people who are visitors or are not regular churchgoers take
part. In these cases the bell as a signal is entirely appropriate and
is sometimes necessary. To conclude: usually a signal with the
bell should be given, at least at the two elevations, in order to
elicit joy and attention."

Q. When we proclaim the mystery of faith after the Consecration, one of the acclamations says, "When we eat this
bread and drink this cup, we proclaim your death, Lord
Jesus, until you come in glory." Isn't this a denial of transubstantiation to call the Body of Christ "bread"? —
R.D.R., Ohio, and J.R.B, Ohio

A. When the word "bread" is used after the Consecration, it
refers either to the continuing appearance of bread (Eucharistic
Prayer IV: "this one bread") or to bread in a qualified sense

(Eucharistic Prayer I: "bread of life," and Eucharistic Prayer II: "life-giving bread").

When various prayers after Communion talk about "bread of life," "one bread," and "bread from heaven," it is in the same sense that Jesus described Himself as bread in John 6:51 ("I myself am the living bread come down from heaven. If anyone eats this bread, he shall live forever; the bread I will give is my flesh for the life of the world").

Q. At Mass recently, the priest and congregation sang this memorial acclamation: "Come Holy Spirit and fill our hearts. Come Holy Spirit and fill our hearts. Come Holy Spirit and fill our hearts that we may praise the Lord our God." Is this legitimate? — F.M., Rhode Island

A. No. The only options permitted are those specified in the *Roman Missal*. Asked if a similar substitution could be made by singing Shalom in place of the *Agnus Dei*, the Sacred Congregation for Sacraments and Divine Worship replied: "No. The Ordinary of the Mass in all its parts must be followed as it appears in the *Missal*" (*General Instruction*, Appendix 2, n. 56e).

Q. During the Eucharistic Prayers, the priest says that Jesus "broke the bread," but the readings we hear during Holy Week say that Jesus "blessed it [the bread], broke it, and gave it to his disciples." Is it wrong for the priest to leave out the part about Jesus blessing the bread? — J.L.N., New Jersey

A. It is not wrong because both versions can be found in Scripture and in the Eucharistic Prayers. Matthew (26:26) and Mark (14:22) both mention that Jesus blessed the bread before He broke it, but Luke (22:19) and Paul (1 Corinthians 11:23-24) do not mention a blessing before Jesus broke the bread.

As for the Eucharistic Prayers, number IV says that Jesus did pronounce a blessing, but numbers I, II, and III do not mention a blessing.

Q. Should the people join with the priest at Mass in saying, "Through Him, with Him, in Him, in the unity of the Holy Spirit ..." at the conclusion of the Eucharistic Prayer? — M.M., Florida

A. The specific roles of the priest and the people at Mass have been spelled out in several liturgical documents. One of them, *Inaestimabile Donum*, was issued by the Sacred Congregation for the Sacraments and Divine Worship to correct "frequent abuses" of the Eucharistic Liturgy, including "indiscriminate shared recitation of the Eucharistic Prayer."

According to this document, the proclamation of the Eucharistic Prayer "is reserved to the priest, by virtue of his ordination," and "it is therefore an abuse to have some parts of the Eucharistic Prayer said by the deacon, by a lower minister, or by the faithful." The people's role is limited to "the responses to the Preface dialog, the *Sanctus*, the acclamation after the Consecration, and the final *Amen* after the *Per Ipsum* ["through Him"]. The *Per Ipsum* itself is reserved to the priest" (n. 4).

Q. At Mass recently, we heard a Lord's Prayer sung that included the words, "which art in Heaven" and "for thine is the kingdom, and the power, and the glory...." Is it appropriate to have this version sung as part of the Sacrifice of the Mass? — P.W., Florida

Q. What is your opinion of the practice in some churches of holding hands during the Our Father and lifting them up while saying, "for the kingdom, the power, and the glory are yours, now and forever"? — J.F.R., California

A. Both of these practices are liturgical aberrations that have no place in the Mass. There is a sung version of the Lord's Prayer that belongs in the Mass, but it is not the one that P.W. heard. As we have said so many times in the past, no priest has a right to change anything in the liturgy on his own initiative.

As for the practice of holding hands during the Lord's Prayer, here is what the *General Instruction*, which describes in detail how the Mass is to be celebrated, has to say:

"The prolonged holding of hands is of itself a sign of communion rather than of peace. Further, it is a liturgical gesture introduced spontaneously but on personal initiative; it is not in the rubrics. Nor is there any clear explanation of why the sign of peace at the invitation: *Let us offer each other a sign of peace* should be supplanted in order to bring a different gesture with less meaning into another part of the Mass. The sign of peace is filled with meaning, graciousness, and Christian inspiration. Any substitution for it must be repudiated" (Appendix 2, n. 112).

Q. Why is the singing of the "Our Father" being done away with more and more these days? — S.M., Michigan

A. It must be the preference of a particular pastor because it is the Church's wish that "great importance should be attached to the use of singing at Mass" (*General Instruction*, n. 19). The

GIRM also says that people should "know how to sing at least some parts of the Ordinary of the Mass in Latin, especially the Profession of Faith and the Lord's Prayer," since the faithful from different countries come together ever more frequently today (ibid.).

Q. When distributing Communion, the priest said, "Body and Bread." Isn't he supposed to say, "Body of Christ"? Maybe he doesn't believe it's the Body of Christ. — R.H.R., Ohio

Q. Our pastor has taken to introducing the Our Father in the Mass with the exclamatory interrogative, "Whose Father?" in the manner of a cheerleader. Apart from the undignified silliness of this introduction to the Lord's Prayer, does a priest have such an option? — R.C.R., Virginia

Q. Our priest announced that we will now sing, "Viva Jesus," during the Consecration because there is a large percentage of Mexicans in our parish. Is this permitted? — J.S., California

A. In the first two instances, the priest was wrong. Regulation of the liturgy is the province of the Apostolic See and the conference of bishops, and no other person, not even a priest, may add, remove, or change anything in the liturgy on his own authority. He could be right in the third situation, however, if he was using the Spanish Sacramentary since two languages may be used at Mass without permission of the bishop.

Q. Is it permissible for a priest to substitute words like "God, our loving Mother and Father" for "God, the Almighty Father," or to leave the word "Father" out of a prayer? — Name Withheld, Louisiana

A. No, it is not permissible.

Q. Why is the doxology "For the kingdom, the power, and the glory are yours, now and forever" added to the Lord's Prayer at Mass when most scholars agree that it is not biblical? Is this a universal practice in the Catholic Church or is it limited to the United States? — E.M., Florida

A. First of all, the doxology is not added to the Lord's Prayer. It is the response to the prayer following the Our Father, which begins, "Deliver us, Lord, from every evil and grant us peace in our day ...." Second, you are correct that these words are not found in the Bible. They were at some point in history written in the margin of the scriptural text by a person who was copying the New Testament and were taken as authentic by Erasmus, whose edition of the Bible lies behind most Protestant Bibles. They have been included in the Mass for their beauty of expression. Third, the doxology is part of the *Roman Missal* that is used to celebrate Mass throughout the universal Church.

Q. A priest told me that the kiss of peace is optional in the Mass, but when it is done it must be done during the Offertory. Is this true? — C.C., California

A. The *General Instruction* says that after the Lord's Prayer comes the "rite of peace: before they share in the same bread, the faithful implore peace and unity for the Church and for the whole human family and offer some sign of their love for one another. The form the sign of peace should take is left to the conference of bishops to determine, in accord with the culture and customs of the people" (n. 56b).

Thus, the rite of peace is not optional, and it belongs after the Our Father and before the Lamb of God.

Q. In your column, you said that the rite of peace is not optional. The late Father Robert E. Burns, longtime weekly columnist in *The Wanderer*, said many times that the laity does not have to take part in the kiss of peace if they so desire. Has the Church changed the rules again? — A.F., New York

Q. In reference to your recent issue, I think C.C. was referring to the exchange of peace, which is optional. — D.D., New York

Q. Your answer about the sign of peace was wrong. You quoted from the *General Instruction of the Roman Missal*, n. 56(b), but if you had read further, you would have seen that n. 112 says that the priest "may" invite the people to offer each other a sign of peace. This is certainly not the verb to use for a mandatory rite. — M.W.D., New Jersey

A. Regarding the first two questions, members of the congregation are free to respond, or not to respond, to the priest's (or deacon's) invitation to share a sign of peace with others in the church, although the *General Instruction* expects that when the invitation is extended, "all exchange some sign of peace and love, according to local custom" (n. 112).

M.W.D. is correct when he says that the priest is not required, after saying "The peace of the Lord be with you always," to add the words: "Let us offer each other a sign of peace." He "may" do so, but it is not mandated. As Fr. Peter Stravinskas of *The Catholic Answer* has written: "It is important to note that the extension of the sign of peace is an option that is left to the discretion of the individual celebrant."

Editor's Note: The following letter regarding the sign of peace was sent to us by the Reverend Thomas J. Paprocki, Chancellor of the Archdiocese of Chicago:

"Recently in *The Wanderer* you addressed the issue of whether the sign of peace is optional at Mass. One opinion indicated that the sign of peace is optional because the rubric states, 'Then the deacon (or the priest) may add: "Let us offer each other the sign of peace."'

"It should be noted that this rubric applies to the invitation to the sign of peace. The next line immediately directs, 'All make a sign of peace, according to the local custom. The priest gives the sign of peace to the deacon or minister.'

"Moreover, the *General Instruction of the Roman Missal*, par. 56(b), says that 'before they share in the same bread, the faithful implore peace and unity for the Church and for one another. The form the sign of peace should take is left to the conference of bishops to determine, in accord with the culture and customs of the people.' The Appendix to the *General Instruction* for the Dioceses of the United States of America, adopted by the National Conference of Catholic Bishops in 1969, par. 56(b), states, 'The Conference of Bishops has left the development of specific modes of exchanging the sign of peace to local usage. Neither a specific form nor specific words are determined.'

"Thus, while the invitation to the sign of peace is optional and the *form* is variable (e.g., handshake, embrace, bow, kiss, etc.), *the exchange of some sign of peace is required*" (emphasis in original).

Q. Is it permissible for a priest to leave the altar to offer the sign of peace to the people in the pews? — W.F.H., Rhode Island

A. There is no specific prohibition against a priest going down the aisle to give the sign of peace, but neither is there permission. The *General Instruction* says that "the priest may give the sign of peace to the ministers" (n. 112), which means to those in the sanctuary, i.e., concelebrants, servers, lectors, extraordinary ministers. That would seem to indicate that the priest should remain at the altar.

Q. Your recent reply that the *General Instruction of the Roman Missal* neither specifically prohibits nor directs the priest to leave the sanctuary during Mass to give the sign of peace to the congregation is not entirely accurate. Sections 82-126 specifically instruct the priest where he is to be every step of the way throughout a Mass with a congregation. By explicitly directing the priest to the appropriate areas of the sanctuary during the Mass, the *GIRM* implicitly tells him he is NOT to be anywhere else. When "the priest may give the sign of peace to the ministers" (n. 112), he is specifically supposed to be at the altar from after receiving the gifts (n. 102) until he distributes Holy Communion (n. 117). — D.H.L., California

Q. In your answer regarding the priest leaving the sanctuary at the sign of peace, you are misinformed or uninformed. The enclosed copy of a newsletter published by the NCCB [National Conference of Catholic Bishops] for February-March 1976 makes it very clear that both the clergy and the members of the congregation are to give the sign of peace "where they are standing. There is no moving around and no disturbance; each offers the sign of peace with the person nearest to him or her." — M.M., New York

A. We thank M.M. for sending a copy of the newsletter from the Bishops' Committee on the Liturgy. In addition to the remarks quoted above, the newsletter also says:

"It is proper therefore that in the *General Instruction* (n. 112) and in the Order of the Mass it is clearly stated that at the invitation addressed to the faithful all exchange the sign of peace according to local custom. It is not a peace that moves out from the altar, a clericalized peace, but a community peace exchanged among those in whose midst is the Real Presence of Christ the Lord.

"The practice where the priest moves out into the nave of the church, among the faithful, to offer personally to them the *pax* is basically a return to the clericalism of the past, oblivious of the reality of the liturgical assembly. Thus, the priest need not move from the altar to offer the sign of peace to this or that person."

Q. Is it permissible for Eucharistic Ministers to pour the Precious Blood from the chalice into individual goblets for

distribution to the faithful? To break the large consecrated Host into smaller pieces? — M.R.M., Pennsylvania

A. Yes to both questions if other priests, deacons, or acolytes are not available to assist the principal celebrant in breaking the large Host and pouring the Precious Blood into other containers (cf. National Conference of Catholic Bishops, *This Holy and Living Sacrifice*, n. 43).

Q. At the Mass our children attend in school, a woman in a miniskirt stands at the altar breaking up Hosts along with the priest, the chalice is a glass water goblet, the container for the Hosts is a glass salad bowl, and after the priest consumes the remaining Body and Blood of Christ, he wipes his hands on a bath towel. Please tell me that our Lord deserves more respect than a salad bowl and a bath towel. — N.K., Ohio

A. As noted in the previous reply, an extraordinary minister can assist the celebrant in breaking up Hosts if there are no priests, deacons, or acolytes available. If she were running out of Hosts while distributing Communion, she could also break the smaller Hosts in half or in quarters to accommodate the number of communicants still waiting to receive. But miniskirts are hardly appropriate attire in the sanctuary.

If you mean a fluffy hand towel — a bath towel would be ridiculously oversized — to wipe his hands after Communion, there is no problem. These are sometimes used for bishops' Masses since the celebrants can actually wash their hands rather than their fingertips.

As for the chalice and ciboria to be used, the *General Instruction* gives the following requisites:

"Chalices and other vessels that serve as receptacles for the Blood of the Lord are to have a cup of nonabsorbent material. The base may be of any other solid and worthy material" (n. 291).

"Vessels that serve as receptacles for the Eucharistic Bread, such as a paten, ciborium, pyx, monstrance, etc., may be made of other materials that are prized in the region, for example, ebony or other hard woods, as long as they are suited to sacred use" (n. 292).

Waterford glass makes an elegant chalice (is it possible that's what you saw?), but there is the question of durability.

Q. In the past, a paten was used to keep particles of the Host from falling to the floor during Communion, and the priest purified his fingers after giving out Communion. Today we have Eucharistic ministers who handle many Hosts and never purify their fingers. Has this problem been addressed by the bishops? — R.K., Texas

A. Yes, it has. The *General Instruction* says that "whenever a particle of the Eucharistic Bread adheres to his fingers, especially after the breaking of the Bread or the Communion of the people, the priest cleanses his fingers over the paten or, if neccessary, washes them" (n. 237). Responding to a question about purifications, Appendix 2 of the *GIRM* says: "The remarks on the priest, deacon, and acolyte are applicable to a special minister who lawfully distributes Communion" (n. 238).

Q. What is the proper method of disposing of the left-over Precious Blood of Christ after Mass? At our parish, it is poured down a "special sink." — F.F., Arizona

A. The special sink is called the sacrarium. Located in the sacristy, it has a drain pipe that leads directly into the ground and not into the sewer system. It is for the disposal of water that was used to cleanse the sacred vessels or linens.

To answer your question, the Precious Blood is to be completely consumed by the celebrant and is not to be poured down the sacrarium. In the words of the Sacred Congregation for the Sacraments and Divine Worship: "The consecrated wine is to be consumed immediately after Communion and may not be kept. Care must be taken to consecrate only the amount of wine needed for Communion" (*Inaestimabile Donum*, n. 14).

The *General Instruction* says: "The vessels are purified by the priest or else by the deacon or acolyte after the Communion or after Mass, if possible at a side table. Wine and water or water alone are used for the purification of the chalice, then drunk by the one who purifies it" (n. 238).

Q. Our priest does not cleanse the vessels at the altar. Is it proper to cleanse them after Mass? — R.W., Missouri

Q. After Communion, the Eucharistic ministers carry vessels containing the Precious Blood to the sacristy and consume what is left over. But if there is too much Precious Blood remaining to be consumed, it is poured down a secret sink. Is this an acceptable practice? — C.F., Kansas

A. Regarding the first question, it is proper to cleanse the vessels after Mass. Here is paragraph 120 of the *General Instruction of the Roman Missal*:

"After Communion, the priest returns to the altar and collects any remaining particles. Then, standing at the side of the altar or at a side table, he purifies the paten or ciborium over the chalice, then purifies the chalice, saying quietly: Lord, may I receive these gifts, etc., and dries it with a purificator. If this is done at the altar, the vessels are taken to a side table by a minister. It is also permitted, especially if there are several vessels to be purified, to leave them, properly covered and on a corporal, either at the altar or at a side table, and to purify them after Mass when the people have left."

Regarding the second question, see the previous answer. Should the celebrant have inadvertently consecrated more wine than was needed, leaving more than he could reasonably be expected to consume, the remaining Precious Blood can be poured down the special sink known as a sacrarium. Before doing so, however, the priest should dilute the Precious Blood with water so that Christ is no longer sacramentally present in the liquid. This should be an extraordinary event and not the habitual method of disposing of the sacred Species.

Q. We have no Mass on Mondays, so the parish priest sometimes celebrates the Mass for the Monday saint on Tuesday and ignores the Tuesday saint. Can he do this? — G.T.C., Indiana

A. It depends on the relative rank of the two celebrations in question. The most important celebrations, including those of certain saints, are *solemnities* and *feasts*. Some are never moved, some can be moved by the Bishops' Conference, and still others by an individual bishop. Of the remaining saints' *memorials*, some are *obligatory* and some *optional*. It would for instance be allowable to omit Vincent the Deacon on Tuesday and celebrate Agnes from Monday; it would not be allowable to move Peter Chanel from Monday to Tuesday and omit Catherine of Siena.

Chapter 11

Christian Marriage

Q. Does the Church have rules against a Catholic mayor or justice of the peace performing marriages for Catholics or those of other religions? — D.J., Iowa

A. A mayor or justice of the peace is a civil official with certain duties, including performing marriages for those who meet the requirements of the civil law for a valid marriage. There is no Church rule against a Catholic mayor or justice of the peace performing such a civil ceremony. The Catholic Church, in fact, recognizes as valid a marriage between two non-Catholics who are free to marry; it recognizes as valid and sacramental a marriage between two baptized persons of other Christian faiths who are also free to marry.

As for performing a marriage for one or two Catholics who had decided not to be married in the Church, a Catholic mayor or justice of the peace would be acting in a civil and not a religious capacity. He most likely would not even know the religious affiliation of the bride and groom, only that they were presenting him with a license indicating that they had satisfied the conditions for marrying in that state. His obligation as a civil official would then require that he perform the ceremony.

But if he did know the background of the couple, and particularly if one or both of the parties had publicly and notoriously rejected the Catholic Church, then the Catholic civil official should in conscience excuse himself from performing that particular ceremony.

Q. Two people in my parish were divorced and have married again. Both of them come to Mass every Sunday with their new spouses and, while they do not receive Communion, they take part in parish activities and seem to be accepted members of the parish. My pastor says that I am wrong to be scandalized by this situation. What do you think? — Name and State Withheld

A. The couples in question apparently recognize that they are in irregular marriages and are unable to receive the sacraments, but they still want to attend Mass every week. This is laudable as long as they stay away from Communion. Instead of you being scandalized by them, you should pray for them that they will be able to straighten out their marriage situations and return to the sacraments.

Q. If a baptized Catholic woman marries an unbaptized man of no religion in a Catholic ceremony, and he later walks out on her, will she be eligible for an annulment under the Pauline Privilege? — E.H., Pennsylvania

A. No, because one of the conditions for invoking the Pauline Privilege (so named because it appears in Paul's first letter to the Corinthians) is that *both* parties must be unbaptized at the time of the wedding.

What would apply in the situation you describe is the Petrine Privilege, which refers to the power of the Holy Father to dissolve a marriage between a baptized person and an unbaptized person in favor of the faith of the Catholic party, allowing him or her to enter into a new marriage with another Catholic. The petitioning process begins on the diocesan level and is then sent to Rome, where it is handled by the Congregation for the Sacraments and Divine Worship.

Q. Would you kindly inform me what is meant by the Pauline Privilege? — R.H.B., New York

A. Based on a passage of St. Paul (1 Corinthians 7:12-15), the Pauline Privilege means that a marriage entered into by two unbaptized persons is dissolved in favor of the faith of the party who has received Baptism and has married again, provided that the non-baptized party departs the marriage either by divorce, desertion, or by making married life unbearable for the convert, and provided that the baptized party did not give the other party just cause for departure (canon 1143).

In other words, the marriage to be dissolved must be one in which both of the parties were certainly non-baptized, and the dissolution depends on one of the parties having been baptized before the second marriage and the refusal of the non-baptized party to remain with the baptized spouse, or to remain peacefully. This can be determined by means of interpellations, i.e., questioning the non-baptized party as to whether he or she wants to be baptized or at least wishes to cohabit in peace with the baptized spouse.

The Pauline Privilege cannot be applied if the non-baptized party is willing to be baptized and is willing to live in peace with the convert. Nor can it be applied if the convert culpably caused the separation, say by committing adultery, and then was baptized with the intention of dissolving the marriage.

Those interested in more details about the privilege should consult canons 1143-1150 of the Code of Canon Law and the commentary that follows them.

Q. Can a practicing Catholic marry within the Church a person who is an atheist because he was reared in a communist country where religion was prohibited? — M.Q., Illinois

A. The impediment to marriage between a baptized Catholic and an unbaptized person is called disparity of cult. Only the bishop of the Catholic party or the bishop of the diocese where the marriage will take place can "for a just and reasonable cause" remove this impediment. Before granting a dispensation for such a marriage, according to canon 1125 of the Code of Canon Law, the bishop must be satisfied that the following conditions have been fulfilled:

"1. The Catholic party declares that he or she is prepared to remove dangers of falling away from the faith and makes a sincere promise to do all in his or her power to have all the children baptized and brought up in the Catholic Church.

"2. The other party is to be informed at an appropriate time of these promises which the Catholic party has to make, so that it is clear that the other party is truly aware of the promise and obligation of the Catholic party.

"3. Both parties are to be instructed on the essential ends and properties of marriage, which are not to be excluded by either party."

Q. Our pastor at first gave permission for a Catholic woman to marry a divorced Protestant man (no annulment had been obtained) in our parish church with a Protestant minister officiating. When some parishioners objected, the pastor withdrew his permission and the wedding took place in a Protestant church. Were the parishioners who objected being uncharitable? — C.L.C., Kansas

A. Was Jesus being uncharitable when He chased the money-changers out of the temple because they had turned a house of prayer into a den of thieves? If a pastor, for whatever reason, chooses to let the parish church be used for a ceremony that is contrary to the teachings of the Church, then parishioners have every right to object to his decision once they have determined the facts. This is not a question of being uncharitable, but is rather a case of wanting to protect the Church from scandal.

Q. In preparing couples for marriage, is receiving the sacrament of Penance stressed, and are couples told how important it is to marry in the state of grace? I have heard young couples joke about Pre-Cana classes and say that they go through these preparations only to please parents. — P.W., Florida

A. Canon 1065 of the Code of Canon Law says that "it is strongly recommended that those to be married approach the sacraments of Penance and the Most Holy Eucharist so that they may fruitfully receive the sacrament of marriage." So marriage preparation ought to include instruction on Penance and the importance of starting married life in the state of grace. Some young couples may indeed just go through the motions to please parents, but the seriousness of the commitment they are making ought to be made clear to them, as well as the consequences of not living up to the teachings of Jesus and His Church.

Some good reading material for young couples preparing for marriage would include *Marriage Is for Keeps* (Foundation for the Family) by John F. Kippley, *A Catholic Handbook for Engaged and Newly Married Couples* (Faith Publishing Company) by Frederick W. Marks, and *Until Death Do Us Part* (Family Apostolate) by Fr. Robert J. Fox and Fr. Charles Mangan.

Q. A priest told a friend of mine that a marriage by a justice of the peace is not considered a valid marriage by the Church and could not be annulled. He also said that it would be okay for a Catholic to marry a person divorced from such a marriage since the Church did not recognize that marriage to begin with. Is this really true? — E.P., Connecticut

Q. What does the Church consider a valid marriage in regard to indissolubility and adultery? Is it a mortal sin to break the bond of matrimony through divorce without a just cause? — Name and State Withheld

Q. Can a Catholic and a non-Catholic be married in the presence of a priest and a minister in the non-Catholic person's church? — T.W.S., Florida, and W.H.P., New York

Q. My wife of 18 years divorced me after she had an affair for several years. She has attempted to get an annulment, but so far has been denied. The man in question is a divorced Protestant, and our local priest recently

allowed this man to become a Catholic despite my protests. Must a priest allow everyone who wants to become a Catholic to enter the Church? — L.S., Minnesota

Q. I was married in a Las Vegas marriage chapel by a woman minister, but my wife divorced me. Can I remarry in the Catholic Church? — T.B., Colorado

A. Canon 1108 of the Code of Canon Law states that a valid marriage in the eyes of the Church must be "contracted in the presence of the local Ordinary or the pastor or a priest or deacon delegated by either of them, who assist, and in the presence of two witnesses." This is the canonical form of marriage that is to be observed "whenever at least one of the contractants was baptized in the Catholic Church or was received into it and has not left it by a formal act" (canon 1117).

Canon 1127.2 says that the local bishop of the Catholic party can grant a dispensation from the canonical form in the case of a mixed marriage "if serious difficulties pose an obstacle to the observance of the canonical form." Some examples of serious difficulties would include obtaining parental agreement to the marriage, avoiding the non-Catholic party's estrangement from family or religious denomination, recognizing the special relationship or friendship with a non-Catholic minister, and considering the particular importance of the church to the non-Catholic party.

A valid marriage creates "a bond between the spouses which by its very nature is perpetual and exclusive" (canon 1134), and "a ratified and consummated marriage cannot be dissolved by any human power or for any reason other than death" (canon 1141). If the two parties divorce, the bond remains intact and remarriage is considered invalid and adulterous. A subsequent marriage is not permitted in the Catholic Church unless the prior marriage is declared to be null.

To answer the questions: (E.P.) A marriage by a Catholic before a justice of the peace is not considered a valid marriage by the Church (unless a dispensation from the canonical form was granted by the local bishop) and does not need to be annulled. It can be taken care of by a tribunal procedure called "A Declaration of Nullity by Defect of Form," which simply involves verifying and documenting the circumstances. The process can be completed in a matter of weeks.

(Name Withheld) A valid and consummated marriage is indissoluble. Canon 1152 says that adultery can be grounds for the separation of the spouses, but not for dissolving the marriage. Depending on one's motives, it could be a grave sin for one party to break the bond of matrimony through divorce. Bear in mind, however, that divorced persons are still in good standing in the Church and can receive the sacraments provided that they do not attempt remarriage.

(T.W.S. and W.H.P.) Catholics can marry in non-Catholic churches before non-Catholic ministers provided that they have obtained a dispensation from the canonical form because of one or more of the serious difficulties mentioned above.

(L.S.) We cannot comment on this situation without knowing all the facts, but it is safe to say that a priest is not obliged to allow everyone who wants to become a Catholic to enter the Church. There are certain criteria that must be met — e.g., the prospective convert must be in a canonically regular situation and must be willing to abide by the laws and teachings of the Church — and the priest apparently felt that the man met these criteria.

(T.B.) If your marriage was not contracted according to the norms of the Church, then it was not valid and you are free to remarry in the Catholic Church.

Q. My baptized Catholic son married a woman of no particular religion in her mother's house 14 years ago. The ceremony was performed by a Protestant minister. They have since been divorced and my son has met another woman whom he wishes to marry. Was his first marriage invalid according to the Catholic Church and, if so, is he free to marry now in the Church? — L.A.P., Michigan

A. The first thing your son should do is to pursue this matter with a priest. But based on what you have told us, his first marriage was invalid because it was not contracted in the presence of a priest or deacon (canon 1108), and there was apparently no dispensation from the canonical form granted by the local bishop (canon 1127). If the woman your son married was not baptized, and there was no dispensation from this disparity of cult, that would also make the marriage invalid (canon 1086). He should therefore be free to marry, but he should check all of this out immediately.

Q. If a person gets married while in the state of mortal sin, would this make the marriage invalid? If a person who was excommunicated because of an abortion got married, would that marriage be invalid? — F.K., Ohio

A. In the first case, while the Church strongly recommends that "those to be married approach the sacraments of Penance and the Most Holy Eucharist so that they may fruitfully receive the sacrament of marriage" (canon 1065.2), it is not necessary that the parties be in the state of grace in order for the marriage to be valid. If they are in the state of mortal sin at the time of the marriage, they will not receive the graces of the sacrament until they have received the sacrament of Penance and been reconciled with God and His Church.

In the second case, a person bound by the censure of excommunication is forbidden "to celebrate the sacraments and sacramentals and to receive the sacraments" (canon 1331.2). If the person involved was publicly known to have been excommunicated, then no priest or deacon could lawfully perform the ceremony.

Q. Regarding pre-nuptial agreements, it is my understanding that in order for a marriage to be valid, it must be made of free will. It would seem that a pre-nuptial agreement would express an inherent reservation and would thus invalidate the marriage. On the other hand, since state laws now allow "no fault divorce," would a pre-nuptial agreement be a legitimate precaution against being taken to the cleaners? — J.C., Illinois

A. A pre-nuptial agreement apportioning a couple's assets in case of separation or divorce would indeed militate against one of the essential properties of marriage, which is indissolubility. How can a man and woman promise to be true to each other until death if they have already signed an agreement to divide up the spoils when the allegedly lifelong commitment goes sour?

Just because civil divorce is now much easier to obtain than a generation ago does not mean that those called to a higher standard by the sacrament of Matrimony should also take the easy road when the going gets tough. One hopes and prays that couples considering marriage would know so much about the values of their future spouse that the thought of some day "being taken the cleaners" would never even enter their mind.

We would not see a problem, however, with a pre-nuptial agreement between a widow and a widower who agree to waive certain survivor rights in favor of the other spouse's children.

Q. Does the Church permit a young couple to get married without the intention of having children? — G.V., New Brunswick

A. Assuming that the young couple has nothing physically wrong that would prevent them from having children, the answer is no. And if the couple conceals their intention never to have children, then the marriage would be invalid.

It is the teaching of the Church that "marriage and conjugal love are by their nature ordained toward the begetting and educating of children. Children are really the supreme gift of marriage and contribute very substantially to the welfare of their parents .... Hence, while not making the other purposes of matrimony of less account, the true practice of conjugal love, and the whole meaning of the family which results from it, have this aim: that the couple be ready with stout hearts to cooperate with the love of the Creator and the Savior, who through them will enlarge and enrich his own family day by day" (Vatican II, *Pastoral Constitution on the Church in the Modern World*, n. 50, and *Catechism of the Catholic Church*, n. 1652).

During the marriage rite, couples are specifically asked, "Will you accept children lovingly from God, and bring them up according to the law of Christ and his Church?" Since the procreation and education of children is one of the essential elements of Christian marriage (canon 1055), "if either or both parties through a positive act of the will" should exclude this element, the marriage "is invalidly contracted" (canon 1101.2).

Q. If a couple plans to practice birth control to prevent any children for the first few years of marriage so they can buy a house, car, etc., is their marriage valid? — T.G., New York

A. If the couple intended never to have children, the marriage would be invalid since the procreation and education of children is one of the essential elements of Christian marriage. If they do intend to have children in a few years, and plan to practice contraception until then, the marriage would be valid, but they would be living in a state of objective sin.

Q. I am a Catholic who remarried in my mid-forties after my first marriage was annulled. I had two children from my first marriage and was practicing birth control at the time of my second marriage, not wanting more children due to my age. I deeply regret my previous sins and have since completely accepted Natural Family Planning. While avoiding pregnancy for the most part, I am open to life. My question is whether my state of mind at the time of my second marriage made the marriage contract invalid? — A.B., Vermont

A. According to canons 1055.1 and 1101.2, a couple that deliberately excludes an essential element from their marriage, such as "the procreation and education of offspring," is not validly married. This may be true in your case, based on what you have told us, but the best way for you to resolve this doubt would be to explain your situation to a priest or marriage tribunal official and ask to renew consent to your marriage. This can be done privately so as not to cause you and your husband embarrassment.

Q. If a couple getting married knows that they will not be able to have children because the removal of a cancerous tumor rendered the woman permanently sterile, is it licit for them to get married and to consummate their marriage? We hope to adopt several children to raise in place of those we will be unable to have together. — F.X.M., Illinois

A. Of course it would be licit for you to get married and consummate your union. The physical impossibility of conceiving a child yourselves is not the result of any deliberate contraceptive or sterilizing act, but rather the unfortunate side-effect of life-saving surgery. We pray that God will bless your marriage and reward you for your willingness to adopt children.

Q. I understand that it would be wrong for a young couple to marry without the intention of ever having children. But what about a couple in their middle forties (one a widow with two teenage children) who plan to marry and are not in favor of more children? Would it be wrong for them to practice Natural Family Planning as a means of avoiding pregnancy? — J.W.W., Florida

Q. Is it a sin for a couple with four children to forego any further children by practicing Natural Family Planning so that they can enjoy some luxuries, like a second home or taking vacations around the world? — R.J.K., Connecticut

A. It is the teaching of the Church that "the true practice of conjugal love, and the whole meaning of the family life which results from it, have this aim: that the couple be ready with stout hearts to cooperate with the love of the Creator and the Savior, who through them will enlarge and enrich his own family day by day" (Vatican II, *Pastoral Constitution on the Church in the Modern World*, n. 50).

In cooperating with the love of God in the practice of responsible parenthood, the same document says, couples "will thoughtfully take into account both their own welfare and that of their children, those already born and those which may be foreseen. For this accounting they will reckon with both the material and the spiritual conditions of the times as well as of their state in life. Finally, they will consult the interests of the family group, of temporal society, and of the Church herself" (*Ibid.*).

Relating these statements to the practice of Natural Family Planning, Pope John Paul II has warned that NFP can be abused "if the couple, for unworthy reasons, seeks in this way to avoid having children, thus lowering the number of births in their family below the morally correct level, [which is] established by taking into account not only the good of one's own family, and even the state of health and the means of the couple themselves, but also the good of the society to which they belong, of the Church, and even of the whole of mankind.

"Responsible parenthood [is] in no way exclusively directed to limiting, much less excluding, children; it means also the willingness to accept a larger family" (*L' Osservatore Romano*, April 11, 1988).

The bottom line for both questioners revolves around trusting in the providence of God and responding with generosity in accepting and raising children. We cannot decide for either couple what generosity means in their particular situations, although we must say that a desire for luxuries is not a serious reason for avoiding pregnancy. We would agree with John Kippley of the Couple to Couple League who says in his book, *Sex and the Marriage Covenant*, that the key is to get a couple "to really ask themselves if they have a truly serious reason to avoid pregnancy, whether they are really answering God's call to generosity in the service of life."

Mr. Kippley recommends a "reflective reading" of sections 49 and 50 of the *Pastoral Constitution on the Church in the Modern World* to help answer those questions. And we would suggest also a reflective reading of his own book, as well as discussing this matter with a priest who is loyal to the teachings of the Church on marriage and family life.

Q. My son is marrying again after being divorced. If he and his new wife, who is also divorced, come to visit me, can I let them stay at my home without giving scandal? — M.J.F., Iowa

A. The situation you describe is one that has caused heartache for many parents who have seen their children fail to remain faithful to the Church's teaching on divorce and remarriage. However, your son's situation is not the same thing as having you attend an invalid wedding ceremony or reception. Catholics should stay away from such ceremonies since it would signify their apparent approval of what is to become an adulterous relationship.

But this does not mean that you must break off all communication with your son. Presumably your son is aware of your disappoinment that he has turned away from the teaching of Christ and His Church on marriage, and you should not feel the least bit guilty for upholding this teaching yourself. However, there is no need for you to shun your son. Jesus associated with sinners and loved them, but He never condoned their sinful actions. In fact, He told them to avoid such sins in the future (John 8:11).

Your role is to continue to communicate your love and concern to your son and to pray that he and his wife might soon conform their relationship to the plan of God.

Q. We avoid weddings of Catholics outside the Church, but what about the reception afterwards? — R.L., Ohio

Q. Is it a sin to go to the wedding of a Catholic outside the Church? Aren't we saying that we approve of this marriage? — M.J.M., Minnesota

Q. You told M.J.F. to keep open the lines of communication with her divorced and remarried son, but you did not answer the question about whether the couple should be allowed to stay at the parents' home. Wouldn't letting them stay over constitute approval of a sinful situation? — J.T.O., New Jersey

Q. We disagree with your answer to M.J.F. about not shunning a divorced and remarried son. We tried communicating with our son after his first marriage outside the Church, but now he's married again and seems only to want our acceptance of his lifestyle and his rejection of God's law. Our Lord does not want us to negotiate a false peace with sin. — P.W., Florida

A. The widespread rejection of the Church's teaching on divorce and remarriage is one of the most distressing situations facing families and friends of those who choose to marry outside the Church. As the questioners indicated, it is no easy task to offer answers that will satisfy everyone while still remaining faithful to the law of God. Some readers think that questions of this type are too complex to treat in this limited format, but because the questioners are sincerely looking for guidance, we are going to try once again to move into an area where even angels fear to tread.

It is not only the teaching of the Church, but also the teaching of our Lord that "everyone who divorces his wife and marries another commits adultery. The man who marries a woman divorced from her husband likewise commits adultery" (Luke 16:18). Adultery is a grave evil, and St. Paul warned that "God will judge fornicators and adulterers" (Hebrews 13:4).

Traditional morality forbids cooperation with the evil act of another. Thus, it would be wrong to cooperate in the procuring of an abortion, or in the selling of illegal drugs, or in the theft of a large sum of money. So, too, it would be wrong to cooperate in the evil act of adultery that will begin on the invalidly married couple's wedding night by attending the attempted marriage or the reception. And it would be wrong to let such a couple stay overnight in one's home.

To those who rationalize attendance at the ceremony or reception by saying that this does not mean approval of the adulterous relationship, or that they have expressed their disapproval verbally, we remind them that actions speak louder than words. How seriously will the couple take the verbal expression of concern when parents or friends are physically present at the wedding?

To those who say that staying away from the ceremony or reception will foster dissension in the family, it should be pointed out that it is the couple, by their disregard for the teachings of Jesus and His Church, who have caused the dissension, not their parents. Peace in the family at the expense of following the Gospel is a false peace, one that will never compel the couple to come to grips with the danger of losing their eternal salvation. Our Lord spoke out against this kind of false peace:

"Do not suppose that my mission on earth is to spread peace. My mission is to spread, not peace, but division. I have come to set a man at odds with his father, a daughter with her mother, a daughter-in-law with her mother-in-law; in short, to make a man's enemies those of his own household. Whoever loves father or mother, son or daughter, more than me is not worthy of me" (Matthew 10:34-37).

Yes, this is a hard teaching, but it would be a disservice to faithful and unfaithful Catholics to water it down in order to avoid pain or hard feelings. Better pain and hard feelings now than for all eternity!

The Church's answer in these situations is to pray constantly for the invalidly married couple, keep the lines of communication open with them, and encourage them, in the words of Pope John Paul II, "to undertake a way of life that is no longer in contradiction to the indissolubility of marriage" (*Familiaris Consortio*, n. 84). But never, by word or example, to signify approval of their adulterous union.

Q. I am deeply disturbed over the answer given to the question in "Catholic Replies." I consulted Fr. Sheedy in the *Sunday Visitor*, a parish priest, a missionary, a deacon, and a religious brother, and all are in opposition to your answer. P.S. So far, your answer is the most convincing and hurting. — A.U., Illinois

Q. I am sending you a copy of a recent article in *Our Sunday Visitor* that deals with a subject you covered in *The Wanderer*. Fr. Sheedy's advice is contrary to yours. I am not looking for a debate here, but would like to get some clarification from you on the subject matter. I still feel that your answer was the correct one. — J.M.T., California

A. In his question-and-answer column in the *Sunday Visitor*, Fr. Frank Sheedy took "Catholic Replies" to task for comments that we made about not attending the weddings and receptions of divorced and remarried children and not letting the couples stay overnight in the parents' home. Among other things, Fr. Sheedy called us "very narrow and fundamentalist," "very legalistic," and unable "to make proper distinctions."

As far as making proper distinctions is concerned, we suggest that it is Fr. Sheedy who has failed in this regard. The question he answered concerned a person who had married outside the Church; there was no indication whether this person had been married before. The question we treated, and which Fr. Sheedy had in front of him when he wrote his answer, concerned a person who had been divorced and remarried and was therefore living in adultery.

It was not fair for Fr. Sheedy to relate our answer to a different situation than the one described by his questioner and then to say that our reply was wrong. Nor was he on target when he cited Jesus' parable of the Prodigal Son, in which "the son was not turned away because he had sinned and failed the father." Surely, Fr. Sheedy is aware that the Prodigal Son was sorry for his sins, while many divorced and remarried couples have shown no sign of repentance.

It would have been more appropriate to cite Jesus' advice to the woman caught in adultery: "But from now on, avoid this sin"

(John 8:11). Or Fr. Sheedy could have used the words of Jesus that we quoted in our reply: "Do not suppose that my mission on earth is to spread peace. My mission is to spread, not peace, but division. I have come to set a man at odds with his father, a daughter with her mother, a daughter-in-law with her mother-in-law; in short, to make a man's enemies those of his own household. Whoever loves father or mother, son or daughter, more than me is not worthy of me" (Matthew 10:34-37).

Fr. Sheedy advised his questioner "to show love and charity to the couple." But is it charitable not to speak the truth about the teaching of Christ and His Church on marriage? What kind of love is it that ignores or at least implicitly condones sinful actions by family members? Wouldn't real love and charity compel us to admonish the sinners (a spiritual work of mercy) and to try to persuade them to face the very real possibility of losing their soul? One can love the sinner without signifying approval of the sin by word or example.

Q. When my sister began dating after her divorce, even dating married men, we refused to allow any boyfriends into family get-togethers. Three priests said our actions were correct since we wanted to avoid scandal to our young children, but many relatives have since accused us of being judgmental and uncharitable. How can we get through to our relatives that we are doing this out of love for my sister and our children? And aren't these relatives being judgmental themselves? — M.A., Pennsylvania

A. As we have noted above, the question of divorce, dating, and remarriage is one of the most emotional issues facing Catholic families today. Family members are torn between love for Jesus and the teachings of His Church and love for relatives and friends who have made the decision to disregard the teachings of our Lord and to live according to the standards of the world. It is not M.A.'s actions that have provoked dissension in the family, but rather the actions of her sister.

We have pointed out on other occasions that it is not uncharitable to speak the saving truth given to us by Jesus or to attempt to correct sinners. Nor is it unloving to refuse approval for the sinful actions of family members; one can love the sinner without condoning the sin. So instead of going over this ground again, let us deal only with the accusation of being judgmental.

When Jesus told us not to judge others, He was referring to their motives, not their actions. We have no way of knowing why people do certain things since we cannot get inside their minds. But we can say, based on our Lord's moral code, that certain actions — murder, adultery, blasphemy — are always objectively sinful. We try to avoid these actions ourselves, and we also try to influence our family members, by word and example, to avoid them.

We have been taught since childhood to stay away from persons who could get us into trouble — persons who might steal, deal drugs, get drunk, vandalize property. We used to call these persons "occasions of sin" because they had the potential of leading us into sin. If we stayed away from them, there was less chance of us going wrong.

Our parents encouraged us to exercise good judgment in our choice of companions when we were growing up. Should that prudent judgment change once we reach adulthood? Shouldn't we still avoid persons who could lead us into sin or get us into trouble? If your sister were a drug dealer and wanted to bring her supplier to a family party, would your relatives approve? If she worked in an abortion chamber and wanted to bring the chief baby-killer to a christening, would your relatives say okay? If she were a prostitute and wanted to bring her pimp to a wedding, would your relatives welcome his presence? Or would they use the same good judgment you have demonstrated and tell her not to bring her companion along?

Granted, these examples are more graphic than inviting a boyfriend to a get-together, but the principle is the same. The invitee is a potential occasion of sin for your sister, and it is your love and concern for her that prompts you to tell him to stay away. To do otherwise would be to compromise your own moral values and religious standards and to give bad example to your children.

We all have to do what we believe to be right, but our decisions ought to be based on the law of God and the teachings of the Church He gave us to help us get to Heaven, not on the standards of the world. To follow Jesus in these matters will not be easy; it could mean estrangement from family and friends. But better to be estranged from them than from our Lord. Whether your relatives can see the merit of your position will depend on how close they are to the position of the Church. Continue praying for them and for your sister, and stick to your principles.

Q. My daughter lives with a man to whom she is not married. Is there a Church rule that says we cannot visit her

or invite her boyfriend to family gatherings? — Name Withheld, New Brunswick

Q. Is there a Church rule that parents cannot visit their children who live together without being married? Five priests have told me there is no such rule and that such a rule would be uncharitable and would cause more family problems. Shouldn't we try to keep the door open so that through communication and love we can help our children? — Name Withheld, Canada

A. First of all, there is no Church rule that covers visiting one's children who are presumably practicing fornication and therefore are objectively living in sin. We are always bound to avoid cooperation in evil and to avoid giving scandal to others, but how does one respond correctly to this situation?

There are two schools of thought. One says that we should keep the lines of communication open while continuing to indicate our disapproval of the situation. In other words, we love the sinners while hating the sin. The other school says that we should sever all ties with the couple until they live according to the teachings of Christ and His Church.

We would advocate the first course of action unless, as some distraught parents have told us, the couple revels in and even taunts heartsick parents with their immoral lifestyle. Communication is a two-way street and, if the couple is intent on ridiculing the parents as old-fashioned and out of touch, then visitations back and forth would serve no good purpose.

If on the other hand the two people are not arrogant about their situation, and parents believe that the values of family love and friendship may influence the couple to change their lifestyle, then visitations may be appropriate within certain parameters, such as not allowing the unmarried duo to stay overnight in one's home or giving any sign of approval, by word or example, of their living together without marriage.

There are no easy answers to this question, and we don't pretend to be the last word on it. Pope John Paul has addressed this problem by urging pastors and other members of the Church to "make tactful and respectful contact with the couples concerned, and enlighten them patiently, correct them charitably, and show them the witness of Christian family life in such a way as to smooth the path for them to regularize their situation" (*Familiaris Consortio*, n. 81).

Q. My divorced sister was remarried by a justice of the peace and regularly receives Communion because her parish priest told her it was all right to do so. My sister and my mother both maintain that it's okay since she is receiving Communion on the advice of the priest, but I say that if you know something is wrong, it is wrong no matter who says it's right. What do you think? — R.B., Georgia

A. Presuming that the priest knows all the facts about your sister's marital situation, he is wrong in advising her to receive Communion. She is living in adultery, according to what you have told us, and is therefore not free to receive the Eucharist since she is guilty of what the Catholic Church has always taught as objective mortal sin.

It is unfortunate that some priests, for whatever reason, are giving the faithful false counsel regarding such gravely sinful matter as abortion, adultery, contraception, and homosexual behavior. If your sister knew of no other view of her situation than that of her parish priest, then her subjective guilt would be diminished.

But since members of her family have reminded her of the Church's teaching, she has an obligation to find out if the priest's advice conflicts with the Church's official position. If it does conflict, then she is bound to conform her conscience to the Church's teaching and to stay away from Communion until she has ended her adulterous relationship. No priest who is faithful to the teaching of Jesus and His Church can say that adulterous conduct does not bar a person from receiving our Lord in the Holy Eucharist.

Q. My son's fiance was baptized a Catholic but not raised in the faith. They were told by the parish priest that she can receive Holy Communion at their wedding because the Church has become much more flexible about such matters in recent years. Can you tell me how to respond? — M.J.G., Ohio

A. A baptized Catholic who has never practiced her faith is presumably in need of instruction about the doctrinal beliefs and moral teachings of the Catholic Church. It is not being judgmental to assume that she is also probably in need of catechesis about, and reception of, the sacrament of Penance. Whatever flexibility exists in the Church today does not include the flexibility to receive Communion while in a sinful state. The responsibility of the priest to prepare the couple for a holy wedding day is clear in canon law.

Canon 1063 of the 1983 Code says that "pastors of souls" are obligated to prepare couples getting ready for marriage by instructing them about "the meaning of Christian marriage and the duty of Christian spouses and parents," and by making sure that they are "predisposed toward the holiness and duties of their new state." Canon 1065 says: "If they can do so without serious inconvenience, Catholics who have not yet received the sacrament of Confirmation are to receive it before being admitted to marriage. It is strongly recommended that those to be married approach the sacraments of Penance and the Most Holy Eucharist so that they may fruitfully receive the sacrament of marriage."

Q. I am a divorced Catholic who was not married in the Church, and I have been going to Confession and receiving Communion. But I ran across an article that said divorced Catholics are not to go to Confession or take Communion. Can you tell me what divorced Catholics are allowed to do? — T.B., Colorado

A. The article you saw presumably referred to divorced Catholics who had remarried without having their first marriage annulled. Unless such couples are living as brother and sister, they are in a state of adultery, which precludes them from receiving the sacraments of Penance or the Holy Eucharist unless they are willing to end what the Church considers an adulterous relationship.

Divorced persons who have not remarried are in good standing with the Church, and there is no obstacle to them receiving the sacraments.

Q. Is it wrong for me to attend the wedding of a couple who have been living together for the past two years? — L.M.C., Minnesota

Q. I find it difficult to attend weddings of Catholic couples who have lived together before marriage. Am I wrong to attend these weddings? — M.F., Maryland

A. Since the couples in question are about to correct an immoral situation through the sacrament of Matrimony, there is no reason to stay away from the wedding. To stay away would imply that they have not repented of their sinful actions, and that is something of which you have no knowledge and should not take it upon yourself to judge. It is to be hoped that couples who lived in sin before marriage have confessed those sins and received absolution so that they can begin their married life in a state of holiness.

It is also good pastoral practice for priests counseling those soon to be married who are living together to demand that they live apart for a certain period of time, say six months, prior to the ceremony as a sign of their good faith and of their remorse for having lived in sin.

Q. Pope John Paul has said that the Church in America is giving too many annulments. Does this mean that my annulment, which was granted in 1982, might not be valid? — F.G.S., Pennsylvania

Q. A priest told my daughter that she would first have to get a divorce before seeking an annulment. If that is true, would it mean she is cut off from the sacraments? Can she remarry? — G.H.G., Wisconsin

Q. In Australia, a petition for annulment can only begin after a divorce has been granted by a secular court. This seems wrong to me because it encourages Catholics to acknowledge that the state has a right to divorce people. — A.J., Australia

A. Let us answer the specific questions first and then offer some background information. (1) If F.G.S. went through the proper channels, then her annulment is valid and would remain valid even if the ground was subsequently declared to be insufficient. (2) A divorced person is not cut off from the sacraments unless that person remarries. Since the first marriage is still valid in the eyes of God and the Church, a second marriage would mean that the couple was living in adultery, which precludes worthy reception of the sacraments of Penance and the Holy Eucharist. (3) Before seeking an annulment, a person must obtain a civil divorce. This does not mean that the Church acknowledges the right of the state to dissolve a valid marriage; it means that the union is ended in the eyes of the state and that there is no possibility of reconciliation.

An annulment or, more properly, a decree of nullity, is a declaration by the Church, through a diocesan agency known as a tribunal, that what appeared to be a valid marriage was defective in some way at the time the couple exchanged their vows. It is not a dissolution of a valid marriage, but rather a decree that a valid marriage never existed. And by the way, it does not make any children of that union illegitimate.

Prior to 1968, when there were 338 declarations of nullity in the United States, the usual reasons for granting an annulment were fraud, force, and fear. It had to be proven that at least one of the parties was not free to marry, lacked the physical ability and mental competence to fulfill the duties and responsibilities of the married state, or was forced into the union by parental or societal pressure.

Since 1968, annulments in the United States have sky-rocketed to about 40,000 a year, causing concern on the part of Pope John Paul. On January 18, 1990, the Holy Father said that while the Church recognized "the great difficulties facing persons and families involved in unhappy conjugal living situations," it could not annul valid marriages "without doing violence to the truth and undermining thereby the only solid foundation which can support personal, marital, and social life."

The Pontiff told marriage tribunal judges that they must always "guard against the risk of misplaced compassion, which would degenerate into sentimentality." He reminded them of canon 1676, which says that before accepting a case, judges are "to use pastoral means to induce the spouses, if at all possible, to convalidate the marriage and to restore conjugal living."

Canon 1095 of the Code of Canon Law says that persons incapable of contracting a valid marriage would include those "who lack the sufficient use of reason; who suffer from grave lack of discretion of judgment concerning essential matrimonial rights and duties which are to be mutually given and accepted; who are not capable of assuming the essential obligations of matrimony due to causes of a psychic nature."

That last phrase — "causes of a psychic nature" — has generated much controversy, with those favoring more annulments saying that not enough attention was paid in the past to psychological causes, and those favoring fewer annulments arguing that too much weight is being given to them today and that psychological grounds are being expanded. The solution to the grave difficulties facing some married couples, as Pope John Paul has suggested, lies somewhere between these two positions.

Q. What is the "internal forum" and how is it used or abused today in regard to marriage annulments? — B.B., Indiana

A. The phrase "internal forum" refers in general to the realm of conscience, as opposed to the realm of law and judicial procedures. In marriage cases, it applies to divorced and remarried Catholics who are "subjectively certain in conscience" that their first marriage was not valid and that they are allowed to receive the Holy Eucharist while living with their second spouse. While some Catholics continue to advocate this "solution," it is contrary to the teaching of Christ and His Church. Writing in *Familiaris Consortio,* Pope John Paul clearly states the reasons why this theory is wrong:

"The Church reaffirms her practice, which is based upon Sacred Scripture, of not admitting to Eucharistic Communion divorced persons who have remarried. They are unable to be admitted thereto from the fact that their state and condition of life objectively contradict that union of love between Christ and the Church which is signified and effected by the Eucharist. Besides this, there is another special pastoral reason: if these people were admitted to the Eucharist, the faithful would be led into error and confusion regarding the Church's teaching about the indissolubility of marriage" (n. 84).

The Holy Father said that the only way divorced and remarried Catholics could receive Holy Communion would be by taking on themselves "the duty to live in complete continence, that is, by abstinence from the acts proper to married couples."

He also urged those couples not to "consider themselves as separated from the Church, for as baptized persons they can, and indeed must, share in her life. They should be encouraged to listen to the word of God, to attend the Sacrifice of the Mass, to persevere in prayer, to contribute to works of charity and to community efforts in favor of justice, to bring up their children in the Christian faith, to cultivate the spirit and practice of penance and thus implore, day by day, God's grace."

Q. A person gets an annulment, then remarries, and later on gets a divorce. Can this person receive Communion? — J.A.W., Massachusetts

A. Yes, if this person was not the cause of the divorce. A person who obtains a decree of nullity, which says that a previous sacramental marriage did not exist, is free to marry in the Church. If that union ends in divorce, the person is able to receive Holy Communion, according to the *Catechism of the Catholic Church* (n. 2386), as long as he or she is the innocent victim of a divorce decreed by civil law and has not contravened the moral law. There is a big difference, the *Catechism* says, between a spouse who has sincerely tried to be faithful to the sacrament of marriage and is unjustly abandoned, and one who deliberately destroys a canonically valid marriage.

Q. The new *Catechism* is right to the point on the sacredness of marriage, but what about annulments? Are they now

no longer allowed? And what about the many questionable annulments before the new *Catechism*? Are they suddenly not recognized as valid by the Church? Also what about the innocent children involved in a divorce, who through no fault of their own have to spend time with a fallen-away Catholic parent who will not take them to Mass? Will the children be denied Communion the times when they are able to attend Mass? — D.L.M., Washington

A. In its section on marriage consent, the *Catechism of the Catholic Church* (n. 1629) says that there are certain reasons that render a marriage null and void and that the Church, after an examination of the situation by the competent ecclesiastical tribunal, can declare the nullity of a marriage, i.e., that the marriage never existed. In this case, says the *Catechism*, the contracting parties are free to marry, provided that the natural obligations of a previous union are discharged.

Repeating what we have said previously, an annulment is a decree by a Church tribunal that what was thought to be a valid marriage at the time it took place was lacking some essential element that rendered the union invalid. In the eyes of the Church, the man and woman are free to remarry since no valid marriage occurred in the first place. The new *Catechism* contains no language that would prohibit these decrees of nullity in the future or that would overturn annulments that have already been granted by the Church, even those that might be considered questionable.

Children are indeed the innocent victims of divorce and, if they live with a parent who does not practice his or her faith, they will be deprived of the opportunity to attend Mass and receive our Lord in the Eucharist. But children in this situation cannot be held culpable for missing Mass, and are therefore able to receive Communion when taken to church by a practicing Catholic.

It is sad but true that for some children today, their First Communion is often their last Communion. Fallen-away parents apparently feel some obligation to have a child prepared for First Communion, but many of these children seldom attend a religion class or see the inside of a church again until it is time for Confirmation.

There are many good religion teachers who try to instill in children the importance of weekly Mass participation and reception of the Eucharist, as well as recourse to the sacrament of Penance, but it is very hard to offset parental indifference or even hostility to the Church and the sacraments.

Q. How can the Catholic Church give an annulment to a non-Catholic? In this case, a Catholic woman married a divorced Lutheran man, and the annulment did not come through in time, so they were married in a Lutheran church with no priest present. A year later, the marriage was blessed in a Catholic church. Why bless a marriage that could not be celebrated in her own church? To my mind psychological immaturity is the same as temporary insanity for murder. — Name Withheld, Pennsylvania

Q. I wish you would address the problem of Catholics who after years of marriage apply for an annulment in order to marry someone else. My non-Catholic friends criticize the Catholic Church for giving annulments to those who have money. I feel so many times this is a very unfair law and contributes to the loss of children from the parent judged guilty. — J.C., Texas

A. Since divine law governs all marriages, and since the Catholic Church is the authoritative interpreter of the divine law, a Catholic tribunal can grant a decree of nullity even to a non-Catholic if the investigation produces clear evidence that one or both of the parties to the non-Catholic marriage were not free to marry, did not really understand what marriage was all about, or were incapable of assuming the essential obligations of matrimony.

The marriage in the Lutheran church could not be blessed by the Catholic Church until both parties were free to marry, which apparently did not happen until a year later.

Yes, as noted above, the ground of psychological immaturity has surely been overused and abused in recent years to nullify some marriages that probably should have remained intact.

As for the conventional wisdom that only people with money can obtain a decree of nullity, that is a falsehood. Some dioceses impose a $50 filing fee (sometimes absorbed by the parish) to discourage frivolous or impulsive requests and send no further bill (usually $300 to $400) until after the process is concluded. Money is never the issue.

Q. Could you explain how some prominent people can call themselves Catholics and still be able to receive the sacraments when they are divorced and have remarried outside the Church? — J.B., Missouri

A. Without knowing all the facts of any particular case, and without knowing the state of any person's soul except our own, we can't explain why certain people whose marital status has apparently disqualified them from being able to receive the sacraments worthily nevertheless march up to Communion in full public view. All we can do is state the Church's teaching and let God be the judge of these persons. One restatement of that teaching was contained in a letter sent to the world's bishops on October 14, 1994, by the Sacred Congregation for the Doctrine of the Faith:

"In fidelity to the words of Jesus Christ, the Church affirms that a new union cannot be recognized as valid if the preceding marriage was valid. If the divorced are remarried civilly, they find themselves in a situation that objectively contravenes God's law. Consequently, they cannot receive Holy Communion as long as this situation persists.

"This norm is not at all a punishment or a discrimination against the divorced and remarried, but rather expresses an objective situation that of itself renders impossible the reception of Holy Communion:

"'They are unable to be admitted thereto from the fact that their state and condition of life objectively contradict that union of love between Christ and his Church which is signified and effected by the Eucharist. Besides this, here is another special pastoral reason: If these people were admitted to the Eucharist, the faithful would be led into error and confusion regarding the Church's teaching about the indissolubility of marriage'" (n. 4).

The letter also said that "the Church is in fact the body of Christ, and to live in ecclesial communion is to live in the body of Christ and to nourish oneself with the Body of Christ. With the reception of the sacrament of the Eucharist, communion with Christ the head can never be separated from communion with his members, that is, with his Church.

"For this reason, the sacrament of our union with Christ is also the sacrament of the unity of the Church. Receiving eucharistic Communion contrary to the norms of ecclesial communion is therefore in itself a contradiction. Sacramental communion with Christ includes and presupposes the observance, even if at times difficult, of the order of ecclesial communion, and it cannot be right and fruitful if a member of the faithful, wishing to approach Christ directly, does not respect this order" (n. 9).

Q. What is the significance of a priest "blessing" a marriage when one or both parties have not gone through the annulment process? I realize there is an outward signifi-

cance — a priest gives a blessing as a representative of the Church — but I am unsure as to whether there is a spiritual, grace-giving aspect to such a blessing. I am writing because of a number of very public "blessings" of second marriages which I thought were illicit in the Church's view. As I am currently going through a painful annulment process, and will continue to do so to remain in total communion with the Church, I can't help but feel that, given the spate of public "blessings," the annulment process exists for those powerless dupes who are willing to go through with it. — J.S., Virginia

A. The blessing of a marriage involves a simple ceremony in which the man and woman renew their vows before a priest and two witnesses. When a priest presides over such a renewal of vows, he is saying that the union is in accord with the marriage laws of the Catholic Church, i.e., that the parties are not married to anyone else and are free to marry each other. There certainly is a spiritual, grace-giving aspect to this blessing since, as J.S. said, the priest is acting as a representative of the Church.

If, on the other hand, one or both of the parties had been married before, and no decree of nullity had been obtained for the first marriage, then it would be a sacrilege for any priest to "bless" the second marriage since that union would be an adulterous one in the eyes of God.

The annulment process can be very painful and it is not made any less painful when it appears that some public figures are able to circumvent the rules, or at least to claim that the Church has given its blessing to their second marriages. We are not privy to all the facts about these claims and would not presume to judge whether these unions have truly been blessed or not.

What we would say to J.S. and others in her situation is to pray for the strength to see their own process through to completion and to ignore media reports of other people's situations. It is quite enough to be concerned about keeping one's own spiritual house in order without worrying about the spiritual or marital status of certain public personalities.

Q. Is a Catholic wife still obliged to obey her husband or has this teaching by St. Paul and Pope Pius XI been changed? — J.R.L., New York

A. The relationship that should exist between husband and wife was spelled out by Pope John Paul in *Familiaris Consortio*, his 1981 apostolic exhortation on "The Role of the Christian Family in the Modern World." Among other things, he said:

"Authentic conjugal love presupposes and requires that a man have a profound respect for the equal dignity of his wife: 'You are not her master,' writes St. Ambrose, 'but her husband; she was not given to you to be your slave, but your wife .... Reciprocate her attentiveness to you and be grateful to her for her love.' With his wife a man should live 'a very special form of personal friendship.' As for the Christian, he is called upon to develop a new attitude of love, manifesting towards his wife a charity that is both gentle and strong like that which Christ has for the Church" (n. 25).

Q. Our pastor said that St. Paul was dead wrong, because he felt the end of the world was at hand, when he told men and women not to marry and to live as virgins. Would you please comment? — M.M., Texas

A. St. Paul may have thought that the end of the world was near, but the principal reason why he urged men and women to remain unmarried was so they would have more time to devote to the work of the Lord: "The unmarried man is busy with the Lord's affairs, concerned with pleasing the Lord; but the married man is busy with this world's demands and occupied with pleasing his wife. This means he is divided. The virgin — indeed, any unmarried woman — is concerned with things of the Lord, in pursuit of holiness in body and spirit. The married woman, on the other hand, has the cares of this world to absorb her and is concerned with pleasing her husband" (1 Corinthians 7:32-35).

The Church has long agreed with St. Paul about the superiority of virginity or celibacy for the kingdom of God. "In virginity or celibacy," said Pope John Paul II, "the human being is awaiting, also in a bodily way, the eschatalogical marriage of Christ with the Church, giving himself or herself completely to the Church in the hope that Christ may give himself to the Church in the full truth of eternal life. The celibate person thus anticipates in his or her flesh the new world of the future resurrection" (*Familiaris Consortio*, n. 16).

This in no way puts down marriage, the Holy Father said, explaining that "marriage and virginity or celibacy are two ways of expressing and living the one mystery of the covenant of God with his people. When marriage is not esteemed, neither can consecrated virginity or celibacy exist; when human sexuality is not regarded as a great value given by the Creator, the renunciation of it for the sake of the kingdom of Heaven loses its meaning.

"Rightly indeed does St. John Chrysostom say: 'Whoever denigrates marriage also diminishes the glory of virginity. Whoever praises it makes virginity more admirable and resplendent. What appears good only in comparison with evil would not be particularly good. It is something better than what is admitted to be good that is the most excellent good'" (*Ibid.*).

Q. How does the Catholic Church view a transsexual? My son tried to commit suicide because he thought he was gay and rather than be gay he wanted to die. After doctors pointed out to him that his history revealed a classic case of transsexualism and suggested the possibility of a sex-change operation, his depression left him. We are presently doing what we can to research this condition and be more educated on the subject, but our main concern is how does the Catholic Church view someone in this condition? — M.N., New Mexico

Q. Is there an official Catholic position on whether or not it is even possible for a transsexual who has undergone a sex-change operation to marry? Are there any Catholic books, articles, or agencies to which one can turn in order to get information about this matter? — A.A.H., Indiana

A. First of all, the Catholic Church views every person, whatever their sexual orientation, as a person loved by God and redeemed by Christ. Every person, regardless of their sexual orientation, is called to live a chaste life with the help of prayer and the sacraments and compassionate counseling. The Church is ever ready to provide considerate and kind pastoral care to those faced with difficult problems in the area of human sexuality.

Second, the Church is opposed to sex-change operations because they cause unnecessary mutilation and are always sterilizing and therefore intrinsically evil. Even the medical community has stopped virtually all such operations because of the multiple years of psychotherapy that are necessary both before and after surgery.

Third, since the Church has rejected sex-change operations as immoral, it would certainly not knowingly sanction a marriage involving a person who had undergone such an operation.

Fourth, we don't know of any sources of reliable information on transsexualism, but perhaps Fr. Donald G. Timone, the director of Courage, the Catholic organization that helps homosexual men and women lead chaste lives, could be of some help even though the problem of transsexualism differs from that of homosexuality. The address for Courage is St. Michael's Rectory, 424 W. 34th Street, New York, NY 10001, and the phone number is (212) 421-0426.

Another person who might be helpful is Dr. Joseph Nicolosi of the Thomas Aquinas Psychological Clinic, 16542 Ventura Blvd., Encino, California 91436. Nicolosi is also secretary-treasurer of the National Association for Research and Therapy of Homosexuality, which contends that "homosexuality is primarily developmental in origin, and that in most cases it definitely is responsive to psychotherapeutic measures."

Q. According to the enclosed article, a new book entitled *Same-Sex Unions in Pre-Modern Europe* **will produce evidence that for at least 1,000 years the Catholic Church had special approved rituals for joining two men or two women in wedlock. I would like very much to know if this is true. — H.V., Michigan**

A. We have not seen the book, which was written by a John Boswell, but there is no way that the *Magisterium* of the Catholic Church ever sanctioned special rituals to unite homosexuals or lesbians in marriage. If any Catholic priest ever did such a thing, he was acting contrary to the explicit teaching of God and of the Church.

For a summary of that teaching, see articles 1601-1620 of the *Catechism of the Catholic Church*, particularly article 1604, which says that God created man and woman and intended them to be fruitful and multiply (something that same-sex unions are not capable of doing); article 1605, which says Holy Scripture affirms that man and woman were created for one another ("That is why a man leaves his father and mother and clings to his wife, and the two of them become one body" — Gn. 2:24); and article 1614, which says that in His preaching Jesus unequivocally taught the original meaning of the union of man and woman as the Creator willed it from the beginning.

Editor's Note: Regarding a recent question about a new book by Yale Professor John Boswell that alleges the existence in pre-modern Europe of special Catholic rituals for same-sex "marriages," a specialist in medieval church history at a major Catholic university, who asked that his name be withheld, writes to say that while "no mainstream medievalist is unaware of the serious flaws in Boswell's work, many scholars, however, because of their commitment to gay rights issues, are willing to give him a pass and let him off easily. But you can assure readers that he may be a professor at Yale, but his historical scholarship is by no means widely accepted as trustworthy."

To buttress his argument, our specialist sent along a photocopy of an article in *First Things*, in which Richard John Neuhaus quoted from some negative reviews of Boswell's 1980 book, *Christianity, Social Tolerance, and Homosexuality*, by his fellow historians. While Boswell's theories have repeatedly been invoked by the promoters of homosexuality, said Fr. Neuhaus, the scholarly judgment of his peers "has ranged from the sharply critical to the dismissive to the devastating."

For instance, New Testament scholar Richard Hays of Duke Divinity School said that Boswell's interpretation of New Testament material "has no support in the text and is a textbook case of reading into the text what one wants to find there." Robert L. Wilken, a scholar of early Christianity at the University of Virginia, describes Boswell's book as "advocacy scholarship," by which he means "scholarship in the service of a social and political agenda."

And David Wright, the author of an encyclopedia article on homosexuality, wrote in 1989: "The conclusion must be that for all its interest and stimulus Boswell's book provides in the end of the day not one firm piece of evidence that the teaching mind of the early Church countenanced homosexual activity."

But as Fr. Neuhaus perceptively noted, "the ideologically determined are not easily deterred by the facts. As the churches continue to deliberate important questions of sexual morality, be prepared to encounter the invocation, as though with the voice of authority, 'But Boswell says ....'"

We are seeing that now with Boswell's latest book, *Same-Sex Unions in Pre-Modern Europe*, which even received considerable publicity from cartoonist Garry Trudeau in his comic strip "Doonesbury." This proves once again that the surest way to gain credibility for the most outrageous and unproven allegations is to direct them at the Catholic Church.

Editor's Note: We have received a number of questions dealing with the sexual relationship between husband and wife — what is permitted and what is not. Because the questions are of such an intimate nature, and because they cannot be easily answered in the limited space available to us, we have chosen not to treat those questions either in our column or in this book.

A most reliable source of information on these matters is John F. Kippley of the Couple to Couple League, Post Office Box

111184, Cincinnati, Ohio 45211. In addition to his books already mentioned in this chapter (*Marriage Is for Keeps* and *Sex and the Marriage Covenant*), Mr. Kippley also has some valuable brochures, including *Marital Sexuality: Moral Considerations*, which express moral norms that are a combination of the official teaching of the Catholic Church and the common opinion of Catholic moral theologians who accept the official teaching of the Church.

The brochures are available free of charge from the Couple to Couple League to those who send along a business-size stamped and self-addressed envelope.

Chapter 12

On Human Life

Q. Would you please comment on the article about *Humanae Vitae* in the enclosed Sunday bulletin? — P.G., Ohio
A. The bulletin article said that Catholic couples, after informing their consciences by prayer, study, and consultation, "can make a conscientious choice to use artificial contraceptives." Those who do this, the article said, "are not bad Catholics and certainly are not excommunicated. They are doing what they must in conscience do. But, as the Belgian bishops note, they must continue to pray and reflect about this question."

That the priest who wrote this tried to justify his stance by reaching back to a statement of the Belgian bishops more than 20 years ago shows where he is coming from. Wouldn't a pastor ordinarily quote from the numerous statements on artificial contraception by the reigning Pontiff, whose counsel carries considerably more weight than what one country's bishops said two decades ago? And what kind of a pastor would deny his people the clear guidance they need as they "pray and reflect about this question"?

For artificial contraception has been condemned in this century by Pope Pius XI (1930), Pope Pius XII (1951 and 1958), Pope John XXIII (1961), the Second Vatican Council (1965), Pope Paul VI (1964, 1965, and 1968), Pope John Paul II on many occasions, including *Familiaris Consortio* in 1981 and in major addresses during visits to the United States in 1979, 1987, and 1993, and by the *Catechism of the Catholic Church* (1992).

The clearest explanation of the reasons for the Church's opposition is contained in Pope Paul VI's 1968 encyclical letter *Humanae Vitae*. In brief, the Holy Father said that marital intercourse has a twofold purpose in the plan of God. It is to be procreative (life-giving) and unitive (love-giving), and it is morally wrong for a couple to break this "inseparable connection" either by practicing contraception or by physically or emotionally abusing one's spouse. Couples who for good reasons wish to space out births, recent Popes have said, should resort to Natural Family Planning, which avoids the use of powerful drugs and harmful devices and requires self-control and the loving cooperation of both spouses.

Quoting from *Humanae Vitae*, the *Catechism* said that "'every action which, whether in anticipation of the conjugal act, or in its

accomplishment, or in the development of its natural consequences, proposes, whether as an end or as a means, to render
procreation impossible,' is intrinsically evil" (n. 2370).

Living according to God's plan will not be easy for Catholic
couples, said Pope Paul, "and if sin should still keep its hold
over them, let them not be discouraged, but rather have
recourse with humble perseverance to the mercy of God, which
is poured forth in the sacrament of Penance" (n. 25).

The Holy Father predicted in 1968 that widespread use of
artificial birth control would lead to marital infidelity, the
general lowering of morality, loss of respect for women, and
government imposition of repressive contraceptive programs
upon their peoples (n. 17).

No one can seriously deny that these prophecies have come
true, or that we have experienced an epidemic of sexually
transmitted diseases, teenage pregnancies, and abortions as a
result of ignoring the plan of the Creator.

It seems unlikely that any literate Catholic couple could be
unaware of the Church's clear teaching on human life,
especially since the media delight in reporting polls that show
Catholics dissenting from this and other moral teachings of the
Church.

The other thing P.G.'s pastor neglected to do was to give his
parishioners accurate information on how to form a correct
conscience. Yes, a person "is bound to follow his conscience
faithfully" (Vatican II, *Declaration on Religious Freedom*, n.
3), but in doing so, "the Christian faithful ought carefully to
attend to the sacred and certain doctrine of the Church. The
Church is, by the will of Christ, the teacher of the truth. It is
her duty to give utterance to, and authoritatively to teach, that
Truth which is Christ Himself, and also to declare and confirm
by her authority those principles of the moral order which have
their origin in human nature itself" (*Declaration on Religious
Freedom*, n. 14).

At a time in history when the individual conscience has been
accorded what Pope John Paul has called "the status of a
supreme tribunal of moral judgment which hands down
categorical and infallible decisions about moral evil" (*Veritatis
Splendor*, n. 32), people need to be reminded that conscience
can be culpably erroneous, as in the case of a person "who
cares but little for truth and goodness," or it can by degrees
grow "practically sightless as a result of habitual sin" (Vatican
II, *Pastoral Constitution on the Church in the Modern World*,
n. 16).

In his World Day of Peace Message on December 8, 1990, the Holy Father said: "To claim that one has a right to act according to conscience, but without at the same time acknowledging the duty to conform one's conscience to the truth, and to the law which God Himself has written on our hearts, in the end means nothing more than imposing one's limited personal opinion."

Yes, "each individual has a right to be respected in his own journey in search of the truth," Pope John Paul has said, but "there exists a prior moral obligation, and a grave one at that, to seek the truth and adhere to it once it is known" (*Veritatis Splendor*, n. 34).

P.G.'s pastor does a grave disservice to his parishioners by keeping from them the truth about the evil of artificial contraception and the formation of a correct conscience. Pray for him that he will give them the splendor of truth instead of the squalor of falsehood.

Q. The enclosed article by Fr. John Catoir on conscience and birth control seems to conflict with the Church's teaching. Can you comment? — A.J.P., Pennsylvania

A. Fr. Catoir's column is ambiguous in that he really didn't come down firmly on the side of the Church's teaching against artificial contraception, nor did he explain the reasons for the Church's stand. He said that most Catholics who use birth control "are at peace with their consciences and go to Communion without recourse to the sacrament of Reconciliation," and that the *Magisterium*, or teaching office, of the Church "provides the safest norm of conduct for all and is binding on all members of the Church, but it does not cancel freedom of conscience."

The then-director of the Christophers also said that while "the *Magisterium* is the pre-eminent source of our knowledge, it is not the only source. The Catholic also has access to reason, science, the common thinking of the faithful (the *sensum fidei*), the example of people of esteemed virtue, the opinion of theologians, and the teachings of other traditions. Eastern Rite churches, for instance, even those in union with Rome, have taught that the Church's right to intrude in this matter stops at the bedroom door, and that couples must work this out in the privacy of their own hearts."

All of this may be true, but it gives carte blanche to those who want to practice contraception and still call themselves faithful Catholics.

Fr. Catoir could have done his readers a real service by telling them what the Second Vatican Council said about conscience and contraception. "In the formation of their consciences," the Council taught, "the Christian faithful ought carefully to attend to the sacred and certain doctrine of the Church" because "the Church is, by the will of Christ, the teacher of the truth" (*Declaration on Religious Freedom*, n. 14).

The Council Fathers agreed that parents themselves have to make the decision on how many children to have, but added that, "in their manner of acting, spouses should be aware that they cannot proceed arbitrarily. They must always be governed according to a conscience dutifully submissive toward the Church's teaching office, which authentically interprets that law in the light of the Gospel" (*Pastoral Constitution on the Church in the Modern World*, n. 50).

Nothing there about consulting science, the opinions of theologians, or the teachings of other traditions. Oh, Fr. Catoir urged people to "read the relevant Church documents and look into Natural Family Planning before closing their minds on this issue," but he never quoted any of those documents. And he left the very clear impression that one could be at peace with one's conscience and go to Communion while practicing contraception. What Catholic seeking the truth would find it in this uncertain trumpet?

Editor's Note: In a recent column, we restated the Church's clear condemnation of artificial contraception in order to rebut the contention of a priest in Ohio that Catholics could make a conscientious choice to use artificial contraceptives and remain in good standing in the Church. Dr. P.R.B. of Ohio writes to remind us that some so-called contraceptives, such as the Pill, are also abortifacients, which makes the use of them an even graver evil. Here are his comments:

"These drugs act in three major ways: First, they usually prevent the release of a new egg from the ovaries. Secondly, they thicken the mucus in the reproductive tract, thus making it more difficult for the sperm to reach the egg. Finally, should an egg be released, and should a sperm manage to join with the egg, a new unique individual human is formed, which then passes down the tube to the uterus where it attempts to embed in the wall and complete its development.

"It is here that the third effect of 'the Pill' (and most other so-called contraceptives) causes the wall of the uterus to be unable to allow implantation, and so the new child is thus aborted. Contraceptive pills are not just contraceptive; they are also abortifacient. Although this effect does not occur every cycle, it does occur from time to time, and thus a mother aborts her child without knowing it.

"I enclose a news item which states that the Vatican has condemned the use of RU-486 and morning-after pills which act similarly to 'the Pill.' One must also condemn the use of the IUD, which does not prevent conception, but rather causes the fertilized egg to be aborted. True contraceptives include the diaphragm, condoms, and various spermicidal gels. Depoprovera and Norplant also have abortifacient effects."

Q. I seek literature that clearly elaborates the Church's position on contraception. Not vague or scholarly information, but something that vividly explains how birth control pills not only prevent fertilization, but how they destroy the embryo when fertilization does occur. — M.S., Florida

A. Regarding the abortifacient effect of the pill, see the previous reply.

For literature that clearly states the Church's opposition to artificial contraception, see Pope Paul VI's encyclical on human life (*Humanae Vitae*), Pope John Paul's exhortation on the Role of the Christian Family in the Modern World (*Familiaris Consortio*), Lawler, Boyle and May's book *Catholic Sexual Ethics* (Our Sunday Visitor), *Why Humanae Vitae Was Right: A Reader*, edited by Janet E. Smith (Ignatius Press), *Humanae Vitae: A Generation Later* by Janet E. Smith (Catholic University of America Press), and John F. Kippley's book *Sex and the Marriage Covenant* (Couple to Couple League).

There are also excellent pamphlets available from the Couple to Couple League, P.O. Box 111184, Cincinnati, Ohio 45211, for 15 or 20 cents apiece plus a business-size self-addressed stamped envelope.

Q. Since the objective of both artificial contraception and Natural Family Planning is to avoid pregnancy, why does the Church support the natural form when it clearly has the same objective as the artificial means? — S.H., New Jersey

A. Both methods do indeed aim to avoid pregnancy, but morally they are not the same. Contraception involves taking direct and deliberate steps before, during, or after the marital act to prevent pregnancy. Natural Family Planning involves no marital act at all. In other words, contraception means doing something, while NFP means doing nothing.

There's a big difference, morally speaking, between acting against something and not acting against it. In the case of a terminal cancer patient, for example, it would be morally wrong to kill the patient with a drug injection, but it would not be wrong to forego an operation that at best might only keep the patient alive for a short time.

A couple who for serious reasons seeks to practice responsible parenthood by spacing out the births of their children can abstain from marital relations without harboring a hostile and immoral attitude toward human life. They are not attacking life at its very beginning through chemical or mechanical means, but are rather allowing every marital act to remain open to the transmission of life.

Another significant difference between contraception and NFP is the fact that the latter method requires the loving cooperation of both parties instead of placing the burden only on one partner. This mutual involvement of husband and wife, which will demand real communication between them, can enhance the respect, increase the affection, and deepen the love that they feel for each other.

Q. If the Church teaches that every act of marital intercourse must be open to the conception of children, what does that mean for marriages where one partner has been surgically castrated for medical reasons? And also, should couples abstain from marital relations after menopause, when conception is no longer possible? — Name and State Withheld

A. Pope Paul VI answered these questions in *Humanae Vitae*: "These acts, by which husband and wife are united in chaste intimacy, and by means of which human life is transmitted, are, as the [Second Vatican] Council recalled, 'noble and worthy,' and they do not cease to be lawful if, for causes independent of the will of husband and wife, they are foreseen to be infecund, since they always remain ordained toward expressing and consolidating their union" (n. 11).

The Holy Father also said the Church "does not at all consider illicit the use of those therapeutic means truly necessary to cure diseases of the organism, even if an impediment to procreation, which may be foreseen, should result therefrom, provided such impediment is not, for whatever motive, directly willed" (n. 15).

In other words, marital intercourse is meant to be life-giving and love-giving. If the life-giving aspect is no longer possible due to sterility, whether organic or as a result of surgery to cure a disease, or following menopause, couples are free to continue marital relations since they are fulfilling the love-giving purpose of the conjugal union.

Q. Is there any moral difference between onanism and modern-day methods of artificial contraception? — Y.L., Alberta

A. The term "onanism" is derived from Onan, the son of Judah, who married his brother's widow but violated the levirate law by withdrawing during intercourse and wasting his seed on the ground (Genesis 38:8-10). Morally speaking, this contraceptive act is no different from contemporary barrier methods of contraception, such as condoms, diaphragms, and foams, which destroy the life-giving meaning of marital intercourse. The Pill and the intrauterine device (IUD), however, are morally worse than withdrawal because both have the potential to cause very early abortions and both can be harmful to a woman's health.

Q. Would you comment on the enclosed article in regard to the use of contraceptives for women at risk of rape? — P.D.L., Massachusetts

A. The Reuters dispatch sent to us quoted from the Jesuit journal *La Civiltà Cattolica*, which said that when a woman is in danger of being raped, such as nuns working in dangerous places like Bosnia, "it is morally licit that she take recourse in the only means available, contraceptives, to avoid a possible pregnancy."

Germain Grisez, an outstanding Catholic moral theologian who is a firm supporter of the Church's teaching against artificial contraception and who believes that "contraception is always wrong," has argued that "preventing conception due to rape need not be contraception." Writing in *Living a Christian Life*, volume 2 of his projected four-volume work, *The Way of the Lord Jesus*, Professor Grisez says:

"Rape is the imposition of intimate, bodily union upon someone without his or her consent, and anyone who is raped rightly resists so far as possible. Moreover, the victim (or potential victim) is right to resist not only insofar as he or she is subjected to unjust force, but insofar as that force imposes the special wrong of uniquely intimate bodily contact. It can scarcely be doubted that someone who cannot prevent the initiation of this intimacy is morally justified in resisting its continuation ...."

In a footnote to this section, Grisez rules out the use of certain alleged contraceptives (e.g., the IUD) because they may cause an early abortion.

Q. The "Catholic Replies" answer to use of contraception for women at risk of rape never clarifies that this is not Church teaching. If Germain Grisez is an outstanding theologian, he wouldn't propose such strange arguments. It would follow that not only nuns in Bosnia but all women in Bosnia (a dangerous place) would also be in danger of rape. It would follow that inner city women are also in danger. Dissident theologians are looking for cracks to make strides against *Humanae Vitae*. James Drummey has given his stamp of approval to this argument by Grisez. — J.O., Massachusetts

Q. I know nothing about Germain Grisez, whom you describe as an outstanding moral theologian, and speak with only the authority of a young wife and mother, but I'm absolutely certain he is wrong in this case. "Preventing conception due to rape need not be contraception." What nonsense! I simply can't believe you printed that without comment. In whatever situation, contraception is always contraception. — R.M.T., Arizona

A. First of all, J.O. is correct in stating that the *Magisterium* of the Church has not taken a clear stand one way or the other as to whether women may use contraceptives to prevent pregnancy resulting from rape. However, this question keeps coming up these days, and Catholic theologians thoroughly familiar with the Church's teaching on contraception, and completely loyal to that teaching, have proposed what this writer considers to be a reasonable and moral justification for the use of barrier contraceptives (cervical cap or diaphragm), but not abortifacients (the Pill or the IUD), to prevent possible pregnancy in the event of rape.

The remarks that follow are taken from the writings of three of these solidly orthodox Catholic moralists — Germain Grisez, John F. Kippley, and Fr. Brian W. Harrison, O.S.

Germain Grisez, Professor of Christian Ethics at Mount St. Mary's College in Emmitsburg, Maryland, has been arguing for the intrinsic immorality of contraception at least since 1964, when he published a book entitled *Contraception and Natural Law*. He wrote an article, with John C. Ford, S.J., in the June 1978 issue of *Theological Studies*, reprinted in *The Teaching of Humanae Vitae: A Defense* (Ignatius Press), contending that the Church's teaching against contraception meets all the conditions for infallibility set forth by the Second Vatican Council. He is the author of two monumental summaries of Catholic moral teaching, *Christian Moral Principles* and *Living a Christian Life* (Franciscan Press), each of them nearly a thousand pages in length. And he was a consultor to Pope John Paul II in the preparation of *Veritatis Splendor*, the Holy Father's 1993 encyclical on morality.

John Kippley, who along with his wife Sheila founded the Couple to Couple League in 1971 to help other married couples with Natural Family Planning, has co-authored, with his wife, *The Art of Natural Family Planning*; written a wide range of articles, brochures, and booklets related to NFP and the traditional truths about human love; and has thoroughly demolished arguments for unnatural birth control in two books: *Birth Control and the Marriage Covenant* and *Sex and the Marriage Covenant*.

Fr. Brian Harrison, who lives in Puerto Rico, writes frequently for orthodox Catholic publications, is well known as a defender of *Humanae Vitae*, and had published in the Spring 1993 issue of *Faith & Reason* a 54-page article arguing that the encyclical of Pope Paul VI is an infallible statement of the Church's teaching on human life.

The impressive credentials of this trio are listed to show that their reflections on artificial contraception are not the shallow opinions of publicity-seeking dissenters, but rather the carefully considered and scholarly views of men who are unquestionably faithful and articulate proponents of Catholic truth.

As pointed out in a previous reply, Professor Grisez believes that contraception is always wrong. He argues, however, that if the victims (or potential victims) of rape are unable to prevent the violent act itself, they are "morally justified in trying to prevent conception insofar as it is the fullness of sexual union. The measures taken in this case are a defense of the woman's ovum (insofar as it is a part of her person) against the rapist's sperms (insofar as they are parts of his person)" (*Living a Christian Life*, p. 512).

Grisez contends that using true contraceptives, such as a diaphragm and/or spermicide, in anticipation of rape is not the moral equivalent of a married couple's use of them to impede a new human life. This is not a "strange argument," or an effort to undermine *Humanae Vitae*, but rather a plausible conclusion by a man who has the confidence of the reigning Pontiff.

In his 1991 book *Sex and the Marriage Covenant*, John Kippley talks about a "contralife will" on the part of the couple practicing contraception. He defines a contralife will as "the positive will that a possible person should never come into being." Kippley goes on to say, however, that "it is not clear to me that every contralife will put into contraceptive practice is intrinsically evil. For example, take the case of a woman who is in danger of being raped, e.g., a public health nurse working in a notoriously high crime area. May she use a true contraceptive device — a diaphragm or cervical cap — to prevent pregnancy from rape? I think the common answer of orthodox Catholic theologians is that it would be morally permissible for her to use such a true contraceptive device" (p. 302).

Kippley concedes that the nurse has taken "a premeditated contraceptive action," but he says that "protection from the consequences of rape is hardly what the contraception controversy is all about; and I would certainly agree that such protective action is not the marital action considered and condemned by *Humanae Vitae*, etc."

In a letter published in the November 1992 *Fidelity* magazine, Fr. Harrison argues that Paul VI never addressed the issue of contraceptives to prevent pregnancy from rape. He says that the Holy Father's condemnation of contraception referred only to its use before, during, or after "intercourse freely chosen by both spouses" (p. 14). This obviously has nothing to do with a woman attacked by a rapist.

In the October 1993 issue of *Fidelity*, Fr. Harrison admits that the issue is "a confused one because 'contraception' is an ambiguous word. It can mean: (a) 'any action which aims to prevent the conception of a child'; or (b) 'any action which aims to prevent one's own sexual act from conceiving a child.' Let's call these two 'contraception A' and 'contraception B.'

"My understanding is that Pope John Paul II has contraception B in mind when he says that 'contraception' is intrinsically evil and admitting of no exceptions. I accept that absolutely. I think contraception B is intrinsically evil mainly because in each and every case it perverts one's own God-given genital faculty, suppressing any possible gift of new life while grasping at the lesser goods of intercourse: physical and emotional satisfaction.

"Contraception A, however, would include also the woman who uses a contraceptive device in view of possible rape; and the Church has never condemned this more broadly defined class of behavior as intrinsically evil" (p. 4).

This is not an issue that is easily understood, and trying to explain it is a "no-win" battle, says John Kippley, because you will be accused of undermining the Church's teaching. As we enter that battle, let it be emphasized once more that there is no doubt in our mind that contraception in marriage is intrinsically evil. As Pope John Paul II has said: "When, therefore, through contraception, married couples remove from the exercise of their conjugal sexuality its potential procreative capacity, they claim a power which belongs solely to God: the power to decide in a final analysis the coming into existence of a human person" (Seminar on "Responsible Parenthood," September 17, 1983).

Q. A friend told me that the Church would give permission for sterilization if a woman's life or health would be endangered by her getting pregnant. Is this true? I thought that only Natural Family Planning could be used. — R.W., Wyoming

A. It is not true. The Church has long taught that direct or contraceptive sterilization is immoral because it frustrates the life-giving aspect of marital intercourse. In his encyclical on human life (*Humanae Vitae*), Pope Paul VI first rejected abortion as a "licit means of regulating birth" and then said: "Equally to be excluded, as the teaching authority of the Church has frequently declared, is direct sterilization, whether perpetual or temporary, whether of the man or of the woman" (n. 14).

Immoral means cannot be used to justify the end of protecting the woman's life or health. That desired end could be achieved by the moral means of Natural Family Planning.

For a good discussion of the Church's teaching on this and other matters involving human sexuality, see the book *Catholic Sexual Ethics* by the Reverend Ronald Lawler, O.F.M. Cap., Joseph Boyle Jr., and William E. May.

Q. What are some of the moral implications for a married man who has had a vasectomy and now regrets his action and currently practices his Catholic religion with a high level of commitment (daily Mass and Communion and weekly Confession)? Are there guidelines regarding

marital intercourse? What kind of reparation should be made? — J.Z., New Jersey

Q. I know that obtaining vasectomies and tubal ligations are gravely immoral acts. If a penitent confesses that he or she purposely became sterilized, are such persons morally required to reverse the sterilization procedures? Are there any magisterial proclamations/declarations on this matter? If a person is not required to reverse the situation medically, or if it is not possible, would he or she with his or her spouse be required to abstain from conjugal relations during normal fertile times? — J.S.R., South Dakota

A. We know of no magisterial teaching on this particular question, but we do know of some valuable insights from respected moral theologians. Because the Church teaches that these sterilizing procedures are gravely sinful, moralists loyal to the *Magisterium* believe that persons who have sincerely repented of vasectomies or tubal ligations ought to take additional steps as a sign of their genuine contrition. Otherwise, these couples would be psychologically able to enjoy the fruits of their sin every time they had intercourse during the fertile time.

The first thing the couples should do is seek to have the sterilization reversed, a step that has become increasingly possible with the advances in microsurgery. This effort to return one or both of the spouses to their normal state of fertility would be a clear sign of true repentance.

If reversal of the vasectomy or tubal ligation is not medically possible, or if the cost is beyond the means of the couple involved, then they ought to practice Natural Family Planning, that is, to abstain from intercourse at those times when the wife would normally be fertile. They would then be acting in the same way as unsterilized couples who believe that they have a serious reason for avoiding pregnancy.

For a more detailed presentation of the obligations incumbent upon repentant sterilized couples, see pages 208-215 of John Kippley's book *Sex and the Marriage Covenant.*

Q. If a Catholic couple who has had infertility treatments for a year or two decides to discontinue the treatments even though there is a possibility that further treatments could result in a pregnancy, are they guilty of sin? — Name Withheld, New York

A. If a couple has made reasonable efforts over a period of time, such as two years, to determine the cause of the infertility and to undergo treatments that might make pregnancy possible, they would not be guilty of sin if they decided to discontinue the treatments. Infertile couples are not obliged to continue seeking treatment that may be costly and unpleasant and that holds no guarantee of success.

In its 1987 *Instruction on Respect for Human Life in Its Origin and on the Dignity of Procreation*, the Sacred Congregation for the Doctrine of the Faith expressed sympathy for infertile couples, saying that "sterility is certainly a difficult trial." The instruction called on the community of believers "to shed light upon and support the suffering of those who are unable to fulfill their legitimate aspiration to motherhood and fatherhood."

The Vatican document also quoted from Pope John Paul II, who said that sterile couples must not forget that "even when procreation is not possible, conjugal life does not for this reason lose its value. Physical sterility in fact can be for spouses the occasion for other important services to the life of the human person, for example, adoption, various forms of educational work, and assistance to other families and to poor or handicapped children" (*Familiaris Consortio*, n. 14).

Q. What is the Church's position on the use of fertility drugs? What is it when there is the possibility of a multitude of embryos being conceived at one time and therefore many or maybe none will grow to term? What if the doctor says twins or triplets are the probable outcome? These could survive but have some probability of birth defects. The woman involved in these decisions is pro-life and would not consider "pregnancy reduction." The drugs being considered are Pergonal and Clomid. — M.A.S., Michigan

A. We turn gratefully for assistance to Peter J. Cataldo, Ph.D., Director of Research for the Pope John Center for the Study of Ethics in Health Care, 186 Forbes Road, Braintree, Massachusetts 02184. Dr. Cataldo writes:

"Given that 'pregnancy reduction' is ethically out of the question, the use of these drugs seems to be morally permissible, with certain qualifications, to overcome an infertility problem of a married couple. The drugs could not licitly be used as part of a prohibited procedure such as in vitro fertilization. Rather, they could only be used to help the spouses' conjugal act 'reach its natural objectives.' ['If the technical means facilitates the conjugal act or helps it to reach its natural objectives, it can be morally acceptable. If, on the other hand, the procedure were to replace the conjugal act, it is morally illicit' — *Donum Vitae*, II, B, 6].

"The spouses must be fully aware of the risk for multiple ovulations from these drugs. If possible, the couple should learn whether some dosages have a greater risk of multiple ovulations and avoid such a dosage, depending upon what it is. Multiple ovulations can result in multiple conceptions, which can lead to serious pregnancy complications. The couple must be prepared to care for more than one child in the event that there are multiple births due to the use of the drugs. The couple should also consider other morally acceptable procedures."

Q. Is a Catholic couple who has a child via in vitro fertilization automatically excommunicated? Is the child born by this method allowed to be baptized as a Catholic? — T.K., Maryland

A. No to the first question; yes to the second. Conceiving a child via in vitro fertilization is immoral, according to Catholic teaching, but there is no penalty of excommunication attached. The child resulting from this process, said *Donum Vitae*, "must in any case be accepted as a living gift of the divine Goodness and must be brought up with love" (part II, B5).

As explained by the Sacred Congregation for the Doctrine of the Faith in its *Instruction on Respect for Human Life in Its Origin and on the Dignity of Procreation*, the Church certainly recognizes "the suffering of spouses who cannot have children," but it teaches that "the act of conjugal love is ... the only setting worthy of human procreation." It teaches that the conception of life in the laboratory and transfer of the new life to the womb of the mother is "illicit and in opposition to the dignity of procreation and of the conjugal union, even when everything is done to avoid the death of the human embryo" (part II, B5).

The Church believes that the child conceived "must be the fruit of his parents' love. He cannot be desired or conceived as the product of an intervention of medical or biological techniques; that would be equivalent to reducing him to an object of scientific technology" (part II, B4).

Q. As you can see from the enclosed article, actress Ann Jillian played the role of a grandmother who became a surrogate mother for her own grandchild. I am sure that Jillian is no authority on Catholic faith and morals, but a

lot of people reading the enclosed will think so. Let me know if I'm wrong. — R.S., New Jersey

A. According to the article, Miss Jillian, who had a child herself after 15 years of a childless marriage, empathized with the surrogate grandmother, saying that "we're both Roman Catholics, so we had questions of faith, and I'm happy to say the Church did support her. As far as I can see, every child comes from God. It's a miracle. For us, with our finite minds, to question such a miraculous result is not something I'm going to tackle."

We don't know who in the Church supported the grandmother, but the *Magisterium* of the Church has condemned surrogate motherhood as immoral because "it is contrary to the unity of marriage and to the dignity of the procreation of the human person." In its *Instruction on Respect for Human Life in Its Origin and on the Dignity of Procreation*, the Congregation for the Doctrine of the Faith had this to say:

"Surrogate motherhood represents an objective failure to meet the obligations of maternal love, of conjugal fidelity, and of responsible motherhood; it offends the dignity and the right of the child to be conceived, carried in the womb, brought into the world, and brought up by his own parents; it sets up, to the detriment of families, a division between the physical, psychological, and moral elements which constitute those families" (part II, A3).

The Church is not unsympathetic to the suffering of childless couples. She insists, however, that "marriage does not confer upon the spouses the right to have a child, but only the right to perform those natural acts which are per se ordered to procreation.

"A true and proper right to a child would be contrary to the child's dignity and nature. The child is not an object to which one has a right, nor can he be considered as an object of ownership: rather, a child is a gift, 'the supreme gift' and the most gratuitous gift of marriage, and is a living testimony of the mutual giving of his parents. For this reason, the child has the right, as already mentioned, to be the fruit of the specific act of the conjugal love of his parents; and he also has the right to be respected as a person from the moment of his conception" (part II, B8).

Editor's Note: In a recent column, we took issue with a statement attributed to actress Ann Jillian in which she expressed her belief that the Catholic Church was supportive of a surrogate grandmother (played by Miss Jillian in a TV movie) who had carried a child to term for her daughter. The following comments are taken from a letter sent to us by Andy Murcia, husband and manager of Miss Jillian:

"With a good natured smile on my face I want to relate that my wife is very proud of her faith and has had the benefit of a wonderful Catholic education. She also continues to read and converse weekly with our dear priests at our parish about being a Catholic. I also want to assure your readers that Ann is a person of high morals. As manager of her career, I can testify that the reason we don't see Ann acting on the big movie screen is because she has a stop order in effect at her agent's office on any scripts that have any type of foul language or sex or nudity in them. That uncommon high moral stand has cost her well into the millions in lost income over her thus-far thirty-five-year career. Ann acts mainly in TV movies now that have no language, sex, or nudity in them.

"Re [the film] 'Labor of Love' ... the daughter's egg was fertilized by her husband's sperm while the egg was in her and then because her medical problem would not allow her to carry the baby to term, they then placed the egg in the grandmother's womb until birth. All Granny did was hold her grandchild. Not to do this would mean the baby would die inside its mother....

"Now that you are armed with these facts (and if necessary I could send you a tape of the movie for you to view), I hope you will convey them to your many readers as it is our understanding from the real people involved that their priest did give them his blessings."

First of all, let us express our congratulations to Ann Jillian for sticking to her high moral standards in an industry that seems to have virtually no moral standards. We have nothing but the highest admiration for her courageous witness to Catholic moral teaching.

Regarding the main issue, the gist of our previous reply was that the Catholic Church has condemned surrogate motherhood as immoral because "it is contrary to the unity of marriage and to the dignity of the procreation of the human person."

Instead of repeating the reasons for that position that we quoted in our previous reply, let us note that the same condemnation is contained in the *Catechism of the Catholic Church*, which says that techniques that entail the dissociation of husband and wife, by the intrusion of a person other than the couple (donation of sperm or ovum, surrogate uterus), are "gravely immoral" (n. 2376).

We understand how difficult it is to accept this teaching, especially when a childless couple wants children so desperately. We also understand Ann Jillian's empathy for the family in the TV movie, and we have no reason to doubt her husband's statement that the real people portrayed in the film had their actions blessed by their priest.

But our point then, and now, is that no faithful Catholic, priest or layperson, should give approval to something that the *Magisterium* of the Church has condemned. The Church is not unsympathetic to the plight of childless couples, but the *Catechism* (n. 2378) reminds us that a child is not something owed to anybody, but is a gift, and that a child possesses genuine rights, including the right to be the fruit of the specific act of the conjugal love of his parents, and the right to be respected as a person from the moment of conception.

The *Catechism* (n. 2379) goes on to say that the Gospel shows physical sterility is not an absolute evil. Spouses who still suffer from infertility after exhausting legitimate medical procedures should unite themselves with the Lord's Cross, the source of all spiritual fecundity, it says, adding that they can give expression to their generosity by adopting abandoned children or performing demanding services for others.

This is one of those hard teachings, along with no remarriage after divorce, where deep emotions and feelings make it difficult to see the wisdom of the Church's stand. But as Catholics we are expected to adhere to all the teachings of the Church, even those which severely challenge our faith.

Q. Is it a sin to buy shares in a mutual fund that invests in companies which make and sell contraceptives and abortion-producing drugs? Could this be considered cooperating with and profiting from contraception and abortion? — R.E.B., New Jersey

A. There are two kinds of cooperation in the sinful actions of others: formal and material. Formal cooperation, which means actually taking part in the sin of another, is always sinful because one shares in the sin. Helping a doctor perform an abortion would be an example of formal cooperation in a sin, as would making contraceptives or abortion-producing drugs since those things are used for sinful purposes.

Material cooperation, which means assisting in another's wrongdoing without approving it, is sinful if the cooperation is proximate. It is a sin against charity to aid another in the commission of a sin, even if one's own action is lawful. Thus, a bartender who sells liquor to a patron cooperates materially toward the patron's drunkenness when he sells him alcohol knowing that he will drink himself into oblivion.

However, it is not wrong to cooperate materially in the sin of another if the cooperation is remote and there is a sufficiently grave and proportionate reason. A nurse, for example, could cooperate in abortion by caring for the patient and cleaning the operating room if failure to do so would mean losing her job, and she could not easily get another job.

In answer to R.E.B.'s question, her cooperation in the sinful actions of the company producing and selling contraceptives and abortifacients is material and remote. However, since she does not have a suffcently grave reason for remote cooperation in an evil action, she should not buy shares, or she should sell whatever shares she already owns, in the mutual fund that invests its clients' money in the aforementioned company.

Q. Your example of when material cooperation would be remote and not sufficiently grave — and thus not sinful — was dangerously inadequate. You said: "A nurse, for example, could cooperate in abortion by caring for the patient if failure to do so would mean losing her job, and she could not easily get another job." So much is unclear here that some might be apt to rationalize seriously sinful behavior. What is meant by "caring for the patient"? Does the nurse assist the doctor with the abortion or only take care of the woman as she recovers from the procedure? How difficult would it be for the nurse to obtain another job elsewhere (preferably where no abortions are performed)? — J.A.S., Iowa

A. We disagree that the example was "dangerously inadequate." It was taken from *Outlines of Moral Theology* by the late Fr. Francis J. Connell, one of the most reliable moral theologians of our time, and it was offered as a general moral principle, not as a thorough analysis of every possible nuance of the situation. As for lack of clarity about the nurse's role, we had already defined formal cooperation earlier in the reply as "helping a doctor perform an abortion." Since "caring for the patient" came in the discussion of remote material cooperation, it referred to helping the patient recover *after the abortion*.

Q. About 30 years ago, I invested in funds which I now find include among their many investments drug com-

panies that probably manufacture contraceptives. I'm now retired and have no knowledge or interest in the stock market. What if I sell these shares, switch to another fund, and later find that fund invests in companies that make contraceptives? Do I sell again? Do you still say it's seriously sinful to own these funds? — J.K., Minnesota

A. We have never said that it was seriously sinful for someone like yourself to own such funds. What we have said was that cooperation like yours in the sinful actions of companies producing and selling abortifacients and contraceptives was material and remote. Formal cooperation means to take part in the sin of another and consent to the evil intention of the sinner, as in the case of one who assists a doctor in the performance of an abortion. Formal cooperation is always wrong.

Material cooperation means the cooperator has no evil intention but knows that his or her assistance may be used for evil purposes. Such cooperation is not sinful if there is sufficient reason for the cooperation. If a person was looking to invest money in a company that was known to the person to be involved in sinful actions, it would be wrong to invest money in that company.

In J.K.'s situation, however, the shares were bought 30 years ago with no idea that they might one day be invested in companies producing abortifacients and contraceptives. Furthermore, it would be difficult for J.K. to sell the shares and invest the money elsewhere. Thus, it would not be sinful to hold onto those shares since there is sufficent reason for the material and remote cooperation.

Q. On a recent talk show, I heard the pro-abortion host state that the Catholic Church, and certain Popes and saints, such as Augustine, Thomas Aquinas, and Alphonsus Liguori, did not always teach that abortion was immoral. Is there any truth to this? — J.W., Maryland

Q. How has the Catholic teaching on abortion evolved over the centuries? Did the Church ever advocate abortion and later change its position? — K.T., Texas

A. No, the teaching of the Catholic Church against abortion goes back to the *Didache*, a first-century collection of apostolic teachings, which states: "You shall not procure abortion. You shall not destroy a newborn child." This condemnation was repeated by, among others, Athenagoras in the second century, Jerome in the fourth century, Augustine in the fifth century,

Pope Stephen V in the ninth century, Aquinas in the 13th century, Pope Sixtus V in the 16th century, and by virtually every Pope in this century, as well as by the Second Vatican Council, which called abortion an "unspeakable crime" (*Pastoral Constitution on the Church in the Modern World*, n. 51), and the *Catechism of the Catholic Church.*

Since the first century, says the *Catechism*, the Church has affirmed the moral evil of every procured abortion. This teaching has not changed and remains unchangeable. It says that direct abortion, that is, abortion willed either as an end or a means, is "gravely contrary to the moral law" (n. 2271).

There was a time in the Middle Ages when it was believed that the soul was not present in the unborn child until weeks after conception. So a distinction was made in the evaluation of the sin and the gravity of the penalty imposed for abortions performed in these first few weeks and those performed after the soul was thought to be present. But at no time did those Catholic moralists holding this opinion ever deny that procured abortion was an objectively grave evil.

Q. In his autobiography, C. Everett Koop says that the Catholic Church allows abortion when the mother's life is threatened. I believe this is incorrect. Am I right? — J.F., Pennsylvania

A. Yes, you are right. If Dr. Koop did say such a thing, he is mistaken. The Catholic Church does not permit the direct and intentional killing of an unborn child for any reason. If the mother's life is endangered, the Church expects the doctor to do everything possible to save the life of the mother and the baby.

Now it is possible that what you read referred to an indirect abortion, which is morally allowable if the death of the unborn child is not directly willed, but is rather the unintended side effect of a legitimate medical procedure. For instance, it would not be contrary to Catholic teaching to remove a cancerous uterus in order to save the mother's life, knowing that the operation would cause the death of the child who was growing inside that uterus but who was not yet able to live outside the mother.

Q. You seem to contradict yourself when you state that a doctor can remove a cancerous uterus knowing that the unborn child will die. This doesn't seem to square with your earlier statement that the Church does not permit the

direct and intentional killing of an unborn baby for any reason. I would greatly appreciate a clarification. — J.M.T., California

A. This situation is covered by what is known in Catholic morality as the principle of the double effect. That principle says that it is morally allowable to perform an action that will produce a good effect and a bad effect provided the following conditions are met:

(1) The action to be performed must be good in itself or at least morally neutral. Removal of the cancerous uterus is a good thing.

(2) The good effect must not come about as a result of the evil effect. The death of the unborn child is not the cause of the good effect, but is only an unintended side effect of the operation to remove the cancerous uterus.

(3) The evil effect must not be desired in itself but only permitted. There are no bad feelings toward the unborn baby and no wish that he or she should die.

(4) There must be a sufficiently grave reason for permitting the evil effect to occur. The reason is to save the life of the mother.

This situation is quite different from the direct and intentional killing of an unborn child and is morally permissible as long as all four conditions are satisfied.

Q. The answer you gave some time ago about using the principle of the double effect in a case where the removal of a cancerous uterus resulted in the death of an unborn child contradicts what I learned in Catholic education in the 1950s. We were taught that the life of the unborn had priority since the mother had already accomplished God's plan in this life. Where did the principle of the double effect come from? — D.T., Idaho

A. The principle of the double effect has long been used in moral theology (at least since the 17th century). While attending a Catholic college in the late 1950s, the principle first came to our attention in a book by Vernon J. Bourke entitled *Ethics: A Textbook in Moral Philosophy*, which was published in 1951. There is also a lengthy explanation of the principle in Fr. Francis J. Connell's *Outlines of Moral Theology*, which was published in 1952.

If there ever was a time when the life of the mother or the child was given priority, that is not true today in either morals or medicine. The doctor's duty is to do all that he or she can to save the life of both patients, mother and child. And if faced with an action that could have good and evil results, the principle of the double effect can be invoked.

Q. Is it permissible for a woman to abort a tubal pregnancy? Won't she have internal bleeding due to her fallopian tubes bursting, and couldn't this result in death? I am very much pro-life, but I don't know how the Church views this. — D.B., California

A. The Catholic Church has always forbidden direct abortion, that is, a procedure whose intent is to end the life of the unborn child. The Church does not forbid indirect abortion, that is, where the unintended side effect of an operation to save the mother's life is the death of the unborn child. This might happen, for example, when a pregnant woman is diagnosed with uterine cancer and must have the cancerous uterus removed. Or it could happen in the situation described by D.B., where the fertilized ovum lodges in the fallopian tube and begins to develop there.

The damaged section of the tube, containing the growing baby, may be removed if the surgery is clearly and imminently necessary to save the life of the mother. The operation is morally justifiable under the principle of the double effect because there is no intentional killing of the unborn child, and the death of the baby is the unintended side effect of surgery necessary to preserve the mother's life. Morally, the operation is considered to be an indirect abortion; legally, it is not considered to be an abortion at all.

Q. The nun in charge of our RCIA program told me that since the Pope has not spoken infallibly on abortion, a new Catholic can make her own decision and follow her conscience on this matter. Can a person consider themselves a practicing Catholic in good standing with the Roman Catholic Church and still maintain a "pro-choice" position? — R.C.C., Texas

A. The answer to the question is no. Since the Catholic Church has virtually from the beginning expressed firm and unequivocal opposition to abortion, no one who supports this evil can be objectively considered a faithful Catholic.

As for the point about the Pope not having spoken infallibly against abortion, Catholics are still obligated to assent to the teachings of the Pope even when he does not speak infallibly (Vatican II, *Constitution on the Church*, n. 25), particularly on an issue like abortion, which the Church has so vigorously condemned for 20 centuries.

But in 1995, Pope John Paul came about as close to an infallible statement as is possible when he declared:

"Therefore, by the authority which Christ conferred upon Peter and his successors, in communion with the bishops — who on various occasions have condemned abortion and who ... have shown unanimous agreement concerning this doctrine — *I declare that direct abortion, that is, abortion willed as an end or as a means, always constitutes a grave moral disorder*, since it is the deliberate killing of an innocent human being. This doctrine is based upon the natural law and upon the written word of God, is transmitted by the Church's tradition and taught by the ordinary and universal Magisterium" (*Evangelium Vitae*, n. 62).

Q. Is a Catholic who counsels others to have abortions excommunicated? — M.H.T., Massachusetts

A. Canon 1398 of the Code of Canon Law says that "a person who procures a completed abortion incurs an automatic (*latae sententiae*) excommunication." This means that all those involved in the deliberate and successful effort to bring about a completed abortion, including the doctor, the woman, and family members, friends, and counselors who advised the abortion, would be automatically excommunicated, provided that each of these persons knew the Church's penalty for this action but went ahead with it anyway.

According to canons 1323 and 1324 of the Code of Canon Law, excommunication would not be automatically incurred if a person was truly ignorant of the penalty attached to procuring an abortion, was under the age of 16, thought that the law applied only to the person having the abortion and not to her accomplices, acted out of serious fear about parental or societal reaction to the pregnancy, or erroneously believed that the abortion was necessary to preserve the mother's life.

Q. If a person obtains an abortion or participates in the act, then this person brings excommunication upon themselves automatically. Is absolution by a bishop required to have the excommunication lifted? — J.T.R., California

A. If the person willingly takes part in the abortion, knowing that the penalty is automatic excommunication, then the person is excommunicated. If that is the case, only a bishop can absolve the penalty. However, if it would be very difficult for the penitent to remain in a state of serious sin until the absolution of a bishop can be obtained, then any confessor can remit the censure temporarily until he can request a permanent remission from the bishop. In some dioceses, all confessors have the authority to remit the censure for abortion without going through the bishop.

Q. You have said that anyone favoring abortion or helping in any way would be excommunicated from the Church. What about pro-abortion nuns who seem to be operating as usual despite acting contrary to the teachings of the Church? — A.C.R., Kentucky

A. We have never said that anyone favoring abortion or helping in any way would be excommunicated. What we did say was that persons procuring a completed abortion, and all those involved in the deliberate and successful effort to bring about the completed abortion, would be automatically excommunicated, *provided* that each person knew the Church's penalty for this action but went ahead with it anyway. Here is the way Pope John Paul put it:

"The excommunication affects all those who commit this crime with knowledge of the penalty attached and thus includes those accomplices without whose help the crime would not have been committed. By this reiterated sanction, the Church makes clear that abortion is a most serious and dangerous crime, thereby encouraging those who commit it to seek without delay the path of conversion. In the Church, the purpose of the penalty of excommunication is to make an individual fully aware of the gravity of a certain sin and then to foster genuine conversion and repentance" (*Evangelium Vitae*, n. 62).

This teaching applies to all Catholics — clergy, Religious, and laity. Therefore, nuns who speak and act on behalf of abortion ought to be publicly chastised and removed from any office or position in the Church not only because they are rejecting one of its fundamental teachings, but also because of the scandal they are giving to others.

Q. My Ob-Gyn is a Catholic man who refuses to perform abortions, but at the same time admits to performing tubal ligations and most likely prescribes the Pill and other contraceptives. Is there an apostolate of Catholic physicians I can refer him to to help clarify things and support this physician? — M.K., Vermont

A. Try the National Federation of Catholic Physicians Guild, 850 Elm Grove Road, Elm Grove, Wisconsin 53122. They publish *The Linacre Quarterly*, an excellent resource that always reflects the Church's position on contraception and sterilization.

Q. Since Democratic presidential nominee Bill Clinton is "pro-choice" on abortion, would it be a sin for a Catholic to vote for him for President? — J.R.L., New York

A. Before answering the question, let us reiterate that the Second Vatican Council called abortion an "unspeakable crime" (*Pastoral Constitution on the Church in the Modern World*, n. 51); the Sacred Congregation for the Doctrine of the Faith, in its 1974 *Declaration on Procured Abortion*, said that "a Christian can never conform to a law which is in itself immoral, and such is the case of a law which would admit in principle the licitness of abortion. Nor can a Christian take part in a propaganda campaign in favor of such a law, or vote for it. Moreover, he may not collaborate in its application" (n. 22); and the U.S. Catholic Bishops said in November 1989 that "no Catholic can responsibly take a 'pro-choice' stand when the 'choice' in question involves the taking of innocent human life."

For some sound advice on the question asked, we turn to Bishop John Myers of Peoria, Illinois, who on June 1, 1990, issued a pastoral letter entitled *The Obligations of Catholics and the Rights of Unborn Children*. Among other things, Bishop Myers made these comments:

"A public official who would deny unborn children the protection of laws enjoyed by other citizens is guilty of grave injustice. Ordinarily it is morally illicit to help such a person achieve an office in which he or she will be in a position to do such an injustice. Those who assist such candidates because of their position on abortion are guilty of complicity in the abortions their election would make possible....

"One is formally complicit in the injustice of abortion when one votes for a candidate even partially on the basis of his or her pro-abortion positions .... One who supports legal abortion cannot avoid formal complicity by maintaining that he or she wills not abortion as such, but only the freedom of others to choose abortion. Anyone who supports legal abortion seeks to remove from one class of human beings a basic protection afforded to others. By helping to make abortion available, a person becomes formally complicit in its basic injustice whether or not he or she would actively encourage anyone else to have an abortion. From the ethical point of view, there is no distinction between being 'pro-choice' and being 'pro-abortion.'... All formal cooperation in abortion is gravely immoral. So is most material cooperation in abortion."

Since Mr. Clinton is adamantly pro-abortion, and supports the so-called Freedom of Choice Act that would allow unrestricted abortion on demand in the United States, any Catholic who votes for him in November *because* of his position on abortion is guilty of an objectively grave immoral action. The same is true, of course, of a vote for any pro-abortion candidate for political office. The subjective sinfulness of the action would depend, as always, on whether the voter acted with sufficient reflection and with full consent of the will.

Q. I understand your reply that it would be a sin to vote for a pro-abortion political candidate like Governor Clinton. But what should we do if faced with a choice between President Bush, who would permit abortion in cases of rape, incest, and the life of the mother, and a third-party candidate who is solidly pro-life but has no chance of winning? Would it be wrong to vote for Bush on the basis that he is the only one who has a realistic chance of defeating Clinton? — G.A., Arizona

Q. You have written before on the question of Catholics voting for political candidates who are pro-abortion. What is one to do when faced with a choice between a candidate who is moderately pro-abortion and one who is fanatically pro-abortion? — J.V., California, and J.H., New Jersey

A. Bear in mind, now, that the following reply is not to be construed as an endorsement of any political candidate. It is a summary of the moral principles that should enter into such a decision, and it is based on the writings of John Cardinal O'Connor of New York ("Abortion: Questions and Answers," *Origins*, June 28, 1990) and Bishop John Myers of Peoria, Illinois ("The Obligations of Catholics and the Rights of Unborn Children," *Origins*, June 14, 1990).

(1) If all candidates support abortion equally, one could in good conscience refrain from voting for that particular office altogether even though voting is normally a moral obligation. Or one could vote for the challenger on the grounds that he would have less clout in office and would not be able to push abortion as forcefully as the incumbent.

(2) If one candidate is less supportive of abortion than another, one could vote for that candidate with the intention of helping to prevent the election of someone whose pro-abortion position is even more extreme and, in so doing, perhaps save the lives of some unborn babies. Or one may hope to influence the moderately pro-abortion candidate to modify his stance even more or possibly to reverse it completely.

(3) If a third-party or independent candidate is pro-life, but has no realistic chance of winning, one could still vote for that candidate as a matter of conscience, or write in the name of a pro-life person.

(4) One should always strive to vote for worthy candidates, or to abstain if all candidates are equally unworthy. One should never vote for a candidate *because* of his or her pro-abortion stance; in fact, it would be wrong not to count such advocacy as a very weighty reason *against* the candidacy. But there may be what Bishop Myers called "certain limited circumstances" when it would not be immoral for a Catholic to vote for a pro-abortion office-seeker.

Q. What can we do to unmask those political candidates who hide the "right to kill" behind the expression "the right to choose"? — G.A., Indiana
A. Keep hammering home the point that the "choice" they are advocating results in the death of an unborn child who is never given the choice of whether to live or die. The only choice involved is whether the baby will be killed by a powerful vacuum-like device, sharp and deadly surgical instruments, salt poisoning, chemicals or drugs like RU-486, or suffocation or neglect following a mini-Caesarean section that usually produces a live baby.

Don't ever use the phrase "pro-choice" — always say "pro-abortion" or "pro-death." Don't ask a politician how he or she stands on abortion; ask them how they stand on killing unborn babies. Ask them why they are not concerned about the second victim of every abortion — the women who suffer a myriad of physical and mental complications from so-called safe, legal abortions. Ask them to comment on a statement by Nancyjo Mann, whose abortion led to a hysterectomy at the age of 22. One of the founders of the organization Women Exploited by Abortion, Ms. Mann has said that "legal abortion is the most destructive manifestation of discrimination against women today" (cf. David C. Reardon, *Aborted Women: Silent No More*, p. xi).

Q. If the federal government starts to use tax money to pay for abortions, should Catholics withhold some of their taxes from the government? — M.T., South Dakota; A.D., Illinois; P.M.D., Kansas; and G.H., New York

A. First of all, the federal government has for a long time used tax money to pay for abortions. Millions of dollars have gone to abortion providers like Planned Parenthood and to so-called family planning programs that have pushed the Pill (which functions as an abortifacient in some cases) on American women, as well as on women in foreign countries.

But to answer the question, if a person can determine what percentage of the federal budget is used to finance abortions, one could withhold that same percentage of taxes due to the government from an individual or a family. In taking such a step, of course, one must be prepared to pay the penalty, perhaps even time in jail, should the government decide to prosecute.

Those who may be considering such a course of action should bear in mind that even if all taxpayer financing of abortion were eliminated, it would not halt the abortion holocaust. More than 1.6 million babies would still die in the abortion chambers of America each year. Each pro-lifer must decide in conscience whether effort expended on withholding a portion of one's taxes might be better directed at trying to enact laws that would protect innocent life from the moment of conception until its natural end.

Q. Do Catholics have a moral obligation to boycott corporations which financially support Planned Parenthood, this country's number one abortion provider? Knowing that a company like General Mills supports Planned Parenthood, would it be a sin to purchase General Mills products? — K.P.C., Ohio

A. If there is clear evidence that General Mills contributes money to Planned Parenthood, which is indeed the nation's number one killer of unborn babies, then one does have a moral obligation not to buy General Mills products. And you should write to General Mills and explain why you intend to stop purchasing their products. If the company gets enough letters from pro-lifers, it may be persuaded to stop sending money to Planned Parenthood.

It is always a sin to cooperate in evil, but the gravity of the sin depends on the nature of one's cooperation. If the cooperation is formal and proximate (contributing money directly to

Planned Parenthood), such an action would probably be a mortal sin. If the cooperation is material and remote (buying products from a company which contributes money to Planned Parenthood), such an action would probably not be a sin if one had a good reason for buying the products (they are necessary for one's health and are not available elsewhere) or if all producers of a given product do the same objectionable thing.

But since K.P.C. can buy similar products from other companies, then he certainly should not continue to let General Mills use some of the money from his purchases to help finance abortion.

Q. Should we contribute to the March of Dimes? I have been told that they are involved with abortion. — N.M., Massachusetts

A. Right-to-life groups have for more than a decade urged people not to contribute to the March of Dimes because MOD funds are used for prenatal testing to identify abnormal babies, who are then killed by abortion. While the March of Dimes has not used its money directly to promote or pay for abortions, it has set up genetic testing centers across the country that use amniocentesis in the second trimester (a procedure that is dangerous to the baby) to determine if the baby is handicapped.

March of Dimes funds, says Dr. J.C. Willke in his book *Abortion: Questions and Answers,* "pay for and facilitate only the search and identify portion," which then leads to the killing of 97 to 98 percent of those babies thought to have handicaps. Willke says that "Right to Life has repeatedly asked them to stop doing mid-trimester amniocentesis (not late ones, which benefit both baby and mother). Such testing has only one purpose: to identify the child's condition. There is no medical problem identifiable in the mid-trimester that is treatable in the mid-trimester."

MOD argues that by identifying "normal" babies, their testing often saves babies who would otherwise be aborted. Willke answers this argument with the analogy of "a testing center outside Auschwitz where suspected Jews would be taken. Some would be found to be 'normal' Aryans and their lives would be spared. Of course, the Jews would be gassed. Would you contribute money to such a testing center?"

Responding to an MOD memorandum on its policies and practices, Dr. Willke has pointed out that "the March of Dimes has never publicly denounced abortion. Rather, it subscribes to the Supreme Court decision that says every woman has the choice to kill if she wishes." He has noted, too, that "a free booklet offered in the MOD publication catalog and prepared in part by MOD is titled *Adolescent Perinatal Health*. On page 25 it states: 'Whatever the reason, abortion is the last available line of childbirth prevention and must be considered in the spectrum of services offered to pregnant adolescents.'"

Q. Does the Fifth Commandment and Proverbs 24:11 ("Rescue those who are being dragged to death") give Catholics a moral obligation to blockade abortion clinics or risk being guilty before God of consent to murder? — M.C., Kentucky

A. While we are morally obligated to oppose the killing of unborn babies, we are not obligated to blockade the abortion chambers where the slaughter is taking place and risk arrest and jail. Reasonable people who are adamantly opposed to abortion can disagree on the tactics to be employed in the battle and can in good conscience choose peaceful prayer vigils or rescue operations.

Q. What does the Church teach about taking up arms in the defense of others and in the defense of the unborn? — D.M., New Jersey

A. The Catholic Church has always taught that one may take up arms in self-defense against an aggressor, whether that aggressor is an individual criminal bent on doing you mortal harm or a nation intent on subjugating your country and taking away your freedom. In both cases, the use of arms must be a last resort to which we turn only after all efforts to resolve the situation peacefully have been unsuccessful and the serious threat remains.

The Catholic Church has never taught that it would be morally right to take up arms against those who are involved in killing unborn babies. Those who shoot and kill abortionists or employees of abortion mills are gravely wrong. The violence and killing taking place inside the abortuaries are no justification for engaging in more violence and killing either inside or outside the facility. Yes, the abortion holocaust is an abominable and unspeakable crime, but no true follower of Jesus can legitimately take up arms and go around shooting abortionists.

Editor's Note: In response to a question about taking up arms in defense of the unborn, we stated recently that there was no moral justification for shooting and killing abortionists. Several readers have expressed disagreement with that reply, asserting that a Florida man was justified in killing an abortionist. They have contended that man's action was morally equivalent to defending an innocent third party from imminent death at the hands of an aggressor. We do not agree. God alone has power over life and death, and no one may take the life of another person without having been given that power by God, as in the case of the state's authority to impose capital punishment or conduct a just war. God has never delegated that power to private individuals.

In the case of defending one's own life, or that of an innocent third party, there are certain conditions that must be fulfilled. First, we must never intend to kill another person, only to defend our own life or the life of another. Second, we must use the lowest level of force necessary to resist the attacker. If maiming the aggressor or running away will give sufficient protection, this should be done. Third, the use of force must be imminently necessary to save the person's life.

Applying these conditions to the Florida situation, Michael Griffin was apparently intent on killing Dr. David Gunn, he did not the use the lowest level of force necessary to protect the unborn children in the Pensacola abortuary (he might, theoretically, have broken Gunn's arm), and the shooting took place in the parking lot before Gunn had entered the building.

But the bottom line is that the end of stopping abortion does not justify the means of executing abortionists. As A.J. Matt put it in the pages of *The Wanderer*: "Nothing in Sacred Scripture or Christian belief can be cited to justify murder — even of an evildoer." Fr. Paul Marx of Human Life International has said that "committing additional violence is in no way a response to the daily violence of abortion. Even though babies are daily being killed by the thousands, we have a responsibility to ensure that further bloodshed does not take place. It will only foster more violence and bloodshed in our already stricken society."

And the last word comes from Jesus himself, who commands us to "love your enemies, pray for your persecutors. This will prove that you are sons of your heavenly Father, for his sun rises on the bad and the good, he rains on the just and the unjust" (Matthew 5:44-45).

Q. Are Catholic law enforcement officers permitted to supply protection at abortion clinics to pregnant women

seeking abortions? Are extraordinary ministers of the Eucharist permitted to act as "pro-choice escorts" at abortion clinics? — J.D.C., Pennsylvania

A. Let's start with two facts: Catholics are not permitted to cooperate in evil, and the clear teaching of the Church is that the killing of unborn babies is an objectively grave evil. Let's also note that there are two kinds of cooperation: formal, where a person not only takes an active part in the evil action but agrees with the evil being done (the doctor who performs abortions, staff members who directly assist him, or those who counsel women to have abortions), and material, where a person does not agree with the evil action but helps to facilitate it (a nurse in a hospital or a receptionist or a secretary in an abortion facility). We must also consider whether the material cooperation was proximate (giving a woman an anesthetic before the abortion) or remote (caring for her after the abortion) in determining whether such cooperation is morally justifiable.

Regarding the cases raised by J.D.C., a civilian who volunteers his time as a "pro-choice escort" would be cooperating formally in abortion by encouraging the woman to have her child killed. But even if this "escort service" was only material cooperation in evil, it would still be totally incompatible with service as an extraordinary minister of the Eucharist.

As for a state or local law enforcement officer assigned to duty at an abortion mill, that would probably be proximate material cooperation, even if the officer does not agree with the evil being done, since his presence there helps to guarantee that babies will be killed.

A person employed by the abortuary as a security guard or escort would be guilty of formal cooperation in evil, something not permissible for a practicing Catholic.

Q. Given that the government and the judicial system are clearly on the side of the pro-death crowd and determined to keep abortion-killing an ongoing fact, why is it not proper to use force (not necessarily deadly) to stop an abortion which would kill a child? Am I therefore approving or advocating the killing of abortionists or at least some violent action against them or one of their "clinics"? No, but I confess myself lacking in any solid arguments why. — R.N., New Hampshire

A. Writing in the May 1994 issue of *Homiletic & Pastoral Review*, moral theologian Monsignor William B. Smith offered these clear and solid arguments against shooting abortionists:

"The Church repudiates the direct intent to kill. Justifiable self-defense applies only to that killing that is not directly intended, that is a secondary effect. Moral theology does not permit the faithful Christian individual acting alone (on one's own authority) to intend to kill another human being directly. St. Thomas Aquinas, the usual and classic source of justifiable self-defense, is most insistent about this requirement (cf. *Summa Theologiae*, II-II, q. 64, a. 7).

"Next, the justifiable defense comparison urges that the guilt of a known intentional killing can be outweighed by preventing another, but as yet unknown, evil. But a good end does not justify an evil means (Rom. 3:8). Shooting the abortionist is not the same as killing in defense of home or family because the latter killing could be incidental, unintended, a secondary effect. Whereas the murder [of a Florida abortionist] (from what I have read) was intended, premeditated, and not an accident at all.

"Further, those who kill on their own authority open a dangerous spiral that all pro-lifers want shut. When the attacker attempts intended lethal force against the abortionist, is not the clinic guard free, and the police officer duty bound, to repel the attacker with force, even lethal force? Where does this end? How is it limited? ...

"Direct abortion is murder. And I am sure we are all as tired of abortion as we are tired of murder. But using evil to fight evil shows our impatience with God. We must fight bad things in God's way: 'Do not be conquered by evil, but conquer evil with good' (Rom. 12:21).

"While we can hate evil as God surely does, we must as surely do good to our enemies as the same God teaches us. We must fight murder without conforming to it, nor condoning it in any way, but it makes no Christian sense to try to justify murder to limit murder."

Expanding on this argument several months later (as quoted by John Cardinal O'Connor in a speech to the Pontifical Council for Pastoral Assistance to Health Care Workers on November 25, 1994), Msgr. Smith said:

"No Christian, however fervid or misguided, has the moral right to declare himself the sole detective, district attorney, judge, jury, and supreme court in our democratic society and on his own authority set aside the natural law and the Ten Commandments, allegedly to advance the fifth of those Ten Commandments.

"For the first 300 years of Christian history, the Christians were on the wrong side of unjust laws. Yet they were convinced and taught us that it is better to suffer evil than to cause evil. 'Know this, my dear brothers ... the wrath of man does not accomplish the righteousness of God' (James 1:19-20). That was infallibly true when written and is just as true when read today."

Q. I am a Catholic and a Ph.D. candidate in the program in Neuroscience at Harvard University. A few months ago, I found out that the lab I am in occasionally uses brain tissue from aborted fetuses, mostly to verify in human tissue what has been discovered in animals. I would like your advice on whether I must leave this lab. The head of the lab has agreed to exclude me from participating in such research. Such research forms only a small proportion of the lab's work. I have three questions: (1) What do you think of research on aborted fetuses? (2) Can I as a Christian stay in such a lab as long as I don't participate in fetal research? (3) What should my attitude be towards a fellow Christian who involves himself in such research? Also, do you think that automatic excommunication would apply to those who knowingly perform this type of research? — A.L.R., Massachusetts

A. Since this is such an important issue, we again consulted the Pope John Center for the Study of Ethics in Health Care. This Center was founded more than 20 years ago to provide scholarly, timely, and reliable information from the Catholic moral tradition on questions involving medical ethics.

With a professional staff and consultants who are specialists in such fields as philosophy, law, medicine, theology, and the natural and social sciences, the Center sponsors regional workshops and seminars throughout the country, publishes a monthly newsletter (*Ethics & Medics*), and produces books and pamphlets on a variety of issues, including the family, sexuality, abortion, *Humanae Vitae*, prolonging life, genetic counseling, and in vitro fertilization.

The answers to A.L.R.'s questions were provided mostly by Dr. Peter J. Cataldo, the Center's Director of Research, in consultation with Father Russell E. Smith, the president of the Center. We are grateful to both of them for their assistance.

What do you think of research on aborted fetuses?
There are both ethical and medical problems with research

on aborted fetuses for the purpose of tissue transplantation. There has been a virtual silence about the medical disadvantages with aborted tissue in the press and in recent professional literature. For example, it is estimated that 75 percent of aborted tissue, especially fetal liver, is unusable for transplantation due to contamination from the abortion procedure and maceration. The remaining 25 percent will inevitably have some problems from genetic mutation and from drugs used in the abortion. Some of the potentially treatable diseases require tissue in the second trimester, which accounts for only 10 percent of abortions and usually has medical problems associated with it.

Ethically, the use of aborted tissue amounts to a complicity in the evil of abortions, past, present, and future. Use of the results of an abortion cannot be separated from the past evil means by which those results were obtained. There is a complicity in present and future abortions insofar as the use and success of fetal transplantation influence either the decision to abort or the abortion procedure itself. The evil of abortion is thus also perpetuated by the use of aborted tissue. Moreover, there is no sense in which the mother is qualified to give consent to the use of tissue from her aborted child. There is also every reason to believe that a commercialization of pregnancies for the purpose of using aborted tissue could develop.

Can I as a Christian stay in such a lab as long as I don't participate in fetal research?

Under the described conditions there would be no cooperation with the evil of abortion — neither material nor formal — on the part of the researcher. If the work of the researcher does not involve aborted fetal tissue, then it would be permissible to remain at the laboratory.

What should my attitude be towards a fellow Christian who involves himself in such research?

Even though there are conditions under which it would be morally permissible to work at the lab, there is still a possibility of causing scandal. Scandal is an example which, by its nature, leads another person to sin. The researcher would have an obligation to make his or her disapproval of the use of aborted tissue known to those whom the researcher believes might be led to sin by his continued work at the lab. Scandal is possible with both Christian and non-Christian colleagues.

Do you think automatic excommunication would apply to those who knowingly perform this type of research?

Canon 1398 of the Code of Canon Law says that "a person who procures a completed abortion incurs an automatic (*latae sententiae*) excommunication." According to John Cardinal O'Connor's 1990 statement entitled *Abortion: Questions and Answers*, this canon is normally interpreted to include the adult woman who knowingly has the abortion and anyone who assists willingly and directly in procuring the abortion, such as the doctor, the nurse, the abortion counselor, and family or friends who pressured the woman into having the abortion and perhaps even paid for it. In these cases, the excommunication occurs automatically and immediately after the knowing and willing act of the individual. No action is necessary by the bishop.

Apart from automatic excommunication, said Cardinal O'Connor, individual bishops might impose penalties "on those who support abortion in a general way," or on those who engage in "impermissible forms of cooperation, inconsistent with being a practicing Catholic, which give active scandal within the Church and within society." It does not seem that automatic excommunication would apply to those who perform research on aborted babies, but such complicity in the evil of abortion is certainly gravely immoral and might provide sufficient ground for some bishops to excommunicate individuals engaged in this kind of research.

What about the use of miscarriage tissue in this research?

(This question was not raised by A.L.R., but Dr. Cataldo was good enough to offer the following comments.)

Human fetal tissue transplantation is uncertain and experimental at this point in time. Other means for treating the same diseases targeted by fetal tissue transplantation are equally promising. However, under the right conditions, the use of tissue from miscarriages for transplantation can be morally permissible. Miscarriage tissue has several medical advantages over aborted tissue, and could conceivably be the only reliable source of tissue in the future.

The retrieval, storage, and distribution of miscarriage tissue for transplantation represent a special opportunity for Catholic health care both to witness the dignity of human life and make a contribution to a potentially important medical advancement. Assuming that aborted tissue cannot be used, the central conditions for the moral use of miscarriage tissue are: (1) The miscarriage tissue must meet all the medical requirements and the preborn child must be certifiably deceased. (2) Appropriate consent must be obtained. (3) The use of miscarriage tissue must not positively influence abortions. (4) There must be adequate access to the transplantation treatment.

Q. In my diocese, the bishop has publicly stated that it is perfectly all right to vote for a politician who supports abortion. Yet, on the other hand, he had a letter read in all of the parishes strongly opposing euthanasia, and he had a collection taken up to support this activity. Isn't this somewhat of a double standard? — C.H.E., California

A. If the facts are as C.H.E. has stated them, we are surprised because abortion and euthanasia are two sides of the same pro-death coin. In both situations, innocent lives are being taken because the victims are perceived as an economic or social burden to someone. There is no moral difference between killing an unborn child who is not wanted by his mother or an old or sick senior citizen because she is not wanted by members of her family. Life is a continuum along the spectrum from the womb to the tomb, and to sacrifice it at any point on the spectrum for specious reasons is to place in jeopardy the lives of those at all points on the spectrum. That is why the Catholic Church teaches that life must be protected from the moment of conception to natural death. In the words of Pope John Paul:

"Human life, as a gift of God, is sacred and inviolable. For this reason, procured abortion and euthanasia are absolutely unacceptable. Not only must a human life not be taken, but it must be protected with loving concern .... Society as a whole must respect, defend, and promote the dignity of every human person, at every moment, and in every condition of that person's life" (*Evangelium Vitae*, n. 81).

Q. Will you explain what extraordinary means are acceptable to maintain life? — C.R., Illinois

A. It is difficult to enumerate extraordinary means of prolonging life because advances in medicine have changed the definition of what are ordinary and extraordinary means. Surgical procedures once considered extraordinary are now fairly routine. In its 1980 *Declaration on Euthanasia*, the Sacred Congregation for the Doctrine of the Faith said that the best way to make a correct judgment in these matters is "by studying the type of treatment to be used, its degree of complexity or risk, its cost and the possibilities of using it, and comparing these elements with the result that can be expected, taking into account the state of the sick person and his or her physical and moral resources."

The Congregation went on to offer several clarifications of the general principles:

— A patient may choose the latest medical techniques, even if they are risky and still in the experimental stage.

— The patient may halt the use of these advanced techniques if they are not achieving the desired results or if they are imposing on the patient "strain or suffering out of proportion with the benefits which he or she may gain from such techniques."

— One can refuse advanced medical treatment and make do with normal means as an "acceptance of the human condition," to avoid medical procedures disproportionate to the results that can be expected, or to spare the family or the community excessive expenses.

— When death is imminent, the patient can refuse forms of treatment "that would only secure a precarious and burdensome prolongation of life, so long as the normal care due to the sick person in similar cases is not interrupted."

Discontinuing medical procedures that are burdensome, dangerous, extraordinary, or disproportionate to the expected outcome can be legitimate, says the *Catechism of the Catholic Church* (n. 2278), since this only constitutes the refusal of "overzealous" treatment. The person does not will to cause death in this situation, the *Catechism* says, explaining that one's inability to impede death is merely accepted. But it also says that the decisions should be made by the patient if he is competent and able or, if not, by those legally entitled to act for the patient, whose reasonable will and legitimate interests must always be respected.

Q. What is the current Church law on administering artificial nutrition and hydration to patients in a persistent vegetative state? Is the Church law final and binding? — R.P.G., Indiana

, **A.** There is no specific Church law on this matter, but there are moral standards that bind medical personnel and families in resolving these difficult cases. See, for instance, the September 1989 statement of Bishop James McHugh of Camden, N.J. ("Principles in Regard to Withholding or Withdrawing Artificially Assisted Nutrition/ Hydration") and the January

1992 statement of the Catholic Bishops of Pennsylvania ("Nutrition and Hydration: Moral Considerations").

Space prevents us from discussing this complicated issue in depth (those seeking more information should read the two statements mentioned above), but we can offer a brief answer to the question. First, some definitions. Persistent vegetative state is a form of deep unconsciousness caused by a failure of function in one portion of the brain. The person is alive, but only the brain stem is operating. Nutrition and hydration mean supplying food and water to an unconscious person, either orally, through a tube into the stomach, or through the veins.

Any decision in such a case must take into account the distinction between ordinary means of care (which we are morally obliged to use) and extraordinary means (which we may use, but are not obliged to use), and must ask whether the procedure would be beneficial to the patient in terms of preserving life or restoring health, whether it would add a serious burden, and whether it would only prolong the dying process without actually preserving life.

We must also base our decision on the bedrock principles that God is the Author of all life, that we have only steward-ship, not dominion, over life, that euthanasia and suicide are not morally permissible, and that we may not intentionally end another person's life by a deliberate act or by omission.

Having said all that, here is Bishop Hughes on the situation of a person in a persistent vegetative state:

"In the unconscious, non-dying patient, nutrition and hydration should be supplied. Feeding is not useless because it sustains a human life. There is no indication that the person is suffering, nor is there any clear evidence that the provision of nutrition and hydration is an unreasonable danger or burden. In such a case, the withdrawal of nutrition/hydration brings about death by starvation/dehydration. Absent any other indication of a definite burden for the patient, withdrawal of nutrition/hydration is not morally justifiable."

The *Catechism of the Catholic Church* (n. 2279) says that even if death is thought imminent, the ordinary care owed to a sick person cannot be legitimately interrupted. It says that the use of painkillers to alleviate the sufferings of the dying, even at the risk of shortening their days, can be morally in conformity with human dignity if death is not willed as either an end or a means, but only foreseen and tolerated as inevitable. Palliative care, the *Catechism* says, is a special form of disinterested charity that should be encouraged.

For further elaboration of these principles, see section 65 of *Evangelium Vitae.*

Q. Would you please restate clearly and explicitly the Church's official position on the matter of using or not using extraordinary life-support measures in near-terminal medical emergencies? Are life-support measures mandatory or optional and, if once begun, must they be continued regardless of their efficacy in achieving their purpose? — A.E.L., Michigan

A. On April 2, 1992, the U.S. Bishops' Committee for Pro-Life Activities issued a statement opposing the withdrawal or omission of nutrition or hydration intended to cause a medical patient's death (see the full text in the April 9, 1992 issue of *Origins*). The statement set forth a number of moral principles to guide Catholics in these situations. Two of those principles deal with A.E.L.'s question:

"Everyone has the duty to care for his or her own life and health and to seek necessary medical care from others, but this does not mean that all possible remedies must be used in all circumstances. One is not obliged to use either 'extraordinary' means or 'disproportionate' means of preserving life — that is, means which are understood as offering no reasonable hope of benefit or as involving excessive burdens. Decisions regarding such means are complex, and should ordinarily be made by the patient in consultation with his or her family, chaplain or pastor, and physician when that is possible.

"In the final stage of dying, one is not obliged to prolong the life of a patient by every possible means: 'When inevitable death is imminent in spite of the means used, it is permitted in conscience to take the decision to refuse forms of treatment that would only secure a precarious and burdensome prolongation of life, so long as the normal care due to the sick person in similar cases is not interrupted.'" (That last quotation is from the *Declaration on Euthanasia.*)

Q. For over a year, I have tried to come to a decision as to the advisability of making a "Living Will." I find differences of opinion among Catholic clergy. What is your opinion? — A.R.B., New Jersey

A. "Living Wills" are the creation of the euthanasia crowd, and they have been promoted under such nice-sounding slogans as "death with dignity." Everyone would like to die with dignity, but to the so-called mercy killers, this means bringing about the death of a person so that he or she will no longer be a burden to family or friends, will no longer take up space in a health-care institution that could be better utilized by someone else, and will no longer "waste" funds that could be better spent for more constructive programs.

The Catholic notion of dying with dignity, on the contrary, means that the sick person is surrounded by family and loved ones, is receiving excellent medical and nursing care in an attractive environment, is obtaining the ordinary means of sustaining life and extraordinary means if they choose, and is being provided with religious and spiritual consolation by a member of the clergy.

There are several problems with "Living Wills": (1) They have more to do with dying than with living. (2) It is dangerous to attempt to make a decision now about what kind of medical care we would want for an unknown problem at some unknown time in the future. (3) Sick people often change their minds, something that a legally binding "Living Will" might prevent a patient from doing. (4) Phrases such as "terminal illness," "heroic measures," and "extraordinary means" can be defined differently with time and with advances in medical care.

A better solution would be to choose a mature, trustworthy family member or friend, one with sound moral values, to act as your agent or proxy in the event the time should come when you are unable to make a necessary health-care decision yourself. You should discuss with this person, and perhaps with an alternate in case the first person is not available, your concerns about what life-sustaining measures you would want taken, or not taken, and perhaps even spell out your wishes in writing so that the authority of your agent to make such decisions on your behalf will be clear.

It would be a good idea, too, if copies of this document were available to others, such as doctors, family members, and friends. For more information on this health-care proxy, contact your diocesan pro-life office.

Q. My husband is dying of a liver disease and will soon go to the hospital to see if he is a candidate for a liver transplant. In going through a brochure, it states that the donor organ would be from a person who is brain dead. My question is: Would it be morally valid according to the Church's teaching to receive a liver from a brain-dead person? — E.D., New York

A. Yes, if by brain dead they mean that the whole brain and the brain stem have stopped functioning. If this situation exists, and there is a possibility of organ donations, mechanical ventilation and circulation may be used to keep the organs fresh until they are ready to be transplanted. The key point to remember, as far as the morality of this procedure is concerned, is that organs can only be harvested from the dead, not from the dying.

We will also ask our readers to pray for you and your husband.

Q. I would like to be an organ donor upon my death but have been told that it would be against God's law. Is this true? — V.B.D., Illinois

Q. What is the Church's position on an individual's being an organ donor? I feel that donating my organs would be a good humanitarian act. — M.D. and T.F.D., Pennsylvania

A. Donating one's organs to help another person, whether during life or at the moment of death, is not contrary to the law of God. Speaking at a congress on kidney transplants on April 30, 1990, Pope John Paul said that "those who believe in our Lord Jesus Christ, who gave His life for the salvation of all, should recognize in the urgent need for a ready availability of organs for renal transplants a challenge to their generosity and fraternal love." The Holy Father cautioned, however, that everything in this field "should be done with the utmost respect for the fundamental principles of the natural law and Christian ethics."

It is also not against Christian principles to donate one's body to science, provided that reasonable assurance is given that the remains will be disposed of in a reverent and dignified manner after the scientific research has been completed.

Q. Your answer regarding organ donations is misleading. The Pope's remark that you quote is restricted to renal transplant. As we have two kidneys, we can miss one without harming ourselves. — B.M., Ontario

Q. Perhaps it is true that certain organs can be morally and ethically donated, but it is my understanding that this is an area where extreme caution is required. It would seem that more elaboration in your answer is in order. — T.W., Connecticut

Q. I wish you would clarify your answer to the question

regarding organ donation, and please do not confuse it with donation of the body after the fact of death has been established without doubt. — P.A.B., Ohio

A. The original question dealt with donation of organs at the moment of death, which we said was not contrary to Christian principles. We also noted the Holy Father's praise for those who donate their kidneys out of "generosity and fraternal love," as well as his caution that organ donations "be done with the utmost respect for the fundamental principles of the natural law and Christian ethics."

B.M. and P.A.B., both medical doctors, sent along articles dealing with some of these fundamental principles. Their major concern is defining the moment of death precisely and making sure that organs are not removed from persons who are still alive. One of the articles noted that "there is such a shortage of organs at the present time that there is great pressure to declare potential donors brain dead prematurely, thereby killing them. There is more and more reason to doubt that those diagnosed with whole brain death are fully dead."

Another article was a speech delivered by Pope John Paul on December 14, 1989, to participants at a congress on the determination of the moment of death. In that address, the Pontiff discussed the "tragic dilemma" involved when "it is conceivable that in order to escape certain and imminent death a patient may need to receive an organ which another patient who may be lying next to him in the hospital could provide, but about whose death there still remains some doubt. Consequently, in the process there arises the danger of terminating a human life, of definitively disrupting the psychosomatic unity of a person. More precisely, there is a real possibility that the life whose continuation is made unsustainable by the removal of a vital organ may be that of a living person, whereas the respect due to human life absolutely prohibits the direct and positive sacrifice of that life, even though it may be for the benefit of another human being who might be felt to be entitled to preference."

The Holy Father told the members of his audience to "pursue their research and studies in order to determine as precisely as possible the exact moment and the indisputable sign of death. For, once such a determination has been arrived at, then the apparent conflict between the duty to respect the life of one person and the duty to effect a cure or even save the life of another disappears. One would be able to know at what moment it would be perfectly permissible to do what had been definitely forbidden previously, namely, the removal of an organ for transplanting, with the best chances of a successful outcome."

In an article that appeared in the Fall 1990 issue of *The Pharos*, the journal of the Alpha Omega Alpha Honor Medical Society, P.A.B. and a co-author stated:

"Great care must be taken not to declare a person dead even one moment before death has actually occurred. Death should only be declared after, not before, the fact, as to declare death prematurely is to commit a fundamental injustice. A person who is dying is still alive, even a moment before death, and must be treated as such.

"In conclusion, we believe that destruction of the entire brain can occur, but that criteria to determine this state reliably have not been established. Cessation of brain function is not the same as destruction. In the present state of the art of medicine, a patient with destruction of the entire brain is, at most, mortally wounded, but not yet dead. Death ought not be declared unless and until there is destruction of the entire brain, and of the respiratory and circulatory systems as well."

Writing on this topic more recently in *Evangelium Vitae*, Pope John Paul singled out the "everyday heroism made up of gestures of sharing, big or small, which build up an authentic culture of life. A particularly praiseworthy example of such gestures is the donation of organs, performed in an ethically acceptable manner, with a view to offering a chance of health and even of life itself to the sick who sometimes have no other hope" (n. 86).

Chapter 13

Christian Morality

Q. I have heard it said that the Ten Commandments are Old Testament morality, but didn't Jesus mention them in the New Testament? — M.H., Minnesota

A. Yes, He did. In chapter 19 of Matthew, chapter 10 of Mark, and chapter 18 of Luke, our Lord mentioned several of the Ten Commandments. In the Gospel of Matthew, for instance, a rich young man asked Jesus what he must do to get to Heaven. Christ responded:

"'If you wish to enter into life, keep the commandments.' 'Which ones?' he asked. Jesus replied, 'You shall not kill; You shall not commit adultery; You shall not steal; You shall not bear false witness; Honor your father and your mother; and Love your neighbor as yourself'" (Matthew 19:17-19).

After using this dialogue between Jesus and the rich young man to begin *Veritatis Splendor*, his encyclical on morality, Pope John Paul stated: "God's commandments show man the path of life and they lead to it. From the very lips of Jesus, the new Moses, man is once again given the commandments of the Decalogue. Jesus himself definitively confirms them and proposes them to us as the way and condition of salvation" (n. 12).

Are the Ten Commandments still binding today? Listen to the *Catechism of the Catholic Church*:

"Since they express man's fundamental duties towards God and towards his neighbor, the Ten Commandments reveal, in their primordial content, *grave* obligations. They are fundamentally immutable, and they oblige always and everywhere. No one can dispense from them. The Ten Commandments are engraved by God in the human heart" (n. 2072).

Q. Why is our numbering of the Ten Commandments different from that of other religions? — M.G.L., Florida

Q. A fallen-away Catholic and a Protestant fellow employee ask why the Catholic listing of the Ten Commandments is different from the Protestant listing. What is the Catholic to answer? — D.J., Iowa

A. The numbering discrepancy occurs because Catholics take Exodus 20:2-3 ("I, the LORD, am your God, who brought you out of the land of Egypt, that place of slavery. You shall not have other gods besides me") and Exodus 20:7 ("You shall not take the name of the LORD, your God, in vain") as the first two commandments. Protestants, on the other hand, take the three verses in between, which forbid the carving or worship of idols, and make them the second commandment. They maintain the total number of ten by combining into one commandment the prohibitions against coveting a neighbor's wife or goods (Exodus 20:17) that Catholics list as two separate commandments. The numbering sequence is not as important as the fact that Catholics, Protestants, and Jews all agree on the entire moral blueprint handed down by God.

Q. Have the Beatitudes replaced the Ten Commandments as a guide for examining our consciences before the sacrament of Penance? — L.R., South Carolina

A. A thorough examination of conscience prior to receiving the sacrament of Penance/Reconciliation should include a review of the Ten Commandments; the Sermon on the Mount, especially the Beatitudes; Christ's discourse at the Last Supper; the commandments of the Church; and the corporal and spiritual works of mercy. By considering these moral principles, we can determine whether we have fulfilled or neglected our duties toward God, toward other people, and toward ourselves.

But we must go beyond the Ten Commandments, said Pope John Paul, because Jesus made clear that "it is not enough simply not to kill, we must also not hate our brother or sister; it is not enough not to commit adultery, we must also avoid desiring to do it; it is not enough to respect the formalities of the law on divorce, but we must banish every intention to get a divorce; it is not enough simply not to swear, we must also cultivate inner purity expressed in the direct language of yes when it is yes, no when it is no."

The Holy Father also pointed out the connection between the Beatitudes and the Ten Commandments:

"The Beatitudes are not specifically concerned with certain particular rules of behavior. Rather, they speak of basic attitudes and dispositions in life and therefore they do not coincide exactly with the commandments. On the other hand, there is no separation or opposition between the Beatitudes and the commandments: both refer to the good, to eternal life. The Sermon on the Mount begins with the proclamation of the Beatitudes, but also refers to the commandments (cf. Mt. 5:20-48)" (*Veritatis Splendor*, n. 16).

Q. How can you answer people who say they don't have to follow the laws of God or the Church if they go against their conscience? — T.C., Delaware

A. You can agree with them that we must follow our conscience, but you have to point out that a good conscience must be formed in accordance with God's plan for our lives. Because conscience is a practical and reasoned judgment about the good or evil of a concrete act that we are going to perform, are in the process of performing, or have already completed, the key factor is where we get the information to make the judgment. Just as what we get out of a computer will depend on what we enter into it, so decisions about right and wrong will depend on what information was programmed into those decisions.

If the advice that governs our moral choices comes from our friends, or from the advice column in the newspaper or some talk-show host, the choice may be quite different from one based on Scripture or on the teachings of the Holy Father. Some sources of erroneous moral judgments, says the *Catechism of the Catholic Church* (n. 1792), are ignorance of Christ and His Gospel, bad example given by others, enslavement to one's passions, assertion of a mistaken notion of autonomy of conscience, rejection of the Church's authority and her teaching, and lack of conversion and of charity.

To help us form right consciences, said Pope John Paul in *Veritatis Splendor,* Christians "have a great help in ... the Church and her *Magisterium.* As the [Second Vatican] Council affirms: 'In forming their consciences the Christian faithful must give careful attention to the sacred and certain teaching of the Church. For the Catholic Church is by the will of Christ the teacher of truth. Her charge is to announce and teach authentically that truth which is Christ, and at the same time with her authority to declare and confirm the principles of the moral order which derive from human nature itself'" (n. 64).

Q. I have heard it said that if you break one commandment, you break them all. How is that possible? — A.E.L., Michigan

A. This statement comes from the letter of James (2:10-11), who said: "Whoever falls into sin on one point of the law, even though he keeps the entire remainder, has become guilty on all counts. For he who said, 'You shall not commit adultery,' also said, 'You shall not kill.' If therefore you do not commit adultery but do commit murder, you have become a transgressor of the law." This is true, says the *Catechism of the Catholic Church* (n. 578), because the law of God makes up one inseparable whole, and we are called to follow the example of Jesus, who kept the law in its all-embracing detail, down to "the least significant of these commands" (Matthew 5:19).

Q. If the third condition for a mortal sin is willingly doing what one knows to be gravely sinful, what about those who commit acts of fornication or abortion but don't seem to know the seriousness of the offense? Is this culpable or inculpable ignorance? — M.C., Kentucky

A. Ignorance is inculpable or invincible if the lack of knowledge about a sin is not the person's fault. Thus, if a person was truly unaware of the grave evil of abortion and fornication (not that likely in these days of highly publicized debate about both evils), either because he or she had never been told that these acts were evil, or because one had been given false moral guidance by persons whom they presumed to be telling the truth, there would be no mortal sin.

Ignorance is culpable or vincible if the person makes no effort to dispel the lack of knowledge. Thus, if one suspects that abortion or fornication might be wrong and neglects to search out the truth, that person is guilty of sin. And the person is even more guilty if he or she deliberately chooses to remain in ignorance so as to continue committing the sin.

Q. A priest and several practicing Catholics told me that if a person commits a sin but is unaware that it is a sin, it is not a sin for that person, even if they commit murder, adultery, theft, blasphemy, or any other sin. How can this concept be reconciled with what our Lord said about sin in the Gospels? — A.S., New York

A. The Church has taught at least since the time of St. Thomas Aquinas in the 13th century that for a sin to be mortal, three conditions must simultaneously occur: the object of the sin must be grave matter, and it must be committed with full knowledge and deliberate consent (*Catechism of the Catholic Church*, n. 1857). Since mortal sin requires full knowledge and complete consent, the *Catechism* goes on to explain, unintentional ignorance can diminish or even remove the imputability of a grave offense, and the promptings of feelings and passions can also diminish the voluntary and free character of the offense, as can such things as external pressures or pathological disorders (n. 1860).

However, the same article also says that no one is deemed to be ignorant of the principles of the moral law, which are written in the conscience of every person. In other words, while it is not impossible to be unaware of the evil nature of murder, adultery, theft, and blasphemy, we would think it highly unlikely in this day and age.

Q. I have been called self-righteous, hypocritical, and judgmental by a co-worker for identifying adultery as a sin. I know that I am a sinner and no better than the next person, but does that mean that I am self-righteous if I call specific actions sins? — L.N.B., Illinois

Q. Is there a specific list of mortal sins and how one can differentiate or educate today when there is so much confusion in the Church? — J.M., Wisconsin

A. The catalogue of mortal sins can be found in many places, including the Bible, Council documents, papal encyclicals, and various summaries of Catholic teaching. In Mark 7:21-22, for example, Jesus identified the following as grave sins: "acts of fornication, theft, murder, adulterous conduct, greed, maliciousness, deceit, sensuality, envy, blasphemy, arrogance, an obtuse spirit." There are similar lists in the letters of St. Paul, notably in First Corinthians 6:9 and in Galatians 5:19-21.

The Second Vatican Council listed many mortal sins that harm individuals, "poison human society," and constitute "a supreme dishonor to the Creator." These sins include murder, genocide, abortion, euthanasia, mutilation, torments inflicted on body or mind, attempts to coerce the will, sub-human living conditions, arbitrary imprisonment, deportation, slavery, prostitution, the selling of women and children, and "disgraceful working conditions, where men are treated as mere tools for profit, rather than as free and responsible persons" (*Constitution on the Church in the Modern World*, n. 27).

Other lists can be found in the *Basic Teachings for Catholic Religious Education* (n. 19), *Veritatis Splendor* (nos. 13, 49, 80, 81, 100, 101), and in the section on the commandments in the *Catechism of the Catholic Church* (nos. 2083-2557).

While the actions enumerated in these lists constitute objectively sinful matter, the subjective sinfulness of the persons committing them depends, as always, on the other two conditions for a mortal sin: sufficient reflection and full consent of the will. Only God knows the human heart with certainty, so only God can judge the degree of sinfulness of human actions.

It is not up to us to judge the motives of those we perceive to be sinners; that prerogative belongs to God alone. This does not mean, however, that we cannot label certain actions (adultery, abortion, fornication, murder) as being contrary to the clearly stated law of God. This isn't being self-righteous or judgmental; it is letting others know what the moral teachings of Christ and His Church are and the obligation we have to follow those teachings if we wish to be saved. We wonder if your co-worker would fail to report that his car had been stolen lest he be considered self-righteous or judgmental.

Q. Would you explain the theory called situation ethics and the so-called fundamental option? I seem to be confronted with these in the confessional. — W.F.H., Rhode Island

A. The theory known as situation ethics was popularized by the late Joseph Fletcher in a book entitled *Situation Ethics: The New Morality*. The theory denies any absolute standards of morality and says that the morality of each action is to be determined by the particular situation or circumstances surrounding that action.

The publisher's blurb on the jacket of Fletcher's book is an accurate summary of his thinking: "The sensational deductions which the author draws for this premise include the bold statement that any acts, even lying, premarital sex, abortion, adultery, and murder could be right — depending on the situation. Because 'whatever is the most loving thing in the situation is the right and good thing. It is not excusably evil, it is positively good.'"

Any theory that can transform lying, premarital sex, abortion, adultery, and murder into good actions is far from the teaching of Christ and His Church.

The theory of the fundamental option holds that each person has a basic orientation either toward or away from God and that this orientation can be affected by our actions. But there are two variations of this theory, one of which is in accord with Catholic teaching and one of which contradicts it.

The traditional view is that we can alter our orientation toward God by one evil act of abortion, adultery, contraception, or premarital sex, and that such acts are mortal sins. The extreme view is that these acts are not mortal sins that separate us from God unless we make a fundamental and basic decision, at the core of our being, to refuse God's love and to turn away from Him.

In paragraphs 65-70 of *Veritatis Splendor*, Pope John Paul explained in detail the correct understanding of fundamental option. "'Care will have to be taken,'" he said, "'not to reduce mortal sin to an act of "fundamental option" — as is commonly said today — against God,' seen either as an explicit and formal rejection of God and neighbor or as an implicit and unconscious rejection of love. 'For mortal sin exists also when a person knowingly and willingly, for whatever reason, chooses something gravely disordered. In fact, such a choice already includes contempt for the divine law, a rejection of God's love for humanity and the whole of creation: the person turns aways from God and loses charity. Consequently, the fundamental orientation can be radically changed by particular acts'" (n. 70).

The Holy Father also said that the current notion of fundamental option "involves a denial of Catholic doctrine on mortal sin: 'With the whole tradition of the Church, we call mortal sin the act by which man freely and consciously rejects God, his law, the covenant of love that God offers, preferring to turn in on himself or to some created and finite reality, something contrary to the divine will. This can occur in a direct and formal way, in the sins of idolatry, apostasy, and atheism, or in an equivalent way, as in every act of disobedience to God's commandments in a grave matter'" (*Ibid.*).

Q. Can you explain why the four sins which cry out to Heaven for vengeance — willful murder, homosexuality, oppression of the poor, and defrauding the laborer of his just wages — are so described? Who labeled them as such? Are they related in some way? — R.R.M., Illinois

A. We are not sure who labeled these sins as such, but their connection with each other is that in each case the victims of these sins cried out to the Lord for help, and their cries were heard. The origin of these four sins can be found in Scripture.

Willful murder: After Cain killed his brother Abel, "The LORD then said: 'What have you done! Listen: your brother's blood cries out to me from the soil!'" (Genesis 4:10).

Sodomy or homosexuality: Before He destroyed the cities of Sodom and Gomorrah, the Lord said to Abraham: "The outcry against Sodom and Gomorrah is so great, and their sin so grave, that I must go down and see whether or not their actions fully correspond to the cry against them that comes to me" (Genesis 18:20).

Oppression of the poor: After the flight of Moses from

Egypt, "A long time passed, during which the king of Egypt died. Still the Israelites groaned and cried out because of their slavery. As their cry of release went up to God, he heard their groaning and was mindful of his covenant with Abraham, Isaac, and Jacob" (Exodus 2:23).

Defrauding laborers of their wages: In warning the rich of their impending miseries, James writes: "Here, crying aloud, are the wages you withheld from the farmhands who harvested your fields. The cries of the harvesters have reached the ears of the Lord of hosts" (James 5:4).

These are not necessarily the four *worst* sins — in the early Church, the worst sins included murder, adultery, blasphemy, and apostasy — and today we might add public profanation of the Eucharist. But they have been singled out in Scripture because the cries of their victims were heard by God.

Q. A priest told me that he sometimes keeps people in their ignorance about their sins because to tell them the truth would drive them away from the Church. He feels that as time goes on, and as these people grow in their faith, an opportunity will arise to explain the Church's teachings to them, and they will then be able to accept the truth. I am sorry, but I consider this attitude scandalous. Am I wrong? — J.L. California

A. No, you are not wrong. Jesus said that the truth would set us free from the slavery of sin (John 8:31-36), but how can that happen in your parish if the priest denies his people the truth about their sins? Our Lord called upon the people of His time, and ours, to "reform your lives and believe in the gospel!" (Mark 1:15). How can we reform our lives if our spiritual shepherds neglect to point out where we have gone wrong? We do not know the hour or the day of our death and judgment, so is it prudent to keep the truth from people who may be on the road to Hell? And if they are comfortable in their sins, how can they grow in faith? Jesus did not hesitate to admonish or warn the sinner, and your priest should follow the example of the Lord in exercising this spiritual work of mercy.

Q. Responding some time ago to a question about a priest who didn't always tell a person about his sins because it might cause him to lose heart, you said that a priest should never do that. Well, you are very zealous for what you believe in, but sometimes zeal has to be tempered with mercy and wisdom. The enclosed articles about Pope John

XXIII and Pope St. Gregory the Great urge priests to do just what the priest you criticized did. As you are well aware, Jesus came to give mercy, healing, and forgiveness. He was never hard or dogmatic with sinners or the other lost sheep. — E.M.C., Ohio

A. This excerpt from a much longer and very interesting letter does not accurately reflect the question that we answered. We agree with the first part of E.M.C.'s statement, and with the comments of the two Popes, but the question we treated described a situation where the priest was keeping people in complete ignorance of their sins.

It is one thing to warn a person about serious wrongs while temporarily overlooking lesser wrongs so as not to discourage the person, and quite another matter to overlook all wrong-doing in order to allow sinners to "grow in their faith" and then later "be able to accept the truth" about their sinfulness (as the priest in question had suggested). Our concern was that people not admonished for their sins might grow comfortable in their sinful state and perhaps delay reforming their lives until it was too late to avoid eternal punishment.

As for the last part of E.M.C.'s statement, we agree that Jesus came to give mercy, healing, and forgiveness, but only to those who were truly repentant. The Samaritan woman at the well, the woman caught in adultery, and the good thief on the cross come to mind. We disagree, however, that Jesus was never hard or dogmatic with unrepentant sinners. Consider His words to the hypocritical scribes and Pharisees:

"Woe to you scribes and Pharisees, you frauds! You travel over sea and land to make a single convert, but once he is converted you make a devil of him twice as wicked as yourselves. It is an evil day for you, blind guides! ... You are like whitewashed tombs, beautiful to look at on the outside but inside full of filth and dead men's bones .... Vipers' nest! Brood of serpents! How can you escape condemnation to Gehenna?" (Matthew 23:15ff.).

Q. What are sins of omission? — V.A., Illinois

A. A sin of omission is when one willfully neglects or positively refuses to perform some good action that one knows should be performed. The seriousness of the sin depends on the importance of what should have been done, on the willfulness of the person who failed to do it, and on the circumstances of the situation. Thus, if a person chooses to play golf all day Sunday instead of going to Mass, then he is guilty of the sin of missing Mass even if he does not specifically say to himself, "I am not going to Mass today."

Other sins of omission would include deliberately ignoring the material, physical, or spiritual well-being of those in need as spelled out, for example, in the corporal and spiritual works of mercy. Think of the many ways in which we could willfully neglect our obligation to feed the hungry, give drink to the thirsty, clothe the naked, visit the sick, visit the imprisoned, shelter the homeless, bury the dead, admonish the sinner, instruct the ignorant, counsel the doubtful, comfort the sorrowful, bear wrongs patiently, forgive all injuries, and pray for the living and the dead.

Q. If a person has a dream which can be interpreted as either foretelling good luck or bad luck, and the person believes somewhat in the possibility of this happening, would this be superstitious and possibly sinful? — L.N., Minnesota

A. Superstition means giving to a creature or thing power or worship that belongs to God alone, and it is a violation of the First Commandment. Thus, one who tailors his or her daily routine to the advice of a fortuneteller or a horoscope writer would be turning away from God, who alone knows what will happen in the future. One should rely not on the stars but on the God who made the stars.

As far as dreams are concerned, many of us have experienced some unusual and even bizarre dreams, and perhaps there have been times when what we dreamed even came true. Such dreams are common to everyone and are often hard to understand. So there is nothing wrong with thinking about the possibility of our dreams coming true or in sharing them with others in an effort to make some sense out of them. What would be superstitious and sinful would be to become obsessed with our dreams and to revolve our lives around them.

Q. What is sacrilege and is it always a mortal sin? — R.L.Z., Nebraska

A. According to the *Catechism of the Catholic Church*, sacrilege consists in profaning or treating unworthily the sacraments and other liturgical actions, as well as persons, things, or places consecrated to God. Sacrilege is a grave sin, the *Catechism* says, especially when committed against the Eucharist, for in this sacrament the true Body of Christ is made substantially present for us (n. 2120).

Examples of sacrilege would include violence of some kind against a priest or Religious brother or sister, acts of unchastity with a cleric, destruction or defilement of a church or other sacred place, theft or use of sacred vessels or vestments in profane ceremonies, and grave irreverence toward the Eucharist, such as receiving Communion while knowingly in a state of mortal sin.

Objectively speaking, sacrilege is always a mortal sin because it is a grave violation of the virtue of religion, which involves giving God the praise and worship He deserves. Subjective guilt would depend on whether the person had sufficiently reflected on the grave matter and had given the full consent of his will to the act.

Q. How seriously does God take our promises to Him? I love God so very much that I promised Him that I would never marry outside of my Faith. Well, to make a long story short, I found myself engaged to a girl from the United Church of Christ. Can promises to God be broken? Does He realize that we are human? I hate myself for doing this. — S.Y., Wisconsin

A. A vow is a free and deliberate promise to God to do something that is possible, morally good, and better than its opposite would be. The deliberate breaking of a vow is a sin against the virtue of religion, a mortal sin if the violation is grave matter, a venial sin if the matter is light. Because a vow is a very serious action, one should not make such a promise without the help of a spiritual advisor.

Of course God takes our promises to Him seriously, and He wants us to keep those promises that were freely, knowledgeably, and conscientiously made. But there is not enough information in your letter to help us determine whether your vow was valid or not, whether your breaking of the vow was truly deliberate, or whether there is grave or light matter involved. We would suggest that you consult a reliable spiritual advisor for assistance in resolving this dilemma.

Q. A relative whose children accompany friends to a Protestant service says that this is a substitute for Sunday Mass. Would you please comment? — J.R.B., Ohio

A. Under no circumstances can one equate the Mass with a Protestant worship service. Any Catholic who thinks they are the same apparently never learned much about the profound nature of the Holy Sacrifice of the Mass, which is the central act of worship for Catholics. While there are certainly elements of truth and sanctification at the services of non-Catholic denominations, it is only at a Catholic Mass that Jesus, the Son of God, becomes truly present on the altar when the priest pronounces the words, "This is my body .... This is my blood."

This stupendous miracle is what places the Mass so far above any other liturgical event one can attend. For it was to "His beloved spouse, the [Catholic] Church," said Vatican II, that Jesus entrusted this "memorial of His death and resurrection: a sacrament of love, a sign of unity, a bond of charity, a paschal banquet in which Christ is consumed, the mind is filled with grace, and pledge of future glory is given to us" (*Constitution on the Sacred Liturgy*, n. 47).

Q. At what age is a child required to attend Mass on Sundays and holy days? Would a child with an above-average I.Q. be required to attend Mass at an earlier age? — B.M., Missouri

A. Children are required to attend Mass every week once they have made their First Communion, but parents ought to begin taking children to church from the time they are toddlers so that they will grow to understand and love the Mass and to attend out of love for God rather than as an obligation. The Church has since 1910 set the time for reception of First Communion at the age of reason, about seven, when it is presumed that a child has sufficient knowledge to understand that the Eucharist is the Body of Christ and can receive the Host with faith and devotion.

Children with above-average I.Q.s should not receive Communion prior to the age of seven, and therefore are not required to attend Mass prior to that age.

Q. I am 80 years old and in good health. Since I do not drive, I must depend upon others to get to Mass. Am I obliged to insist that others take me to Mass or am I being too scrupulous? — M.T.W., Florida

A. First of all, you are to be commended for your desire to attend Mass every Sunday. At a time when many Catholics cannot be bothered going to Mass, it is wonderful that you recognize the value of participating in that special worship of the Lord every week. It is also wonderful that you have family and friends who are willing to take you to Church. We hope it's not necessary for you to *insist* that others drive you; a simple request ought to be sufficient, and many parishes have people who are very happy to bring to church people like your-self who have no way of getting there on their own.

As long as you enjoy good health, you should try to attend Mass every Sunday. Your request for transportation not only gives good example to others, but it also provides others with the chance to perform a good deed.

Q. Can the Sunday Mass obligation be fulfilled on any day other than Sunday (or Saturday evening)? If a priest is not available for Mass, does one have an obligation to attend a prayer and Communion service? Does a pastor or even a bishop have the authority to dispense or change the Sunday obligation law? — A.E.R., Michigan

A. Sunday has always been the Lord's Day for Catholics and the day on which we worship God at Mass. If Mass is being celebrated on Sunday in one's parish, the obligation to attend Mass would have to be fulfilled on that day. One could not, for instance, decide to go to Mass on Monday because one was busy the day before.

In recent years, however, the availability of Masses has been sharply reduced in some areas of the United States due to a shortage of priests. Some priests find themselves, like missionaries, traveling great distances on a Sunday to say Mass for Catholics in different regions. If there is no priest available on Sunday, obviously there would be no way of fulfilling one's obligation, and no sin would be attached to missing Mass under those circumstances.

Communion services (where consecrated Hosts are available) are being substituted where there are no Masses and, while we are not sure what the regulations are in every diocese, we can foresee a bishop insisting that the obligation to worship as a faith community does not cease when the highest form of such worship, the Mass, is not available to the faithful.

Under normal circumstances, no pastor or bishop can dispense or change the Sunday obligation requirement. But as circumstances become other than normal, a conference of bishops could conceivably require Catholics to attend Mass on a different day.

Q. If I attend Mass for a wedding or Confirmation on Sunday, does this fulfill my Sunday obligation? I have gotten different answers from two priests. — C.F., Illinois

A. Any Mass attended on Sunday fulfills your obligation, whether it's the regular Sunday liturgy or a Mass in conjunction with the sacraments of Matrimony or Confirmation. If you attend a wedding Mass after 4:00 p.m. on Saturday, that would satisfy your Sunday obligation, but a wedding Mass earlier than 4:00 on Saturday would not.

Q. Can a Catholic fulfill his Sunday obligation by attending a Byzantine Catholic liturgy and receiving the Eucharist? — T.B., Florida

A. Catholics may fulfill their Sunday obligation by attending Mass in any Catholic rite, including the Byzantine, which is in full communion with the Roman Catholic Church. This is so, said the Second Vatican Council, because "such individual Churches, whether of the East or of the West, although they differ somewhat among themselves in what are called rites (that is, in liturgy, ecclesiastical discipline, and spiritual heritage), are, nevertheless, equally entrusted to the pastoral guidance of the Roman Pontiff, the divinely appointed successor of St. Peter in supreme governance over the universal Church. They are consequently of equal dignity, so that none of them is superior to others by reason of rite. They enjoy the same rights and are under the same obligations, even with respect to preaching the Gospel to the whole world (cf. Mk. 16:15) under the guidance of the Roman Pontiff" (*Decree on Eastern Catholic Churches*, n. 3).

Q. Please explain the reasoning given for permission to celebrate anticipated Masses on the eve of holy days and Sundays. Must a person have a good reason for attending Mass on Saturday evening? If the Sabbath begins at sundown on Saturday, are we obliged to abstain from servile work and unnecessary shopping? — J.D.K., Pennsylvania

A. The permission for attending Mass on the eve of holy days and Sundays was granted by the Sacred Congregation of Rites in 1967, and pastors were told to explain the meaning of the change carefully to the faithful and to "ensure that the significance of Sunday is not thereby obscured" (*Eucharisticum Mysterium*, n. 28). The purpose of the change, the Congregation said, was "to enable the Christians of today to celebrate more easily the day of the resurrection of the Lord."

The SCR may have had in mind those who had essential jobs on Sundays (nurses, bus drivers, police officers, firefighters, etc.), but today a lot of people with no particular commitments on Sunday go to Mass on Saturday. The preferred day to attend Mass ought to be Sunday, and we should make every effort to begin this day of rest by worshiping at Mass.

The anticipation of Sunday begins at 4:00 p.m. on Saturday (it is only tied to sunset on the Vigil of Easter), but the Church has never indicated whether abstinence from unnecessary work and shopping is obliged after four o'clock on Saturday.

Q. My life as a working mother and the pro-life sidewalk counseling I do on Saturdays leaves me only Sunday nights to do my grocery shopping. Is this wrong? — B.A.M., Rhode Island

Q. Sunday is supposed to be a day of rest, but I see Catholics washing windows, painting their houses, and so forth. And some of them are retired people who could do these things during the week. Should I mention it to them? — V.B.D., Illinois

Q. Regarding the Third Commandment, is servile work any work that tires the body? What if your employer calls you into work on a Sunday? What about doing household chores, sewing, or crafts? If my husband's company has a banquet at a fancy restaurant on a Sunday, can we attend? — A.M., Wisconsin

Q. I know that Catholics are supposed to attend Mass on holy days, but are we also to refrain from servile work on those days? — J.O., California

Q. Please tell me specifically what activities the Sunday rest requires Christians to refrain from. — J.H.B., Maryland, and M.D., Michigan

A. First, let us state the general requirements of the Third Commandment regarding what used to be called servile work, and then answer some of the specific questions. According to the *Catechism of the Catholic Church* (n. 2185), on Sundays and other holy days of obligation, the faithful are to refrain from engaging in work or activities that hinder the worship owed to God, the joy proper to the Lord's Day, the performance of the works of mercy, and the appropriate relaxation of mind and body. Family needs or important social service, the *Catechism* says, can legitimately excuse from the Sunday rest. It cautions, however, that we should see to it that legitimate excuses do not lead to habits prejudicial to religion, family life, and health.

Sundays, the *Catechism* also says, should be devoted to good works and humble service of the sick, the infirm, and the elderly; to spending time with families and relatives; and to engaging in reflection, silence, cultivation of the mind, and meditation which furthers the growth of the Christian interior life (n. 2186).

Finally, the *Catechism* says that every Christian should avoid making unnecessary demands on others that would hinder them from observing the Lord's Day. It concedes that traditional activities, such as sports, and social necessities, such as public safety, require some people to work on Sundays, but adds that everyone should still take care to set aside sufficient time for leisure. With temperance and charity, the *Catechism* says, the faithful will see to it that they avoid the excesses and violence sometimes associated with popular leisure activities. It also urges public authorities to assure citizens a time intended for rest and divine worship, and says that employers have a similar obligation toward their employees (n. 2187).

To B.A.M.: You are to be commended for your efforts to save unborn babies, and you should not discontinue your life-saving work, but perhaps you could reduce those efforts just enough to do your grocery shopping on Saturday and leave Sunday nights for time with your children and for your own rest and relaxation.

To V.B.D.: Washing windows or painting a house on Sunday is not wrong if there is no other time that these tasks can be performed and they do not keep us from Mass or from enjoying the Lord's day. As for whether you should suggest to your retired neighbors that they might do certain chores during the week, you could tactfully remind them of the law regarding Sunday observance and even show them the pertinent paragraphs from the *Catechism*. They may have slipped away from this observance and your gentle reminder might bring them back to it.

To A.M.: Servile work is more work that is unnecessary than work that tires you out; if your employer calls you in on a Sunday for a good reason, you don't have much choice if the job is essential to your economic well-being, but you ought to indicate to your employer your feelings about the special nature of Sunday; routine household chores are permitted on Sunday, as are such things as sewing and crafts, which could be considered restful and relaxing activities; and attending a company banquet on Sunday would not be wrong.

To J.O.: We are supposed to refrain from unnecessary work on holy days, too, but the key word is "unnecessary." Since several holy days in the United States fall on week days when people have to work, it would be difficult, if not impossible, to refrain on those days from labors and business concerns. The obligation to attend Mass on holy days still binds, but one may engage in work that is necessary for one's livelihood.

Q. I am 65 years old and have never voted in an election. Is this a mortal sin? — J.A.T., Kentucky

A. Among other things, the Fourth Commandment ("Honor your father and your mother") obliges us to be good citizens of the nation in which we live. This means that we should love our country, defend it against aggression, pay just taxes, give proper respect and obedience to public officials, study current political issues and candidates for public office, and vote intelligently, or refrain from voting if we have little or no knowledge of the issues or the merits of the candidates in an election.

Never to have voted would certainly be a venial sin since one has failed in his obligation to be a good citizen. These sins of omission would not be mortal since there apparently was no grave matter involved and there may not have been sufficient reflection or understanding of one's duty to vote.

Q. The *Baltimore Catechism* does not state that one must vote in order to be a good citizen and keep the Fourth Commandment. I would like to know under what authority you extend the Fourth Commandment to voting. — P.V., Pennsylvania

Q. I find myself in serious disagreement with you on the matter of the "sinfulness" of a 65-year-old who has never voted. I accept as a given that Republicans and Democrats are statists — and statists are evil persons. If that citizen has never had an opportunity to vote for anyone from a third party or of Independent status, then to vote at all would have been to join in bringing harm to our Republic. — J.O.B., Pennsylvania

A. Two versions of the *Baltimore Catechism* that we have both stress under the Fourth Commandment the duty of a citizen to vote as a sign of sincere interest in the welfare of one's country. In the New Confraternity Edition (No. 3, 1949), and in the New Saint Joseph Baltimore Catechism (No. 2, 1969), it says that "a citizen shows a sincere interest in his country's welfare by voting honestly and without selfish motives." Fr. Francis J. Connell, in the Confraternity Edition, goes on to comment: "Citizens should exercise their right to vote. This is a moral obligation when the common good of the state or the good of religion, especially in serious matters, can be promoted."

This obligation was reaffirmed by the Second Vatican Council: "Let all citizens be mindful of their simultaneous right and duty to vote freely in the interest of advancing the common good" (*Pastoral Constitution on the Church in the Modern World*, n.

75). And the *Catechism of the Catholic Church* (n. 2240) says that submission to authority and co-responsibility for the common good make it morally obligatory to pay taxes, to exercise the right to vote, and to defend one's country. It recalls the words of St. Paul: "Pay each one his due: taxes to whom taxes are due; toll to whom toll is due; respect and honor to everyone who deserves them" (Romans 13:7).

Since we have an obligation to vote that stems from the Fourth Commandment, failure to exercise that obligation over a lifetime would violate a requirement of that commandment and would therefore constitute at least a venial sin.

J.O.B.'s contention that we don't often have much choice between statists of the two major parties may be true, but what about other races on the same ballot, or what about ballot questions involving serious issues, such as abortion, rights for homosexuals, distribution of condoms in public schools, etc.? Or what about state and local elections? One does not have to vote for the lesser of two evils for President or Senator or Governor; you can write in the name of a good person for those offices or skip those contests and vote only for good people for some other office, all the way down to the local town council or school board.

The point of the earlier reply was that the reader from Kentucky must over some four decades have missed some significant elections for local, state, or national candidates or issues. Missing a few elections during that time for good reason (illness, away from home) would not be wrong, but not voting at all in some 44 years shows a careless disregard for the welfare of one's country.

Q. What is the Church's teaching on military service and pacifism? — P.M., Virginia

A. As indicated in the previous reply, it is morally obligatory to defend one's country. Pope John Paul on several occasions upheld "the principle of legitimate defense" and rejected the course of pacifism. In his World Day of Peace message in 1984, the Holy Father said that a "person who deeply desires peace rejects any kind of pacifism, which is cowardice, or the simple preservation of tranquillity. In fact, those who are tempted to impose their domination will always encounter the resistance of intelligent and courageous men and women, prepared to defend freedom in order to promote justice."

Speaking to Italian soldiers in 1989, the Pope said that "the military profession is defined as the task of defending the justice and freedom of the nation, and consequently of contributing to the tranquillity and peace of the entire world." He said that "peace must be defended" because "it is out of love of neighbor, of one's loved ones, of the weakest and most defenseless, as well as the love of the spiritual values and traditions of one's nation, that one must agree to self-sacrifice, to struggle, and even to give up one's life, should it be necessary."

Addressing participants at the Third International Convention of Military Ordinaries on March 11, 1994, John Paul said that those who serve in the armed forces "should be considered, according to the apt expression of Vatican II [cf. *Constitution on the Church in the Modern World*, n. 79], custodians of the security and freedom of their fellow-countrymen."

Q. What is the Church's specific teaching regarding "justifiable homicide" in the defense of life? — D.G., Michigan

Q. Does the Catholic Church allow the use of lethal force to protect life, liberty, or chastity? I am speaking here of a private citizen facing a criminal attack, not police or military personnel. If so, does this extend to the protection of family members or a neighbor who seeks refuge from a criminal attack? — J.J.W., Missouri

A. Yes to both of J.J.W.'s questions, provided that a person does not intend to use more force than is necessary to repel the aggressor. In that section of the *Catechism of the Catholic Church* that deals with the Fifth Commandment, there are moral distinctions made between legitimate self-defense of persons and societies (nos. 2263-2267), which is permitted, and the intentional killing of persons and groups of persons (nos. 2268-2269), which is always gravely sinful.

Regarding an individual case of self-defense, the *Catechism* (n. 2264) says that love toward oneself remains a fundamental principle of morality and, therefore, it is legitimate to insist on respect for one's own right to life. It cites St. Thomas Aquinas in stating that someone who defends his life is not guilty of murder even if he is forced to deal his aggressor a lethal blow: "If a man in self-defense uses more than necessary violence, it will be unlawful; whereas if he repels force with moderation, his defense will be lawful .... Nor is it necessary for salvation that a man omit the act of moderate self-defense to avoid killing the other man, since one is bound to take more care of one's own life than of another's."

As for defending the lives of others, the *Catechism* (n. 2266) says that preserving the common good of society requires rendering the aggressor unable to inflict harm. For this reason, it says, the traditional teaching of the Church has acknowledged as well-founded the right and duty of legitimate public authority to punish malefactors by means of penalties commensurate with the gravity of the crime, not excluding, in cases of extreme gravity, the death penalty. For similar reasons, it says, those holding authority have the right to repel by armed force aggressors against the community in their charge.

The *Catechism* also says (n. 2267) that if bloodless means are sufficient to defend human lives against an aggressor and to protect public order and the safety of persons, public authority should limit itself to such means because they better correspond to the concrete conditions of the common good and are more in conformity to the dignity of the human person.

Q. What is the Church's stand on the death penalty? — P.Y., Georgia; C.L., Kansas; D.M., Massachusetts; and A.P., New York

A. It has long been a part of Catholic teaching that the state has the right to inflict the death penalty on persons convicted of grievous crimes, but it is not obligated to do so. The right is based on passages in the Old and New Testaments and has been reiterated in the *Catechism of the Council of Trent*, by some Popes, and in the *Catechism of the Catholic Church*.

For example, it says in Genesis 9:6: "If anyone sheds the blood of man, by man shall his blood be shed; For in the image of God has man been made." In Romans 13:4, St. Paul says: "It is not without purpose that the ruler carries the sword; he is God's servant, to inflict his avenging wrath upon the wrongdoer."

Commenting on the Fifth Commandment, the *Catechism of the Council of Trent* said: "Another kind of slaying is permitted, which belongs to those magistrates to whom is given the power of condemning to death, by the legal and judicial use of which [power] they punish the guilty and protect the innocent (Rom. 13:4); in which function, provided they act justly, they are not only not guilty of murder, but they eminently obey this law [the Fifth Commandment] which prohibits murder; for, as the proposed end of this law is to provide for the life and safety of men, to the same end also tend the punishments [executions] inflicted by the magistrates, who are the legitimate avengers of crimes, giving security to life by punishing and thus repressing audacity and outrage."

Addressing the First International Congress on the Histopathology of the Nervous System on September 14, 1952, Pope Pius XII said: "Even when it is a question of the execution of a man condemned to death, the state does not dispose of the individual's right to live. Rather, it is reserved to the public authority to deprive the criminal of the benefit of life, when already, by his crime, he has deprived himself of the right to live."

However, as the years went by, Popes, as well as the Catholic Bishops of the United States, without denying the compatibility of capital punishment with Catholic teaching, began coming out against the death penalty for a variety of reasons. They said that capital punishment was not a deterrent; that it could lead to the death of an innocent person; that it prevented the conversion of a criminal; that it was most commonly inflicted on blacks and persons of low economic status; and that it could lead to the further erosion of the respect for life in our society.

Catholics who favored the death penalty countered that it definitely deterred the criminal executed from committing any more crimes; that one would have to abolish all laws to avoid completely the punishment of innocent persons; that a criminal was more likely to repent when facing death rather than life in prison; that many crimes were committed by blacks and persons of low economic status, frequently against persons in the same environment; and that respect for life might be improved if those guilty of horrendous crimes were swiftly and permanently punished.

In 1994, the *Catechism of the Catholic Church* reaffirmed the use of capital punishment in cases of extreme gravity (n. 2266). But as noted in the previous reply, the *Catechism* went on to say that if bloodless means are sufficient to defend human lives against an aggressor and to protect public order and the safety of persons, public authority should limit itself to such means because they better correspond to the concrete conditions of the common good and are more in conformity to the dignity of the human person (n. 2267).

In summary, then, there is a long Catholic tradition in favor of imposing capital punishment on those convicted of terrible crimes, but a reluctance today by our custodians of faith to have it inflicted on anyone.

Q. What is Pope John Paul's most recent stance concerning capital punishment? — D.S.B., Texas

A. In his encyclical *Evangelium Vitae* ("The Gospel of Life"), Pope John Paul said that in order to give a criminal offender "an incentive and help to change his or her behavior and be rehabilitated ... the nature and extent of the punishment must be carefully evaluated and decided upon, and ought not go to the extreme of executing the offender except in cases of absolute necessity: In other words, when it would not be possible otherwise to defend society. Today, however, as a result of steady improvements in the organization of the penal system, such cases are very rare if not practically nonexistent" (n. 56).

Q. When I converted to Roman Catholicism 37 years ago, I was taught that suicide, for any reason, was a mortal sin. Recently in Washington, D.C., a Catholic who committed suicide was given a funeral Mass. Has the teaching of the Church on this matter changed in recent years? — C.M.S., Virginia

A. No, the teaching of the Church on suicide has not changed. "Suicide is always as morally objectionable as murder," said Pope John Paul in *Evangelium Vitae* (n. 66). "The Church's tradition has always rejected it as a gravely evil choice. Even though a certain psychological, cultural, and social conditioning may induce a person to carry out an action which so radically contradicts the innate inclination to life, thus lessening or removing subjective responsibility, suicide, when viewed objectively, is a gravely immoral act.

"In fact, it involves the rejection of love of self and the renunciation of the obligation of justice and charity toward one's neighbor, toward the communities to which one belongs, and toward society as a whole. In its deepest reality, suicide represents a rejection of God's absolute sovereignty over life and death as proclaimed in the prayer of the ancient sage of Israel: 'You have power over life and death; you lead men down to the gates of Hades and back again' (Wis. 16:13; cf. Tb. 13:2)."

In the past, the Church denied a funeral Mass to a suicide victim on the grounds that the act was a violation of the Fifth Commandment and that it also constituted a sin of despair in that it signified rejection of the merciful forgiveness of God. Today the Church celebrates a Mass for those who take their own lives on the grounds that we cannot know with certainty the state of the victim's mind when the suicide took place. Killing oneself is so contrary to human nature that there is the presumption that the person was not mentally capable of the sufficient reflection and full consent of the will necessary to commit a mortal sin that would send him to Hell.

In other words, the Church gives the victim the benefit of the doubt and leaves the judgment of that tormented soul to God. The Church offers the funeral Mass not only for the salvation of the deceased but also for the consolation of family members and friends.

Q. Are there definite, absolute standards of modesty for female dress at this time in the United States as stipulated by the Catholic Church? — A.M., Pennsylvania

A. No, there is no dress code as such that defines what attire is modest and what is not, but it is obvious that standards of modesty have fallen far in recent decades. People today parade around in states of undress that are scandalous. That this would happen was predicted in 1920, when Jacinta, one of the three children to whom the Blessed Mother had appeared at Fatima in 1917, said: "The sins which cause most souls to go to Hell are the sins of the flesh. Fashions will much offend our Lord."

Modesty may be compared to the security system that protects our home from intruders. Once that system is breached, those living in the house are endangered. The same is true of the virtue of chastity, which involves using our sexual powers according to God's plan. If we are immodest in the way that we dress — or act, speak, dance, etc. — then we endanger our chastity or that of others. We must be careful that we do not dress provocatively, not only for our own sake but also for the sake of others for whom our lax standards could become an occasion of sin.

Common sense has to be our guide in this matter. One can dress stylishly without exposing more of the body than is covered. One can be fashionably clothed without arousing sexual desire in others. Perhaps a good standard to adopt would be to ask oneself: "If I were going to meet Jesus and His mother, would I dress like this?"

Q. When I was in high school 40 years ago, one guiding principle that was emphasized over and over was that we were not entitled to sexual gratification outside the context of a valid marriage. That principle was the basis for practically all Church rules regarding the virtue of purity — rules against impure pictures, magazines, songs, jokes, movies, entertainment, masturbation, adultery, fornication, and all the other "sins of the flesh." I never hear any reference to this principle of "no sexual arousal." Is it no longer valid? — L.W., Illinois

A. The principle certainly is still valid, but we don't hear enough about it. We hear far more about condoms than we do about chastity, which explains why there is so much sexual immorality in our society today, with all its disastrous consequences. There ought to be much more emphasis — in the home, from the pulpit, and in our religious education classes — on what the U.S. Bishops said in their *Basic Teachings for Catholic Religious Education*:

"In the area of sexuality, the Christian is to be modest in behavior and dress. In a sex-saturated society, the follower of Christ must be different. For the Christian there can be no premarital sex, fornication, adultery, or others acts of impurity or scandal to others. He must remain chaste, repelling lustful desires and temptations, self-abuse, pornography, and indecent entertainment of every description" (n. 19).

Q. My 22-year-old daughter and her female roommate share their apartment with a male student who attends a nearby Catholic law school. She says the arrangement is strictly for financial purposes, with absolutely no sexual relationships. I say it's an occasion of sin that should be terminated. What do you say? — R.J.K., Connecticut

A. We say that such an arrangement is not morally wise for any of the three persons living in the apartment. Each of the roommates may have the highest of ideals, and no intention of getting involved in a sexual relationship, but the close proximity of the trio certainly makes such a relationship a distinct possibility, especially in this day and age when sexual relationships are so graphically portrayed on television as to put immoral thoughts and desires in the minds of even those who think that they are relatively immune to such temptations.

And by the way, are there no females in the area where your daughter lives who would be interested in sharing a room with her and her friend?

Q. We joined the St. Vincent de Paul Society to help the poor in our parish. But some of the people we are called upon to help with food, rent, utilities, etc., are couples living together without marriage. Is it right to assist these people? Should we say something about their immoral lifestyle? — G.E.D., Washington, and A.J., Colorado

A. Obviously, if we run across individuals or couples who are desperately in need of food, clothing, or shelter, our first obligation is to help them with these necessities, regardless of their lifestyles. Having met the physical needs of these people, however, we think that their spiritual welfare is even more important, and that efforts should be made to get them to marry or to live apart. It hardly seems appropriate for a Church agency named after a man whose holiness earned him sainthood to assist people in continuing an immoral or unholy lifestyle.

Q. Why are all directly voluntary sins against the Sixth and Ninth Commandments mortally sinful? A priest once told me that you can argue all points of view against the other Commandments, but when it comes to the Sixth and Ninth, the case is closed. Can you suggest a good book which treats of moral theology? — M.F.S., Pennsylvania

A. The priest who said this was exaggerating. The conditions for a mortal sin, as we have mentioned before, are grave matter, sufficient reflection, and full consent of the will. Therefore, the knowing and deliberate violation of the grave matter of all Ten Commandments, not just the sixth and ninth, constitutes a mortal sin. There is no mortal sin involved in violating any commandment if grave matter, sufficient reflection, or full consent of the will are lacking.

Three good books on the Church's moral teaching are William May's *An Introduction to Moral Theology* (Our Sunday Visitor), Carlo Caffara's *Living in Christ* (Ignatius Press), and Heribert Jone's *Moral Theology*.

Q. Our supposedly future son-in-law has challenged us to show him if he is living in sin by being with our daughter. They intend to marry in two years. Some priests have told them that it was not stated anywhere in the Bible that young couples could not live together. My son-in-law-to-be wants proof that it is wrong to be "shacked up." Please help me. — G.V., New Brunswick

A. If your daughter and her male friend are living together and are engaging in sexual intercourse, the dictionary calls those acts fornication. The Bible is quite clear about the evil of fornication. For instance, Jesus said: "Wicked designs come from the deep recesses of the heart; acts of fornication, theft, murder, adulterous conduct, greed, maliciousness, deceit, sensuality, envy, blasphemy, arrogance, an obtuse spirit. All these evils come from within and render a man impure" (Mark 7:21-23).

St. Paul echoed our Lord and said that sins like fornication would keep the unrepentant from reaching Heaven: "Do not deceive yourselves: no fornicators, idolaters, or adulterers, no sexual perverts, thieves, misers, or drunkards, no slanderers or robbers will inherit God's kingdom" (1 Corinthians 6:9-10).

Q. Your recent reply quoted Jesus as condemning "acts of fornication" (Mark 7:21), but my New Catholic Edition of the Bible, a revision of the Challoner-Rheims version, does not contain the word "fornication." Can you explain? I also have a close relative who is living with a woman prior to marriage. He said he has been told by a priest it is not wrong. — E.T., New Jersey

A. Different translations of the Bible use different words for sexual immorality between unmarried persons. The quotation we used was from the New American Bible, 1970 edition. Some of the other Bible translations that use the word "fornication" in chapter 7 of Mark are the King James (1928), the Ronald Knox (1944), and the Jerusalem Bible (1968).

The word "immorality" is used in the version you cited, but if you turn to 1 Corinthians 6:9, you will see the word "fornicators" used. Skip down to verse 18 and it says, "Flee immorality." So that edition of the Bible uses those two words to mean the same thing.

The New American Bible uses "fornicators" in 1 Corinthians 6:9, while in verse 6:18 it says, "Shun lewd conduct. Every other sin a man commits is outside his body, but the fornicator sins against his own body."

The King James Bible talks about "fornicators" in 6:9 and says in 6:18, "Flee fornication."

The Knox version renders 6:9 "the debauched" and 6:18 "debauchery," but then says, "Any other sin a man commits leaves the body untouched, but the fornicator is committing a crime against his own body."

In 6:9 of the Jerusalem Bible, fornicators are "people of immoral lives," but 6:18 says, "Keep away from fornication."

So whichever word you use, sexual intercourse between two unmarried persons, whether they are living together or not, is contrary to the plan of God and therefore seriously sinful. According to the *Catechism of the Catholic Church* (n. 2353), fornication is carnal union between an unmarried man and an unmarried woman. It is gravely contrary to the dignity of persons and of human sexuality which is naturally ordered to the good of spouses and the generation and education of children. Moreover, says the *Catechism*, it is a grave scandal when there is corruption of the young.

Q. Can you tell me where it is authoritatively stated that extramarital sexual activity by the husband is morally wrong? — R.G., Texas

A. There is only one word to describe extramarital sexual activity by a husband, or by a wife, and that word is adultery, which occurs, says the *Catechism*, when two partners, of whom at least one is married to another party, have sexual relations (n. 2380). Adultery has been authoritatively forbidden by God the Father (Deuteronomy 5:18), God the Son (Matthew 15:19 and 19:18), and by the Catholic Church.

Christ condemns even adultery of mere desire, the *Catechism* (n. 2380) reminds us, noting that the sixth commandment and the New Testament forbid adultery absolutely and recalling that the prophets denounced adultery because they saw it as idolatry.

Adultery is also an injustice, says the *Catechism* (n. 2381), because the person who commits it fails in his commitment, does injury to the marriage bond, transgresses the rights of the other spouse, and undermines the institution of marriage by breaking the contract on which it is based. Such a person, it says, compromises the good of human generation and the welfare of children who need their parents' stable union.

Q. My husband has engaged in many affairs over the years, but when he reached out to his mother for help with his sexual addiction, she told him that he didn't need to go to Confession because God was watching over him. What do you think? — S.Q., New Jersey

A. Looking at the situation from the viewpoint of objective morality, the husband is guilty of adultery, which Jesus said would keep a person from sharing in everlasting life (Mark 10:17-19). The only ordinary way for a Catholic to obtain forgiveness for this violation of God's law is through the sacrament of Penance. Not only is Confession necessary for S.Q.'s husband to be reconciled with God and with the Church, but it would also seem necessary for him to discuss his sexual addiction with a priest in order to obtain counseling to help overcome that addiction.

Q. Advice columns in the newspapers often say that the Catholic Church has changed its teaching on masturbation and that medical experts believe that masturbation is a healthy and normal way to relieve sexual tension. Can you tell me how to respond to these columnists? Is there a scriptural reference? — P.L., Massachusetts

A. First of all, the Catholic Church has not changed its teaching on the objective sinfulness of masturbation or self-abuse. In its 1975 *Declaration on Certain Problems of Sexual*

Ethics, the Sacred Congregation for the Doctrine of the Faith stated that "masturbation is an intrinsically and gravely disordered action" because "the deliberate use of the sexual faculty, for whatever reason, outside of marriage is essentially contrary to its purpose. For it lacks that sexual relationship demanded by the moral order and in which 'the total meaning of mutual self-giving and human procreation in the context of true love' is achieved. All deliberate sexual activity must therefore be referred to the married state" (n. 9).

Second, there is no scriptural condemnation of masturbation by name, but the tradition of the Church, according to the *Declaration on Sexual Ethics*, "has rightly taken it to have been condemned by the New Testament when it speaks of 'uncleanness' and 'unchastity' and other vices contrary to chastity and continence." See, for instance, Romans 1:24.

Third, the Church is very much aware that its traditional teaching on the grave sinfulness of masturbation "is frequently doubted nowadays if not expressly denied," and that modern psychologists and sociologists, not to mention advice columnists, are claiming that, especially in adolescents, "it is a normal concomitant of growth towards sexual maturity and that for this reason no grave fault is involved." However, the *Declaration* said that these opinions are "contrary to both the teaching and the pastoral practice of the Church."

The document conceded that psychological or sociological factors, including "adolescent immaturity, which sometimes outlasts adolescence, the lack of psychological balance, and ingrained habit can influence a person's behavior, diminishing his responsibility for his actions, with the result that he is not always guilty of subjectively grave fault." But it said that such a determination would have to be made by one's confessor.

The *Declaration* also said that one's confessor should take into account "the habitual general conduct of the person concerned," the "care given to the observance of the special precept of chastity," and whether the person was using the "necessary natural and supernatural helps" which "age-long Christian ascetical experience recommends for curbing passion and making progress in virtue."

It is unlikely that these comments will have any effect on advice columnists. Their popularity is due in part to telling people what they want to hear, rather than what is morally right. But just because they quote "experts" as saying that masturbation is widespread does not mean that it is morally okay to engage in it.

Q. Everything I've read about masturbation seems to refer to males. What does the Church teach about female masturbation? — Name Withheld, Georgia

A. The Church teaches that masturbation by females and males is wrong. The following summary of that teaching is from the book *Catholic Sexual Ethics* by Rev. Ronald Lawler, O.F.M. Cap., Joseph Boyle Jr., and William E. May:

"Masturbation is the deliberate stimulation of the genital organs to the point of orgasm which is not a part of sexual intercourse. Thus understood, masturbation can be done either by a person acting on himself or herself (thus, its frequent description as 'self-abuse'), or by one person acting on another. Throughout her history the Church has consistently held that masturbation, when it is a freely chosen act, is seriously wrong, for it always involves a failure to respect the human goods which all sexual activity should take into account. The Fathers of the Church, the medieval Scholastics, and all moral theologians until most recent times have been unanimous in condemning every deliberate act of masturbation as a serious violation of the virtue of chastity. This same teaching has been proposed by the magisterium of the Church from the time when it was discussed by Pope Leo IX in 1054 to the present" (p. 187).

The teaching was reaffirmed by the Sacred Congregation for the Doctrine of the Faith in its 1975 *Declaration on Certain Problems Concerning Sexual Ethics* and by the *Catechism of the Catholic Church*, n. 2352.

Q. I am unable to convince my students that masturbation is a serious sin. Will you please refer me to some authoritative source for your observations? — J.N., Michigan

Q. Regarding masturbation, the *Catechism of the Catholic Church* states: "To form an equitable judgment about the subjects' moral responsibility and to guide pastoral action, one must take into account the affective immaturity, force of acquired habit, conditions of anxiety, or other psychological or social factors that lessen or even extenuate moral culpability" (n. 2352). I understand the cases of immaturity and psychological reasons, but it seems that anyone could find an excuse in the other exceptions if they wanted to. Could you explain what those other exceptions mean? — P.G., Ohio

A. First of all, the *Catechism* makes clear in the same paragraph that both the *Magisterium* of the Church, in the course of a constant tradition, and the moral sense of the faithful have been in no doubt and have firmly maintained that masturbation is an intrinsically and gravely disordered action. The deliberate use of the sexual faculty, for whatever reason, outside of marriage is essentially contrary to its purpose, says the *Catechism*. For in this case, sexual pleasure is sought outside of the sexual relationship which is demanded by the moral order and in which the total meaning of mutual self-giving and human procreation in the context of true love is achieved.

These statements come from section 9 of the *Declaration on Certain Problems of Sexual Ethics*, a careful reading of which would be helpful, as would studying pages 187-195 of the Lawler, Boyle, May book *Catholic Sexual Ethics*. These moral theologians demonstrate that "the objections to this teaching are based on poor arguments or perspectives contrary to the received teachings of the faith. There is no doubt therefore that the Christian ideal of chastity excludes masturbation, and that it is possible for Christians to acquire the ability to live in accord with this teaching."

Conditions that might lessen a person's moral guilt would include ignorance, fear, concupiscence, habit, temperament, and mental disorders. These conditions cannot be used as an excuse to sin, and sincere efforts must be made to overcome them through prayer and the sacraments, and the counsel of a good confessor.

It is difficult for adolescents (and some adults) to recognize the distinction between objective and subjective morality. J.N. will have to convince them of the objectively grave nature of masturbation, while pointing out subjectively mitigating conditions, without providing them with alibis for sinful actions. Not an easy task!

Q. Are impure actions while asleep or semi-awake mortal sins? Does an impure action have to end in ejaculation to be a mortal sin? Are thoughts which lead to ejaculation without any physical action sinful? How does one confess these sins to a priest? If a person dies for the Faith with an unconfessed mortal sin on their soul, do they go to Hell? — J.G., New York

A. Without knowing all the particular circumstances, we can only state general moral principles. Those with questions about these matters ought to discuss them with a confessor who is faithful to the Church's teaching on sexuality. But perhaps the following comments will be helpful.

(1) One is not responsible for actions which occur while asleep since the full consent of the will is lacking. Thus, noc-

turnal emissions are not sinful. However, should such emissions consistently follow the reading of pornographic literature or the viewing of pornographic films, then the person would not be blameless. Lacking a clear definition of "semi-awake," we cannot respond to that part of the question except to say that using such a term could be a convenient way of trying to escape responsibility for a sinful action.

(2) No, an impure action would not have to end in ejaculation to be a mortal sin. If the subjective intention was to bring about ejaculation, but the person was physically unable to do so despite prolonged self-abuse, it would still be a gravely sinful act.

(3) Impure thoughts are not sinful in themselves unless we dwell on them and take pleasure in them. Doing so to the point of ejaculation would certainly constitute an objective mortal sin. The subjective guilt of the person would have to be determined in Confession.

(4) The proper way to confess these sins is to state them plainly and simply. Tell the priest that you find it difficult to talk about them and ask for his help. There is nothing you can tell him that he hasn't heard before.

(5) A person who dies with an unconfessed mortal sin on his soul, and who has not expressed sorrow for that sin through an act of contrition, has turned away from God and has chosen Hell, where the souls of the damned are eternally turned away from God. It doesn't seem likely that a person in that state of mind would give up his life for his Faith. On the other hand, a person who had committed a mortal sin, but who had said an act of contrition and had the intention of going to the sacrament of Penance when he was killed for his Faith, would eventually go to Heaven.

Q. Could you please give the Church's position on cross-dressing? — F.F., California

A. We are not aware of any official Church statement on cross-dressing, but there is this passage from Deuteronomy 22:5: "A woman shall not wear an article proper to a man, nor shall a man put on a woman's dress; for anyone who does such things is an abomination to the LORD, your God." This would not apply, of course, to those in theatrical productions or to those who dress up for Halloween.

Q. Is it a sin for young men to wear earrings? I thought St. Paul condemned men for dressing like women. — R.J.K., Connecticut

A. Persons who adopt the dress and often the behavior of the opposite sex are known as transsexuals. They are confused or ambivalent about their sexual identity and in need of psychological counseling. A young man who wears an earring is usually making a social or cultural statement, or just trying to drive his parents crazy, rather than exhibiting transsexual tendencies. So, we would not consider it a sin for a young man to wear an earring.

Q. A local priest says that "the Bible has nothing to say about homosexuality in the context of contemporary society — a committed relationship between two people of the same sex." Is he correct? — T.C.D., Virginia

A. No, he is not correct. The Bible is quite clear on the evil of homosexual behavior, and the prohibitions enunciated in Scripture are just as applicable in contemporary society as they were thousands of years ago. For instance, the Lord said to Moses: "If a man lies with a male as with a woman, both of them shall be put to death for their abominable deed" (Leviticus 20:13). And St. Paul said: "God therefore delivered them up to disgraceful passions. Their women exchanged natural intercourse for unnatural, and the men gave up natural intercourse with women and burned with lust for one another. Men did shameful things with men, and thus received in their own persons the penalty for their perversity" (Romans 1:26-27).

Bear in mind, however, the distinction the Church makes between homosexual orientation, which is not sinful provided there is no genital relationship with a person of the same sex, and homosexual acts, which "are intrinsically disordered and may never be approved in any way whatever" (*Declaration on Certain Problems of Sexual Ethics*, n. 8).

Q. I never did get an answer from you about why the U.S. Catholic bishops allowed Dignity, a gay organization, to propagate its teachings within the confines of numerous Catholic parishes for about ten years. I thought that Catholic bishops were supposed to follow the directives of the Pope in regards to sexual teachings. — M.C., New York

A. We don't know why some bishops permit activities in their dioceses that are contrary to the teachings of the Catholic Church, as expressed in directives from the Pope and the congregations at the Vatican, and we would not attempt to guess at their motives. You would have to write directly to a specific bishop and ask him the reason why such things happen. Of course, bishops are supposed to follow what the Holy Father says, but we know that this is not always the case. Pray for the bishops that they will be courageous and faithful shepherds of their flocks.

Q. How can I obtain a copy of the Congregation for the Doctrine of the Faith's advisory to the U.S. Catholic Bishops regarding legislative proposals on discrimination against homosexuals? — A.M.B., Oregon

A. The advisory, dated July 23, 1992, was published in the August 6, 1992 issue of *Origins*, the documentary publication of the Catholic News Service. Single copies of this issue of *Origins* can be obtained for $3.50 by writing to the Catholic News Service, 3211 4th Street, N.E., Washington, DC 20017-1100, or by calling (202) 541-3290.

The advisory, which should be read in conjunction with the Congregation's 1986 *Letter to the Bishops of the Catholic Church on the Pastoral Care of Homosexual Persons*, says, among other things, that "there are areas in which it is not unjust discrimination to take sexual orientation into account, for example, in the placement of children for adoption or foster care, in employment of teachers or athletic coaches, and in military recruitment" (n. 11).

That letter can be found at the back of Fr. John Harvey's excellent book *The Homosexual Person: New Thinking in Pastoral Care* (Ignatius Press). Fr. Harvey, who has counseled homosexuals for more than 30 years, is a founder of Courage, the organization that helps those with a homosexual orientation to live chaste lives through an active spiritual life that includes frequent reception of the sacraments of Penance and the Holy Eucharist.

Q. The lead article in the March 1993 *Atlantic Monthly* offers strong evidence that homosexuality may be caused wholly or in large part by a genetic predetermination. If there should be conclusive evidence that homosexuals are not acting out of free will, but rather are genetically programmed to act that way, then what will happen to the Church's teaching on that matter? — J.C., Illinois

A. Even if it should ever be established that homosexuals are genetically programmed to act that way, there would be no change in the Church's teaching that everyone, homosexual or heterosexual, is called to lead a chaste life. The Church teaches that while homosexual orientation is objectively disordered, it is not sinful unless one engages in a homosexual act. Those with an orientation toward any kind of sinful activity, whether sexual or not, must strive to control that inclination through spiritual counseling, prayer, and frequent recourse to the sacraments.

For persuasive evidence that homosexuality is not genetically predetermined, see chapters 2 and 3 of *The Homosexual Person*. Fr. Harvey devotes considerable space to the studies of British psychologist Dr. Elizabeth Moberly, who holds that a homosexual orientation "does not depend on a genetic dispositional hormonal imbalance or abnormal learning processes, but on difficulties in the parent-child relationship, especially in the early years of life." Fr. Harvey's discussion of research done by Moberly and others, and of the fine work being carried on by groups like Courage, makes his book a valuable resource.

Q. Would you please explain how and when the homosexual community adopted the word "gay." I realize that this is not a religious question, but in view of the growth and acceptance of the Dignity organization by some in the Church, the question seems relevant. — R.L.W., Texas

A. According to *The Barnhart Dictionary of Etymology* (H.W. Wilson), the word "gay" commonly meant joyous or merry from the end of the 14th century until the middle of this century. "The slang sense of homosexual is first recorded in 1951, apparently shortened from an earlier compound *gaycat*, homosexual boy (about 1935, in underworld and prison slang), but used earlier for a young tramp or hobo, often one attached to an older tramp and usually with a connotation of homosexuality."

"Gay" has been used as a noun for a homosexual since about 1971. For a more detailed explanation of the evolution of this word, see *Webster's Word Histories* (Merriam-Webster).

Q. What exactly is homosexuality? Are they born that way? Why does God permit some people to be afflicted with this condition? Can a homosexual fall in love with a member of the opposite sex and have a happy marriage and family? — J.M., New York

A. In *The Homosexual Person*, Fr. John Harvey says that homosexuality has traditionally been described "as a persistent and predominant attraction of a sexual-genital nature to persons of one's own sex. I use the term predominant to indicate that there may be a lesser degree of erotic interest in the other sex .... I use the term persistent to indicate that these erotic feelings toward someone of the same sex have persisted beyond the adolescent phase" (p. 27).

Fr. Harvey also says that "we have to distinguish between transitory homosexuality, which may be a phase of development, especially during adolescence, and chronic homosexuality, the latter being the type of homosexuality that is generally meant when one uses the term."

As for the other questions asked, Fr. Harvey presents compelling evidence that homosexuals are not born that way, that their disordered condition may be the result of defects in the parent-child relationship in the early years of life, and that homosexuals can change their orientation and enter into happy and successful heterosexual marriages. For a fuller treatment of this evidence, see Fr. Harvey's book.

Why does God permit some people to be afflicted with this condition? The same question could be asked about those afflicted with alcoholism or cocaine addiction or heterosexual promiscuity. We don't know the full answer, except to say that these and other disorders are the result of original sin and the personal sins that we ourselves commit.

Some people, of course, freely choose evil, and influence others to do likewise, and any bad consequences that result are their fault, not God's. Others who get caught up in these addictions can get help if they want it, and they can reform their lives through an active spirituality that includes prayer and frequent recourse to the sacraments of Penance and the Holy Eucharist.

Q. I am glad that you answered the question regarding the word "gay" in a previous column, but I would like to provide you with some additional and important information about the word, and about the "gay" movement as well. The two words cannot be used interchangeably. While "gays" are normally homosexual, homosexuals are possibly not at all "gay." I have enclosed some material written by "gay" activists, and a letter written by a homosexual. This material can explain better than I the difference between "gay" and homosexual. — Name Withheld, California

A. Our reader sent along photocopies of articles from *Patlar*, a monthly magazine that describes itself as the "Voice of Lesbian/Gay America." In the May 1991 issue, Nancy Lyn Define declares that "we all realize that being homosexual is not the same as being gay. That the first is merely a sexual preference; the second, a complete lifestyle. There are a whole lot of homosexuals out there who have nothing in common with those of us who are proudly, openly, socially, politically, personally GAY."

In the June 1991 issue of *Patlar*, Tim Campbell wrote: "Call me gay, call me lesbian, you can even call me queer. Just don't call me 'a homosexual,' please and thank you."

In a letter published in the May 26, 1993 issue of the *Wall Street Journal*, Mark Dennis of California said that many of his fellow homosexuals despise the term "gay" because it "bespeaks noisy, self-indulgent brats who make every decision based on sexual urges with members of the same sex. Some of us are embarrassed by the gay agenda, which plans the end of 'breeders' (heterosexuals) through a takeover of public education. Some of us are angry that the mass media rolls over so easily, giving credibility to the absurd term 'gay.' It's homosexual, stupid!"

After criticizing gays for refusing "to admit that gay sex clubs are a danger" and that "unbridled use" of cocaine and crack among gays is "the single most important element in the spread of AIDS," Dennis concluded his letter:

"As a homosexual man dying of AIDS, I take full responsibility for my situation. My death will not be this government's fault or Ronald Reagan's fault. I don't need more funding by taxpayers as much as I need gays to admit that they are part of the problem and impeding a solution. I will die a homosexual but I will not die 'gay.'"

Further insight into this distinction has been given by Fr. John Harvey in *The Homosexual Person*. Explaining why he seldom used the word "gay" in his book to describe the homosexual person, Fr. Harvey said:

"In thirty-two years of counseling homosexual persons, I have yet to meet a practicing homosexual person who could be called 'gay' in the sense of joyful. In a penetrating article ["Are Homosexuals Gay?" *Commentary*, January 1979, pp. 20-22], Samuel McCracken shows by a critical analysis of data in pro-homosexual books that the claim that homosexuals are as happy as other people has not been established; in particular, he points to data that show that suicide attempts are significantly higher among homosexuals than among others — for example, 3% for white non-homosexual males, 18% for white homosexual males.

"The unhappiness of so many so-called gay persons is rooted in their mania for sexual pleasure, coupled with their unwillingness to accept responsibility" (p. 103).

Fr. Harvey's book is also valuable for its exposure of the organization known as Dignity, which brings together under the aegis of Catholicism homosexual persons who have no intention of abandoning their immoral homosexual behavior. After quoting from several Dignity newsletters, Fr. Harvey concluded:

"Dignity has established itself within the Church with support of clergy, religious, and laity, but against the teaching of the Church. It uses every means in its power to undermine that teaching on homosexual activity" (p. 169).

Editor's Note: E.M. of Texas writes to say that "I was glad to see your quite extensive coverage of the subject of homosexuality in your column. Besides Fr. Harvey's book, there is another excellent book on the subject which perhaps you could recommend. It is *Homosexuality: Ten Questions — Scriptural, Church, and Psychiatric Answers* by Herbert F. Smith, S.J., and Joseph A. DiIenno, M.D. The book is published by the Daughters of St. Paul and should be available in any Catholic bookstore for $5.95. Dr. DiIenno is a psychiatrist, and the book has a preface by another psychiatrist. They are firm in asserting that people are seduced into homosexuality and not 'born that way.'

"It is a puzzle to me why the Church — and individual priests — do not have more to say about the obligation of a homosexual to change his 'lifestyle.' If someone has a strong inclination to steal, we don't tell him to just go ahead and steal. Or to do any number of other wrong things that he has an inclination to do."

Q. What is the definition of "homophobia"? Our church has prayers of the faithful that ask us to pray "not to be homophobic." I am a tolerant person, but this says to my thinking that we are supposed to be accepting of the homosexual lifestyle. I pray daily for all homosexuals to be converted to Christ, but this surely does not mean I will pray that their lifestyle will be accepted. Am I correct? — J.L.P., Washington

A. The dictionary says that homophobia is "hatred or fear of homosexuals or homosexuality." As followers of Jesus, we are forbidden to hate anyone, although we may certainly hate evil actions and behavior. We are called to hate the sin, but to love the sinner, that is, to pray that the sinful person will turn away from evil.

One of the favorite tricks of the homosexual movement is to label as homophobic anyone who says that the homosexual lifestyle is contrary to the plan of God and harmful to society. Thus, the Catholic Church is often accused of homophobia, even though the Church makes a distinction between homosexual orientation (which is not sinful) and homosexual behavior (which is sinful).

We agree with J.L.P. that the use of the adjective "homophobic" in a prayer of the faithful sends the wrong message. It implies that we ought to accept homosexual activity as a permissible alternative lifestyle, and suggests that anyone who calls attention to the biblical condemnations (Genesis 19, Leviticus 18:22, Romans 1:26-27) of this lifestyle is a promoter of hatred and fear.

Q. Is there any difference from the moral point of view between bestiality and sodomy? Is one more horrible than the other? — G.A., Indiana

A. Both evils are contrary to the purposes of sex in the divine plan and are equally condemned in the Bible. Regarding bestiality, the Lord told Moses: "If a man has carnal relations with an animal, the man shall be put to death, and the animal shall be slain. If a woman goes up to any animal to mate with it, the woman and the animal shall be slain" (Leviticus 20:15-16).

Regarding sodomy, which takes its name from the ancient city of Sodom that was destroyed by God because of the homosexual behaviour of its inhabitants (Genesis 19), that evil has been condemned in the Old Testament (Leviticus 18:22, 20:13) and the New Testament (Romans 1:24-27, Jude 7).

One could argue that bestiality is a more profoundly disordered choice because the object is not even human.

Q. In one of your columns, you stated that we have a moral obligation to avoid doing business with companies that promote abortion. But there is also the problem of doing business with sponsors of TV shows that glorify immorality (the American Family Association lists many of these companies every month), or with stores that sell or rent immoral books, magazines, and videos. Does God expect us to drive 60 miles to find a store that does not deal in these things? — F.Z., Ohio

A. You raise a dilemma that has troubled many persons concerned about the tide of immorality that had deluged American society. There is hardly an aspect of our lives that is not tainted by this tide in some way, and it is extremely difficult to stay completely clear of it.

Obviously, we cannot boycott every company or store which in some way promotes immorality. Nor should we have to drive 60 miles to shop at an establishment that is not part of the problem. What one must do is to make every reasonable effort to refrain from giving financial support to those promoting evil in our society.

This would mean, for instance, boycotting companies, magazines, and newspapers that advertise or glorify immorality or that engage in "Catholic-bashing" because of the Church's opposition to immoral practices. It would mean not shopping at grocery or department stores that feature pornographic literature or videos.

But one may have to choose between two stores that sell objectionable materials, or two newspapers or television stations that feature immoral advertising or programming, and patronize the one that is less offensive. An effort must be made, of course, to persuade the proprietors of the stores, newspapers, or TV stations to discontinue the sale or promotion of such materials, or at least to stay away from the particularly gross ones.

But the bottom line is that if more Americans, and Catholics in particular, were sensitive to this problem and made it clear that they would not shop at a certain store, or watch a certain TV network, or read a certain newspaper because it was promoting immorality, the people in charge would soon change their direction lest they lose the support necessary to stay in business.

Q. Observing that some of my friends have been viewing R-rated movies, I am wondering if the table suggested by the Catholic Church for appropriate movie selection has been changed. I had always understood that we would only view movies with ratings of G, PG, or PG-13. Could you inform me as to what is permitted for Catholic viewing? — M.H., Maryland

A. Prior to 1965, the Legion of Decency issued movie ratings that had considerable influence on Catholic moviegoers. The Legion was then absorbed by the U.S. Catholic Conference's Department of Communications, and its ratings of films are not as widely disseminated today, nor do Catholics pay much attention to them.

The ratings mentioned by M.H. are those assigned by the movie industry itself, which is not at all interested in Christian moral values, and those ratings have undergone considerable slippage as movies that were once rated R are now labeled PG-13. Much of this has become academic with the advent of the VCR, which makes possible home viewing of the foulest films, and with the increasing nudity, sex scenes, sexual innuendo, violence, and coarse language on prime-time television shows every night of the week.

What should Catholics watch on television or in the movies? They should watch programs and films that uphold Christian moral values and do not promote or glorify repeated violations of the Ten Commandments. Even the best-intentioned Catholics can become desensitized to the evil of fornication, adultery, homosexual acts, abortion, murder and mayhem, foul language, misuse of God's name, and many other examples of sinful conduct if they watch these things portrayed in a favorable light night after night in their own homes.

Individual Catholics have to establish their own rating system, one that keeps them away from occasions of sin or from movies and programs (and books and magazines) that so preoccupy their minds that there is little or no room left for spiritual thoughts or actions.

Q. Are the following actions sinful — laziness at work or absenteeism without a good reason, cheating on your income tax, and abusing your body by drinking or eating to excess? — R.L.Z., Nebraska

A. Yes to all of them. Whether they are mortal or venial sins depends on the degree of laziness, cheating, and bodily abuse and the scandal that our actions give to others.

Regarding laziness or missing work without a good reason, a person owes his or her employer a day's work for a day's pay. If you fail to live up to your commitment, i.e., you accept a week's pay without doing your job or without doing it well, then you have cheated your employer. You have taken money from him without earning it, and that's stealing.

In the second case, if you underreport your income or claim false deductions, you are defrauding the government by failing to pay your share of the cost of government. You may think that the government takes too much of your income in taxes, or that it uses your tax money wastefully or for unconstitutional or even evil purposes (funding abortion, for example), but the answer is to lobby your elected representatives to put the government on the proper course, not to engage in sinful actions yourself.

Eating or drinking to excess is called gluttony. It is one of the seven capital or deadly sins because it can lead to other sins.

Q. If a person stole from different stores for a long time, must he give back the exact amount stolen? What if some of the stores have gone out of business? Can the person approximate the amount stolen from all the stores and give that amount to charity? — Name and State Withheld

A. As the questioner realizes, there is an obligation to make restitution for the property stolen, that is, to give back to the lawful owner what belongs to him or the value of what was taken. How can this be done? In the case of those stores that are still operating, the person must either return the items that were stolen or the approximate value of them. This can be done anonymously if necessary to preserve the reputation of the person who is not known to be a thief and who is sorry for his actions and wants to atone for them.

As for those stores which have since gone out of business, the approximate value of the goods taken can be given to charitable causes. Churches and charitable agencies often receive anonymous contributions, sometimes accompanied by a note indicating that the donation is "conscience money."

Q. How many commandments of the Church are there, and are we required to obey them? — A.H., Massachusetts

A. To answer the second question first, Jesus gave His Church the authority to make laws when He told Peter: "Whatever you declare bound on earth shall be bound in heaven" (Matthew 16:19). Since Jesus said that He would back up in Heaven whatever laws or precepts Peter and his successors would make on earth, Catholics are obliged to observe Church laws faithfully.

We grew up knowing six commandments or precepts of the Church (and the *Catechism of the Catholic Church* lists only six), but since they issued their *Basic Teachings for Catholic Religious Education* in 1973, the U.S. bishops have listed seven, adding one about joining in the missionary work of the Church that we think originated with Pope Paul VI. But whatever listing we use, the purpose of these positive Church laws is to help us lead holy lives on earth so that we can get to Heaven. Briefly, then, here are the seven commandments of the Church:

(1) To participate actively at Mass every Sunday and holy day of obligation, and to avoid unnecessary work on those days.

(2) To receive Holy Communion frequently (but at least once a year) and the sacrament of Penance or Reconciliation regularly

(but at least once a year if one is conscious of having committed a mortal sin).

(3) To study Catholic teaching in preparation for the sacraments of Penance, the Holy Eucharist, and Confirmation; to be confirmed; and then to continue to study the Catholic Faith.

(4) To observe the marriage laws of the Church; to give religious training to one's children; and to use parish schools and religious education programs.

(5) To contribute to the support of the Church (parish, diocese, and worldwide) and the Holy Father.

(6) To fast from food and abstain from meat on the days appointed by the Church (at least Ash Wednesday and the Fridays of Lent).

(7) To join in the missionary spirit and apostolate of the Church by spreading the Catholic Faith to others through word and example.

Q. In your column, you said that Catholics must obey the commandments of the Church. But the *Baltimore Catechism* says that these commandments can be changed, and Fr. Peter Stravinskas says in his *Catholic Encyclopedia* that "the commandments were never officially approved by the Church." Can you explain this? — D.L.S., Washington

A. The *Baltimore Catechism* says (q. 1325) that because the commandments of the Church were made by God's authority, "we are bound under pain of sin to observe them." Question 1328 says that the Church gave us these commandments "to teach the faithful how to worship God and to guard them from the neglect of their religious duties."

Fr. Stravinskas traces the origin of the commandments of the Church to St. Peter Canisius in 1555 and says that they "foster a sense of personal responsibility by reminding the faithful of their minimal responsibilities toward the Church." He also says that while these precepts were never officially approved by the Church, they have a "long-standing acceptance by the Church," and "obedience is to be demanded to the extent required by the common good of the Church and the well-being of the faithful."

Before listing six of the precepts, the *Catechism of the Catholic Church* said that the obligatory character of these positive laws decreed by the pastoral authorities is meant to guarantee to the faithful the indispensable minimum in the spirit of prayer and moral effort, in the growth of love of God and neighbor (n. 2041).

Chapter 14

Miscellaneous Matters

Q. Is the program of Alcoholics Anonymous compatible with my practice of the Catholic Faith? It seems to me, given my five years of contact with these (largely irreligious) people that it is not. They condemn "institutionalized, hierarchical" religion as "man-made" and therefore somehow inherently incapable of restoring any man to contact with the divine, and say that one should worship "one's own conception" of God. Are my fears well-grounded? — S.B., New York

A. We know people who are faithful Catholics and who have been members of A.A. for more than 25 years. According to them, A.A.'s program is compatible with the Catholic Faith. They pointed out, for instance, that A.A.'s 12 steps are based on the Ten Commandments and that one of the authors of these steps was Fr. Edward Dowling, a Jesuit priest. Step 11 says that "we sought through prayer and meditation to improve our conscious contact with God as we understand Him, praying only for knowledge of His will for us and the power to carry it out."

Our friends said that A.A. is not a religious organization, but an organization to help people stop drinking. A.A. says that people must meet God as each person understands Him, but it operates under the banner of "But for the grace of God," and the Lord's Prayer is said at all meetings.

This has always been the thrust of Alcoholics Anonymous, but our friends said that they have noticed in recent years an effort by some A.A. members, perhaps reflecting the trend in society as a whole, to eliminate references to God and to take A.A. in a different direction. This may be what S.B. has run into in his New York chapter. The solution, our friends told us, is for S.B. to find a group that is more in line with the original objectives of A.A., such as the one expressed in Step 11 of the organization's 12-step program.

Q. Has the Church ever taken a position regarding the sport of boxing? I have a problem with the goal of knocking unconscious a person whose body is a temple of the Holy Spirit. — J.B.P., California

A. We are not aware of any official statement by the Church

on boxing. Some Catholic moralists, however, have questioned the morality of a "sport" whose goal is to hurt an opponent and ultimately to knock him senseless. How does this goal square with Christ's command to love our neighbor? Some would make a distinction between amateur boxing, where skill and finesse are the rule, and professional boxing, where violence and even savagery are the norm, and that distinction has some merit.

Another factor that has to be considered is the bloodthirsty behavior that professional boxing calls forth from spectators, who clamor for more brutality and viciousness as a fight progresses. Is it a good thing to stir up the primitive violence that is never very far below the surface in the supposedly civilized men and women of today? Perhaps the time has come for the Church to take a position on the morality of boxing.

Q. Is there anything wrong with undergoing hypnosis to stop smoking or overeating or to correct a fault such as stealing? — G.V., New Brunswick

A. There is nothing wrong with hypnosis in itself, and the Church has long permitted its use for a serious reason, such as a legitimate therapeutic purpose, and provided that it is conducted by a competent and morally sound hypnotist. The guidelines to be followed were set forth by the Vatican's Holy Office (now the Sacred Congregation for the Doctrine of the Faith) on July 26, 1899, and on August 4, 1956.

The Church requires certain conditions because hypnotism denies a person full use of reason and free will, and because subjects can be persuaded to commit immoral acts that they would not normally commit. For these reasons, Catholics should not allow themselves to be hypnotized for the sake of amusement. They should bear in mind, too, that while hypnotism may help a person to give up smoking or lose weight, the person will still have to exert plenty of willpower.

Q. What is the official Church teaching on the practice of tatooing? — G.J., New Mexico

A. We are not aware of any Church law against getting a tatoo. What would have to enter into such a decision, however, would be our obligation not to do anything that would harm our bodies. We are not allowed to mutilate our bodies (amputation of a diseased limb would be a permitted exception) or make them vulnerable to any disease that might be transmitted through careless use of dirty needles in the tatooing process.

Q. What is the feeling of the Church about Nostradamus? Is he considered a true prophet? — P.G., Ohio

A. Nostradamus (1503-1566), the chief astrologer to Catherine de Medici of France, made a number of predictions of the future that, from our perspective four centuries later, can be made to fit events in this century. The predictions were expressed in very general terms, like the daily horoscopes in the newspaper, which means that people can read into them whatever their imagination dictates.

For instance, Nostradamus wrote: "At the rising of the sun, a great fire shall be seen, noise and light tending to the north and all around about — death and cries shall be heard...." That could mean almost anything, but some have related it to the dropping of the atomic bomb on Japan in 1945 because Japan is the "Land of the Rising Sun." Of course, it could also relate to various volcanic eruptions around the world.

The Church made clear its attitude toward Nostradamus in 1781 when it put his works on the Index of books that Catholics were forbidden to read without ecclesiastical authorization. That Index no longer exists, but the reasons why the Church included the unreliable writings of Nostradamus on it are just as valid today. Only God, and those whom He has chosen to be His prophets, can know the future with certainty.

Q. Could you please tell me where I could obtain a list of Catholic magazines published in the United States? — M.L.H., Louisiana

A. You will find such a list in the *Catholic Almanac*, in the section dealing with "Communications." The *Almanac* should be available in any Catholic bookstore.

Q. Where can I get a copy of the Code of Canon Law? — J.M., California

Q. How can I get the publications you mention in your column, such as the documents of Vatican II, the *General Instruction of the Roman Missal*, *Inaestimabile Donum*, etc.? — M.S., Tennessee

A. The Code and the other publications should be available at any Catholic bookstore in your area, or the store should be able to order them for you. You can purchase a book containing the 16 documents of the Second Vatican Council, copies of the individual documents themselves, or Austin Flannery's two-volume work entitled *Vatican Council II* (St. Paul Editions), which contains all 16 documents, as well as the *General Instruc-*

tion of the Roman Missal, Inaestimabile Donum, and more than 100 other post-Vatican II Church and papal statements, instructions, and decrees.

The *General Instruction* is also published as a separate document by the Office of Publishing Services, U.S. Catholic Conference, Washington, D.C.

Q. Can you give me the address and subscription rate of the English edition of *L'Osservatore Romano*? — L.C., California

A. The address is *L'Osservatore Romano* - English Edition, Via del Pellegrino, 00120 Vatican City, Europe. Telephone: 39-6-698-85315. Fax: 39-6-698-85164. The subscription rate is $80 a year for surface rate and $108 a year for air mail.

Q. I enclose a list of summer reading recommended by the deacon in my parish. As a reader of *The Wanderer* for many years, I know that some of these authors have consistently challenged basic articles of faith and statements by the *Magisterium*. I would like to show the deacon concrete examples of this. Can you help? — V.M., Virginia

A. There are sixteen books on the list, including five by Fr. Raymond Brown, one by feminist theologian Monika Hellwig (*Jesus: The Compassion of God*), and one by Fr. John P. Meier (*A Marginal Jew: Rethinking the Historical Jesus*). From what we know of these authors, reading their books would only confuse a Catholic seeking to deepen his or her faith.

For instance, Fr. Meier says in his book that "... the historical Jesus is not the real Jesus, but only a fragmentary hypothetical reconstruction of him by modern means of research" (p. 31). Contrast this statement with what the Nicene Creed tells us about the Jesus who entered human history in the womb of the Virgin Mary, was crucified, died, and was buried, rose from the dead, and ascended into Heaven. That is the real and historical Jesus whom we worship, not some fragmentary hypothetical reconstruction.

As for Monika Hellwig, you can read about her contributions to the radical Catholic feminist movement in Donna Steichen's book *Ungodly Rage*. And Fr. Brown's scriptural heterodoxy has been well documented in Fr. William Most's book *Free From All Error*.

V.M. can try to point these things out to his deacon, but the list of books he recommended suggests to us that the mind of the deacon will not be easily changed.

Q. In the catechumenate class my wife is taking, they are using two books: *Christ Among Us* by Anthony Wilhelm and *A Catholic Learning Guide for Adults* by the Rev. Alfred McBride. I would like your opinion of these two books, and can you recommend additional materials that would help my wife to gain a more complete understanding of the Catholic Church? — G.B., Kansas

Q. A national distributor of Catholic products (AUTOM of Phoenix, Arizona) offers in its current catalog Anthony Wilhelm's *Christ Among Us*. The catalog states: "Fifth revised edition, over two million copies sold." In about 1981, I attended classes in my parish which were based on this book. I subsequently began hearing cautions against it. My question is: Have the revisions over the years made this book a true and clear catechism of the Christian faith, or does it still lead astray those who seek to know, love, and serve the Lord? — R.D.H., Maine

A. We are not familiar with this book of Fr. McBride's, but we know from his other books, including *Essentials of the Faith* (Our Sunday Visitor), his guide to the *Catechism of the Catholic Church*, and from having heard him speak, that he is a thoroughly orthodox and articulate proponent of the Catholic Faith.

The same cannot be said about Anthony Wilhelm, whose book is bad news for anyone who wants to know what the Catholic Faith is all about. More than a decade after it was first published in 1968, the Vatican's Sacred Congregation for the Doctrine of the Faith ordered that the imprimatur be removed because the book was doctrinally unsound. Harper & Row, a secular publisher, reissued the book in 1984, without an imprimatur, and it apparently continues to sell a lot of copies. We have not seen the latest revision, but we believe that it would have to have been entirely rewritten to qualify as a reliable catechism of the Christian faith.

For examples of this book's doctrinal deficiencies, see pages 124-133 of Msgr. Michael J. Wrenn's book *Catechisms and Controversies* (Ignatius Press). In the words of Msgr. Wrenn: "This religion textbook by Anthony Wilhelm is typical of many modern religion textbooks in that it uses Christian terminology — 'grace,' 'heaven,' and so on — but fits them into a totally different framework than the framework of historic Christianity or Catholicism .... It seems pretty clear that anyone using this book would probably end up very confused about just who Jesus Christ is. He might grasp that Jesus was an unusual person of great abilities and influence, but it is hard to say what other firm conclusions about Jesus he might be able to arrive at on the basis of the kind of confused and sometimes contradictory information provided in this religion text."

As for other materials that would help a catechumen gain a more complete understanding of the Catholic Church, we would recommend *Essentials of the Faith*, the *Catechism of the Catholic Church*, the *Basic Catechism* of the Daughters of St. Paul, *Catholicism and Reason* by Hayes, Hayes, and Drummey, and *One Faith, One Lord* by Msgr. John F. Barry.

Q. I have received a pamphlet with a recent issue of *The Wanderer*. It states that the Sophia Institute Press is now "the premier publisher of classic Catholic works for laymen." But I have seen an article that makes a critical reference to "creation spirituality, goddess worship, Sophia." I am confused by Sophia's apparent double life. Can you clarify it for me? — S.M., Massachusetts

A. We called the Sophia Institute Press and asked them why that name was chosen. In 1983, said John L. Barger, editor and publisher of the Press, he and a friend decided to start a publishing house that would reissue out-of-print books with a Catholic philosophy. They chose the name Sophia to represent Christian wisdom. "Sophia is an ancient Christian term that refers to the Holy Spirit and the wisdom of God," Barger said. "We publish books that we hope are returning that wisdom to Catholics and to society in general."

He said that the name was chosen before radical feminists began promoting Sophia as some kind of earth goddess or "Mother Wisdom," but that his publishing house has gotten some criticism from Catholics who are wary of the feminist agenda. "Please judge us by our books," said Barger, referring to such Catholic classics as Dietrich von Hildebrand's *Trojan Horse in the City of God* and *The New Tower of Babel*, Romano Guardini's *The Art of Praying* and *The Rosary of Our Lady*, and St. Thomas Aquinas' *Devoutly I Adore Thee* and *Light of Faith*.

Q. Regarding your reply in which you said you were not familiar with Gabriele Uhlein's book on Hildegard of Bingen, you may be interested in the enclosed information. — N.H., Florida

A. N.H. sent along excerpts from Fr. Mitch Pacwa's book *Catholics and the New Age*, and some comments from Donna Steichen that appear in her book, *Ungodly Rage*. Fr. Pacwa said that in a speech he heard Sister Gabriele give in 1987, "This very bright woman spoke about changing paradigms, that is, the key concepts for understanding the world. She insisted that since we all come from the earth, she is our mother. Further, the sun is our grandmother and the universe is our great-grandmother."

He also said that "Dr. Barbara Newman, an expert on St. Hildegard of Bingen at Northwestern University, is skeptical of [Matthew] Fox's work on St. Hildegard. In a footnote, she says of Gabriele Uhlein's *Meditations with Hildegard of Bingen* and Fox's *Illuminations of Hildegard of Bingen* that the 'so-called translations in these volumes are not to be trusted.'"

In a section of her book dealing with the Franciscan Sisters in Wheaton, Illinois, Donna Steichen wrote: "The altered consciousness of the Wheaton Franciscans led *National Catholic Reporter* to say that they 'have gone to meet the 21st century.' In fact, what they have gone to meet is the New Age. The understandably shrinking community has run pleas for new members in the back of Matthew Fox's *Creation* magazine under 'Opportunities.'

"Wheaton Sister Gabriele Uhlein, who studied with Fox, is the author of *Meditations with Hildegard of Bingen,* one in the series of ICCS [Institute for Culture and Creation Spirituality] *Meditations* with books distributed by Bear & Company. At Our Lady of the Angels Convent in Wheaton, Sister Gabriele has presented 'enlightenment' classes to 'explore' Jewish, Buddhist, Islamic, Indian and Wiccan 'traditions' and rituals and to introduce the I Ching, a Chinese fortune-telling system. Sister Gabriele explained her quintessentially New Age motives:

"'We no longer have the luxury of a leisurely religious search. We are in the process of unfolding a new human identity, and in the balance hangs our ability to successfully navigate our initiation as planetary people. The convergence is upon us as surely as the evolution of the species'" (p. 251).

Editor's Note: Regarding the question of why Matthew Fox, the "creation spirituality" guru and Catholic priest turned Episcopalian, has promoted the writings of Hildegard von Bingen, the 12th century Benedictine nun and visionary, W.G.T. of Pennsylvania sends along the Summer 1992 issue of *Touchstone* magazine. The publication contains an article by Dr. Barbara Newman, a professor of English and Religion at Northwestern University, author of two books on Hildegard, and a member of the Orthodox Church in America.

Touchstone describes itself as "a journal of ecumenical orthodoxy" and includes on its masthead such solid Catholic writers as Mitch Pacwa, S.J., and Donna Steichen. The Summer 1992 issue, in fact, contained a fine review by Mrs. Steichen of Fr. Pacwa's book, *Catholics and the New Age*.

In her lengthy *Touchstone* article, Dr. Newman shows that Fox is able to use the writings of Hildegard only by omitting some of her key beliefs and taking others out of context. She says, for example, that "Bear & Company's [Fox's publishing arm] translation of the *Scivias*, the first volume of Hildegard's theological trilogy, is abridged to about half its original length. The omitted sections are those which the editor deemed 'irrelevant or difficult to comprehend today.'

"Among these are lengthy passages promoting orthodox sexual ethics, commending virginity, expounding the theology of baptism and Eucharist, condemning heresy, upholding priestly ordination and celibacy, defending the feudal privilege of nobles, and exhorting the obedience of subjects. In other words, Hildegard is welcome to Fox's mystical pantheon so long as she refrains from being a twelfth century Catholic.

"Her holistic cosmology is acceptable, but not her defense of social and ecclesiastical hierarchies. Fox is delighted to stress her 'womanly wisdom' but ignores the fact that she was a consecrated virgin, blithely ascribing to her his own ideas about 'the recovery of Eros.' Since he also wants to make her a feminist, he rigorously edits her trinitarian thought to fit the standards of an inclusive-language lectionary. The divine Mother, who figures prominently in Hildegard's visions, is allowed to remain; but the Father and his Son are ushered firmly out the door. Fox does not overtly criticize these unpalatable aspects of Hildegard's thought; he simply ignores them....

"My point is not that Hildegard is right and Matthew Fox wrong. What disturbs me is that he makes her the mouthpiece for ideas she never held, and in fact explicitly rejected. Fox may believe he is announcing what Hildegard would have said if she were alive today, but that is a judgment no one has the right to present as historical fact."

Q. What is the Church's position on the writings and philosophy of Meister Eckhart? — J.P., Indiana

A. In his *Modern Catholic Dictionary*, Fr. John Hardon offers these comments on the German Dominican mystic who lived from 1260 to 1327:

"In 1329, Pope John XXII condemned twenty-eight of Eckhart's sentences as heretical or dangerous, e.g.: 'We are totally transformed into God and changed into Him .... Though a person commits a thousand mortal sins, if he is rightly disposed, he should not wish not to have committed them .... A good man is the only begotten Son of God.' Investigation of his doctrine has since indicated Eckhart's personal orthodoxy, while admitting indiscretion in language and the fact that his writings have been used by persons unfavorable to the Church, as Kant to defend agnostic idealism, Hegel to defend pantheism, and Rosenberg to defend Nazism."

Q. During a daily Mass sermon, one of our priests mentioned one of his favorite theologians, Teilhard de Chardin. When I told this priest that the Vatican had issued various censures against de Chardin, the priest said that he asked other priests and a bishop about him and was told that there was nothing wrong with de Chardin. Do you have any other facts? — P.W., Florida

Q. Please explain the Church's opinion on the writings of Teilhard de Chardin. — M.C.O., Rhode Island

A. Pierre Teilhard de Chardin (1881-1955) was a French Jesuit priest and paleontologist whose evolutionary theories were expressed primarily in two books: *The Phenomenon of Man* and *The Divine Milieu*. On June 30, 1962, the Vatican's Holy Office issued a warning about the writings of Teilhard, saying that his works "are full of such ambiguities, nay more even of grave errors, as to offend Catholic doctrine." We are not aware of any repeal or reversal of that warning in the years since it was first issued.

In his critique of Darwinism (*Darwin on Trial*), Phillip E. Johnson makes some comments about Teilhard that may indicate why the Church issued its warning:

"Teilhard de Chardin's aspiration to reformulate the Catholic faith with evolution at its center illustrates the difficulty of disentangling religious and scientific motives on both sides of the evolution controversy. Teilhard was not only a theologian but a major figure in paleoanthropology. He was closely involved with the amateur fossil hunter Charles Dawson and Sir Arthur Smith Woodward in the discovery of the fraudulent 'Piltdown Man' in 1912-1913.

"There are strong grounds for suspecting that Teilhard's religious enthusiasm for evolution led him into participation in fraud. Many persons familiar with the evidence (including Stephen Jay Gould and Louis Leakey) have concluded that Teilhard was probably culpably involved in preparing the Piltdown fraud, although the evidence is not conclusive and Teilhard's admirers insist that he was too saintly a man to consider such a thing. Gould's essays 'The Piltdown Conspiracy' and 'A Reply to Critics' in *Hen's Teeth and Horse's Toes* (1983) provide a good introduction to the subject" (pp. 186-187).

Q. I have seen many messages from "The Little Pebble," a so-called seer from Australia who says that Jesus told him that he would be the next Pope, Peter II. Is he authentic or a hoax? — M.J.G., New Jersey

Q. Have you any knowledge of pronouncements by the Church about "The Little Pebble," a "seer" from Australia who sends out numerous messages containing prophecies? — S.M.V., Wisconsin

Q. Could you give me some information and advice regarding the prophecies coming from Little Pebble of Australia? Has the Church taken a position on these prophecies, especially those relating to the end times? What is the best stance to adopt under the circumstances? — Name Withheld, Canada

A. All that we know about the Little Pebble is that he is an adult convert from atheism who lives in Australia and who claims to have received messages directly from our Lord. In one of the alleged messages, dated June 19, 1987, the Little Pebble quotes Jesus as having told him:

"Rest assured ... you will be the real and only successor to John Paul II and you will be called Peter the Roman, Peter II. You will not be elected as the other Popes have been, but according to divine plans for the last Pope ... you will reign until the end of time .... An anti-Pope will seat himself on the throne of Peter after the death of John Paul II, and his name is Casaroli, a demon worshipper. I make this known to you directly, my son, so that the entire Church may know it...."

There has been no Church approval of the "prophecies" of Little Pebble, nor do we expect any approval of statements as bizarre as this one. It is certainly a false prophecy since it contradicts Christ's promises that the gates of Hell will not prevail against His Church (Matthew 16:18), and that He will be with His Church "always, until the end of the world!" (Matthew 28:20).

The best stance to adopt is to pray constantly that all may be prepared for the end times whenever they come, whether for each person individually or for the world as a whole.

Q. Is it true that Maria Valtorta's *The Poem of the Man-God* is on the Index of forbidden books? — H.S.S., Texas

Q. I have been told that *Poem of the Man-God* is not approved. Do you know anything about it? — E.W., New York

Q. I recently read that *The Poem of the Man-God* was on the Index and has been described as a "poorly romanticized life of Jesus." — B.M., Ontario

A. The *Poem of the Man-God* purports to be a day-by-day account of the lives of Jesus and the Blessed Mother as revealed to Maria Valtorta (1897-1961), an Italian woman confined to a sickbed who wrote *Poem* and other spiritual works from 1943 to 1953. It is divided into five lengthy books — The Hidden Life, The First Year of the Public Life, The Second Year of the Public Life, The Third Year of the Public Life, and Preparation for the Passion, The Passion, and The Glorification.

Poem was placed on the Index in 1959 and, even though the Index was abolished seven years later, "it still retained all its moral value," according to a letter from Cardinal Ratzinger of the Congregation for the Doctrine of the Faith, dated January 31, 1985. In that letter, the Cardinal advised against any distribution or recommendation of *Poem* because the condemnation of it was made after serious investigation and study and because its contents could be harmful to faithful Catholics.

Along with his letter, Cardinal Ratzinger enclosed an article which said that the second edition of Maria Valtorta's work "remains a monument of childishness, fantasy, and false history and exegesis. It is diluted in an atmosphere that is subtly sensual, through the presence of a flock of women following Jesus. In short, this is a monument to psuedo-religiosity. Therefore, the judgment of the Church's condemnation retains its validity also for the second edition of the work."

Some have attributed this characterization of *Poem* to Cardinal Ratzinger himself, but the words are apparently from the above-mentioned article, the author and date of which were not cited, and not from the prefect of the Congregation for the Doctrine of the Faith. It should be noted too that in the variety of materials sent to us there were different translations of the Cardinal's letter, as well as conflicting dates for and different translations of articles about *Poem* that appeared in *L'Osservatore Romano*. So be careful what you write or say about the books.

The point is that *The Poem of the Man-God* has been condemned by the Church as an unreliable and spiritually harmful account of the life of Jesus and His mother. Catholics could better spend their time reading the Gospels or a good life of Christ.

Q. I have never seen reference in your column to Fr. Nicholas Gruner of the *Fatima Crusader*. Do you agree with his writings? Is it true that the real consecration of Russia to the Immaculate Heart of Mary was never done properly? — M.B.S., New Jersey; Name Withheld, West Virginia; M.N., Illinois

Q. I enclose two recent Vatican statements dealing with the apostolate of Fr. Nicholas Gruner. They appear somewhat contradictory. Just what is Fr. Gruner's standing? — R.H., Saskatchewan

A. Regarding the two statements, one is a copy of an Apostolic Blessing given to Fr. Nicholas Gruner by Pope John Paul II "for his sixteen years priestly service and for his very important apostolic work with the 'Fatima Crusader.'" The other is a declaration issued by the Congregation for the Clergy in October 1992. In that declaration, the Congregation said that "the international meeting on the topic, Peace in the World and the Immaculate Heart of Mary, scheduled for 8-12 October in Fatima, Portugal, and organized by Fr. Nicholas Gruner, has not been approved by the competent ecclesiastical authorities. The Congregation also declares that the same Fr. Nicholas Gruner does not have faculties from the Diocese of Leiria-Fatima to perform ministerial acts."

The statements do appear to be contradictory, but the one carrying more weight is the declaration from the Congregation for the Clergy, which for reasons that were not spelled out expressed its disapproval of the conference that Fr. Gruner had planned in Fatima in October 1992. Fr. Gruner held his conference and, according to the Winter 1993 issue of *The Fatima Crusader*, was physically attacked at the Fatima shrine by a person or persons whom he said had been seen in the residence of the Bishop of Fatima and who were ordered to assault him by the rector of the shrine.

We only know Fr. Gruner's side of this story, and we find it hard to believe. Just as we find hard to believe some of the other things he has said over the years, most of which revolve around whether the consecration of Russia to the Immaculate Heart of Mary has ever been accomplished. Some Fatima experts, like Fr. Robert Fox, contend that Pope John Paul's act of consecration in 1984 met all the requirements, and Fr. Fox says that Sister Lucy, the only surviving member of the trio to whom the Blessed Mother appeared in 1917, has confirmed the authenticity of the 1984 consecration.

Fr. Gruner, however, disputes this and talks about "plots" and "conspiracies" to silence our Lady. He says that "there remains today a small but powerful group within the Church actively working to suppress Our Lady's full message." He says that Sister Lucy has been silenced since 1960 and that she made some statements in an interview in October 1992 that "are so bizarre and out-of-character that it has led some Fatima scholars to go so far as to suggest that she was drugged, brainwashed, or even replaced with an impersonator."

It is one thing to express doubt about whether the consecration of Russia has really taken place; it is quite another to say that Sister Lucy has been drugged and brainwashed and perhaps even replaced by an imposter. It is these kinds of allegations that keep us from recommending the writings of Fr. Gruner or his *Fatima Crusader*. He may sincerely believe these things, but we do not find them credible. We have enough trouble trying to persuade people of the truthfulness of those things that we can prove, without trying to convince them of things that we think would be virtually impossible to prove.

Regarding the consecration of Russia, we have read the arguments pro and con and wish that all those who are devoted to Our Lady of Fatima would spend more time praying and less time fighting each other over this issue. Perhaps we should all ask our Lady, under her title of Queen of Peace, to bring peace of mind and heart to those who are so disturbed and distraught about the Fatima consecration.

Q. Would you please inform me about the late Father Charles E. Coughlin, the famed radio priest from Royal Oak, Michigan? Why was he rejected by both civil and Church authorities? — J.V.M., Wisconsin

A. Charles Edward Coughlin (1891-1979) was ordained to the priesthood in 1916 and taught for ten years at Assumption College in Windsor, Ontario, before becoming pastor of the Shrine of the Little Flower in Royal Oak, Michigan. After broadcasting primarily religious homilies over the radio in the late Twenties, Fr. Coughlin began in the early Thirties to talk on political and economic issues, denouncing Communism, "modern capitalism," and the "money-changers on Wall Street." His national audience on Sunday afternoons was estimated in the tens of millions.

At first a backer of Franklin Roosevelt, Fr. Coughlin turned against FDR because, the priest said, "he recognized the atheistic, godless government of the Communists in Russia." Coughlin founded the National Union of Social Justice and published a magazine entitled *Social Justice* that carried his views to a million subscribers. Critics of Fr. Coughlin accused him of anti-Semitism and of harboring sympathies for Fascism. After the United States entered World War II, the Federal Government forced *Social Justice* to stop publishing, and Church officials ordered the priest to end his radio broadcasts.

"I could have bucked the government and won — the people would have supported me," Fr. Coughlin said after he was silenced. "But I didn't have the heart left, for my Church had spoken. It was my duty to follow, for disobedience is a great sin."

Fr. Coughlin remained as pastor of the Shrine of the Little Flower until his retirement in 1966. He died in 1979 at the age of 88.

Q. **What is your opinion of the book *Pope John's Revolution* by Ursula Oxfort? She claims Pope John XXIII's Second Vatican Council was heresy and that the Pope was influenced by the devil. — S.J., California**

Q. **Have you ever read this [Ursula Oxfort's publication *Christian Counter-Revolution*]? I send it to you because of the answer you gave to the question, "If Modernism was condemned by St. Pius X, how could Vatican II come about?" — M.F., Pennsylvania**

A. We have not read the book by Ursula Oxfort, but we did read the September-December 1994 issue of *Christian Counter-Revolution*, which told us all we need to know about this writer. She has said, among other things, that the *Catechism of the Catholic Church* is filled with "blatant heresies and moral perversion"; that Pope John Paul II is "the powerful ecumenical one-world ruler"; that Pope Paul VI was an "apostate"; and that "Vatican II is Antichrist."

Pray for this misguided woman.

Q. **What is the Church's attitude toward such secular groups as the Rotary Club and the Kiwanis Club? — J.H.B., Maryland**

Q. **What is the Vatican's position on the Rotary Club and the Moose Lodge? I am given to understand that Catholics were once prohibited from seeking membership in them. — I.O.M., Florida**

A. We are not aware that the Church has ever taken a position on the Kiwanis Club or the Order of Moose, but the Vatican Holy Office in 1950 did forbid priests to join the

Rotary Club and warned Catholic laymen against becoming affiliated with any Rotary International group. No reason for that ban or warning was given, although there was speculation that Rotary International had some connection with Freemasonry and was anti-Catholic.

No evidence to support this speculation has come to our attention and, while the ban has never been officially reversed, the Church has shown no indication that it intends to enforce it. In a 1965 talk to a group of Rotarians, Pope Paul VI referred to "possible problems" that had existed in the past, but praised the work of Rotary International.

Q. What is RENEW? Is it a good thing for the Catholic Church? — G.H., Maryland, and J.R., Maine

A. The program known as RENEW came into existence more than a decade ago with the stated goal of renewing spirituality at the parish level through small groups that would get together and study. While the intention of the program was worthwhile, in practice some problems arose in the study groups.

For one thing, we have learned, many important doctrines of the Church were never covered in the discussions. And, second, when the Church's spiritual and moral teachings did come up, there were no right or wrong answers; everyone's opinion was treated as equally valid by the group leaders, who were known as "facilitators."

Complaints about RENEW led to an investigation by the U.S. Bishops' Committee on Doctrine. The committee concluded that there were some praiseworthy features to the program, but asked those in charge to correct the problem areas. Whether that was ever done or not, we don't know.

Q. Can you tell me anything about an organization called Communion and Liberation and how I may contact them? — R.O., Texas

A. Communion and Liberation is an international Catholic organization of lay people that was founded in Italy in the mid-1950s. In addition to encouraging its members to pursue lives of personal holiness through recourse to the sacraments and adherence to the *Magisterium* of the Church, the organization also urges those members to bring the Gospel values into the world and to seek the transformation of our secular society. Pope John Paul has given the movement his support.

You can reach Communion and Liberation by writing to the organization at Via Marcello Malpighi 2, 00161, Rome, Italy.

Q. Many in our parish belong to Pax Christi. What can you tell me about this organization? — G.E.F., New York

A. Pax Christi was started in France by French and German Catholics after World War II in an effort to reconcile enemies from that war. It became international in scope after spreading to Italy and Poland and merging with the British organization Pax. The stated purpose of Pax Christi is to bring about "the unity and pacification of the world through the promotion of a new international order based on the natural law and on the justice and charity of Christ." It seeks to achieve this purpose by sponsoring conferences on peace.

Pax Christi USA, the American branch of Pax Christi International, was founded in 1973, according to the *Catholic Almanac*, "to establish peacemaking as a priority for the American Catholic Church, to work for disarmament, primacy of conscience, a just world order, education for peace, and alternatives to violence."

In fact, however, both the European and American organizations have often been involved in leftwing and secular causes to the detriment of the Church. We cannot recommend becoming involved with Pax Christi.

Q. I know people who are involved in "The Way." Do you have any information on this group? — V.F.M., Minnesota

A. According to books by Fr. Albert J. Nevins (*Strangers at Your Door*) and William J. Whalen (*Strange Gods*), The Way is a cult that was founded in Ohio in the late 1950s by Victor Paul Wierwille, a former minister of the Evangelical and Reformed Church who claims that God spoke to him and revealed truths about the Bible that had been lost since the first century.

Some of those "truths" are that Jesus is not God, that there is no Trinity, that the Gospels are part of the Old Testament and are therefore meaningless, that the only books of the Bible that have value are the letters of St. Paul, and that there is no life after death.

Although it often presents itself as merely a Bible-study group, The Way has ordained male and female ministers who conduct worship services and perform marriages. It actively recruits young people, particularly on college campuses, and offers courses on speaking in tongues and other charismatic gifts. It expects its dedicated followers to meet on a daily basis and to tithe their incomes, with the tithe money going to its headquarters in New Knoxville, Ohio, where there is a printing plant that publishes Wierwille's books and *The Way* magazine.

The cult also has a training center for its missionaries in New Emporia, Kansas, a College of Biblical Research in Rome City, Indiana, and a Total Fitness Institute in the California Sierras, where members learn about Scripture and survival skills.

Q. Would you have any information about an organization called Focolare? — V.M.C., Utah

A. In the *Catholic Encyclopedia* edited by Fr. Peter Stravinskas, there is this information about Focolare:

"This movement was begun in Trent, Italy, in 1943 by Chiara Lubich. It is an association of men and women which is officially approved by the Church. The purpose of this association is one of making a contribution to Jesus' last prayer: 'That they may all be one' (Jn. 17:21). The spirituality of unity proper to the Focolare has proven to be a powerful means of introducing the Gospel into modern life, bringing a greater unity to society. Centers of the movement have been established in sixty countries throughout the world. U.S. centers are located in New York City, Chicago, Boston, Los Angeles, San Antonio, Washington, D.C., and Columbus, Ohio; a center for spirituality is located in Hyde Park, New York."

Q. I noticed a book entitled *Cursillo: To Deceive the Elect.* What is this movement all about? — J.L.P., Washington

A. In his *Modern Catholic Dictionary*, Fr. John Hardon describes the Cursillo Movement as "a method of Christian renewal originated by a group of laymen, assisted by Bishop Hervas y Benet, on the island of Mallorca, Spain, on January 7, 1949. The term literally means a 'little course,' and the program itself comes in three stages of three days each: preparation (pre-cursillo), the course proper (cursillo), and the follow-up (post-cursillo). Its objective is to change the world by changing one's mind according to the mind of Christ and then reshaping one's life accordingly.

"The cursillo proper is an intensive weekend built around some fifteen talks, of which ten are given by laymen, and living together as a close Christian community. Those who participate are called cursillistas, who meet regularly after the initial program in what is called the ultreya, in small groups to pray, share their experiences, and plan apostolic action. An essential part of the cursillo, as conceived by Bishop Hervas, is the Spiritual Exercises of St. Ignatius, to give doctrinal foundation and spiritual structure to the movement."

That is what the cursillo was intended to be, and we have friends who have made a cursillo and found it to be a wonderful spiritual experience. The authors of *Cursillo: To Deceive the Elect*, however, contend that the movement is heretical and that it uses brainwashing techniques to switch the loyalty of participants away from the Church to the cursillo group. That has not been the experience of people we know who have made a cursillo.

Q. What is the difference between the heresy of Montanism and the Charismatic movement? — V.F., Florida

Q. Is the Charismatic movement approved by the Catholic Church? — J.M., California

A. Montanism was a second-century heresy whose believers considered themselves to be the true prophets of the Holy Spirit in preparing for the Second Coming of Christ. They saw themselves as elite possessors of charismatic gifts who could replace bishops and even the Pope. Montanism was eventually condemned by several Popes and its leaders were excommunicated from the Catholic Church.

Catholic Charismatic Renewal, which publishes a magazine called *New Covenant*, originated on the campus of Duquesne University in 1967 and has since spread to many other campuses and cities in the United States. It holds weekly meetings that focus on a special relationship with the Holy Spirit through spontaneous prayer, singing, and personal testimonies. Some of its members claim the spiritual gifts listed by St. Paul in First Corinthians, chapters 12-14, including prophecy and speaking in tongues.

Some Catholics have been critical of those Charismatics who bear a strong resemblance to Protestant Pentecostals in their denial of Church authority and their attitude of elitism. But there is no reason to criticize Catholic Charismatics who leave the judgment of the genuineness and proper use of their gifts to the Church, "not indeed to extinguish the Spirit, but to test all things and to hold fast to that which is good" (Vatican II, *Constitution on the Church*, n. 12).

Speaking at the Vatican on March 14, 1992, Pope John Paul told several hundred international leaders of the Charismatic Renewal that there should be "no conflict between fidelity to the Spirit and fidelity to the Church and her teaching authority." He asked them to "seek increasingly effective ways" to show "complete communion of mind and heart with the Apostolic See and the college of bishops, and to cooperate ever more fruitfully in the Church's mission in the world .... Whatever shape the Charismatic Renewal takes — in prayer groups, in covenant communities, in communities of life and service — the sign of its spiritual fruitfulness will always be a strengthening of communion with the universal Church and local churches."

Q. One of the families in our Catholic home-schooling group attends Mass at a church that is affiliated with the Order of St. John of Jerusalem. This family claims that their church is a Catholic church, but the Archdiocese says that it does not recognize the Order of St. John or the Mass as valid. Can you tell me anything about this Order? — G.R.S., Indiana

A. All we can tell you is what appeared in *L'Osservatore Romano* on December 9, 1976: "Enquiries have been received from various parties asking for further information regarding the 'Sovereign Order of St. John of Jerusalem' and in particular how the Holy See looks on this Order.

"We are authorized to repeat the clarifications previously published in our newspaper in this regard. The Holy See, in addition to its own Equestrian Orders, recognizes only two Orders of Knighthood: The Sovereign Military Order of Saint John of Jerusalem, called the Order of Malta, and the Equestrian Order of the Holy Sepulchre in Jerusalem.

"No other Order, whether it be newly instituted or derived from a medieval Order having the same name, enjoys such recognition, as the Holy See is not in a position to guarantee its historical and juridical legitimacy. This is also the case with regard to the above-mentioned 'Sovereign Order of St. John of Jerusalem,' which assumes, in an almost identical form and in such a way as to cause ambiguity, the name of the Sovereign Military Order of Saint John of Jerusalem, more commonly known as the Sovereign Military Order of Malta."

Thus, the Sovereign Order of St. John of Jerusalem is not the same thing as the Sovereign Military Order of St. John of Jerusalem and is not recognized by the Church as a legitimate organization.

Q. Does the teaching of the Catholic Church call for separation between church and state? — J.R.L., New York

A. The question was answered this way in Vatican II's *Constitution on the Church in the Modern World*, n. 76:

"It is highly important, especially in pluralistic societies, that a proper view exist of the relation between the political community and the Church .... The role and competence of the Church being what it is, she must in no way be confused with the political community, nor bound to any political system. For she is at once a sign and a safeguard of the transcendence of the human person....

"It is always and everywhere legitimate for her to preach the faith with true freedom, to teach her social doctrine, and to discharge her duty among men without hindrance. She also has the right to pass moral judgments, even on matters touching the political order, whenever basic personal rights or the salvation of souls make such judgments necessary. In so doing, she may use only those helps which accord with the gospel and with the general welfare as it changes according to time and circumstance."

See also paragraphs 2244-2246 of the *Catechism of the Catholic Church*.

Q. Scripture condemns usury in many places, yet the Vatican has many investments in banks. Has the Church changed its position on usury? — C.B., Michigan

A. Usury in Scripture involved the taking of interest for a loan of money, and it was condemned as a sin against justice. As economic systems changed from barter economies to economies based on money, which could increase in value, the Church recognized a distinction between a lender taking exorbitant interest (usury) for a loan and taking a fair return for the risk involved in making the loan.

The Church's basic teaching in this area never changed. It still condemns the charging of excessive interest for money loaned because it means unjust gain for the lender. When the unjust situation that had existed in certain economic systems changed, the Church calibrated its moral principles to the new situation and permitted what was no longer unjust.

Q. What is the Church's position on "out of body" experiences where people apparently dead are brought back to life and report having seen a brilliant light and having experienced a feeling of great peace? — R.E.B. New Jersey

Q. I have heard of people that have "died" and then had some experience with the hereafter before being restored to life. What is the Church's teaching on this? — H.P., New York

A. Our readers are referring to what are called "near-death" experiences. There have been books written about them, and people who have gone through them have told their stories on television. The stories they tell are strikingly similar: after "dying" on an operating table, or in an automobile accident, the person reports finding himself above the scene, watching doctors or emergency medical personnel trying to restore him to life.

The person then recalls going down a dark tunnel and being resistant to leaving this life. After a while, however, the person sees a light that grows brighter and brighter and eventually envelops him in a wonderful feeling of love and peace. Christians who have had this experience associate the light with Jesus, and they find themselves not wanting to return to this life.

When they are revived, most if not all of these people report coming away from their "out of body" experience with a greater appreciation for life, a lessened fear of death, and a desire to be a better person.

As far as we know, the Church has taken no position on these "near-death" reports. Perhaps these people did have some brief hint of what all of us will experience on the day of the particular judgment, when Christ will demand an accounting of our lives. But the lesson that we should learn from these interesting reports is always to be ready spiritually for the moment when actual death will occur for each one of us.

Q. What is the official judgment of the Church on the existence of unidentified flying objects? — J.B., Delaware

A. As far as we know, the Catholic Church has never made any official or unofficial statement on the existence of UFOs, beings from outer space, or life on other planets. These are matters of speculation and, even if proven true sometime in the future, would not be incompatible with our faith since God's Revelation does not require intelligent life only on this planet.

Q. What is the Church's teaching about dinosaurs on earth, and does the "Behemoth" described in Job 40:15-24 refer to a dinosaur? — D.C., Oklahoma

A. We are not aware of any teaching of the Church regarding the existence of dinosaurs. As for the "Behemoth" mentioned in the Book of Job, notes in the Confraternity Catholic edition of the Bible (1961), the New American Bible (1970), and the New World-Dictionary Concordance to the New American Bible all agree that the huge animal was probably a hippopotamus, not a dinosaur. And the Leviathan mentioned in Job 40:25 was probably a crocodile.

Q. What is biofeedback and is it permissible for Catholics? — R.F.K., Florida

A. Biological feedback involves the use of electronic equipment to monitor the functioning of the human body so as to provide a person with visual or auditory evidence that will enable him or her to control responses once thought to be exclusively dictated by the nervous system. For instance, musical tones, lights, or direct visualization of scales or meters can guide a person to control such things as skin temperature, blood pressure, and muscle response in an effort to deal with certain diseases.

Clinical biofeedback is an emerging science that has produced some encouraging results in the treatment of insomnia, phobias, some types of epileptic seizures, cardiac arrythmias, paralysis, and spasticity. We see no reason why a Catholic could not take part in such clinical treatments if they are supervised by competent and ethical medical personnel.

Q. An acquaintance of mine says that all the Crusaders did was kill people. Can you give a brief summary of how long the Crusades lasted and what they accomplished? — A.E.Y., Ohio

A. The term "Crusades" usually refers to some eight European military expeditions ordered by the Popes between 1095 and 1270 to drive out of the Holy Land Moslems who had profaned the sacred places and killed and enslaved thousands of Christians. In commissioning the first Crusaders, so called because of the cross that appeared on their clothes and banners, Pope Urban II freed from canonical penalties all those who took up the crusade "from motives of earnest and sincere devotion." He also promised remission of temporal punishment attached to sins that had been forgiven to every Crusader who "died truly penitent."

The Crusades never did accomplish their goal of achieving Christian control of the Holy Land, and the cruel and rapacious excesses of some Crusaders cannot be denied. But many of the hundreds of thousands who joined in these mighty expeditions did so with the highest religious motives, fighting and dying against overwhelming odds out of love for Christ and the holy places where He lived.

Information on the Crusades can be found in Steven Runciman's *A History of the Crusades* (3 vols.), R.W. Southern's *Western Society and the Church in the Middle Ages*, or the summary that appears in the *Cambridge Medieval History*.

Q. Would you please tell me exactly what the official position of the Church was on the Galileo affair in the 17th century? We need to address this since it has to do with the confidence we place in the Church's teaching authority, infallibility, etc. — **J.F.M., Ohio**

Q. Please refer to the attached letter on the Galileo incident. Apparently, there has been some kind of apology by John Paul II for the trials of Galileo, although without disqualifying expressly the tribunal which sentenced him. Can you provide me with some information on this? — **J.M.T., Puerto Rico**

A. Though critics of the Catholic Church have tried to use the Galileo affair to attack the infallibility of the *Magisterium*, there is no evidence to support their attacks. We are indebted to the *Catholic Encyclopedia*, edited by Fr. Peter Stravinskas, for telling us why:

"In 1616, theological experts working for the Holy Office responded to a court of the Inquisition concerning the orthodoxy of views supported by Galileo. The views in question were first, that the sun, as the supposed center of the universe, was immobile, and second, that the earth was mobile. The opinion of the theological experts was that both views were dangerous, the assertion of the immobility of the sun more so, and it was judged to be formally heretical.

"A sense for what was at stake may be gained by recalling that asserting the immobility of the sun is at least apparently inconsistent with scriptural references to the motion of the sun; for example, see Joshua 10:12-13, in which the usual motion of the sun is presumed. Until Galileo's hypothesis could be harmonized with the Scriptures, it would remain suspect in faith. In any case, in light of the in-house opinion of the consulting theologians, the Pope simply directed Cardinal Bellarmine to have Galileo agree to cease holding the opinion and supporting it.

"In 1632, Galileo was brought to the Inquisition court again by several private enemies for various personal faults and for breaking his earlier agreement by publishing *Dialogue on the Two Great World Systems*. He was cleared of the charges concerning personal faults, but was found guilty of the same errors he repudiated years before. He renounced those errors as ordered, and the sale of his book was stopped.

"In the 1632 court records, the 1616 opinion of the theological consultants was mentioned, the first public mention of the view that the heliocentric assertion of the sun's immobility was regarded as heretical by the consultants. Such hardly qualifies as a public announcement of what the Church considered the good news to the nations. Since neither the Pope nor any official promulgated the theological opinion as if it were official Church teaching, the credibility of the infallibility of the ordinary *Magisterium* cannot be undermined."

On October 31, 1992, Pope John Paul II said that the Church had been wrong in its judgment of Galileo. At the same time, a special commission that had reviewed the matter issued this statement:

"The philosophical and theological qualifications wrongly granted to the then new theories about the centrality of the sun and the movement of the earth were the result of a transitional situation in the field of astronomical knowledge and of an exegetical confusion regarding cosmology. Certain theologians, Galileo's contemporaries, being heirs of a unitarian concept of the world universally accepted until the dawn of the 1600s, failed to grasp the profound, non-literal meaning of the Scriptures when they described the physical structure of the created universe."

Q. I would like to know something about the massacre that took place in France on St. Bartholomew's Day. — D.M.B., Pennsylvania

A. The massacre to which you are referring took place in Paris on August 24, 1572, the feast of St. Bartholomew, and in the provinces of France in the weeks that followed. There is a lengthy article about this in *The Catholic Encyclopedia*, which is available at most public libraries, but here is a brief summary of what happened.

There had been three outbreaks of fighting between Catholics and Protestants in France from 1562 to 1570 and Catherine de Medici, mother of King Charles IX, and others had been considering the idea of assassinating some of the Protestant leaders, including Admiral de Coligny of the Calvinist party, to put an end to the civil discord. Parliament had even offered a reward of 50,000 ecus for the apprehension of Coligny, and the King had said that the sum would be given whether the admiral was delivered alive or dead.

An attempt was made on Coligny's life on August 22, 1572, but he was only slightly wounded. Catherine then pushed for a massacre of the Protestants and persuaded her son to order a mobilization of the royal troops. On the night of August 24th, the King's forces killed Coligny and all the Protestant nobles in the admiral's neighborhood. The number of victims in Paris is not known, but it may have been as many as 2,000. Thousands of others were killed in the provinces over the next several weeks.

Considering all that is known about these events, the author of the *Encyclopedia* article concluded that "the royal decision of which the St. Bartholomew massacre was the outcome was in nowise the result of religious disturbances and, strictly, did not even have religious incentives; the massacre was rather an entirely political act committed in the name of the immoral principles of Machiavellianism against a faction that annoyed the [royal] Court."

Q. Will you please explain what "Liberation Theology" is? — L.C., California

A. The phrase or movement first gained international attention in 1973 with the publication of a book entitled *A Theology of Liberation*. Written by Gustavo Guttierez, a Peruvian Jesuit priest, the book stressed the need for the Church to take a leading role in helping the poor, particularly in Latin America. However, the laudable goal of liberating people from poverty has been undermined by the means advocated by those members of the movement who have sought to portray Jesus as a Marxist revolutionary and to interpret Sacred Scripture from a Marxist perspective.

In his 1975 encyclical on evangelization (*Evangelii Nuntiandi*), Pope Paul VI said that "the Church is in duty bound ... to proclaim the liberation" of millions of people living "on the border line of existence: hunger, chronic epidemics, illiteracy, poverty, injustice between nations, and, especially in the commercial sphere, economic and cultural neocolonialism which are often as bad as the old political colonialism."

The Pontiff warned, however, that in the pursuit of a more humane and just existence for the poor and the oppressed, "the Church cannot accept any form of violence, and especially of armed violence — for this cannot be restrained once it is unleashed — nor the death of any man as a method of liberation. She knows that violence always provokes violence and inevitably gives rise to new forms of oppression, new forms of servitude even more grievous than those from which men were supposed to be emancipated."

During a visit to Mexico in 1979, Pope John Paul II reiterated papal concern about false characterizations of Jesus. He told Latin American bishops that it was wrong "to depict Jesus as a political activist, as a fighter against Roman domination and the authorities, and even as someone involved in the class struggle." The Holy Father said that "this conception of Christ ... as the subversive from Nazareth does not tally with the Church's catechesis."

In August 1984, the Vatican's Sacred Congregation for the Doctrine of the Faith issued a document stating that any "authentic theology of liberation will be one which is rooted in the Word of God, correctly interpreted," and not in a Marxist analysis "which seriously departs from the faith of the Church and, in fact, actually constitutes a practical negation."

The document, which was signed by Joseph Cardinal Ratzinger and approved by Pope John Paul, said that "the class struggle as a road toward a classless society is a myth which slows reform and aggravates poverty and injustice." It called attention to the millions of people who have been deprived of their basic freedoms "by totalitarian and atheistic regimes which came to power by violent and revolutionary means, precisely in the name of the liberation of the people .... Those who, perhaps inadvertently, make themselves accomplices of similar enslavements betray the very poor they mean to help."

Additional information on the origins of liberation theology and its ties with Marxism can be found in Laurene Connor's excellent monograph entitled *Catholic Educators and Marxist Ideology: An Unholy Alliance.* The 20-page monograph is available for $2.50 per copy from The Wanderer Forum Foundation, P.O. Box 391, Marshfield, WI 54449.

Q. I'm concerned about a friend of mine who is involved with a group that plays "Dungeons & Dragons" every Saturday. I have told him that this could be diabolical, but he just laughs it off. Can you suggest something sound he could read on the subject? — L.M.M., Illinois

A. One good source of information about the emotional, spiritual, and physical dangers of the so-called game of "Dungeons & Dragons" is Pat Pulling's book *The Devil's Web*, particularly chapter 6, which deals with "Fantasy Role-Playing Games." The book is published by Huntington House, Inc., Post Office Box 53788, Lafayette, LA 70505.

Mrs. Pulling is a leading authority on occult-related criminal activity and the founder of B.A.D.D. (Bothered About Dungeons & Dragons and Other Harmful Influences on Children). She started the organization in 1983, one year after her 16-year-old son committed suicide following a brief journey into the world of the occult. You can reach her by writing to

B.A.D.D., Post Office Box 5513, Richmond, VA 23220. The phone number is (804) 264-0403.

Q. Is it morally wrong to play Dungeons & Dragons? Sometimes I'll play and get this burning feeling that I'm doing something wrong; then other times I'll think that it's only a game. I'll admit that in the older versions of D&D there were demons and devils, but this has all been taken out of the second edition. If you play it with good intent and only as a game, then the line is no longer crossed between fantasy and reality. I realize that my time could be better spent in serving the Lord, but these games are enjoyable to play every once in a while so long as you don't let it consume your time. What is your opinion? — M.G., California

A. We do not have enough personal knowledge of older and newer versions of D&D to compare different editions and give M.G. an informed answer as to whether it is less dangerous to play the newer version. We would say, however, that if he has serious doubts about playing it on some occasions, then he shouldn't play it at all. And we would recommend that he go to a Catholic bookstore and get a copy of *Satanism: Is It Real?* (Servant Publications) by Fr. Jeffrey J. Steffon, a Catholic pastor in Los Angeles who counsels victims of satanic ritual abuse.

In chapter 5 of the book, Fr. Steffon summarizes the dangers of the fantasy role-playing employed in D&D:

"From a Christian perspective, D&D can be a dangerous game. Its philosophical basis is contrary to the Christian worldview. D&D tends to be graphically violent in its fantasy play. It can also be dangerous because it may intensify psychological problems in some players, or may even be linked to an act of violence by troubled teenagers....

"D&D can be dangerous because it may become an entrance into the occult through its teachings and practice of magic and witchcraft. Inasmuch as it treats Christ as a fantasy character and as one among many gods, D&D may undermine the faith of Christians who play it. For a follower of Jesus Christ, there is no good reason to role-play fantasy characters who regularly practice magic and witchcraft which God condemns" (pp. 71-72).

Q. At a recent parish retreat, we were directed to a table of books and told to further our study by reading some of them. Many were about the New Age and Enneagrams. Both the nun in charge and the pastor gave their approval of Enneagrams. Please help me with this. — C.R. Florida

Q. Our parish is holding an Enneagram Basic Workshop. Just what is that and how does our Catholic Church see it? — G.C., Indiana; S.C., Pennsylvania; and K.D., Indiana

A. For some good information about the Enneagram, and its incompatibility with Catholic teaching, see chapter five ("Occult Roots of the Enneagram") of Fr. Mitch Pacwa's book *Catholics and the New Age.* Moral theologian Msgr. William B. Smith has also cautioned Catholics about the dangers of the Enneagram. Writing in the March 1993 issue of the *Homiletic & Pastoral Review,* Monsignor Smith said:

"The Enneagram is a circular diagram on which nine personality types are systematically represented at nine equidistant points on the circumference. Lines connect various points to each other. It is this diagram itself which is the Enneagram, and it is used as a psychological tool of self-discovery. Each of the nine personality types (numbered 1 through 9) is described negatively by some compulsion, fixation, or basic driving force to avoid something unpleasant. This compulsion is seen as one's basic psychological orientation. To discover your number, you have to realize what you seek to avoid, what your compulsion is....

"The basic premise of the Enneagram is that there are nine and only nine personality types; this is simply given as true, it is nowhere demonstrated as proven. To my knowledge, there are no scientific studies to determine whether Enneagram theory can be integrated with other typologies; but that would not really bother some advocates one way or the other .... The more you read about it, the more it begins to resemble a college-educated horoscope; and that is not compatible with Catholic doctrine or practice....

"As a tool for spiritual direction, it seems to me most deficient, even dangerous. The Enneagram is really built on a theology (?) — perhaps ideology — of self-renewal and self-regeneration that is a far cry from (perhaps contradiction of) the Gospel teaching: 'Amen, Amen, I say to you, unless a grain of wheat falls to the ground and dies, it remains just a grain of wheat; but if it dies, it produces much fruit' (John 12:24)....

"[Pope John Paul II said on November 1, 1982]: 'Any method of prayer is valid insofar as it is inspired by Christ and leads to Christ who is the Way, the Truth, and the Life' (John 14:6). The Enneagram is not the Way, nor is it the Truth, and on those bases not truly compatible with — much less essential to — the Life in Christ."

Bibliography

Anderson, Joan Wester. *An Angel to Watch Over Me*
_____. *Where Angels Walk*
_____. *Where Miracles Happen*
Balducci, Corrado. *The Devil: ... Alive and Active in Our World*
Barry, Msgr. John F. *One Faith, One Lord*
Basic Teachings for Catholic Religious Education
Catechism of the Catholic Church
Catholic Almanac
Catholic Encyclopedia. Edited by Fr. Peter M.J. Stravinskas
Catholic League for Religious and Civil Rights. *Pius XII and the Holocaust*
Cochini, Christian, S.J. *The Apostolic Origins of Priestly Celibacy*
Code of Canon Law
Connell, Fr. Francis J. *Outlines of Moral Theology*
Cristiani, Msgr. Leon. *Satan in the Modern World*
Cruz, Joan Carroll. *Relics*
Daniel-Rops, Henri. *Daily Life in the Time of Jesus*
_____. *Jesus and His Times* (2 vols.)
Denton, Michael. *Evolution: A Theory in Crisis*
Dictionary of the Liturgy. Edited by Fr. Jovian P. Lang, O.F.M.
Dictionary of Saints. Edited by John J. Delaney
Documents of Vatican II, The. Edited by Walter M. Abbott, S.J.
Encyclopedia of Catholic History. Edited by Matthew Bunson
Fox, Fr. Robert J. *Fatima Today*
_____. *Protestant Fundamentalism and the Born-Again Catholic*
_____ and Mangan, Fr. Charles. *Until Death Do Us Part*
Freze, Michael, S.F.O. *The Making of Saints*
Fuentes, Antonio. *A Guide to the Bible*
Gesy, Fr. Lawrence. *Today's Destructive Cults and Movements*
Graham, Henry G. *Where We Got the Bible*
Grisez, Germain. *Christian Moral Principles*
_____. *Living a Christian Life*
Hahn, Scott and Kimberly. *Rome Sweet Home*
Halligan, Nicholas, O.P. *The Sacraments and Their Celebration*
Hardon, John A., S.J. *The Catholic Catechism*
_____. *Modern Catholic Dictionary*
_____. *Question and Answer Catholic Catechism*
Harvey, John F., O.S.F.S. *The Homosexual Person*
Hayes, Fr. Edward J., Hayes, Msgr. Paul J. and Drummey, James J. *Catholicism and Reason*
Index of Watchtower Errors. Edited by David A. Reed

John Paul II, Pope. *Christifidelis Laici*
_____. *Crossing the Threshold of Hope*
_____. *Dominicae Cenae*
_____. *Dominum et Vivificantem*
_____. *Evangelium Vitae*
_____. *Familiaris Consortio*
_____. *Ordinatio Sacerdotalis*
_____. *Reconciliatio et Paenitentia*
_____. *Redemptoris Mater*
_____. *Salvifici Doloris*
_____. *Veritatis Splendor*
Johnson, Phillip E. *Darwin on Trial*
Jone, Heribert, O.F.M., Cap. *Moral Theology*
Jurgens, William A. *The Faith of the Early Fathers* (3 vols.)
Keating, Karl. *Catholicism and Fundamentalism*
_____. *What Catholics Really Believe*
Keller, Werner. *The Bible as History*
Kippley, John F. *Marriage Is for Keeps*
_____. *Sex and the Marriage Covenant*
_____ and Kippley, Sheila. *The Art of Natural Family Planning*
Kreeft, Peter. *Everything You Ever Wanted to Know About Heaven*
_____. *Fundamentals of the Faith*
_____. *Making Sense Out of Suffering*
_____ and Tacelli, Ronald K. *Handbook of Christian Apologetics*
Lawler, Ronald, O.F.M. Cap., Boyle, Joseph Jr. and May, William E. *Catholic Sexual Ethics*
Lawler, Ronald, O.F.M. Cap., Wuerl, Bishop Donald W. and Lawler, Thomas C. *The Teaching of Christ*
Marks, Frederick W. *A Catholic Handbook for Engaged and Newly Married Couples*
May, William E. *An Introduction to Moral Theology*
McBride, Alfred, O. Praem. *Essentials of the Faith*
Myers, Bishop John. *The Obligations of Catholics and the Rights of Unborn Children*
Morton, H.V. *In the Steps of the Master*
Most, Fr. William G. *Catholic Apologetics Today*
_____. *The Consciousness of Christ*
_____. *Free From All Error*
Nevins, Albert J., M.M. *Answering a Fundamentalist*
_____. *Catholicism: The Faith of Our Fathers*
_____. *Strangers at Your Door*

O'Connor, Cardinal John J. *Abortion: Questions and Answers*
Ott, Ludwig. *Fundamentals of Catholic Dogma*
Pacwa, Mitch, S.J. *Catholics and the New Age*
Paul VI, Pope. *Credo of the People of God*
_____. *Humanae Vitae*
Pelletier, Fr. Joseph A. *The Sun Danced at Fatima*
Pius XII, Pope. *Humani Generis*
_____. *Mystici Corporis*
Pontifical Biblical Commission. *The Historicity of the Gospels*
Pontifical Council for Promoting Christian Unity. *Principles and Norms of Ecumenism*
Pulling, Pat. *The Devil's Web*
Rader, Fr. John S. and Fedoryka, Kateryna. *The Pope and the Holocaust*
Reardon, David C. *Aborted Women: Silent No More*
Ricciotti, Giuseppe. *The Life of Christ*
Sacred Congregation for Divine Worship. *Christian Faith and Demonology*
Sacred Congregation for the Doctrine of the Faith. *Declaration on Certain Problems of Sexual Ethics*
_____. *Declaration on Euthanasia*
_____. *Declaration on Procured Abortion*
_____. *Instruction on Certain Aspects of the "Theology of Liberation"*
_____. *Instruction on Respect for Human Life in Its Origin and on the Dignity of Procreation*
_____. *Letter to the Bishops of the Catholic Church on the Pastoral Care of Homosexual Persons*
Sacred Congregation for the Sacraments and Divine Worship. *Inaestimabile Donum*
Sheed, Frank. *Theology for Beginners*
_____. *Theology and Sanity*
_____. *To Know Christ Jesus*
Sheen, Bishop Fulton J. *Life of Christ*
Smith, Herbert, S.J. and DiIenno, Dr. Joseph A. *Homosexuality: Ten Questions — Scriptural, Church and Psychiatric Answers*
Smith, Janet. E. *Humanae Vitae: A Generation Later*
Steffon, Fr. Jeffrey J. *Satanism: Is It Real?*
Steichen, Donna. *Ungodly Rage*
Stenhouse, Paul. *Catholic Answers to Bible Christians* (2 vols.)
Stravinskas, Fr. Peter M.J. *The Bible and the Mass*
_____. *The Catholic Answer Book*
_____. *The Catholic Answer Book 2*

_____. *The Catholic Church and the Bible*
_____. *The Catholic Response*
Surprised by Truth. Edited by Patrick Madrid
Vatican Council II: The Conciliar and Post Conciliar Documents. Edited by Austin Flannery, O.P.
Whalen, William J. *Christianity and American Freemasonry*
_____. *Faiths for the Few*
_____. *Strange Gods*
Why Humanae Vitae Was Right: A Reader. Edited by Janet E. Smith
Willke, Dr. J.C. *Abortion: Questions and Answers*
Wrenn, Msgr. Michael J. *Catechisms and Controversies*

Index

HOW TO ORDER

MORE COPIES OF

CATHOLIC REPLIES

Additional copies of *Catholic Replies* can be obtained
for $17.95, plus $3.50 for shipping and handling. (Add
$1.50 for each additional copy. Massachusetts residents
add 5 percent sales tax.) Send check or money order to:

**C.R. PUBLICATIONS
345 PROSPECT STREET
NORWOOD, MA 02062**

For credit card orders, call:

(800) 879-4214

American Express, Discover, MasterCard, Visa accepted.
(Shipping charges for credit card order slightly higher.)

Book Stores, Parishes, Schools, Organizations:

Order *Catholic Replies* at a trade discount.

Call or fax inquiries to (617) 762-8811